*Human Nature and
the Social Order*

Human Nature and the Social Order

Edward L. Thorndike, 1874 - 1949

Edited and Abridged by
Geraldine Jonçich Clifford

M.I.T. PRESS

Cambridge. Massachusetts. and London. England

Original unabridged edition
copyright by the Macmillan Company, 1940

Abridged edition
copyright © 1969 by
The Massachusetts Institute of Technology

Set in Photon Times Roman.
Printed and bound in the United States of America
by The Maple Press Company, York, Pennsylvania

SBN 262 20016 3 (hardcover)

Library of Congress catalog card number: 75– 76291
75 - 87291

To Frederick Paul Keppel
a cherished friend for nearly fifty years

Preface

This book presents certain facts and principles of psychology which students of human affairs need to know. Psychology cannot as yet claim to be an adequate science of human behavior, upon which all the social sciences rest and with which they must agree. Indeed it probably has much more to learn from them, especially from anthropology and history, than they from it. But human biology and psychology make a substantial contribution. They settle certain questions outright and turn the balance for others.

The welfare of mankind now depends upon the sciences of man. The sciences of things will, unless civilization collapses, progress, extend man's control over nature, and guide technology, agriculture, medicine, and other arts effectively. They will protect man against dangers and disasters except such as he himself causes. He is now his own worst enemy. Knowledge of psychology and of its applications to welfare should at least diminish some of the errors and calamities for which the well-intentioned have been and are responsible. It should reduce greatly the harm done by the stupid and vicious.

I am indebted to the trustees of Teachers College, Columbia University, and to the Carnegie Corporation for the freedom from routine duties which made the writing of this book possible.

E. L. THORNDIKE

New York, August 1939

Contents

ix

Introduction

E. L. Thorndike was disappointed by the lack of response to the publication in 1940 of *Human Nature and the Social Order*. In contrast with the popular interest shown in 1939 in his statistical study of American cities, *Your City*[1]—itself the subject of numerous newspaper features—this later book aroused remarkably little attention. The irony of this neglect was that *Human Nature and the Social Order* was the outcome of nearly a decade of planning and effort, and the massive result was the largest single work of an immensely productive forty-year research and writing career. Insouciance describes the reaction of most general book-review editors. Typical of the reviews fitfully proffered in professional and scientific journals was that of sociologist Talcott Parsons; after a mixture of tame approvals and equally mild reproofs, came his leaden conclusion: "The main criticism of Thorndike's book is that it should be entitled something like 'One Kind of Approach to the Scientific Study of Human Nature and the Social Order.' "[2] Equally unprovoking of interest was Kimball Young's analysis, ending with the judgment that "students of society may easily overlook some of the larger contributions of this volume, for in spite of these limitations this book has considerable merit."[3] That its contributions might indeed be overlooked was made most likely, however, by certain other reviews which noted the congruence of *Human Nature and the Social Order* with Thorndike's earlier work, thereby implying that stimulating novelty was not to be found therein.

His own intentions for the book were recorded by Thorndike in his proposal to the Carnegie Corporation (for financial support) and in his reports as director of the psychological division of the Institute of Educational Research of Teachers College, Columbia University, where the project was housed. As was his wont, he limited his public expression of disappointment with the book's impact to a few words appended to an autobiographical sketch reprinted posthumously:[4]

It seemed to me that psychology should strive to become a basic science on which Anthropology, Sociology, Economics, Political Science, Law, Criminology, and Philanthropy could count for certain fundamental facts and principles, especially concerning human abilities and wants.... *Human Nature and the Social Order* so far is not used by these fields. [My] articles . . . in these fields have not been accepted. It seems more a distrust of psychology than of me.

Another original hope of the Carnegie study was that employing historians, political scientists, lawyers, and economists on the project might encourage careers in making psychology a basic part of these social sciences and professions. That, too, failed to happen. Of the various Carnegie Fellows and research assistants, only Abraham Maslow, Steuart Britt, and Raymond Cattell continued active; but they were already psychologists, and none turned his professional and intellectual interests permanently along the particular lines that Thorndike believed most wanted development.

One explanation of the frustration of Thorndike's expectations for *Human Nature and the Social Order* lies in the condition of the social sciences in the United States in the late 1930s. The majority of social scientists probably agreed with Max Weber that "it can never be the task of an empirical science to provide binding norms and ideals from which directives for immediate practical activity can be derived."[5] Even the lesser tasks of constructing applications and offering advice seemed to many at best premature. Moreover, the social sciences displayed (as they still do) a "status-anxiety" that limited their willingness to speak to practical problems and give counsel on commonplace activities, much less on controversial social issues; rather than compromise their insecure reputations as basic sciences they preferred for themselves a narrower role, even at the cost of being charged with creating "a science of that which is not worth knowing."[6]

The empirical youthfulness of the social sciences is acknowledged everywhere in *Human Nature and the Social Order*. An absence of popular knowledge of the newer of them and a degree of tentativeness are implied by Thorndike's occasional enclosing in quotation marks the terms sciences of man and the social sciences. Culture—in the anthropological, not the humanistic sense—was an unfamiliar enough concept so that Thorndike invariably set it off by quotes.

Anthropology was perhaps that social science which Thorndike himself knew best after psychology. The two fields had been closely allied in the empiricist and evolutionary crusades of the latter half of the nineteenth century. They had often shared a temporary common academic department in the struggle to assert themselves as scientific disciplines in the universities; they had published their papers in the same journals and been linked in the scientific societies. Thorndike had first learned about statistical methods from the influential anthropologist Franz Boas at Columbia University in 1897–1898.[7] While Thorndike used anthropological data freely in *Human Nature and the Social Order,* they were mostly those gained in field studies of primitive peoples; anthropology's applied contributions to modern industrial societies were still largely inferential as far as Thorndike knew them.

Linguistics, a specialization within anthropology, had become an interest of Thorndike's from his researches into the psychology of reading shortly after 1910, grew with his vocabulary studies and lexicographic work during the next two decades, appeared here and there suggestively in *Human Nature and the Social Order,* and culminated in his "babble-luck" theory of the origin of human language.[8] Comparative (or historical) linguistics had developed in nineteenth-century Germany as a study of the relations among languages. In its subsequent struggles to free itself from philology's assumptions about modern languages as the decayed products of the classical tongues (i.e., in turning linguistic paradigms into a Darwinist channel), it paralleled psychology's efforts to be free of a rationalistic philosophy. And in shifting its concerns from written to spoken language and from the language of the cultivated to that of the common man, linguistics nicely complemented psychology's conversion away from abstract mental states to the datum of observable, ordinary behavior.[9] The two fields also come together, of course, in their inquiries into speech origination, and social psychology is interested, as is linguistics, in the factors that enhance and inhibit communication among individuals. Had Thorndike more fully developed, in *Human Nature and the Social Order,* its psycho-linguistic potential, he might thereby have roused to greater interest a natural and sympathetic ally of psychology.

As it was, however, economics received, after psychology, Thorndike's preponderant attention. In the original edition, half of the total pages of Part II of *Human Nature and the Social Order* ("applying" the psychological and other facts and theories of Part I to policy areas in modern life) dealt directly with economics, while economic issues ran prominently through the remaining chapters on law, government, and welfare. In part, of course, the times explain this: economic suffering stood in the foreground of the social malaise that was the Great Depression and that spurred Thorndike and the Carnegie Corporation to undertake the project.

In addition, economics was a well developed, if not an altogether dependable, member among the sciences of man. A fairly systematic study of political economics antedated even Adam Smith's *Inquiry into the Nature and Causes of the Wealth of Nations* (1776). Elaborations of socialistic alternatives to unrestrained capitalism as an ideal type for national economic organization, in the nineteenth century and again during the 1930s, furnished ample material for Thorndike's perusal.[10] Moreover, since his own pioneering work in 1914 in devising personnel-selection tests for the American Tobacco Company and Metropolitan Life Insurance Company, applied psychology had become active in some of America's larger business and industrial enterprises.[11]

It was "political economy" as Thorndike learned it as a young man—the study of wealth (welfare) and its production—that engaged him most in *Human Nature and the Social Order*. But he did reject its older appeals to authority, because economic science can no more avoid embracing induction for its principles than can physics or psychology. Hence he denied the nineteenth century's confidence in economics as a neat compilation of general propositions deduced from theories of "natural rights" or from suspect observations of "natural law." The classical concept of "Economic Man" was thrown out on two counts, one empirical and one theoretical: first, human actions show no con-sistent positive relationship to man's uncontaminated economic best-interests; second, it does more harm than good to describe man by *any* abstract and discrete faculties having no counterpart in the reality assumed by a stimulus-response behaviorism. Because of the book's numerous allusions to the accomplishments of laissez-faire economics, plus Thorndike's personal experience with annoying New Deal taxing policies, plus his sober reflections on Beatrice and Sidney Webb, plus such radical proposals as taxing those of the rich who live in more rooms than they comfortably need, this book's economic discussions are hard to characterize. Therefore, Thorndike's economics emerges as a less consistent "science" than does his psychology.

Among the various social sciences, *Human Nature and the Social Order* treated sociology the least adequately. While this book offers them other worthwhile perspectives, younger sociologists had good reason to ignore it for its exposition of their *own* field. Social class, a major concern of academic sociology and the social professions, Thorndike conceived of narrowly, primarily by its economic parameters. The Webbs were quoted to ridiculously great lengths, but Max Weber was not mentioned, although E. L. Thorndike was a near-perfect living example of the Protestant ethic, as Weber conceived it. Thorndike knew the work of W. I. Thomas and Florian Znaniecki on the Polish peasant, and he referred to Thorstein Veblen often; he liked Veblen's concept of the instinct of workmanship and theory of conspicuous consumption especially: the former because psychology itself deals with instincts and Thorndike himself behaved toward work as if such an instinct was powerful in him; and the latter because of a contempt for ostentation bred in him in a boyhood ethic derived from seven generations of experience in Yankee New England.[12]

Despite his own community investigations, Thorndike paid virtually no attention to the active Chicago school of urban sociologists of the 1930s, except for noting Clifford Shaw's work on delinquency.[13] The fact that Thorndike attended too much to social theorists and too little to the work of even his younger sociologist colleagues on the Columbia University campus, Robert Merton and Robert MacIver, is not, however, the critical factor. It is rather that Thorndike only approached the essential conceptual "stuff" of sociological inquiry. Thus he attended to customs because they are the generalized expressions of *individual* behavior (and hence in psychology's province), but not to *social* institutions, which have a life of their own and which are something more than the mere aggregate of the individuals who express them and give them life. Only one of the reviewers of *Human Nature and the Social Order* showed himself adequately sensitive to this distinction: Morris Ginzberg, Professor of Sociology at the University of London and the London School of Economics. In the prestigious British journal, *Nature,* Ginzberg wrote:[14]

Something must be said, however, on the adequacy of the general theory of human nature and society which is here adopted as the basis of inquiry. We must ask, to begin with, whether a theory of society can be built up on the basis of a psychology of individual differences. Prof. Thorndike seems to think that the differences between communities resolve themselves ultimately into differences in endowment of the individuals composing them or in the range of the distribution. But social structure can scarcely be interpreted in these terms . . . social classes . . ., for example, are not in the main determined by differences in individual endowment, and changes from one type of stratification to another have nothing to do with changes in genetic endowment. Similarly, on the basis of very similar genetic endowment very different social institutions can be built up. A science of society must therefore be largely a study of social forces, that is, of the forces which arise out of the relations between human beings. . . . *Psychology cannot do the work of sociology.*

Where sociology focuses upon used social systems, social psychology's primary subject matter is the personality system: in this case the social nature of the individual person. There is greater affinity here to Thorndike's individualistic mind-set, which he amply recorded in *Human Nature and the Social Order*. "It may be taken as certain that the welfare of society will never be cared for by society acting by itself, but only by the acts of persons" (p. 272), he writes in one place; or "The observable phenomena of political science are the behavior of persons" (p. 276). Thorndike consequently denied any "Voice of the People" and was skeptical of high hopes for governments by the collective decisions of parliaments and of administration by committees; he even approvingly cites Harold Lasswell's contention that the discussion method is much overrated (p. 306).

The peripatetic requirements imposed upon its clergy by nineteenth-century Methodism deprived Edward L. Thorndike of a sense of community. He was never to know Williamsburg, Massachusetts, the place of his birth in 1874; and so it was with the numerous other towns of his youth. All his adult life he was beset by awkward shyness, by doubt that others liked him, and by that compulsive assertiveness which occasionally plagues the socially insecure. Casual gatherings of mere acquaintances were a torture, and he turned inward: to self, to family, and to a very few intimates, but mostly to his work. He well knew of what he wrote in explaining that, "the feeling of 'security,' i.e., the complete absence of fear, antagonism, caution, and 'tension,' may play a large part in liking to be alone, liking to be with friends, and liking to be in one's own familiar habitat and lair" (p. 57).

Because he exemplified the quintessence of selflessness and a "tough-minded" (but helpful) compassion for individuals—including penurious graduate students, his staff, and even street waifs and the local loafers around his Montrose, New York, home—Thorndike's lack of a generalizable social consciousness, even amidst the encompassing suffering of the Depression, merits an attempt at explanation. Is there any cause beyond those youthful experiences in a family that sought emotional security within itself, that habitually withdrew from dependence upon and unnecessary interaction with a succession of strange and watchful villages? Richard Niebuhr offers an explanation from the sociology of middle-class Protestantism. Methodism, especially, erupted late and escaped the persecutions visited upon Baptists and other sects. As Methodism rapidly grew respectable, it quickly transcended its origins as a sect of the poor. "Its martyrs die for liberty, not for fraternity and equality; its saints are patrons of individual enterprise in religion, politics, and economics, not the great benefactors of mankind or the heralds of brotherhood."[15] Thus the interests of the family are made superordinate to appeals for social justice or brotherhood. One's intimates receive the major benefits of one's habits of accountability and need for engagement. Social idealism loses to a personalistic ethic; misfortune and success alike become the property of individuals, not of social classes or social forces, not of mass injustices nor public benefactions.

By the time of his graduation from Wesleyan University in 1895, Thorndike, the minister's son, was an agnostic, although generally undogmatic in his rejection of religion. He did, however, speak out autobiographically for fellow disbelievers who "in spite of resulting difficulties with friends and risk of general unpopularity, have probably deserved extremely high ratings for private and public virtues. Those, whom we may call 'conscientious objectors' to immortality, are men and women whom all the world except the ignorant or bigoted, honors" (p. 72). In an attitude of live-and-let-live, he was unwilling to heap his own, the scientist's, doubts upon the faithful, although he did make some observations about churchgoers and lawbreakers (pp. 72 & 202):

Some persons of mean natures living selfish and depraved lives assert disbelief in a supernatural world and have no affiliations with bodies of religious believers, but they seem to be exceptional. Criminals ... [are found to be] as often believers and communicants as non-criminals. The village drunkard, rake, or crook who avoids the churches may do so partly because his character is so well-known that he would be made uncomfortable there, partly because, by a perverted logic, his disbelief serves him as an excuse for not being a decent man, and partly because the avoidance permits him to respect himself as not a hypocrite.

Nevertheless, let those who would have their religion and even their churches; after all, in a sense, *Thorndike had his own:* the secular religion of progressivism.

"The idea of progress as the controlling force in history, with America at the forefront of advance toward a millennial fulfillment, was the true secular theology of this country in the nineteenth century."[16] The early career of E. L. Thorndike was forged in the progressive era. He also shared with the bulk of progressive reformers similar origins in a segment of middle-class, Protestant, small-town society that was heading for the cities, meanwhile transforming those American universities where one formerly could have taken a Ph.D. in economics (as did Scott Nearing in 1909) without having heard mention of Marx and Engels.

An individualist-orientation characterized most of the progressives. This was somewhat paradoxical in that progressivism once tried to offer collective solutions to social problems. As Otis Graham has noted. however, an inbred and stubborn Protestant individualism caused many old-time progressives to reject the New Deal's massive approach through social action and to turn back instead toward "private solutions through the bracing of character": they sought for solutions in moral regeneration and appeals to thrift and hard work.[17] In Thorndike's own belief, individual salvation and public welfare lay most securely in the *recourse to facts*, a more trustworthy base than is character-building. given Thorndike's essentially pessimistic views of human nature in the abstract.

Loren Eiseley was one reviewer who very much liked *Human Nature and the Social Order*:[18]

This is not a book concerned with paper Utopias. It is meaty with shrewd practical suggestion. ranging all the way from the public encouragement of scientific genius through financial grants to the better management of industry. It attempts to find ways of scientifically encouraging the better side of that obstreperous. blundering. but precocious primate *homo sapiens*.... Although much has happened in the short while since this book was published. its sane and forward-looking optimism is still not unjustified. It is a work extensive in scope but compact in purpose. It is an education in common sense.

No higher praise could be offered to Thorndike. whose ideal was the common-sense man of good will.

In important ways, however. Thorndike wrote a book whose concerns looked backward. over his shoulder, to the economic preoccupations of the Depression years. He had read Marx. of course. but this book's comparisons of Capitalist and Communist economics as much reflected the "Red Scare" of the past as it forecast the wider idealogical and political sweep of the Cold War. There is also an inevitable quaintness about a volume that echoes the intellectuals' laments of twenty-five years earlier on "the late war" when a new and greater holocaust had already erupted in Europe and Asia. If social change—the events to which Eiseley's review alluded. events that distracted the nation and that help to explain the ignoring of the book—was not to relegate *Human Nature and the Social Order* to permanent and deserved oblivion. it would have to be that Thorndike also addressed himself to certain universals of the human condition. to persistent American traits. to still-viable social policy questions. Do its key ideas do so? The answer. I think. is yes.

A recurring theme in Western intellectual history has been the dialectics surrounding naturalism and primitivism—the essence, "goodness," deterministic power of nature. Concerning what is *natural to man*, psychology and philosophy had for some three centuries past been particularly interested in man's sensory reception to the outside world of natural and social objects and events. Among the outcomes of sensing (beside perceptions), the role of pain and pleasure—first as motivators of action and later as agents somehow neurologically explaining learning—had become important. Logical and empirical inquiries into ethical and psychological hedonism ran in a continuous line through such men as Bentham, J. S. Mill, Freud, and Pavlov, to present-day experimentalists. Sketching out the confirming reaction and his own research on reward and punishment (in Part I of *Human Nature and the Social Order*), Thorndike offers then a succinct conceptualization of an interest of historical primacy.

In Part II, especially, Thorndike throws himself clearly against primitivist opinion; he lends support instead to a characteristic American *irreverence* toward nature—but with one difference: while a dread of the wilderness, combined with the careless economics of frontier life, encouraged most Americans habitually to regard physical nature primarily "as a storehouse of raw materials awaiting exploitation,"[19] Thorndike would conserve the natural environment for quite practical reasons. But he was also most unimpressed with the supposed "beauties" of original *human* nature. He still believed, without sentiment, as he did in 1913, that[20]

the original tendencies of man have not been right, are not right, and probably never will be right. By them alone few of the best wants in human life would have been felt, and fewer still satisfied. Nor would the crude conflicting, perilous wants which human nature so largely represents and serves, have had much more fulfillment. Original nature has achieved what goodness the world knows as a state achieves order, by killing, confining or reforming some of its elements. . . . Only one thing [in man's nature] is unreservedly good, the power to make it better [, this] power of learning. . . .

A romanticizing of "Natural Man" had been fostered by the age of discovery, which put civilized, Western man in contact with primitive peoples. The arousal of conscience at social injustice, as in Rousseau, strengthened primitivism further. So, too, did Darwinism, in that "the natural" came to be viewed as the outcome of evolutionary development; as evidence of the successful struggle of the species to survive, the natural was presumed to be the good. To this latter point, Thorndike speaks thus (p. 66):

Man does not put first those wants the satisfaction of which ensures survival, the production of offspring and their survival, and attend to others only after these have been satiated. His craving for social intercourse and the approval of self and others is for greater amounts and different sorts than are needed for survival; his craving for sex pleasures is out of all proportion to what is needed for the production of offspring; his craving for entertainment may even operate against the nourishment of the young and the protection of the community.

About one thing then a psychologist and a utopian, Thorndike and Bellamy for example, might agree: the demand for "bread and circuses" will have a greater chance of expression, even in a bettered future society, than will a passion for justice or an expectation of a rational polity. The reformer must meet nature part way, but attending much more to the rewarding of desirable impulses than to the punishing of the undesirables.

One fact of nature to which Thorndike paid absolute respect was the variation among individual humans, where even a stringent policy of selective breeding could do no more than very slowly narrow the range and raise the average of a population a tiny, if critical, amount. While some of the later utopians tolerated an irremediable inequality in human nature, Thorndike placed this inequality first among the *laws* which the sciences of man offered to government, law, education, philanthropy.[21]

For a literate technical society, differences in intelligence—or the capacity to learn and to choose appropriate responses—is the most important among human variations. (Indeed, because of Thorndike's certainty that above-average intelligence correlates with other favorable traits, an index of intelligence is a very rough quotient of the general merit of a total individual.) During World War I, large populations were tested for the first time in history. This spawned criticisms of the tests, their legitimacy, assumptions, conclusions, and implications. Walter Lippmann's series in the *New Republic* in 1922 was typical. He attacked psychology's claims that any individual's intellectual *potential* was circumscribed by his genetic legacy—by heredity; science would, said Lippmann, undermine democracy if it supported notions favoring an "intellectual caste system."[22] The debate prompted Raymond Franzen's observation that "judgments of human nature are warped by the milk of human kindness . . . [and] dominated by ideals of democracy instead of by the evidence."[23] An editorial in *The Outlook* seemed to bear Franzen out: it suggested that while high test scores would locate talent, low scores did not signify dullness nor mental incompetence.[24] So, yet another chapter in the nature-nurture controversy was being written.

As with other social visionaries, most public school leaders could not accept Thorndike's hereditarian conclusions. Their own professionalism, however, caused them to agree with the position that he accorded to trained leadership, to expert judgment—another of the key ideas of *Human Nature and the Social Order.*

The expert is usually the only one much interested in uncommon, special knowledge; indeed, in a sense, he is as much possessed by it as he is its possessor. Moreover, the expert is qualified to use the facts because he not only knows them (as an ordinary man might), but is far more liable than is the nonexpert to know also their importance *relative* to other facts. If, in an open society, the expert cannot limit the relevant knowledge to a circle of competent colleagues, he must seek to arm himself against incompetents by his professional claims. It was for this reason that psychologist Guy Whipple ridiculed Lippmann's interpretation of the Army test, calling it a dangerous misunderstanding emanating from inexpertness; the test "was not prepared for journalistic use," he jibed.[25]

The expert thinks himself not cause- but profession-oriented. And Thorndike's *Ultimate Expert* was the scientist, or the scientifically informed and fair-minded man of public affairs. Such men are drawn into this work by the nature of their genes. Good genes, plus the scientific habits of mind learned and powers trained, he believed to be the superior predictors of those who would function best as the impartial, objective benefactors of mankind—if only the men in power would share their monopoly on leadership, or at least consult seriously with them.

It would seem that in this age of scientific revolutions, science and the scientist might well gain that place in guiding the social order that Thorndike fervently espoused. Yet, when a society is gripped by unsettling social change, ideologies seem to gain at the expense of disinterested intelligence. It may appear true again, as it was in the 1930s when Lincoln Steffens wrote, "Now is not the time for the open mind. Now is the age of decision."[26] Thorndike's faith in the classless social engineer might be made to appear as inconsequential as Thorndike believed the good intentions of the reformer to be.

Despite his willing admission of the immaturity of the sciences of man, including psychology, Thorndike admitted of no doubt that they were to stand in the same ultimate relationship to the management and enrichment of the social life as the physical sciences stand to the facts and possibilities of the natural world. The Psychological Corporation's onetime interest in creating a typewriter "improved on psychological and physiological lines" barely suggested the possibilities of technological application.[27] But, beyond that, Thorndike took it as a given fact that the future philanthropist or politician or city planner could apply the basic science of psychology in a manner analagous to the physician's dependence upon biochemistry, or the engineer's upon physics, or the agronomist's upon plant genetics.

Thorndike was, then, a consistent limner of the engineering possibilities of social science—however much it is true that "to manage human beings is a more complex and difficult task than to manage chemicals or electrical currents," and that "it takes longer to acquire competence as a human engineer than as a civil or mechanical engineer." Of the future teacher, he once wrote[28] that he will

think out from scientific principles the best way to teach a given child to subtract or divide, as the engineer thinks out the best way to bridge a given river or tunnel a given hill. The study of these principles and their applications will demand as great talents and as close application as the study of the principles upon which medical or engineering practice rests.

If the demands for talent, industry, creativity are indeed greater, the game is surely worth the candle. For it remains as true today as when stated in the Introduction to *Human Nature and the Social Order* that the probability is great that man is his own worst enemy and that the *sciences of things* cannot by themselves insure civilization.

College students of the 1960s (and very probably those of the 1970s) certainly believe so, and many are willing to assume the commitment of personal engagement. Where those of the so-called "Silent Generations" of students crowded psychology courses, the torch has been passed to the university's sociology department. Where the young person only recently professed most the desire to know and to understand himself better, to improve his personality, and to perfect his interpersonal social skills, there has been a dramatic shift, and on a wide front of student opinion: exploring social problems, studying the mechanisms of social control, climbing about the social system all represent an enlargement of focus, a bringing of the self into the mass society in a new way in the history of education in the United States. With the student radicals' demand that professors *do more* than describe and investigate society—that they engage their knowledge in efforts to improve society—E. L. Thorndike would agree.

The guiding principle in abridging *Human Nature and the Social Order* (a work which in the original numbered slightly over one thousand pages) was that repetitive exposition and excessive illustration be eliminated without depriving the reader of that opportunity to understand the workings and qualities of Thorndike's mind and the revealing aspects of his personality that obtained in the original volume. Many long quotations were removed altogether and the rest was drastically shortened; but so that the reader might be informed of all the authors and works originally quoted or referred to by Thorndike, the Bibliography has been left unaltered.

Other published writings of Edward L. Thorndike can be located through the bibliographies printed in three issues of the *Teachers College*

Record: Vol. 27 (February 1926): 466–515; 41 (May 1940): 700–725; 51 (October 1949): 43–45. For biographical studies see Geraldine Jonçich, "Edward Lee Thorndike," *International Encyclopedia of the Social Sciences* (New York: Crowell-Collier and Macmillan, 1968), Vol. 16, pp. 8–14 and *The Sane Positivist: A Biography of Edward L. Thorndike* (Middletown, Conn.: Wesleyan University Press, 1968).

GERALDINE JONÇICH CLIFFORD

Berkeley, California
September, 1969

Notes

1 New York: Harcourt, Brace, 1939. From this remarkable study, examining 297 characteristics of each of 310 cities (and this before the computer was available), much methodological profit can be gained—an opinion shared by Eugene J. Webb, *et al., Unobtrusive Measures: Nonreactive Research in the Social Sciences* (Chicago: Rand McNally, 1966), pp. 72f.

2 *American Sociological Review,* 6 (April 1941): p. 277.

3 *American Journal of Psychology,* 54 (July 1941): p. 448.

4 E. L. Thorndike, *Selected Writings from a Connectionist's Psychology* (New York: Appleton-Century-Crofts, 1949), p. 10.

5 Max Weber, *The Methodology of the Social Sciences,* edited and translated by E. A. Shils and H. A. Finch (Chicago: The Free Press, 1949), p. 52.

6 This was how Karl Mannheim once coupled a too-cautious sociology with an arid, academic philology; in *Essays on Sociology and Social Psychology* (New York: Oxford University Press, 1953), p. 192.

7 To an extent anthropologists returned the favor. George Murdock and Clyde Kluckhohn, for example, employed a neo-Thorndikean stimulus-response theory in explaining role, cultural interaction, and the like; in Gardner Lindzey, editor, *Handbook of Social Psychology* (Cambridge, Mass.: Addison-Wesley, 1954), I, p. 86.

8 See, for example, his "Mental Dynamics Shown by the Abbreviation and Amelioration of Words in Hearing and Remembering," *American Journal of Psychology,* 54 (January 1941): p. 132; "The Origin of Language," *Science,* 98 (July 2, 1943): pp. 1–6; *Man and His Works* (Cambridge, Mass.: Harvard University Press, 1943); "On Orr's Hypothesis Concerning the Front and Back Vowels," *British Journal of Psychology,* 36 (September 1945): pp. 10–13; "The Psychology of Semantics," *American Journal of Psychology,* 59 (October 1946): pp. 613–632.

9 The "ease theory" in linguistics proposes that sounds that are easy to pronounce will be preserved, while difficult pronunciations will be rejected; the indebtedness here to Darwin's principle of natural selection is obvious. (My former student, John Waterhouse, called this illustration to my attention.)

10   Thorndike read Edward Bellamy's utopian novel, *Looking Backward* (1888), as a young man, but does not quote from it in *Human Nature and the Social Order*. Based on Thorndike's conclusions about human nature, the socialist-utopian's concern with the distribution of wealth and the organization of labor are not crucial questions for a science of economics.

11   Although the president of The Psychological Corporation, James McKeen Cattell, could find few psychologists in 1922 who earned their living by industrial work, by 1934 the Corporation's Market Division (providing research services in consumer studies, advertising, and selling) accounted for nearly 70 per cent of its receipts; in *Important Records of the Psychological Corporation* (New York), microfilm, courtesy of the Corporation.

12   Although Thorndike chided Veblen for the moralizing that lies beneath his urbane analysis, *Human Nature and the Social Order* shows that Thorndike also occasionally fell victim to the temptation to point the moral; it seems to be a powerful American tendency, particularly for those most influenced by Puritan culture norms.

13   Useful here is John Madge, *The Origins of Scientific Sociology* (New York: Free Press, 1962).

14   "Man as a Social Organism," *Nature,* 148 (September 27, 1941): p. 353, italics added.

15   H. Richard Niebuhr, *The Social Sources of Denominationalism* (New York: Henry Holt, 1929), esp. pp. 64–76, 87f.

16   Henry Nash Smith, editor, *Popular Culture and Industrialism, 1865–1890* (New York: Doubleday-Anchor Books, 1967), p. xii.

17   Otis L. Graham, Jr., *An Encore for Reform: The Old Progressives and the New Deal* (New York: Oxford University Press, 1967), esp. p. 126.

18   In *Social Education,* 5 (March 1941): p. 236.

19   Smith, note 16, p. xiii.

20   E. L. Thorndike, *Educational Psychology, Vol. I: The Original Nature of Man* (New York: Teachers College, 1913), pp. 281f.

21   See Lewis Mumford, *The Story of Utopias* (New York: Boni and Liveright, 1922).

22   See, for example, Lippmann's "The Mental Age of Americans," "The Abuse of the Tests," and "Tests of Hereditary Intelligence," *New Republic,* 32 (1922): 213f, 297f, 328–330. Also F. L. Wells, "Multiple Choice Minds," *School and Society,* 47 (January 15, 1938): p. 85, and B. Hoffman, *The Tyranny of Testing* (New York: Crowell-Collier, 1962) for continuations of objections to testing.

23   *Educational Review,* 65 (April 1923): p. 266.

24   In *The Outlook,* 143 (1926): p. 46.

25   Guy M. Whipple, "The Intelligence Testing Program and its Objectors— Conscientious and Otherwise," *School and Society,* 17 (May 26, 1923): pp. 561–568.

26   *Lincoln Steffens Speaking* (New York: Harcourt, Brace, 1936), p. 302. See also, Graham, note 17, esp. pp. 129–150.

27   Psychological Corporation *Records,* note 11. Thorndike would probably not have accepted David Bakan's *distinction* between the social role of the physical scientist and the psychologist: that the former's knowledge is

applied and made socially useful without necessarily *teaching* understanding to its consumers, while "The value of the understanding of human
functioning does not inhere in its application in the usual sense, but in its
possession."—"The place of the psychologist in society is more as a teacher
than as expert or technician, helping man to understand himself and his
relations to others. . . . teach[ing] people to use that knowledge in self
understanding, effective life, and management of their affairs;" in David
Bakan, *On Method* (San Francisco: Josey-Bass, 1967), pp. 47, 48.

28   E. L. Thorndike, *Education, A First Book* (New York: Macmillan, 1912),
pp. 257, 258.

PART I
GENERAL FACTS
AND PRINCIPLES

Chapter 1
The ABC of Human Behavior

Competent thinkers agree about the need to understand persons and institutions so as to predict and direct their activities. It is the purpose of this volume to present to students of government, law, economics, business, social work, and education some facts and principles of the basic sciences of man, especially of psychology.

Psychology, as the science of the fundamentals of human nature, is concerned with the mind, but also with the movements of man's muscles and with many other events in his bodily organs outside the brain. The word behavior is convenient to cover sensing, thinking, feeling, willing, acting, and anything else of which a person is capable.

The social sciences need knowledge of how the human animal behaves, of what he thinks, feels, and does. They need also knowledge of what behavior persons are able to manifest, what they *can* be and do and of what they *want* to be and do and experience. The abilities which condition and limit human behavior, and the desires and aversions, likes and dislikes, which instigate and direct it, are often more important and instructive than the actual behavior observed.

Much of the work of improving the world, and many of the problems which economics, government, law, business, philanthropy, and education refer to psychology, concern the nature, causation, and modification of either abilities or wants.

3

A man is a physical mass and behaves in accordance with physical laws. He is a factory and storehouse of chemicals. He is a living animal, capable of biological activities, some psychobiological or mental. A man's life would be described by a list of all the situations which he encountered and the responses which he made to them, including every detail of his sensations, percepts, memories, ideas, judgments, emotions, desires, choices, and other so-called mental facts.

Using S and R as symbols for 'situation or state of affairs encountered by the man' and 'response made by him,' and using $\rightarrow$ as a symbol for 'leads to,' a man's life would be expressed as a list of millions of events like

$$S_1 \rightarrow R_{146}, \quad S_{29564} \rightarrow R_{17361}, \quad S_{104618} \rightarrow R_{3184}, \quad S_{21} \rightarrow R_{269}, \quad \text{etc.}$$

A man's nature at any given stage would be expressed by a list of the R's which he would make to whatever S's could happen to him, somewhat as the nature of a molecule of sugar might be expressed by a list of all the reactions that would take place between it and every substance which it might encounter.

There would be one important difference, however. If each $\rightarrow$ had attached to it a number expressing the probability that the S in question would evoke the R in question, most of these probabilities would be near 0 or near 1.00 for the behavior of the molecule of sugar; but in the case of the behavior of a man our knowledge would not often suffice for that. In human behavior our ignorance often requires the acknowledgment of the principle of *multiple response* or *varied reaction*. Instead of $S_{79} \rightarrow R_{261}$ with a probability of 1.00 and $S_{79} \rightarrow$ any other R than R_{261} with a probability of 0, we often have to expect something like

$$S_{79} \rightarrow R_{261} \quad \text{with} \quad \text{a} \quad \text{probability} \quad \text{of} \quad .80$$
$$S_{79} \rightarrow R_{2612} \quad \text{,,} \quad \text{,,} \quad \text{,,} \quad \text{,,} \quad .04$$
$$S_{79} \rightarrow \text{all other R's} \quad \text{,,} \quad \text{,,} \quad \text{,,} \quad .02$$

If John Doe were really the same person in every particular he would always respond to S in one same way; even when we can detect no differences in him there will be subtle variations in metabolism, blood supply, etc.

Important sorts of change are the strengthening of previously existing tendencies, the growth of new tendencies, the weakening and the abolition of previously existing tendencies. All four sorts are best thought of in terms of S, R, and $\rightarrow$. When $S \rightarrow R$ with a probability of K changes to $S \rightarrow R$ with a probability greater than K, a previously existing tendency has become stronger. When $S \rightarrow R$ with a probability near 0 acquires an appreciable probability, a new tendency has appeared. When $S \rightarrow R$ decreases its probability, there is weakening. When the decrease is to 0, the tendency has been abolished.[1]

The number of different situations which life can offer a man in a modern civilized community is practically infinite. To these he can make millions of different responses. We know them fully for no man. The sciences of man are far below complete knowledge and prophecy but a psychologist who knew the life history of a man to age twenty-five and observed his reactions in ten or twelve hours of testing could make prophecies of the R's he would make to any thousand important S's which would be enormously better than prophecies made by chance. It is as correct to say that human behavior is often predictable as to say that it is often unpredictable. A teacher can predict with few errors which of his students will pass in a state examination, but will make large errors in predicting their vocational status at age 50. Economists and business-men can predict closely the amount of wheat that the world will consume in a year at a given price, but can predict changes in the fashions of women's clothes much less safely. The man in the street is constantly assuming that certain persons will do so and so, and is right perhaps ninety-nine times out of a hundred, namely in those cases where habitual routines and ordinary motives are usually decisive.

Very important among a man's responses are liking, satisfaction, welcoming and, on the other hand, dislike, discomfort, annoyance, rejection. He is born with certain wants and proclivities and acquires more by growth and experience. A man is an organization of $S \rightarrow R$ connections operating in the service of a group of such wants, "drives" or proclivities.

The Person Who Responds

A person develops into an adult, partly by forces residing in him, partly by forces acting upon him from outside. The situations which he experiences and the responses which he makes register themselves by preserving or changing his nature, sometimes in infinitesimal amounts, as in the casual sounds of an hour devoted primarily to sleep, sometimes in impressive amounts, as when one reads a stimulating book, falls in love, joins the church, is wronged by a close friend, or inherits a fortune. $S \rightarrow$ R connections made in him attain increasing strength as knowledge,

---

[1] $S \rightarrow R$ with a probability of 1.00 may become still stronger in the sense that it will still occur under more adverse conditions and will remain after longer periods of lack of exercise.

habits, prejudices, and ideals. Nurture acting on inborn nature thus forms the genes into a person whose probabilities of behavior are as describable as his external bodily form and features.

It used to be customary to divide a person into a unitary mind and the multifarious knowledges, habits, interests, skills, etc., which it had and used. It is better to hold that no clear line can be drawn between the unified organization which we call a person's nature or self and the knowledge, habits, wants which it possesses, or the acts which it does. What a person is really means what he will think and feel and do in response to the various situations of life. Certain parts of him are more or less regnant over other parts, certain parts are tools in the hands of other parts, certain parts are more or less permanent features whereas certain parts easily vanish or change. But it may be misleading to separate off the ruling, purposive, permanent parts into a unitary being and call it the soul, mind, self, or personality. Such a separation does not parallel reality. Biologically all are organized in man's brain, which has no such clear separation, and in the history of any person there is constant interplay.

Elements of Situations, Persons, and Responses

A situation often acts unevenly upon a person, parts of it being prepotent because he is more attentive or responsive to them. So we may be able to predict that a certain element will, no matter what accompanies it in the total situation, evoke a certain response. A thirsty man will tend to respond to water in a glass, water in a cup, and water in a bottle by drinking the water. In his response to foods on the breakfast table, his knowledge of Greek and fear of thunderstorms count for little. Both common practice and science treat persons as containing characteristics whose behavior we may predict more or less irrespective of the rest of the person. So we expect that hunger and purchasing power will make a traveler buy food regardless of whether he is a Republican or a Democrat, a scholar or a dunce.

The total response of a human in even a very brief unit of time is usually very elaborate. When a man casts his vote, or signs a contract, or robs a till, he may also be calm or excited, reminiscent or anticipative, energetic or fatigued. The sciences of government, economics, and criminology concern themselves with certain parts of the total responses.

Of the millions of responses which the person might make he makes in fact not one but a dozen or a score. The picture is not "S in person P evokes R," but "S in person P evokes R_a or R_b or R_c .... R_n." It is largely by selection from among these varied reactions to the same stimulus that human learning occurs.

All the general principles which hold good for the responses of a person to external situations hold also for responses to states within the person. Connections leading from ideas, desires, delusions, and fears very in strength, exhibit multiple response, and involve parts as well as totals. "9×7, how many?" as an inner question put by a person to himself may call up "the idea of 63" as surely as when spoken by another or seen in a book.

Purposes and Mechanisms

Of very great importance are the connections between a situation and chains of responses *until a certain result is attained.* So the sight of the hit ball evokes (in the fielder) a series of movements until his hands grasp the ball. So a line of print to be read leads a reader to move along it until he has got the words. Much of human behavior is purposive, and guided almost incessantly by its consequences in the form of the satisfyingness of the person's status or progress step by step. If one response to a situation does not satisfy the person it is abandoned in favor of another.

This is not to say that human behavior is ruled arbitrarily or mystically by forces that transcend ordinary knowledge and control. On the contrary, we know perhaps more about the biological processes by which purposes influence behavior than about those by which sheer habit influences behavior.

Individuals, Groups, and Homo Sapiens

Facts and principles true of all humans are of special importance, but great caution is required in attributing a trait to all members of the species. The early students of morals, economics, government, and other sciences of man erred often by imputing as universal traits those which were largely caused by civilizations with which they themselves were familiar, and which men in different circumstances lack.

Equal caution is desirable in attributing or denying a mental trait to one sex or age or race. Each individual's behavior is caused in part by certain tendencies which he has in common with all members of the species, in part by tendencies peculiar to his sex, in part by tendencies peculiar to his ancestry, in part by the stage of development or maturation which he has reached, in part by tendencies peculiar to the "culture" of his land and time, and in part by the circumstances which characterize his own peculiar life-history. The reader's behavior in even so simple a routine as his breakfast this morning would doubtless involve humanity, age, western civilization, and personal experiences.

Changes in Behavior

It is convenient to have a word to use in place of the symbol → or the phrase "has a certain probability of evoking"; and the words *connect* and *connection* are so used.[1] So we say that in a person who knows French there is a connection between "roi" and "king."

We may then say that a person's behavior depends upon a system of connections between situations and his responses, between what can happen to him and what he will do in return. The strength of a connection means the amount of the probability that the S will evoke the R. The permanence of a connection means maintenance over a period of time. The formation of a new connection is the increase of the S → R probability in question from zero value to some considerable amount. Changes in a person's nature are changes in his repertory of connections.

A S → R may change by the mere growth or maturation of the person. So at a certain stage an infant laid on its back will stay so, whereas later it will often roll over. The influence of maturation appears most strikingly in the life of sex, but it is potent in many other abilities and proclivities.

Every occurrence of a modifiable S → R in a person will, other things being equal, increase the probability of that →. If saying "dog" occurs as a response to seeing *d o g,* the probability that *d o g* will evoke "dog" will be increased. Interest and satisfaction will raise the amount of increase, but the sheer occurrence of a modifiable connection strengthens it. Unless some force acts upon him in a contrary direction a man will continue increasingly to think and act as he has thought and acted.

Mere frequency of occurrence is, however, a relatively weak strengthener of connections. A more important factor is their accompaniments or immediate after-effects. Man's adaptations to his environment are largely caused by the consequences of his behavior. In typical experiments one

---

[1] Thus use of *connection* to express the fact that there is a certain probability that the person will behave in a certain way to a certain state of affairs is useful whatever the physiology of the process may be. They are specially appropriate words because the brain is a system of neurones which do connect sensitive surfaces of the body with muscle and glands, and which have billions of interconnenctions among themselves. But the words would still be useful regardless of that fact. They do not involve adherence to an associationist psychology or physiology. The words "evoke" or "connect with" and the symbol → designate the basic fact of living behavior.

rewarded occurrence adds six times as much strength to connections as a non-rewarded occurrence.

A Theory of the Operation of After-Effects

What evidence is available shows that the strengthening influence of a relevant satisfying after-effect is as natural a fact as any of nerve physiology. The physiological processes are unknown, but it does not depend on interaction or any other doctrine of the relation of mind to matter. It does not act logically or teleologically. Its influence does not pick out the "right" or "useful" connection by any mystical or logical potency. It is, on the contrary, as natural in its action as a falling stone, a ray of light, a line of force, a discharge of buckshot, a stream of water, or a hormone in the blood. It will strengthen not only the connection which is the most preferred, but also to some extent connections which are wrong, irrelevant, or useless, provided they are close enough to the satisfier in the succession of connections.

This reaction of neurones which is aroused by the satisfier and which strengthens connections may be called the *confirming reaction*. Though its intimate histological basis and physiological nature are no better known than those of facilitation, inhibition, fatigue, or strengthening by repetition, certain facts about it are known.

The confirming reaction is independent of sensory pleasures; indeed, a pain may set it in action. The confirming reaction, though far from logical or inerrant, is highly selective. It may pick out and act upon the words one is saying, leaving uninfluenced one's gross bodily movements and all that one is seeing. The confirming reaction seems often to issue from some overhead control in the brain. This overhead control may be rather narrow and specific, as when a swallow of liquid satisfies thirst and the satisfaction confirms the connection which caused the swallowing and makes the animal repeat that connection. This may happen while the main flow of his purposes concerns the work he is doing or the game he is playing or the book he is reading. It may be very broad and general, as when the purpose is to do well and win a game or to pass the time pleasantly, and is satisfied by any one of many movements. It may be stimulated to send forth its confirming reaction by a rich sensory satisfier, such as freedom, food, and companionship, or by a symbolic satisfier, such as the announcement "Right" in an experiment in learning.

If a connection has a satisfying after-effect which causes a confirming reaction, and if the S continues, the confirming reaction tends to cause a continuance of the R, and often with more vigor and shorter latency. If the situation has vanished, the strengthening of the connection can only manifest itself when S recurs, which may be months later.

The potency of a confirming reaction may bear little relation to the intensity of the satisfier. A "self" may be as well satisfied, and so issue as full and adequate a confirming reaction, by a moderate reward as by one much larger. There seems to be an upper point beyond which increases in a reward add only excitement. Toward the low end there is a range where the reward fails more frequently to arouse an adequate confirming reaction. A state of affairs below this degree of satisfyingness is satisfying to the extent of being tolerated, and nothing is done to abolish or evade it. At the other end of this neutral zone begin states of affairs which are annoying and stimulate one to do whatever his repertory provides as responses to the annoyance in question.

The confirming reaction solves the conflict between commonsense teleology, which asserts that we do as we do largely because we thereby get what we want, and mechanistic science, which asserts that the mind is as truly determined by natural forces as is a dynamo or a radio set. Our purposes, though teleological, are a part of nature; they exist as parts of what I have called the overhead control or ruling set of the mind; they act by the natural force of the confirming reaction; this is as truly a mechanism as the knee-jerk or lid-reflex or strengthening influence of sheer repetition, but it has the special property of working back upon connections to strengthen those which are satisfying to a man's purposes. It is teleological in the sense that it enables the purposes to modify behavior. Consequences as well as antecedents determine thought and action.

Occurrences and after-effects are two real and potent forces changing a person's behavior by strengthening $S \rightarrow R$'s. Other forces such as imitation, "telescoping" (the omission of intermediate links so that $S_1 \rightarrow R_1 \rightarrow S_2 \rightarrow R_2 \rightarrow S_3 \rightarrow R_3$ becomes $S_1 \rightarrow R_3$), and movement toward a mental equilibrium of some sort, have been suggested by certain psychologists, but these are probably secondary results of repetition and the confirming reaction. We shall not invoke them until these two simple biological facts are found inadequate.

The Modification of Behavior by Associative Shift and the Conditioned Reflex

In much human learning there is multiple response to a situation with strengthening of one response and relative weakening of the others. But in some there is only one response, the learning consisting in shifting this response from one situation to another. So we say "Whoa!" and pull the horse's head back hard. He stops as a response to the pull. We repeat, gradually decreasing the force of the pull until eventually he stops at the mere "Whoa!" This is the general principle of *associative shifting*.

The phenomenon of the *conditioned reflex* as discovered by Pavlov and studied by his followers is the special case of associative shifting where the R is a reflex (such as the flow of saliva, or the dilation of the pupil of the eye in darkness or the jerk of an arm at an electric shock) and where the shift is made from the situation S_u, which normally evokes the reflex, to a different one, S_c, by presenting S_c along with S_u. The conditioned reflex is of great theoretical interest and is of practical importance in connection with the control of certain reflexes and habits.

In the actual work of influencing and changing men by government, industry, trade, education, and social work, the selection of more desirable responses to a situation and the shifting of a response to a situation where it is more desirable to have it, often work together in complicated ways. So also the two forces by which they operate, occurrence and after-effect, usually work together. But the changes can always be analyzed into differential strengthenings of responses to the same situation or into differential attachments of the same response.

By sufficient skill any response of which a person is capable can conceivably be attached to any stimulus to which he is sensitive. But in fact some situations so inevitably arouse a certain response that it is practically impossible to put any other response in its place, and some responses are so inevitably attached to only a certain sort of situation that it is practically impossible to shift them. Many investigators have tried to teach men to increase the flow of saliva at a given signal, but without sure success, though it is easily done with dogs. It is easy to teach a child to wave his hands, but very hard to teach him to quicken his pulse. We learn to control the flow of tears to some extent, but not to control the flow of gastric juice.

Chapter 2
Abilities

Human abilities are multifarious and practically innumerable. John Doe can digest this food, spell this word, understand that sentence, jump over yonder fence, solve such and such problems. Whatever classificatory scheme is used, there will not be groups sharply distinguished, but a continuum with intermediate or doubtful borderline cases. So a man's mental or psychological abilities shade off into "bodily" or muscular. Sensory abilities shade off into perceptual.

Three sorts of classification of abilities are of special interest. The first lists abilities according to the operation used, such as moving, secreting, absorbing, perceiving, imagining, attending, discriminating, reasoning, deciding, acting. The second lists them according to the end attained, as to digest starch, to manufacture certain hormones, to read, business ability, executive ability. The third lists them according to the degree to which they can be increased or decreased. So the ability to distinguish reddish grays from greenish grays cannot be greatly increased by any known means. The ability to digest carbohydrates is very hard to modify by training, but may be easily reduced by disease and restored with insulin, and some mental abilities may similarly be obdurate against education but submissive to drugs. The ability to spell a certain thousand words can be increased from near zero to perfection by training with repetitions and rewards, but the ability to learn to spell a thousand new words in half the time required hitherto is very hard to acquire. The ability to understand such words as elephant, rhinoceros, daffodil, portulaca, beige, croquignole and watermelon is easy to acquire; but the ability to understand such words as analytical, derivative, conditional, coordinate, chemistry, proteid, and potentiality is extremely hard to acquire.

A common method of thinking about mental abilities has been to assume that certain entities properly named attention, memory, imagination, reasoning, exist in a man and constitute his nature, and that certain combinations of these, together with certain traits of character and temperament, produce business ability, literary ability, executive ability, ability to read, and the like when the circumstances of life favor their production. The facts are very different from this.

Human abilities are known from human behavior—from what men think and feel and do. Also, they are among our means of predicting it. So the ability to spell *cat* means that the person will respond to certain requests, needs, or the like by saying or writing *c-a-t,* if he has the desire to accede to the request, satisfy the need, etc. Very often the assertion is that he will respond to a situation by any one of many combinations of such which produces a certain result. So the ability to find the correct sum of 1126, 1309, and 1495 does not specify that the person will proceed in any one way. He may write the numbers in a column, or leave them on the line; he may add 5 and 9 first, or 6 and 9; he may write 20 or write only 0; and so on. The attainment of the specified result in response to a situation may involve the trial of various procedures, the abandonment of some, and a more or less long course of deliberation, experimentation, and criticism.

If a person can attain the same result in half the time another person takes or than he himself took before, we shall say that the two abilities were the same in kind but differed in speed of achievement. If a person can attain the same result in the same time with half the effort that another person suffers, the two abilities were the same in kind and speed of achievement but differed in the strain involved. If a person can attain the same result in the same time and with the same effort but by a procedure that is more elegant or instructive or pleasurable or healthful or refined, the two abilities differed in respect of so and so. That is, let us make what is achieved primary, the time required secondary, the strain tertiary in our thinking, and deal with other values which the ability may have as may be required. If we identified no two abilities unless they were alike in every particular we should have an unmanageable list. Indeed, in most work, it has been found desirable to disregard the amount of strain or effort, and limit investigation to what is achieved and the time required, both of which can be determined objectively.

Even with these limitations, the number of distinct abilities is legion and it is obviously desirable to group them further.

(1) As a first means of grouping we may put together abilities which differ only by small and unimportant differences in situation, but are identical in achievement and time required. For example, suppose that the situations are "How many are 9 and 6?" "Add 9 and 6, what is the sum?" "9+6=?" "9 and 6 make how many?" and "9 plus 6 equal how many?" The ability to achieve the right answer in 4 seconds is not identical in the five cases, and persons could in fact be found who had some of these five abilities and lacked others, but we may group them together with little harm.

(2) As a second means of grouping, we may put together abilities which differ only by small and unimportant differences in the achievement. If the ability is that of translating a certain French sentence, or of drawing a line 4 inches long, certain minor variations in what is done may be thus neglected, especially when the performances though different are equally "good." Where they are not equally "good," the limits of tolerance may be stated in the description of the ability. For example, the ability to tell reds from greens could be defined as the ability to detect any such color-differences greater than a certain amount. This last is not a very good illustration of the neglect of "small and unimportant" differences; for the differences among those who are not color-weak, and who would all be credited with the ability, may for certain purposes be rather important. It was chosen precisely as an introduction to the statement that neglecting small differences in the achievement is risky.

As criteria of "small" and "unimportant" which decide whether it is legitimate to group abilities in these two ways, we use first the degree of correlation of the abilities among individuals; that is, the frequency with which the existence of one of them involves the existence of the other in that same person, and second the accidentalness or "chance" causation of such discrepancies as appear. For example, suppose that abilities A_1 and A_2 in a thousand persons show the following correlation: 600 have both A_1 and A_2, 11 have A_1 but not A_2, 9 have A_2 but not A_1, 380 have neither A_1 nor A_2. The degree of correlation is about .96.

If A_1 was the ability to spell *antagonist* when tested at home and A_2 was the ability to spell *antagonist* when tested in school, and if the eleven who manifested A_1 but apparently lacked A_2 spelled *antagonist* wrong to spite the teacher, our confidence that the two abilities were nearly the same would be increased. The accidental and irrelevant forces will show themselves by not acting often in the same direction in the same person. Such high intercorrelations justify us in thinking about the ability to add integers, the ability to multiply decimal fractions, the ability to say the Lord's prayer, without bothering with the rare gaps and mutilations in these abilities.

(3) As a third means of simplification, we may put abilities together when there are no differences except in the time required to achieve the result. Speed is often an indication of important differences in the inner constitution of an ability, the method by which the person achieves the result, and consequently of the significance of it for other abilities, and also because in education and productive labor speed is often important in itself.

(4) As a fourth means of grouping we may put together abilities which almost always go together, the possession of any considerable number of them almost always involving the possession of all or most of the rest. Thus the ability to write any word that one knows how to spell so commonly implies the ability to write any others that the person knows how to spell, that we replace thousands of abilities by the "ability to write."

Groupings of this sort may be divided into those where the abilities go together chiefly because of fundamental biological relations, and those where the abilities go together chiefly because of education, customs, and the like. Ability to walk, to hear, and to call up visual images are samples of the former; ability to write, to run a punch-press, and to dress oneself are samples of the latter.

Two very important means of reducing the list are by grouping together all the abilities which achieve results similar in general character, but differing in extent or "goodness." Thus all the abilities to name correctly this, that and the other plant which is seen may be grouped as "the ability to name plants," which varies in extent from the ability to name none to the ability to name ten thousand or more. All the abilities to draw circles may be grouped as "the ability to draw circles," but with variations in "goodness" from the work of an expert artist down to the faulty products of a tyro. The "goodness" in question may be precision, evenness, beauty, or any other characteristic.

A still more important means of reducing the list is like the above save that the achievements or results vary in what is commonly called the "difficulty" of achieving them. Thus the thousands of abilities to solve an arithmetical problem may be grouped under "ability to solve arithmetical problems," which varies according as the problems are very easy, a little harder, still harder, very hard, and so on, as in the following scale:

LEVEL F: Will is 5 years old now. How old will he be in 2 years?
LEVEL H: What number taken from 35 leaves 27?
LEVEL J: 12 is $\frac{3}{5}$ of what number?
LEVEL N: Five sixths equal how many thirds?

Similarly the millions of abilities to supply specified numbers of words to complete sentences so as to make good sense may be grouped under the ability "to complete sentences," which varies only in difficulty, as shown in these samples:

LEVEL G: The ice . . . . melt when hot weather comes.
LEVEL I: The first . . . . after June is . . . .
LEVEL K: No . . . . is powerful . . . . to . . . . two and two be five.
LEVEL M: Modern . . . . of communication should . . . . closer to each other.

Extent or Range or Width

Suppose that all English words were equally easy to learn to spell, and that all spellings except the correct ones were equally "wrong." The enumeration of the particular words which a person was able to spell could then be replaced by their number. The ability to spell any one ten-thousand would be in an intelligible and useful sense the same as the ability to spell any other ten-thousand and would differ from the ability to spell any five-thousand by being twice as "extensive" or "wide."

Suppose that the ability to earn a dollar by washing n dishes, hoeing n rows of corn, shoveling n pounds of dirt, scrubbing n square feet of floors, or any other variety of unskilled manual labor was entirely unskilled or equally skilled and equally easy to acquire, and that there were no degrees of "goodness" or merit. Then the enumeration of the various abilities at that level of skill possessed by a person could usefully be replaced by their number. John who had fifty such abilities would differ from James who had only forty or Joe who had sixty in extent or range of ability as an unskilled or low-skill laborer.

I cannot give important cases of extent or width pure and simple, because there are none. There are no abilities differing *only* in the number of included abilities. But informational groupings such as knowledge of geography, history, French vocabulary, acquaintance with tools and their uses, or acquaintance with the rocks, currents, and tides of a harbor as constituents of ability as a pilot, do rest upon a certain approximate equivalence of constituent abilities.

Goodness or Quality

Ability to sing the same song, but varying from "very badly" to "very well," is a series of abilities differing in goodness or quality. If various abilities to cook various dishes equally difficult to cook are grouped into one ability by our fourth principle (of affiliation by nature or circumstances), the resulting ability may vary according to the quality of the cooking of each item, and so have as its "quality" the total or average quality of all. There are many abilities of consequence in which the situation is the same and the result or product produced is the same in general nature but differing more or less widely in goodness or quality. These are of consequence as abilities which keep persons alive, are marketable in productive labor, or give pleasure to performers or audience or both.

The varying goodness or quality may be varying degrees of precision, beauty, smoothness, harmony, sweetness, or whatever. In the ability of a mason the probable stability and endurance of his product are prime features of its goodness, but in the ability of a cook they are not. We may not even know what the goodness consists in, but simply rate it by a scale of specimen products as in the case of the goodness of paintings, qualities of voice, witticisms, designs, and decorations.

Difficulty

The concept of difficulty is used widely and loosely in human affairs. Thus we say that "to lift 200 pounds and to lift 225 pounds require the same sort of ability, but the latter is harder." Or we say that carpentry, pattern making, and instrument-making all require mechanical ability; but that the last, being harder, requires a higher degree of that ability.

We are specially concerned with variations of an ability which are clearly variations in difficulty as defined above. Let us call such variations of an ability "levels" of the ability and call the achievements which any given level of the ability can just barely accomplish, achievements of that level. But we will bear in mind that the gradation in an ability from worse to better, may or may not correspond to the gradation in level. It might, for example, require a higher level of ability to control the throat and chest muscles to breathe or swallow *imperfectly* (as in an actor imitating being choked or asphyxiated) than to breathe or swallow normally.

As examples of abilities differing chiefly in level, we may take the ability to understand sentences, the ability to complete them, the ability to decide correctly more and more difficult points of law, the ability to perform an appendectomy with variations in the adhesions of the appendix, or the ability to manage a more and more irritated and disaffected body of soldiers.

When scientists deliberately group the abilities of a graded series which are alike in the situations and the achievements attained but differ only in the fact that of the persons who can succeed at the easiest level fewer and fewer can succeed with each harder and harder level, they are not likely to mix abilities which are really unlike in general nature. When the grouping is taken over from common usage (as in the ability to solve arithmetical problems or the ability to play harder and harder music) there is greater danger that important differences in the situations will be neglected and that the achievements will be alike only in name.

The first task is to determine whether all persons who possess the highest level ability, possess all the lower level abilities, whether all persons who possess the next highest level ability possess all lower than it, and so on. If they do, the abilities may be regarded as of the same general nature. For, if they were different in nature, they would be imperfectly correlated among individuals, and some persons possessing ability A at level L would lack ability not A at a level lower than L.[1]

Even after grouping abilities by the principles described above, their number will be so great as to discourage students of human nature from listing and describing them, and still more from the work of devising means of measuring them, observing their functioning and their values, determining their relations one to another, and experimenting with ways of improving them. There is a strong temptation to combine them further in order to have fewer units of study. There is also the hope that the resulting larger abilities will be better worth studying. For example, abilities comprising knowledge of the meanings of single Latin words, understanding of the uses of various Latin endings, and understanding of Latin constructions or locutions may be combined into "ability to understand Latin."

The harm is less in proportion as the different abilities in the mixture are highly correlated among individuals. Suppose, for example, that strength of grip, strength of back, strength of jaw, and other particular abilities to exert force with particular groups of muscles were correlated each with any other approximately as shown in Fig. 1, which indicates a

[1] The operation of this criterion may be illustrated by extreme cases. Suppose, for instance, that in the completion abilities we inserted the ability to complete "The . . . . of the hypotenuse is equal to the . . . . of the . . . . of the two . . . . in a right triangle." Some persons of high level in completions would fail with the easy mathematical task.

correlation coefficient of about .90. The combined ability consists chiefly of something common to all of them; the use of it for any person or group instead of an inventory of the separate abilities can do little harm to offset its greater convenience.

The criterion of close correlation among components is not, however, infallible. Under certain social conditions there might be a very close correlation between ability to read Latin and ability to demonstrate propositions in geometry because both were required of high-school pupils and acquired by almost no other persons, but the combination of

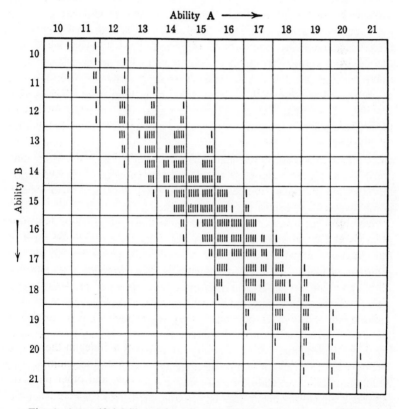

Fig. 1. An artificial illustration of a correlation between two abilities so close that little harm is done by mixing the two abilities into one. Each little line represents one individual's scores in two abilities; his score in Ability A is shown by the relative position of the line from right to left, and his score in Ability B by its relative position from the top down.

the two abilities would, save for a very few purposes, be misleading and much inferior to the consideration of them separately.

Neither popular thinking and reasoning about human abilities nor the sciences of economics, business, government, law, education, etc., have advanced far enough. The universal custom has been to deal verbally with phrases alleged to refer to large total abilities, such as digestion, muscular strength, the ability to learn, to remember, to reason, ability as a weaver, as a mason, as an entrepreneur, the ability to distinguish right and wrong, to control one's temper, to make friends.

These abilities name groups of achievements which are more impressive than the more definite and specific abilities such as to swallow, to walk, to know the letters of the alphabet, to know a thousand plants, to draw a circle. Some (such as the ability to reason or executive ability) are often very complicated mixtures of imperfectly known ingredients so that one does not know what one is thinking about when one considers them. Some (such as the ability to remember) are supposedly common elements of many abilities, but with so little agreement about what abilities they are elements of, that they are extremely vague and uncertain. A few of them (like ability as a mason) are totals or averages of groups of abilities at different levels of goodness which give promise of being analyzable each into a few describable and identifiable abilities. More than nine tenths and probably more than nineteen twentieths of the scientific investigation of human abilities has been of such ill-defined mixtures and components, and we must try to make the best of it.

Science in such cases begins with a name like intelligence or executive ability and a provisional inventory of the behavior put into the form of the situations in which the ability is used and the results attained or products produced by it. So intelligence is taken to mean the ability to obtain good answers to certain questions, good ideas for certain emergencies, good choices or compromises among certain alternatives.

Such an ability-inventory often may be divided conveniently into features of form and features of content. So, in the abilities to remember, the formal elements, such as ability to retain and recall after a few seconds, ability to retain and recall after days, ability to recall in perfect detail, and ability to retain the essential facts and use them appropriately (so-called logical memory) may be separated from the content elements, such as memory for words, for numbers, for connected discourse, for musical phrases, for odors, for shapes and sizes, etc.

The general opinion still is that the formal elements are the chief constituents of abilities, so that a person who has a high degree of an ability with one sort of content will have approximately that degree with other sorts. The investigations of the past forty years, however, have demonstrated an enormous specificity in abilities. This specificity is of theoretical and practical importance wherever human abilities are important, and we may note that it has been found so ubiquitously that it is prudent to expect that managerial ability will vary greatly with the kind of issue that is to be decided, that ability to learn will vary with the subject or trade or accomplishment to be learned and similarly with most of the abilities which figure in the social sciences and human engineering.

Common Factors

The probabilities of achievement included under a certain name can sometimes be represented by one factor common to them all plus certain group factors each of which is common to a considerable number of them, plus many specific factors each of which is limited to few of the "situation → result attained" facts of the inventory.[1]

In proportion as the common factor outweighs the group factors and the specifics, it becomes more and more justifiable to neglect them.

Principal Factors or Components

Common factors and principal factors may best be illustrated by an imaginary case. Suppose that ability as a salesman has been investigated and found to consist of three factors common to almost all sorts of selling, wholesale and retail, by personal interview and by correspondence, to producers and consumers, of sugar, steel mills, bonds, insurance, underwear, seeds, of five broad group factors, and of many specifics, as listed below:

Common factors:
 intelligence, interest in people, ambition.

Broad group factors:
 enjoyment of a conflict of wits, popularity, ability to talk interestingly, pertinacity.

[1] Strictly speaking, the term *specific factor* is applied only to a factor which operates in only one of the achievements included in the inventory. Strictly speaking, the term *group-factor* is used for a factor which is common to two or more achievements included in the inventory, though not to all. But it is usually very difficult, and not very useful, to be sure whether a factor operates in only one, so that "narrow" group factors are often lumped with specifics.

Specific or narrow group factors:

knowledge of product A, knowledge of product B, etc.

knowledge of customer A, knowledge of customer B, etc.

When analyzed into principal, second, third, factors, it might be found that the principal factor was closely allied to knowledge of the particular product sold, which would be determined in part by his intelligence and ambition; and the second factor might be allied to a special sort of popularity which comes in part from a sincere interest in people. It is my opinion that the real elemental factors are so numerous that the analyses will not reach them, but only more or less useful statistical composites of them.[1]

The Causation of Abilities

It is important to distinguish the abilities which may appear as a result of elaborate stimulation and modification by people, books, customs, institutions, and all other products of the past. Using the term "culture" as the anthropologists do to mean the man-made or man-chosen environment of a human group, we may distinguish the features of a man's abilities which are parts of his original, inborn, unlearned equipment from the features which are due to the culture in which he lives and grows. The former are known only very inadequately and have to be inferred from human achievements in devious ways, and with varying probabilities.

For example the locomotor ability of man has as its original roots capacities to roll over, hitch the body along on its back or belly, creep, climb, walk and run on four legs, and later on two.[2] Out of these, or by adding to them stimulation from the culture, are developed various marchings, dancings, pole vaulting, roller-skating, ice-skating, etc. In a liquid medium, the original tendencies are (1) to flounder, which helps one learn to swim, and (2) to reach out to grasp for a hand-hold, a tendency which has to be overcome to make swimming or floating a success.

---

[1] Interested readers should consult C. Spearman, '27, *The Abilities of Man;* T. L. Kelley, '28, *Crossroads in the Mind of Man;* L. L. Thurstone, '35, *Vectors of Mind;* G. H. Thomson, '39, *Factorial Analysis of Human Abilities.*

[2] The incompetence of ordinary observation is well shown by the fact that until a short time ago people could believe that birds had to be taught to fly and babies to walk. Birds fly, snakes wriggle, horses go on four legs and men go on two all by original nature. Their respective genes provide these behaviors as truly as they provide feathers, scales, hoofs, and toes.

The abilities of men as leaders in the hunt or warfare, in parliaments and strikes, banks and factories, are probably rooted in certain traits of so-called dominance, social intelligence, courage, and energy, in the leaders and certain tendencies to approve and submit to size, strength, courage, and gorgeous display, in the led, both provided by the genes. But leadership by the literati in old China or by churchmen in medieval Europe was determined largely by cultural forces.

General Characteristics of Abilities

It is rarely possible to analyze an ability into an inborn capacity and acquired capacities. Science often must take persons as they are and study their abilities to learn, reason, draw, play the piano, sell goods, trade, cooperate, govern, make friends, love, enjoy life, and so on through the long list of achievements which the world needs or desires, and which the sciences of man must know about.

One important fact about them is that most are compounds involving many responses to many different situations. A second fact is that most of them are mixtures of items of width, quality, and level. For example, if A has more ability to govern than B, A can govern more people, or govern them better, or govern people who are harder to govern, or do any two or all three. A third is that most of them include sub-abilities which are very imperfectly correlated so that a person's status in the ability is really an average of the sub-abilities which he possesses. Great sensitiveness to the beauties of line and color may coexist with mediocre appreciation of poetry.

Some alleged unitary ability like leadership, inventiveness, originality, self-control, or business ability turns out to be a multitude of imperfectly correlated powers, a fact still underestimated by thinkers unfamiliar with recent psychology. They are misled by the utterly false notion that a person is a trinity of intellect, will, and emotion, comprising a small group of faculties or powers each of which is a unitary force, a sort of machine or fairy that sits in the person's brain. A word like imagination or leadership or coordination is used vaguely but helpfully to name certain facts in human behavior. Then it is misused as a name for the unknown causes of behavior. Then it is further misused as an excuse for thinking that because one word is used to name the cause, the cause is as neat, simple, and unitary as the word.

Thinkers about civilized life made a similar mistake. Phrases like intelligence, mathematical ability, linguistic ability, salesmanship, manual dexterity, political sense, criminality, useful as convenient names for groups of facts of behavior, led people to fancy that some simple unitary entities existed which were these abilities and caused the behaviors in question. In the case of certain features of intelligence, there is some possibility that a simple cause may operate.[1] But for the most part human genes and brains developed into their present constitutions before civilization, and are not departmentalized in abilities for mathematics, music, trading, politics, law and the like.[2]

The departmentalization to be expected is rather toward ability in running and dodging, in pursuing and catching, in investigating the edibility of small objects, in dismembering larger objects, in keeping in contact with a familiar group of human beings, in soliciting food from them and sharing it with them, in behaving so as not to outrage their instincts, in certain paternal and maternal arts, and in other behaviors typical of men living in small hordes, a hundred thousand or a half-million years ago, without any furniture, books, pianos, pencils, shops, or elections.[3]

Experts in this part of psychology today define the ability by the behavior. Musical ability is the ability to maintain certain specified standards of rhythm, pitch, tone-quality, etc. Intelligence is the ability to succeed with an adequate sampling of all intellectual tasks. The careful now define managerial ability by the difficulties surmounted and achievements made in an adequate sampling of all managerial tasks.

In some cases there are tests which give definite intelligible information about the ability to do said tasks, but knowledge is lacking or imperfect concerning what they imply about the ability in an adequate sampling of all the tasks which they are supposed to represent. So, for example, of three sets of tests of ability to draw and paint (the Christensen, Meier, and Lewerenz tests), no competent person would dare to say just how closely any one of the three would correlate with an adequate sampling of all tasks of an artist; ability at one of these tests is easily determined, and may be a very valuable fact if its

[1] The general amount of energy of the higher brain centers has been suggested by Spearman, and the number of units of neurone to neurone contacts in the cerebrum by the writer.

[2] Original organization for language is probably an exception, though the close association of speech functions with the posterior part of the third left frontal convolution of the brain may be a matter of the movements of the throat and mouth parts and of enunciation and pronunciation rather than of the intellectual control of verbal symbolism.

[3] It is indeed somewhat puzzling that so many children should take to music and mathematics so early, nearly as "naturally" as to running about, picking berries off bushes, and begging from parents and friends, and that the distinction between those who have much and those who have little should be nearly as clear for musical ability or mathematical ability as for chasing or cajolery. This puzzle deserves more attention.

limitations are kept in mind. There are hundreds of such tests, each of which has some correspondence with ability in a wider sampling of tasks, but with inadequate identification and inadequate knowledge of the closeness of correspondence.

The correlations between desirable abilities are usually positive but not high. Nature does not compensate a man for weakness in some by strength in others, but gives to them that have. Her favoritism is, however, not so extreme as it might be. The thousand men now living who have the highest ability to think and reason will be above the average in the various abilities to remember, in ability to understand people, even in musical ability or such arts of skill as shooting, billiards, and carpentry; but they will not be the top thousand in any one of these.

Changes in Abilities

Many abilities improve with age as the organism matures. Intelligence and the ability to learn, for example, improve from birth to the early twenties. Most abilities are improvable by any training which gives the ability exercise and makes its successful operations satisfying to the person. The amount of improvement varies from very great, as in very specific knowledges and skills, to very little, as in what is called general intelligence or in ability to reason, and perhaps to zero as in ability to respond to reds and greens of equal intensity. Old age weakens most abilities, especially those requiring energy and speed, but the drop from age fifty to age seventy-five is probably only one or two percent per year. It may be partly compensated for by increases in certain abilities related to wisdom and experience.

Writers about government, economics, and education are often guilty of a serious error of fact, and men who manage are often guilty of a serious error of policy, in connection with changes in abilities. The first error is to assume that training of an ability in one narrow field with one sort of situations will improve it equally in all fields and problems. This error leads to fantastic expectations, and schools, military service, political responsibility and other forms of training pursue rainbows and go on wild-goose chases when they might be making substantial improvements in men. The second error is to keep young people of great abilities at unimportant work in subordinate posts until facts absolutely compel us to see their merits. The doctrine that, because the average man under our present system reaches his top at forty, we should consider nobody for a top post until he is about forty is unsound, timid, and wasteful.

Abilities and Interests

As a rule one enjoys doing what he can do well. The order of his abilities corresponds fairly closely to the order of his liking for the activities. There is a natural harmony whereby an arrangement by which the world's work is distributed among men so as to maximize achievement will also increase enjoyment greatly. Conversely, if everybody was allotted the work which he liked best to do, the world's work being distributed to maximize enjoyment, there would be a very high status of achievement.

Quasi-Abilities and Traits of Character and Temperament

The common distinctions between abilities and traits of character and temperament are not fundamental. If it is a question of what a person can do if he wishes to, some term like *ability* is customarily used; if it is a question of what he would do if he could, some term like *proclivity, want,* or *like* is customarily used; if it is a question of what he does in fact do, some term like *trait* or *tendency* is customarily used.

The statements of these two chapters about abilities are true of any trait of character, disposition, or temperament. The facts and principles about identification, classification, complexity, specificity, individual differences, correlation rather than compensation, and failure of training of a particular sort to spread its influence widely all apply to all traits of character, disposition, or "personality." Little needs to be added to the psychology of abilities and wants to cover the psychology of traits, tendencies, or characteristics.

Chapter 3
Great Abilities[1]

Common sense and psychology use freely a scaling of abilities from little to great. It would be difficult to frame a rigorous definition of "great" as applied to all the multifarious works of man. And it is not necessary, and probably not even advisable, to try to do so at present. But it is well to have in mind three notable varieties of such scaling. The first includes cases where the upper end of the scale denotes chiefly ability to do *harder* things. The second includes cases where the upper end of the scale denotes chiefly ability to do the same thing *better*, more exactly, more elegantly. The third includes cases where the upper end denotes chiefly ability to do *more* things; the third is much less important than the others and is rarely dealt with by itself alone as a high ability.

Common sense and the social sciences freely assume the existence in men of qualities or combinations which are the causes of some achievement. High musical ability is the ability to achieve thus, to produce such a product, of harmony, pleasure in the listeners, etc. High entrepreneurial ability is the ability to hire materials, labor, and tools and achieve a product that can be marketed at enough to pay the bills with a large surplus. But of what musical ability and entrepreneurial ability consist or how they are related to other abilities little is known. Something real and

---

[1] Much of this chapter is based upon an article ['38 A] by the author in the *Scientific Monthly*, vol. 47, pp. 59–72.

biological doubtless does correspond to these terms, but it may be different in different persons, and the trait in A which, along with other traits in him, gives him high military ability, may, along with other traits in B, make B a great captain of industry, or may, along with certain features of C, permit C to be a great reformer.

Causation

The causation of specially high degrees of ability is, like everything else in human individual differences, the action of certain events or conditions upon the genes. The doctrine of the irrepressibility of genius by any environment, no matter how unfavorable (often attributed to Galton) is unsound, though very high inborn capacities do have a notable tendency to seek and find an environment that favors them and a training that heightens them. General intelligence and singing are cases where training is relatively weak as a cause of very high abilities. Ability in diagnosing diseases and ability in translating Indian languages are cases where it is relatively strong.

In many of the abilities which are called upon in our civilization, we have made arrangements whereby the training without which a person can hardly manifest very high ability is denied to those who have only mediocre genes in that respect. They cannot get into medical schools; they cannot practice entertaining audiences; they cannot, except rarely by nepotism, get training as executives or be elected to public office. So only the originally able receive the training, and we cannot tell how much or little the training could do for persons of low natural capacity. And in general, partly because we give training in relation to capacity and partly because individuals of high capacity seek and find opportunities for training, the two sorts of causation act together in close correlation.

A high capacity may fail to manifest itself by lack of the adequate stimulus. Military ability may lie dormant if there are no wars. The ability to manage a great enterprise through a hierarchy of subordinates could hardly show itself in a pastoral civilization.

Frequency

Common observation reveals that very high abilities are rare. This holds good even when almost everybody has adequate early opportunities and whoever shows fairly high ability as a result of early opportunities is likely to be given more. The number of tenors as good as Caruso and Jean de Reszke will always be very small, unless some new discovery in the physiology of the voice overcomes present limitations, or some new practice in human breeding multiplies these rare individuals.

Observation is likely to be misled by two opposite prejudices in estimating the rarity of men able to solve difficult scientific problems, manage great firms, invest a million dollars wisely, or the like. If one thinks of the persons who are by common consent at the top level of ability and then moves down to estimate how many there are who are nearly as good, they seem very scarce. Close seconds to Carnegie or Caruso or Theodore Roosevelt in their respective generations do not readily come to mind. Such abilities are likely to make us belittle those who are really not far below them on the scale in question. In actual fact there may be many businessmen and singers not far below the best.

The Discovery of Specially High Abilities

Specially high abilities are presumably no more subject to chance or miracle than eclipses, the weather, or anything else in nature. Yet our present powers of prediction seem slight in comparison with what can be done about eclipses or even about the weather, but they are far above zero. A prediction much above chance can be made for any child even before he is born. From age 2 years 0 months certain abilities can be predicted from his sensory, motor, and intellectual achievement to date. All predictions are, of course, in terms of probabilities and with a margin of doubt. As a person's development proceeds and records of his achievements accumulate, better predictions can be made. When, however, the ability to achieve a certain result, A, is inferred from anything save very similar achievement, there is a rather large probability of error. The specialization of some abilities is so great that abilities so similar as to be called by the same name may not be perfect indicators of one another. Also the person himself may change, but this latter is probably the cause of much less doubt than has been supposed popularly. Great shifts, like those of Grant, are very rare.

Some abilities, as in abstract intellect and mathematics, appear early; others, as in the management of men and of money, appear later. The guiding principle is that a capacity will show itself when situations are met which demand the ability and reward it. So a child with the capacity *can* show abstract intellect as soon as he knows a substantial number of facts and words. If his activities are rewarded (perhaps only by his own enjoyment of them) he *will* show it. A person with the relevant capacity will similarly manage people and money as soon as he can profitably do so, but this will naturally be later. Cornelius Vanderbilt was an active and success-ful entrepreneur at 12; but school laws, labor laws, and social customs would probably prevent him from repeating this if he were born again.

In his arrangements to utilize all specially high capacities, one should discover and keep track of: (1) children of parents of high achievement, (2) persons who are especially intelligent, (3) persons who are especially sensitive to beauty, (4) persons who are especially creative in the fine arts or useful arts, (5) persons who are especially desirous of excellence and persistent in striving for success, and (6) persons who are especially courageous and independent. It is probable that a continuous account of the superior abilities that appear at ages 14, 18, and 22, with provision to keep careers open for their talents, would be a useful social investment. Even if nine out of ten of the recipients of such attention and aid achieve only moderately, the investment may yet be profitable provided one in a hundred of those near the top is enabled to do a higher quality of work than he would otherwise have done. Even a slight rise in a very high ability is, roughly speaking, priceless. Even a small chance of such a rise is worth a large expenditure.

Business and industrial enterprises have been supposed to discover very high abilities by work "on the job," but this has never been proved. Wise owners and managers of large enterprises are probably eager to find such persons, but the conditions of modern mines, factories, wholesale houses, banks, or railroads may prevent workers from knowing their own abilities and others from observing them. The more the work of an organization is specialized and regularized so that each person's responsibilities are more fully described and prescribed, the less chance there is that persons can show their promise by extraordinary competence in emergencies.

Utilization

The best function of exceptionally high abilities is to perform valuable services which no lesser ability can perform at all, as in scientific discoveries, inventions, masterpieces of the fine arts, difficult feats in inspiring, persuading, and otherwise managing individuals and groups.

In modern civilization very high abilities should never be unemployed, save for recreation. They should never do anything else, save as a luxury or a medicine. From the moment that a man has demonstrated his possession of such ability, society should arrange that he does it. If by a miracle some possible Newton or Dante could shovel as much sand per hour as ten thousand men, so that he could command four thousand dollars an hour as shoveler of sand all over the globe, society should, if possible, persuade him not to take that contract.

But if some individual can do two or more better than anybody else, the matter is not quite so simple; and if the jobs vary in importance and some of the individuals surpass some of the others in several of them, it may be fairly complex. A solution giving maximal utilization can be reached if all jobs, importances, individuals, and abilities are considered together. Table 1 shows the maximal utilization of ten men for twenty jobs of specified importance which none but they can do. For convenience, it is assumed that each job would require the same time as any of the others.

Table 1   Maximal utilization of 10 persons (A, B, C, D, etc.) doing one job each of 20 jobs. The symbol y indicates that the person in question can do the job in question

Job	Importance	Person Assigned	Persons and Their Abilities									
			A	B	C	D	E	F	G	H	I	J
1	10			y	y		y		y	y		
2	10		y	y	y	y	y	y	y			y
3	11		y	y		y	y		y		y	y
4	12		y		y	y					y	
5	14			y			y					y
6	15		y		y	y			y		y	
7	15			y			y		y	y		y
8	16	I	y		y						y	y
9	16		y		y	y				y		
10	18				y			y	y			
11	18	C or F			y			y	y			
12	20	H	y			y		y		y		y
13	20	F or C			y			y	y			
14	20	G		y			y		y			y
15	20	D	y		y	y						
16	21	E		y			y					
17	22			y								
18	22	J	y				y					y
19	24	B		y								y
20	25	A	y									

Psychologically it seems safer to trust as a rule to the individuals themselves plus the guidance they will obtain in the ordinary course of events from their fellow experts. Cases can be cited where a great man did well under the pressure of a publisher's contracts, the need to compose music that the market would buy, a grant for the completion of a specified project, a popular demand, the dictates of a superior. But on the whole what great men have done by choice will probably average much higher for the common good than what they have done by pressure from employers, advisers, or the public.

Three facts need to be considered in this connection. The first is that there is a positive correlation of about .50 between ability and virtue or good will toward men. Consequently, we will do better to trust our fortunes to able persons than to try to pick well-intentioned ones. Second, very able individuals are far likelier to judge correctly *what* work they are likely to succeed at and whether the time is ripe to attack. Third, very able persons usually attach much more interest and devotion to self-chosen work.

But the correlations between special abilities and good will, good sense, cooperativeness, and other multipliers of a man's value, though almost certainly positive, are far from perfect. In the management of his general life the person of high special ability may profit greatly from direction, persuasion, and even coercion *ab extra*. Wise publishers, heads of educational or business institutions, financial managers, patrons and friends may protect them from distractions, irritations and follies and help to keep them healthy and happy. The success of entrepreneurs in utilizing the labor of specialists of very high abilities will probably be more important for their own profits and for the common good than their success in utilizing the rank and file of workers. The success of the public in making conditions such that high abilities work in its interest will also presumably become even more important than it has been. Less than ever can we afford to stone the prophets.

Public assistance may safely be given to the education of very able persons and their relief from labor which makes poor use of their abilities. Present practices are often diametrically wrong, as where a gifted child who at a certain age has advanced far in school is permitted to be sent to work by his parents, while a dull child of the same age must be kept in school.[2]

The public should demand systems of appointment and promotion by merit in all non-elective government services. This would open one set of careers to individuals of high abilities; and, if physicians, lawyers, workers in physical, biological, and social sciences, engineers and men of affairs are given power and freedom in proportion to their demonstrated services, we should have a very useful, though incomplete, insurance against lack of use of these precious national resources.

Indirect provision for utilization of many sorts of high ability is made fairly efficiently by universities, hospitals, museums, foundations and other endowed institutions. These provide living expenses and facilities for work either as a gift or in return for moderate amounts of teaching or

[2] In the case of a random sampling of about a thousand boys in New York City whose careers were studied from 1922 to 1932, the number of years of schooling received by the top twentieth in intellectual achievement averaged less than half a year more than that for the bottom twentieth.

other service. Indirect provision is made by business concerns which employ men of great ability as physicists, chemists, geologists, engineers, architects, economists, statisticians, psychologists, lawyers, and others. Just how high the efficiency of the utilization is cannot be stated. It probably ranges from a low point where the person is put at work which lower abilities could do as well to a point where he is provided with first-rate opportunities to exercise and improve his abilities. But owners, if they interfere at all, will perhaps in the future interfere less with the specialists in a corporation's management than with the high general executives who plan its organization and appoint the top specialists.

With the vexed question of the degree of correspondence between what is good for the business and what is good for mankind we are not here concerned, beyond noting that if the products produced or services rendered are themselves good for mankind and if there is the amount of control over matters of health, decency, justice and the like now prevalent in civilized countries, the correspondence is much above zero. We may not hope that Adam Smith's "invisible hand" holds it at or near 1.00, but no competent economist would rate it as zero or negative.

There are certain sinister neglects and misuses of high abilities due to selfishness, nepotism, envy, and other base human passions, and others due to natural and normal self-esteem. A king may use his power fairly well in most respects, but, for fear of losing it, may make little use of the great abilities of his subordinates. The number of murders of near relatives by kings of old was very large! Dictators, even the most benevolent, seldom take pains to train able successors. Men have resigned positions of great power and dignity in order to retire to monasteries, or by doctor's orders, but not often simply to give some abler man a chance to do their work better. Indeed, it is psychologically very hard for one to believe that some of his subordinates are abler than he, since that conflicts with his long habit of dominance over them.

Very able men cannot then be relied on to do full justice to other very able men. They are, however, more likely to do so than are mediocre men. The ablest kings will tolerate abler ministers, and we may expect that the ablest bank presidents will give way to promising juniors oftener and earlier than the petty magnates of small towns.

Very high abilities may be misused by their possessors because of two important psychological fallacies. The first is that of overrating one's judgments because in one's special field they are excellent. The second is that of assuming that one's might is right on many occasions because it has been right in one's special field. A man who day after day has judged correctly ninety-nine times out of a hundred about legal problems, and who gains a moderate knowledge about politics or art, will feel an unjustifiable confidence in his judgments about the latter. A man who has exercised power repeatedly with benefit to all concerned as a bishop or general or company president, will feel an unjustifiable confidence in his exercise of power that comes to him as a college trustee or senator.

Such misuses are not of very great importance, first, because men of very high abilities usually are too interested in their own specialities to interfere much in other lines; second, because they are intelligent about their limitations, and third because, even if overvalued, their exercise of thought and of power will still be much better than the average, though below that of the expert.

If the leading specialist in treating a certain disease discovers a preventive of it, he may lessen his own income greatly by making the discovery public. Yet, as Professor Cattell has often remarked, the public gives him nothing to offset this. The ablest lawyers make a great financial sacrifice to take posts as judges or as professors in schools of law. Army officers highly competent in engineering and management have attractive chances to leave the service for private employment. The private concern will usually outbid the public. For example, great scholars or scientists will be paid far more for writing textbooks than for doing research. The case is different with low abilities, where the public often pays more money and security than private employers would offer.

The provision of financial aid during training is very uneven and more benevolent than efficient. For example, the aid available for intending clergymen is far richer than that for intending physicians, the latter being indeed almost nil. The theory is rather to reward religious devotion and palliate future poverty than to provide for public welfare. If he has somehow obtained training, the highly gifted engineer, physician, or clergyman can usually make a living at more or less instructive work. The highly gifted scientist or scholar can, if not too eccentric, make a living by teaching or expert service. Poets and other literary men can, thanks to Pulitzer prizes and Guggenheim fellowships, receive financial rewards for the work they most wish to do, or can become entertainers, as so many of the greatest of their kind have done. Public honors by way of financial support are not popular, however, and even in the enormous increase of public expenditures of the last generation, almost nothing has been spent directly to reward great public services.

Nobody knows how many of the very high possibilities in the genes of the ten million persons born in this country from 1870 on who survived to age 50 or later, have been realized. The reader may well make the best guess he can and act upon it when he has a chance, as voter, donor, adviser, or the like, to further the utilization of the nation's most precious asset. The writer's guess would be that our eventual utilization of possibilities existing at age 15 varies from as low as .30 in the case of capacity to govern well to as high as .80 in the case of managerial and entrepreneurial capacities, and to .90 or .95 for trading ability; is about .60 in the case of the fine arts, science, and scholarship; and is about .70 in engineering, invention, law, medicine, and education.[3] These percentages concern the numbers of persons who are doing the sort of work which they should be doing in the world's interest.

The Wages of Specially High Abilities

The difference between distributions of wages and distributions of the few abilities that have been measured is striking.

There will probably remain large discrepancies between the increases in an ability as a psychologist would measure them and the corresponding increases in wages. And this fact may stimulate us to consider certain forces which can and must cause the latter increases.

One force arises from the fact that a small increase in the ability may cause a large increase in sheer volume of the product or service. It is not inconceivable that abilities to plan an advertising campaign which were in the proportions of 10, 11, and 12 might produce returns in the proportions of 10, 100, and 1000. A's abilities being to B's in the ratio of 3 to 2, A might well sell ten times as many books as B.

A second force arises from the fact that a small difference in the ability may produce a crucial difference in the quality of the product or service. A ball player who is just enough better than other minor league players to be hired for a major league team; a scholar who is just enough better than others to be called to one of the great universities; a physician or lawyer who is just enough better than others to cause his patients or clients to recommend him rather than be silent about him—such a one may receive a disproportionate pecuniary return.

A third force comes into action when the small difference in ability enables its possessor to do something which no lesser ability can do at all. For example, it is reported that Dwight Morrow won repute by solving a problem in corporation organization which slightly less able lawyers had found insoluble. So a surgeon who can successfully perform a certain operation with which others fail may receive a monopoly price from those who can afford to pay for the service.

[3] Probably nine out of ten psychologists and sociologists would consider my estimates far too high.

Within the same sort of ability small differences may receive large pecuniary rewards because of volume, quality, and monopoly. The man of very high ability is in fact likely to be sought because volume makes the cost of some of his services per unit specially low, and quality makes some of them specially valued, and uniqueness makes some of them indispensable for certain purposes.

It is a matter of common knowledge that the pecuniary rewards of specially high abilities of different sorts vary widely. The scholar who of his generation adds the most and best to our knowledge of the Indo-European languages or Greek history may perhaps receive $12,000 for this and certain teaching; the top clergyman may double this; the top violinist or pianist may treble or quadruple it; the top engineer may make seven or eight times as much; the top lawyer may make twenty times as much.

These differences between occupations are important because in the case of a person possessed of more than one high ability they may decide which he puts to use. I have therefore collected such facts and estimates as I could without excessive trouble concerning the top ten or top hundred men of their generation in various lines in the United States. These are reported together with some facts for other countries in Table 2.

The causation of these differences is referable in part to the principles of volume, quality, and monopoly or uniqueness. Specially able literary or histrionic entertainers receive much more than specially able physicians because they can serve hundreds of thousands at a time. The movies set a new pecuniary scale for actors by multiplying volume.

Table 2   Approximate annual wage at age 50–55, or at the highest ten-year period of ability in the case of athletes and entertainers, attainable by the ablest half-dozen persons in the United States in the occupation specified, for the period 1931–1940

	Estimated Obtainable Wages per Year	Facts in Defense of the Estimates[4]
Law	$300,000	A very able lawyer says "I expect to receive $1,000 a day, and by a day I mean each day of the year, not each day that I work."
Medicine and surgery	200,000	
The ministry	15,000	

[4] The facts presented as evidence in defense of the estimates do not imply that the persons mentioned are among the half-dozen ablest persons in the activity specified. In cases where one would dare to select certain persons as among the half-dozen, the wages are often not known. I have also used in the evidential column only facts which are public property.

TABLE 2 (*Continued*)

	Estimated Obtainable Wages per Year	Facts in Defense of the Estimates
Teaching, not including income from textbooks	15,000	
Teaching, including income from textbooks	50,000[5]	
Presidents of universities, superintendents of schools, and other educational managers	35,000	In 1934–1935 the highest salary of a president in the 51 land-grant colleges was $20,500; in municipal colleges [1938] the highest salaries were $21,000. The largest private universities pay somewhat more, and some income is received from books, lectures, and special services. The highest reported salaries of superintendents of schools are around $20,000, and may be increased substantially by authorship.
Science and scholarship without managerial duties	20,000	The report of the Treasury to the Ways and Means Committee includes salaries of $21,500 and $15,875 to two men of science, who work with probably as much freedom as is enjoyed by men in universities or non-profit-making institutes.
Science and scholarship with managerial duties	75,000	The five highest salaries reported to the Ways and Means Committee for men in Cattell's starred list were $65,416.87, $54,281.73, $74,140.70, $55,000, and $40,000.
Engineers without managerial duties	35,000	
Engineers with managerial duties	75,000	

[5] A person who teaches something which many wish to learn, has the reputation of great ability to teach it, and who has ability to manage mass teaching and to combine allied enterprises with it may receive much more than $50,000 a year. According to John Kohler, writing in the *American Mercury* of May, 1936, Ely Culbertson, famous as a teacher of card games, was then receiving about $500,000 a year.

TABLE 2 (*Continued*)

	Estimated Obtainable Wages per Year	Facts in Defense of the Estimates
Invention with managerial duties	200,000	C. F. Kettering received $304,000 in 1936.
Management of philanthropic work or public affairs	30,000	
Business management	400,000	The average of 1935 and 1936 salaries for the highest paid officers of General Motors, American Telephone and Telegraph Company, Standard Oil of New Jersey, and American Tobacco Company, were, in order, approximately $420,000; $210,000; $125,000; and $230,000.
Labor leadership	15,000	The salary of John L. Lewis was recently raised from $12,000 to $25,000.
Army	15,000	The salary of a major-general is $8,000 plus allowances amounting possibly to $1,700, but residence at a military post involves certain valuable customary rights.
Civil service	15,000	
Painting and sculpture	15,000	
Portrait painters	50,000	
Cartoonists	125,000	
Literature	75,000	Walter Lippmann's 1935 salary from the Herald Tribune was $54,329.
Music	75,000	
Acting	400,000	Gary Cooper received $311,000 in 1935, and $370,000 in 1936, and presumably substantial amounts for the use of his name. Marlene Dietrich received $368,000 and $269,000 respectively, as salaries.

TABLE 2 (*Continued*)

	Estimated Obtainable Wages per Year	Facts in Defense of the Estimates
Entertainers: athletic	75,000	It must be remembered that the career of a pugilist or a baseball star is short. On the other hand it begins in the early twenties, so that he has long use of whatever he saves.
Entertainers: combinations of writing, acting, and music	400,000	Will Rogers was receiving about a half million at the time of his death.

We are interested in how much is paid to certain persons as evidence of how much is paid for certain abilities. The estimates may, I hope, be regarded as accurate within 20 percent of their amounts, but they are useful even if they are much less accurate. They show that great ability to entertain us is paid about as well as great ability to manage a business, that great ability to save our lives by surgery is paid nearly as well as great ability to save our property by legal advice, that great abilities in literature, art, and music usually get great pecuniary rewards only if they serve a very large number of people; that public servants in the army, navy, and civil service either are lacking in great abilities or are notably underpaid, that great abilities to advance knowledge and to manage public affairs get low wages, in spite of the fact that they are the abilities most productive of welfare for the world.

Two high abilities may make equally strong appeals to equal numbers of persons, but the persons in the one case may have much greater purchasing power. The presidents of banks receive more than the presidents of universities partly because the latter simply have not the money to spend. The pay of labor leaders or heads of scientific associations in comparison with equally able officers of business concerns is probably a still better illustration.

A high ability of one sort may receive a much lower percuniary return than of another sort because such is the custom. The much lower pay of football stars in England than of baseball stars in the United States seems to be a clear case of this. So also perhaps is the pay of major-generals or high naval officers in comparison with that of federal judges, and officers in the Federal Reserve Banks.

Theories which account for differences in wages by differences in the amount of pain, deprivation, or other disutility, or by differences in the amount of time spent in training (without pay) are especially inept in the case of specially high abilities. Within the same sort of work, the ablest and most paid, though not free from drudgery, usually suffer less from their work than their inferiors and often spend less time in training without pay than their inferiors for a considerable distance down the scale. Among different lines of work this holds even more emphatically. The top business men, lawyers, surgeons, and entertainers surely enjoy their work as much as the top scholars, scientists, philosophers, clergymen, and teachers, and spend on the average less time in unpaid training for it.

That specially high abilities receive important transpecuniary returns in enjoyable action, achievement, prestige, the sense of personal worth, praise from fellow-experts, and the like is obvious. These all deserve study. But I will limit myself here to a few conjectures about the total wages which would be adequate to call forth good use of the abilities in economic systems with very little private control of natural resources, capital, or labor.

Human nature is in general highly adaptable and will learn to get a living, reproduce, and enjoy itself after a fashion under physical and social conditions which seem unbearable. Persons of specially high abilities are probably by nature rather more adaptable than the average. They might, especially if brought up to it, do fairly good work as conscripts in the employ of a communistic majority, or servants of an all-possessing dictator. In general, they would tend to use their abilities as well as they could under any system of life and government that was not so foolish, unjust, or brutish as to arouse rebellion.

The contributions of the ablest men in science and scholarship, in art and music, and in the professions are more than twice the average of those in the same sort of work who are paid half as much, more than four times the average of those who are paid a quarter as much, more than ten times the average of those who are paid a tenth as much.

The magnitude of the service of a company's chief executive increases with the amount of property for whose use he is responsible, with the volume of business which it does, and with the number of employees. Other factors count also, such as the complexity, newness, and un-precedented quality of its work, but these three are the main factors. Let us then consider the salary of the chief executives of a company in relation to the following measure of the magnitude of his services:—Total assets of the company in dollars + 2 times the gross revenue in dollars + 20,000 times the number of employees (average during the year).[6]

---

[6] There may be better formulas for weighting property owned, business done, and personnel used. The use of such would make very little difference in what follows.

Using this formula. Thorndike and Beckwith ['37] observed the relation in oil and mining companies. chain stores. department stores. companies manufacturing automobiles or airplanes, chemicals, food. drinks, or tobacco, light machinery, heavy machinery, and metals, transportation, and public utility companies. Except for the last two the relation was much the same in all. Combining all except the transportation and public utility companies. the relation is as shown in Fig. 2.

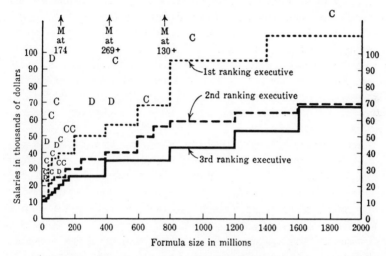

Fig. 2. Median salaries of 1st, 2nd, and 3rd ranking executives, in relation to formula size of company. All companies except railroads and public utilities. C's, D's, and M's are individual salaries of highest paid officers of chemical, drug, and motion picture companies. [Thorndike and Beckwith, '37 A, p. 118.]

To make the matter more realistic let us suppose that the services of the president of the American Telephone and Telegraph Company have in the last ten years added one one hundredth of one percent per year to the cheapness, accuracy, convenience, etc. of telephone use. They probably have done more than that. If every group of persons on the company's payroll for a sum of salaries equal to his salary ($210,000) had done as much, telephone service would have been improved beyond recognition. If by paying him or somebody else $420,000, this addition could have been two hundredths of a percent per year instead of one, it would have been a marvelous bargain. The addition of three hundred switchboard operators to speed up service, or two hundred linemen to reduce breakdowns, which would cost as much or more, would be as one drop to a bucketful of value. The popular objection to the high salaries of business executives thus seems extremely perverse. If any class of business men earns more than it receives, it is probably high executives of great corporations, if they are the ablest men available.

Chapter 4

Wants

The life of a dog or cat or chicken obviously consists largely of and is determined by appetites, cravings, desires, and their gratification. The animal confronts its world with a repertory of these proclivities and does its best to get what it desires and avoid what annoys it. So also does the life of a man, though the appetites and desires are more numerous, subtle and complicated, and the satisfaction is more delayed and indirect. Each man confronts his world with a host of active preferences, being only rarely a mere indifferent recipient of external forces. His acts are directed, on the whole, in the interest of these desires and aversions; when he seems to be doing what he does not wish to do, it is usually because of some other want which is controlling him. All sane and humane persons regard it as desirable, other things being equal, to change nature so that it will satisfy more "good" wants of more human beings. So they plough land, sow crops, bridge streams, destroy disease-germs. They also regard it as desirable to modify the wants themselves, strengthening the "good" ones, such as the cravings for justice, truth, or beauty, and weakening, or exterminating the "bad" ones.

We all recognize the existence and importance of wants. The conduct of individual men and the policies of institutions, communities, and nations are directed (and probably often misdirected) by the current ideas

43

about what men do want, what they ought to want, how they may be taught to want what they ought to want.

This aspect of the sciences dealing with man has shared in the general advancement of knowledge, so that a mediocre mind today can learn more truth and less error about human motives than Euripides and Aristotle had, or than the 19th-century novelists and moralists had. But the great gains of modern science have been elsewhere. For example, physiology has advanced knowledge of how food is digested enormously more than knowledge of why certain foods are preferred. Psychology can give a far better account of the acquisition of ideas than of the interplay of motives. Current practices in education, government, business, philanthropy, and religion abound in mistakes due to ignorance of one or another feature of it; textbooks of psychology, sociology and ethics do not yet present it; it must be sought in observations of animal behavior, experiments with school children, case-histories of pathological cravings, studies of advertising and selling, descriptions of tribal mores, records and statistics of families, churches, courts, prisons. There is no one group of men, nor even any one man, that possesses it, has put it in order, and can bring it to bear at will upon any problem of theory or practice. A gifted and experienced student of government and law has some of it but lacks much. Experts in anthropology, psychology, medicine, social and religious work, criminology, economics, and business possess each a fraction of it, but imperfectly because unchecked by other parts of it.

The importance of increasing it needs no demonstration. It is certain that man should try to match his understanding of masses, atoms, and cells by understanding of himself; it is highly probable that mastery of human nature will greatly increase the value of our mastery of the rest of nature. Many competent thinkers indeed attribute the tragic distress of the civilized world in the last twenty-five years to a lag of scientific direction of human behavior behind that of physical forces.

The Nature, Satisfaction, and Fulfillment of Wants

We are concerned with wants both in the sense of desires or wishes for things which may or may not be good for the person, and in the sense of needs or lacks of beneficial things which the person may or may not desire. We shall use the word *wants* for the former and the word *needs* for the latter. It is somewhat pedantic to distinguish sharply between desires and lacks of desirables when the actual conditions in living men so often fall under both categories. But on the whole it seems best to emphasize the distinction, because it is often crucial in problems of welfare, and also saves the reader the trouble of deciding whether the word *want* in any given case means that the person would be satisfied by a certain state of affairs or that he would be benefited by it. *Want* then = *wish, desire, appetite, liking, craving,* and the like. *Need* = the other common meaning of want and some of the meanings of *drive* as used by psychologists.

The most discussed type of human want is that condition of a person in which he recognizes certain symptoms, is aware that a certain state of affairs will be satisfying, and manifests a certain attitude or behavior toward the attainment of that satisfier. So a thirsty child says "I want a drink of water" or a weary man says "I want to go to bed." In such cases the wanting clearly includes an actual felt condition and an imagined or thought-of satisfier. Many wants, however, vary greatly from this full-fledged occurrence of symptom and idea of satisfier.

The symptom may be only vaguely felt, recognized insecurely, or may not be felt at all. So, for example, a girl seeing a dress in a show-window may want it to the extent of thinking of its possession as satisfactory and of adopting a certain behavior or attitude, with the idea of the satisfier hazy, incomplete, or even entirely absent. So certain restless longings due to sex may exist without any representation of the conditions appropriate to satisfy them.[1]

The essential characteristic of wants is the behavior they cause. This often includes restlessness until the want is gratified; and always includes a tendency to respond to certain satisfiers, in ways different from those used toward non-satisfiers. The essential dynamic quality of wants is preference.

Some wants occur rarely; the reader may never have wanted to know the square root of 1089. Some occur repeatedly; many occur in accord with bodily rhythms. Some seem to be almost perpetual, as the craving for security by the timid, or the craving for success by the ambitious. Some wants are highly specialized, as the mother's desire to see her child after a separation. Some have very general satisfiers; for example, the wish for attention, praise, or success. Some are present in only a small fraction of the population; only a few insane

---

[1] The idea of a satisfier is often of something which will not in fact satisfy the want, as when a man seeks excitement to relieve an irritation which can be relieved much better by vigorous exercise and sleep, or as when a woman craves a career who really wants a husband and home. But such are cases where a person thinks he wants something which he will not in fact prefer. We are here concerned with cases where he does not even think what he wants.

or eccentric souls long to eat grass, lacerate their flesh, or go to bed with corpses. Some are so widespread that we assume their existence in every person. We are, of course, most concerned practically with wants which persist or recur often, which have a range of satisfiers, and which are widespread. But the facts and principles concerning wants in general may often be studied effectively in the case of rare, specialized, and abnormal wants.

A want is a preference. To satisfy a want sometimes means to satisfy the person by putting an end to some annoying thing or lack, as in the drink for thirst, company for solitude, interesting experiences for ennui. In these cases it also often brings a positive state that is welcome in and of itself. The water not only abolishes the thirst but itself feels good; company drives away the wretched loneliness and adds positive comfort and zest. To satisfy a person may mean to produce such enjoyable conditions without any reduction of any annoying thing or lack. A salary increase or good news from a friend satisfies, though one had in no way been suffering from the lack of it, or even aware of the lack. Whether one says that these satisfy a want of the person, or only that they satisfy the person, is not of much consequence.

The satisfier of a want sometimes abolishes or reduces the want, and even predisposes the person to a different one, as when rest satisfies the craving for it and permits the craving for exercise. Sometimes it leaves the want almost or quite unimpaired, as in the case of the cravings for security, power, and affection. A want may even increase by being gratified.

Satisfiers may be defined as states of affairs which the person in question in the state of mind and body in question does nothing to avoid or reject, often doing such things as attain or maintain them. Prominent among them are (1) sensory pleasures, such as sweet, fruity, and nutty tastes, (2) social amenities, such as smiles and approving voices, and (3) the normal healthy functionings of "natural" tendencies, such as overtaking what one chases or subduing what one attacks. But pains may, under certain conditions, be satisfying, as when a painful electric shock is used as a signal that the person's answers are right in experiments in learning; and, in general, things ordinarily annoying may for special reasons become satisfiers. So a fanatic is convinced that the hoots and sneers of mankind signify that he is favored by God and assured of eternal bliss. What is one man's mental meat is another man's poison. And the same man will be variously satisfied according as he is famished, sleepy, in love, in fear of his life, wrestling with another man, or wrestling with a mathematical problem. He is, indeed, strictly speaking, not the same man.

The Modus Operandi of Selection

Although the detailed physiology of wants and satisfactions is yet to be discovered, certain important principles about their dynamics as seen from the outside are known.

The first is the fact of reinforcement,—that one mental tendency may be strengthened by others, that one brain process may be increased in its amount or vigor by another. So, for example, the extent of the knee-jerk, or the force with which one squeezes a dynamometer, may be increased by sensory stimulations of various sorts.

The second is the fact of the special reinforcing or confirming action of a satisfier,—that a satisfier happening to a man reinforces any modifiable mental connection with which it is associated.

This strengthening of a connection is shown in the following ways: If the situation continues, a satisfier will make the person more likely to repeat the response. So a child hitting or biting a novel object will be more likely to hit or bite it again if this response produces an enjoyable sound or taste or parental praise than if it produces no satisfaction. If this second connection of the response with the situation is also followed by a satisfier, and nothing diverts the child, he may repeat the response again and again as long as the situation remains or until the consequence ceases to be satisfying. So a child confronted by his first dish of berries will eat until they are gone or he is satiated. Not so if the saucer had contained little balls of wool or morsels of spinach!

There could be a world in which men changed their behavior in favor of the frequent and not in favor of the satisfying. But experiments in which everything is kept identical save the attachment of a satisfier to the situation $\rightarrow$ response connection at once reveal the satisfier as a powerful force. Its strength at the start may be only .10, the person being as likely to do any one of nine other things in response to the situation as to make the response (call it R_1) which produces the satisfier. But let the satisfier be attached to it once and this strength rises (say to .30), so that it is several times as likely to occur as R_2 or R_3, etc., and is likely to occur once in five seconds instead of once in fifteen. A few more rewarded occurrences and the strength of the connection from S_1 to R_1 is at or near 1.00.

A third item in the dynamics of preference is the fact of "spread" or "scatter" of the confirming action of a satisfier. Suppose, for example, that a hundred men each experienced a sequence of a dozen connections, of which the sixth was rewarded by a satisfier (say, the announcement of "Right" by the experimenter, plus a money bonus), the other eleven being left with no reward or punished by the announcement of "Wrong" and a money penalty. Suppose that the series of situations, S_1, S_2, S_3, S_4, etc. recurs. Then not only will the strength of $S_6 \rightarrow R_6$ be very much increased over what it was at the first occurrence of S_6, but the strength of $S_7 \rightarrow R_7$, and $S_5 \rightarrow R_5$ will also be somewhat increased, and even the strength of $S_4 \rightarrow R_4$ and $S_8 \rightarrow R_8$. Whether the strengthening force of the satisfier *spreads* out beyond the connection or *scatters* in the sense that sometimes it misses entirely the connection to which it is chiefly attached and exerts its influence on some other instead, is not known.

The confirming reaction does not result mechanically from every satisfier and does not exert its force indifferently. A man may experience a condition of intense satisfaction without discharging any confirming reaction. For example, if the experimenter occasionally after a wrong response says "Wrong" but gives ten times the maximum reward, saying "This is for general excellence," the learner may, though much pleased, not strengthen that wrong connection. He is operating in a system where the confirming reaction tends to follow satisfactions of certain special sorts, and tends to attach itself to connections to which it "belongs."

There is, however, a fundamental tendency for a satisfying status to produce a confirming reaction regardless of any reasonableness or relevance. So a cat will learn to claw at the back of a cage in order to get out at the front of it, or to scratch itself to get food, or to lick itself to get freedom. The spread or scatter phenomenon proves that this influence is not logical, rational, or in need of any other than strictly biological principles to explain it. The satisfier does not necessarily strengthen the connection which produces the satisfier, or which is good for the person, or which the person chooses to have strengthened. It does so much more often than chance would allow, but only by virtue of the fact that it strengthens most the connection to which it belongs most closely as a biological event, which is usually the connection immediately preceding it in the strand of experience of which the satisfier is a part. It may strengthen somewhat any connection in the neighborhood, good, bad, or indifferent, desired or not desired, coming before it or after it, left unrewarded or even punished.

By the confirming action of satisfiers a man tends on the whole to get what satisfies him so far as his environment permits, but the procedure is indirect and fallible at its very roots. He cannot make himself do what will gratify his wants by decision and edict, but only by strengthening connections which lead to such action. A main factor in the understanding of human behavior is sound knowledge of the confirming reaction, and a main factor in successful human engineering is ingenuity in arranging matters so that the confirming reaction works on one's side.

Aversions and Annoyers

Men obviously prefer not to be in or experience certain states of affairs as truly as they prefer certain others. They want not to be in pain, terror, confinement, or solitude, not to be scorned, ridiculed, or ashamed. These negative wants or aversions are gratified by getting rid of some annoyer.

Sometimes the same fact of preference may with minor changes be treated as either a positive or a negative. So the same fact may be treated as a desire to get rid of thirst or desire to have a drink. So the desire to avoid solitude and the desire to have company may mean almost the same thing. But there are many clear cases where the want to be rid of a certain status does not imply wanting any specified status in place of it. So with most pains and fears, for example. Among ten thousand who want the pain to cease there are only two or three in whom this want turns into a craving for some particular opiate. Among a thousand who scream or tremble, and crave relief from terror, a score or so may want their God to send them courage or want an abundance of alcohol to create it, but the great majority just want the terror or the terrifying object to cease. In these pure cases of aversion the preference is between some annoyer and the absence thereof, regardless of what, if anything, takes its place.

An annoyer may be defined as a state of affairs which the person in question in the condition in question does little or nothing to maintain, often doing such things as abolish or avoid it. Notable among annoyers are sensory pains, thwartings of certain inborn or habitual tendencies, shock, disgust, shame, melancholy, and irritation.

An aversion is a preference against. An annoyer is a thing *dispreferred;* the aversion is "satisfied" by the abolition or reduction of the annoyer.

The Action of Annoyers

We have seen that a satisfier tends to strengthen tendencies producing it, and that it does this rather uniformly and ubiquitously, though not infallibly, by arousing a confirming reaction which strengthens the connection to which the satisfier is attached. It is natural to think that an annoyer tends to weaken tendencies producing it, with similar uniformity and generality, by arousing directly an inhibitory or depressing reaction which weakens whatever it is attached to. This is not the case. In particular there is no inhibitory or depressing influence aroused by annoyers, comparable to the confirming influence of satisfiers. Attaching satisfiers to mental connections will strengthen them regardless of what else is done; but attaching annoyers to connections will not weaken them save indirectly by causing the person to do something else. Nature might have endowed man at least with a mechanism whereby an annoyer could stimulate the man to do *anything except* the connection followed by the annoyer; but he is not so endowed.

To learn what may be expected from annoyers we must observe what each of them impels the person to do. Some annoyers make him withdraw part of his body, some make him turn and run, some make him scratch, scream, weep, bite and kick, seek about restlessly. After a certain amount of experience some make him seek definitely for what has been found to afford relief from the annoyer in question.

Indirectly some of these behaviors may weaken the connection preceding the annoyer. If a person responds to a certain situation by reaching forth to touch it and then responds by pulling his hand back, the second connection (especially if it is rewarded) decreases the probability of occurrence of the first. But there is no general surety that an annoyer will do so. $S_1 \rightarrow R_1$ followed by the announcement "Wrong" and a painful electric shock may leave the connection as strong as it was before.

If the person understands that the preceding connection caused the annoyer, the occurrence of the annoyer has an informative action. It classes that connection "to be avoided" or the like. A satisfier has a similar informative action, but has its confirming action in addition.

A man will not then tend to get rid of what annoys him in the same way and to the same extent that he tends to keep what satisfies him. Indeed one of the commonest and most serviceable ways of getting rid of an annoyer is by discovering behavior which does get rid of it and making the riddance satisfying (if it is not so already), so that the confirming force of the satisfier strengthens the connections which abolish, reduce, or avoid the annoyers. These facts account for much of the superiority of positive over negative education or legislation.

An Inventory of Human Wants

Suppose that the thoughts and feelings and acts of a random sample of a million representing all human beings during the past year had been recorded and that competent students had estimated from each person's record what that person had wanted and how frequent and intense each want had been. Such an inventory would present an enormous variety. If we tried to present the facts to some dictator who wished to know what the world wanted, or in our prayers to deity, they would be hard to summarize neatly.

It would seem reasonable first to list the wants which were unanimous, but we should be compelled to amend this to "nearly unanimous," for some eccentrics would be found who did not want whatever was listed among the very popular wants. Among those who did manifest the want, there would be variations in its intensity from near indifference to a passion.

The particular forms in which a common craving manifested itself would present a bewildering variety. In spite of custom and standardization the flavors enjoyed by some but not by all would number thousands; the forms of power are multifarious; mothers, nurses, employers, labor-unions, physicians, patent-medicines, science, religions, are wanted to enhance the feeling of safety; tens of thousands of ornaments, styles, accomplishments, and honors are sought variously as means of attaining admiration and avoiding scorn.

The procedure of assigning specific wants is speculative. A person's desire to have an automobile, for example, may be rooted in any one of a large number of combinations of wants (for rapid motion through space, the sense of power over things, mechanisms to tinker with, adventure, the admiring glances of neighbors, ease, and other things) mixed in different proportions. It is relatively easy to find out what people buy, but hard to determine what they buy it for.

A summary which took no risks of giving false weights or of making false inferences would have to stop far short of a compact list of wants with clean-cut estimates of magnitude. Its estimates would be made with wide margins of error. Since such an inventory or even the data for it are lacking, ideas of what the world wants are vague and chaotic in even well-informed and unprejudiced minds. A leading psychiatrist may assert that what mankind universally wants is love and security; a leader in literature may put the prime movers of life as rivalry and adventure; an optimistic reformer may act on the faith that men will cleave to truth and justice once they have experienced them; a pessimist may be equally confident that comfortable superstitions are preferred over truth, and that greed is stronger than justice; one sociologist may think that food, sex, and cheap excitement have been the great satisfiers; another may stress the importance of simple out-door pleasures and family life from the time of our gorilla-like ancestors (the gorilla being now viewed as a model husband and father) to that of Swiss Family Robinson and Little Women; a psychologist may declare that men like what they are used to, whatever it may be; an educator, that men want to express their natures, to be themselves. Samuel Johnson regarded the craving for distinction as of prime importance. It doubtless was to him. Jeremy Bentham allotted nearly a third of pleasures and pains to the intellectual or contemplative part of life.

All neat lists of general names require interpretation in terms of the actual situations, responses, satisfiers and annoyers which they include, if they are to be useful for science. It does little good merely to know that there are pleasures and pains.

It is reasonable to assume that any species of animals enjoys the activities which its inherited nature leads it to engage in—that birds like to fly, pick grains and berries, catch insects, and build nests—that moles like to burrow and fishes to swim. Man is presumably no exception. The pursuits by which man got his living and perpetuated his kind in a state of nature a hundred thousand years ago probably gave him an enjoyable life. Annoyance probably came, not from having to work for a living as hunter, fruit-picker, clam-digger, or whatever, but from sensory pains, deprivations, frustrations, and such annoying states as fear, nostalgia, or shame.

One thing is sure about an accurate inventory, namely, that the desires and aversions pertaining strictly to keeping alive and propagating would form a very small fraction of it. The human food and drink wants necessary to keep the body from wasting away, drying out, or becoming subject to diseases are almost hidden in the prosperous nations by wants for certain accessories in the form of daintinesses and conveniences, and are almost everywhere increased by certain cravings for flavors, intoxicants, narcotics, etc. Clothes and buildings minister not only to cravings for protection from weather and from animals and for sex-appeal, but also to the wants for various social approvals, distinction, protection against magical forces that may injure. Of wants related to sex gratification, family life, and the nurture of the young, a modicum would suffice to perpetuate the human species; most of them relate to gregariousness, sociability, affection, romantic love, display, sex activity far in excess of that useful in producing offspring or enjoyment of the happiness of others.

In the heyday of misuse of the words "evolution" and "the survival of the fit," speculative thinkers were tempted to argue that whatever wants man feels are useful for his survival, or would be so in more primitive conditions. They were also tempted to assume the widespread and intense existence of wants such as those subsumed under the instinct of self-preservation and the parental instinct.

The consideration of an approximate total inventory of human wants could never have been very encouraging to this doctrine and in the present time when nearly every inhabitant of civilized lands wants to own an automobile, go to the movies weekly, and contemplate sports rather than engage in them, and travels in almost every way save by his own legs, when both individual crimes and national wars occur not by passion or impulse, but as elaborate products of the machinations of cold-blooded racketeers and political cliques, when the want not to have children is becoming respectable, the misfit of the doctrine to the facts is beyond question. Indeed, a rather strong case could be made out for the opposite doctrine that the human species wanted on the whole to destroy itself and so was accustoming itself to a wasteful love of amusement devoid of rest and recreation, a dependence upon an unmanageable horde of machines, an intrusting of its life to governmental systems which are well designed to favor the suicide of *homo sapiens*.

Human wants are as natural, as explainable, and as properly subject to matter-of-fact consideration as human bones or blood-vessels; but this is not to say that the human species would be less sure of survival if one after another of men's present wants were annihilated, beginning, say, with the want of A for Love Nest perfumery, of B for national glory, of C for a hundred concubines, and of D for an airplane with gold fittings. Many desires and aversions are man-made, learned in a human environment. Man is a domesticated animal, has been domesticating himself for probably thousands of generations, has selected some of his kin to produce offspring and some to remain childless, has built up customs and institutions, has accumulated paraphernalia of tools, and patterns of conduct. The young man who wants to be a doctor, ride horseback, take an aspirin tablet, or know what time it is, or the girl who wants to be married, first having a diamond engagement ring, to play the piano, have wavy hair, or know how long it will be before spring will come again—in each case wants as he or she does, partly or wholly because of a man-made environment.

It is equally sure that much in the inventory is not man-made, and not learned in a human environment, but is due to the constitution of the genes which form the start of a human life. Neither the old speculative doctrine that a man's mind is a *tabula rasa* to be written on by experience alone nor the recent speculations which attribute omnipotence to the habits established by associative mechanisms will stand the test of facts. Dogs and chimpanzees will not become men in their wants by being treated as men. The chimpanzees might very possibly come to want radios and to go to the movies every week, or even to go to church (if the ceremonial was varied and colorful), but none of them would want to have a large bank account, study algebra, or die for truth and justice.

Acceptance of the fact that man inherits tendencies toward certain desires and aversions as he inherits tendencies to shape of skull, length of arm, etc., leads to another, that he probably shares certain wants with the mammals in general, and certain further wants with the primates, especially the anthropoid apes. But at present so little is known about what chimpanzees are satisfied and annoyed by, that such an analysis of the human inheritance is not of great service in interpreting the variety of human wants.

The split into unlearned components due to the genes and acquired components due to the events of life is helpful for several reasons. First of all, it helps to provide answers to the most important practical questions which can be asked about any human want; namely: "Must we accept it as we accept gravitation, the action of oxygen on metals, or the color of our eyes, and make the best of it, unless and until we can breed it out of the genes? or can we avoid it by eliminating certain features of customs and education, which are responsible for it? Do we get it for nothing as a gift of nature, or must we make sure that the environment is such as to produce and foster it in each generation?"

Other things being equal, the probability of easy control of a human want by customs, laws, schools, is proportional to the probability that the want is a product of "culture." What man has given, man can take away or give in richer measure. Thus the craving called "curiosity" in our supposed inventory would surely include desires (1) to take a cruise around the world, (2) to read the morning's tabloid, (3) to observe the workings of airplanes and gliders, (4) to see the biggest steamship in the world, (5) to discover causes and cures for cancer and infantile paralysis. If these various forms of "curiosity" could be resolved into an unlearned component which the genes of man have to a degree that the genes of whales, sloths, and guinea pigs do not, and learned components, which education can create or prevent, we could probably improve social control.

Furthermore, many of the desires and aversions which have been attributed to original tendencies in man are at least very fundamental. If more searching observation finds one of these to be a product of some environmental condition, that environmental condition is likely to be itself fundamental and widespread. The following list of such candidates seem to the writer to be surely or probably rooted in the genes. This list does not include some which have been imputed to man by various eminent thinkers; on the other hand, it includes some which other eminent thinkers would attribute to training.

Desires

1. bright colors and glitter; sunshine; soft, tinkling, and rhythmical sounds; sweet, fruity, and nutty tastes; touching what is soft and smooth and dry.
2. free bodily movement; rapid motion through space.
3. healthy normal action of the digestive, circulatory, excretory, nervous, and other physiological systems.
4. having something behind one's back when resting; "being in a sheltered nook, open on only one side," as James says.
5. the presence of friendly, or at least not inimical, human beings.
6. "concerted action as one of an organized crowd."
7. to move when refreshed, especially as in running, jumping, climbing, pulling and wrestling.
8. to rest when tired.
9. vocalization; visual exploration; manipulation.
10. mental control; to do something and have something happen as the consequence is, other things being equal, satisfying, whatever be done and whatever be the consequent happening.
11. witnessing the happy behavior of other human beings, especially of children.
12. successful courtship and love between the sexes.
13. voluptuous sensation, however obtained.
14. to manifest affection.
15. to receive affection.
16. intimate approval, as by smiles, pats, admission to companionship, and the like from one to whom he has the inner response of submissiveness; humble approval, as by admiring glances, from anybody.
17. domination, being submitted to by others.
18. to surpass others in the work or play to which original nature leads us and them.
19. submission to a person toward whom it is the "natural" response.
20. In general, when any instinctive behavior series is started and operates successfully, its activities are satisfying and the situations which they produce are satisfying, other things being equal.

Aversions

1. the sight of black; sudden loud sounds; bitter tastes; the odors of putrid flesh; excrement and vomit; sensory pains; over-tension of muscles; impeded or insufficient action of the bodily organs.
2. slimy, wriggling, and creeping things on one's flesh.
3. large animals or objects like animals approaching one rapidly; angry scowling faces; solitude; darkness; being suddenly clutched.
4. pain.
5. severe shock of any sort.
6. being interfered with in any bodily movements which the individual is impelled by his own constitution to make.
7. the intrusion of strangers into the neighborhood of one's habitation and the abstraction of any object therefrom.
8. the seizure by others of an object which one is using.
9. being shut up completely within a small, and especially a strange, enclosure.
10. being subdued by a person to whom (or a thing to which) one does not naturally have a submissive attitude.
11. inattention or neglect by human beings whose attention one solicits.
12. the withdrawal of approving intercourse by masters.
13. looks of scorn and derision from anyone.
14. seeing others approved.
15. being outdone by others.
16. In general, when any instinctive behavior-series is started, any failure of it to operate successfully is annoying.

The effort to divide an inventory of human wants between germinal components and learned components leads to a useful consideration of the range of occurrence of wants, since one indication of a probable inherited basis for a want is its appearance in nearly all members of the human species. Even if the widespread occurrence is due to a widespread occurrence of some environmental cause, it is useful to have emphasis upon such wants.

The unlearned-learned differentiation is also useful in that it emphasizes the essential factors which satisfy or annoy rather than the concrete things or situations which do so. If people list their likes and dislikes, they are likely to report, "I like (or dislike) to dance, play golf, work in a garden, go to church; I like music, art, children, cats, automobile trips, bicycling, horseback riding, swimming; I like to be at parties, alone, in my own home, in new environments, with my mother," and the like. Similarly if one observes the desires and aversions of his fellow men he tends to observe what concrete states of affairs evoke likes and dislikes. This is better than purely speculative assumptions about qualities which are satisfying and annoying. But there probably are factors which in various combinations explain human likes and dislikes. If the sensation of rapid motion through space, for example, is found to be intrinsically satisfying, we can better understand the pleasures of running, riding, bicycling, and the like. The feeling of "security," i.e., the complete absence of fear, antagonism, caution, and "tension," may play a large part in liking to be alone, liking to be with friends, and liking to be in one's own familiar habitat and lair. The effort to discover germinal tendencies is an effort to discover factors independent of all apparatus of civilization, because the genes cannot be expected to be adapted to any such. They do not, so to speak, know a church from a theater, or a book from a roast beef.

Attention to the unlearned gifts of heredity also disposes us to arrange desires and aversions in genetic series, as developments from primitive forms, by way of emphasis, elimination, elaborations, and shifts of various sorts. So if we find reason to believe that man tends by original nature to enjoy human approval in the form of "natural" smiles, admiring or awe-struck looks and cries, we are encouraged to trace the associative links whereby any given symbol of approval in words, wages, honors is very effective for one person, much less so for another, and of nearly zero value for a third. It should be one ideal for science and practice to transform the descriptive inventory into a genetic or developmental chart.

The hope may be cherished that an inventory of human wants will show general facts and principles in spite of its enormous variety and resistance to explanation by any one simple doctrine. We may expect to find some wants pervading many areas of life and developing into multifarious special forms under various stimuli. We may expect to find other widespread wants corresponding to important institutions such as the family, the church, language, numbers, various forms of music and graphic art. We may expect that the eccentricities of individuals will not be chaotic but will cluster about norms or modes.

Obviously no complete and accurate inventory of human wants can be made without a superlative ingenuity which perhaps nobody possesses, and an amount of labor which is prohibitive. A provisional inventory could be tabulated, however, which experts in anthropology, psychology, economics, government, law, business, religion, education, and penology might find useful, and which they could correct and extend in those areas where they have special knowledge. What the population of a given place and time wants is fairly well shown by what it spends its time and money for, and I have been to some pains to collect facts for the population of the United States near 1930.

How We Spend Our Time and What We Spend It For[1]

The best data concerning adults are those given under fifty-nine rubrics by Nelson ['34] for a large group (nearly 500) connected with a Y. W. C. A. From Nelson's records we may summarize the expenditures of waking hours per week as 48 to productive labor, 6 or less to other duties, $33\frac{1}{2}$ or more to pleasure, 24 to eating, personal care, and shopping, and $\frac{1}{2}$ unspecified. If of the 24 hours half are credited to keeping the person alive, well, and presentable for her work and half to the pleasures of the palate, of sociability, and of gaining the approval of others and of oneself by one's appearance, the total for work and duties is 66, not quite three fifths of waking time; and that for pleasure is $45\frac{1}{2}+$, somewhat over two fifths. Of course, some of the productive labor and going to and from it may be pleasurable also.

Moralists generally, and the liberal reformers of the nineteenth century in particular, seem to have expected that if people were enabled to obtain the necessities of life with a part of their energy, they would use a large fraction of the balance in the pursuit of learning, wisdom, beauty, and good works. The fraction is small in these business girls. Yet this group is probably much superior to the average of the population and had convenient and free access to science, literature, and art. They had the time and were obviously not exhausted by their labors, since they resorted to resting other than sleep for less than one hour per week.

Before commenting further on the facts, let us try to translate the schedule of time spent (except in sleep or at productive labor for a wage) into a schedule of wants gratified. For example, how should the hour and a half spent in church activities be allotted among the desires for security, for the approval of others, for self-approval, for the welfare of others, for mental activity, for social entertainment, and for the pleasures of sight and sound? How should the 10 hours for personal care and the $3\frac{1}{2}$ hours for home responsiblities be allotted?

Table 3 shows the allotments from the 55 items according to a jury of six psychologists, and also the summation of the allotments of all the 55 items reporting time spent other than in sleep, work for wages, and

---

[1] This and the following section are quoted in the main from two articles in the *Scientific Monthly* [Thorndike 37B and 37C].

Table 3 The percentages of the time spent in various activities by business girls which gratified certain wants, according to a jury of psychologists

	Personal care	Home responsibilities	Auto-mobile	Talking with family	Writing letters	Reading the news-paper	Church activities	Sum for 55 items, only except sleep, work, and transportation to and from work
1. Protection against hunger, cold, heat and wet. animals. diseases. and bad people, exercise. rest, and sex relief	10.8	15.5	9.7			4.0	4.0	20.2
2. Avoidance or reduction of pain	3.2	1.9	3.0		0.1	0.8	1.1	2.1
3. Pleasures of taste, smell. sight, and sound	5.8	10.5	16.1	2.8		8.3	6.9	14.3
4. Mental activity, curiosity. and exploration		0.3	6.7	5.9	11.6	58.3	3.6	8.1
5. Manipulation and construction	0.8		1.6		0.1			1.0
6. Security (other than in 1)	3.8	10.5	0.3	9.3	4.7	1.7		1.5
7. Affection (to get it)	14.1	3.7	3.5	14.8	15.1		3.6	4.7
8. Companionship	5.3	4.1	12.6	29.6	18.3	5.8	16.7	8.5
9. Approval from others	19.6	16.3	3.5	2.8	11.1	2.5	7.3	7.3
10. Approval from one's self	14.2	9.2	0.3	1.9	5.3	5.8	5.8	4.3
11. Mastery over others	5.3	1.7	0.8	3.7	3.3	0.8	1.1	1.9
12. The welfare of others	0.5	10.2	0.8	9.3	9.7	1.7	7.3	1.9
13. Sex entertainment	11.4	8.5	15.9	0.9	16.7	2.5	5.8	11.5
14. Social entertainment	3.0	6.1	24.2	17.6	3.5	3.3	16.7	10.5
15. Physical entertainment	1.1	0.7	0.8		0.1			1.5
16. Unspecified comfort	0.8	0.7	0.3	0.9		4.2	2.9	0.7

transportation to and from work. In so far as the jury's allotments are dependable, the time spent serves chiefly the desire for entertainment in a broad sense.

Records like these from business girls are not available for business men, farmers, factory workers, housewives, or any large adult groups. We have to rely on general observation helped out by various facts of record. The hours of sleep for adults 20 to 60 may be set at 8 per day or a bit more. In reports by professional, sales, and factory workers (male and female) of a telephone company, less than 2 percent of leisure time was credited to mere rest. The amounts would presumably be larger for persons doing hard muscular work, but they are a small and declining minority; and few even among them are too tired to enjoy the radio.

In ordinary economic conditions the average number of hours of work for wages or about the home, including time spent in going to and from work, is probably not far from 7 per day for adult men and women. The farmer's work is a balance of the seasons; soft-coal miners have tried for years to get 200 days of work per year; the retail dealer and his clerks may work far beyond union hours; many houseworkers add the care of their homes to 8 or more hours for wages. But these great variations are consistent with even greater uniformities.

The care of the body and personal appearance may be estimated at 5 hours a week for men and 8 for women. Routine eating takes perhaps 10 for men and 8 for women (the difference in time being spent by the women in serving and cleaning up, counted in their work records).

About 40 hours a week are left at the adult's disposal. He is free to use these to gratify any of his wants—for security, affection, companionship, approval (of himself, his fellow-men, or his God), power over things or people, the welfare of others, intellectual activity and achievement or entertainment of whatever sort he chooses. A provisional estimate is made by allotting the schedules of leisure time activities reported by professional, sales, and factory employees of a large telephone company to the wants they seem to serve; I shall be guided by the judgments of a jury of psychologists.

For example, games, sports, and other forms of exercise (excluding gardening) account for 12.8 percent, 16 percent, and 21 percent of the leisure time reported by professional, sales, and factory men, and for 7.6 percent, 9.3 percent, and 21.8 percent of that reported by professional, sales, and factory women, respectively. The jury of psychologists allots time so spent as follows:

to the desire for physical—and also sensory, intellectual,
    sex and social—entertainment   76 percent
to the desire for companionship   10 percent
to the desire for approval   6 percent
to other wants   8 percent

In a similar manner the times reported as spent in playing cards and sedentary games are allotted as follows:

to the desire for entertainment   65 percent
to the desire for companionship   15 percent
to the desire for approval   8 percent
to the desire for power or mastery   5 percent
to other wants   7 percent

Similar allotments are shown in Table 4.

Evidence of the use of leisure time for the welfare of others is rare, except in the case of the professional men. They report 9.2 percent of the time as "with family or children." In the other five groups (in order) this figure is 0 percent, 2.0 percent, 1.4 percent, 1.6 percent, and 0 percent. The other evidence is in the time spent in clubs more or less concerned with social betterment. The percentages are 3.3, 0.3, 3.4, 4.3, 0.6, and 1.4. The reports for religious activities give 1.7 percent, 0, 0, 1.5 percent, 1.6 percent, and 2.5 percent. The reports for lectures and studies give 1.4 percent, 6.3 percent, 5.0 percent, 4.4 percent, 4.3 percent, and 5.8 percent. The reports for sewing give 0, 0, 0, 0.5, 1.9, and 8.3 percent.

Table 4   Allotments of leisure time for professional, sales, and factory employees of a large company

	Professional		Sales		Factory	
	Men	Women	Men	Women	Men	Women
Percentage of leisure time reported as spent in games and sports, social gatherings and conversation, radio, theater, movies, reading, music, automobiling, and gardening	76.0	80.9	89.8	85.2	87.2	78.0
Allotted to entertainment	49.2	52.3	61.4	58.3	59.6	54.8
Allotted to companionship	5.0	6.5	9.3	7.2	7.6	7.9
Allotted to approval	8.2	7.7	7.1	6.9	6.9	5.4

Some of the time for these activities should be allotted to entertainment, but we may use this as a factor of safety for the conclusion that over half of the free time of adults in this country, or about 25 hours a week, is spent for entertainment.[1] Another large fraction is spent for companionship, which is itself in part a form of entertainment; a friendly group engaged together without compulsion in almost any sort of activity will entertain itself.

The amount of time spent in physical entertainment by means of games and sports has probably increased within the past generation. But the enormous increase has been in reading magazines, riding in automobiles, going to the pictures, and listening to the radio. The time saved from wage-work and family work by reductions in hours and by gas, electricity, and household appliances has gone for increased entertainment.

Some students of history and sociology will credit the present flood of entertainment to the great increase in the supply coupled with commercial methods of stimulating the demand. They will argue that men will, under fit environmental conditions, spend their free time in serving the state, the church, the family. They will assert that men will follow gods of truth or beauty or virtue or utility or the common good as readily as the false god of entertainment if they are shown the right path by example and have their feet set upon it by habit.

I hope that this is so. But I fear that the craving for entertainment is deeply rooted in man's nature and that very strong counter-attractions will be required. The desire for approval may counteract it widely, as in waves of Puritanism or patriotism. Also, the desire to see others happy, which apparently has been held down by brutal and bigoted customs in most civilizations, may become a more potent alternative, at least in superior souls. The human nervous system is very adaptable and can learn to operate with satisfaction in a humdrum world. But its lines of least resistance go toward cheerful sociability, free play, sensory stimulation and emotional excitement.

What We Spend Our Money For

According to Lynd ['33, vol. 2, p. 889], the people of the United States spent in 1929 8,000 million dollars for clothing, 1,500 million for

[1] Boder and Beach ['36] got statements from 4,000 adolescents (age 13–17) of what they wished that "our government, your parents, your school, and the church should do or be able to do in order that young people of your age might be happier." Three eighths of the statements expressed desires for entertainment directly or indirectly, naming dances, more parties, later hours, and less home-work.

laundry, cleaning, and dyeing, 750 million for death and burial and 3,500 million for life insurance. We inquire how much spent for clothing was to gratify the desires for protection against cold, wet, animals, diseases, pain, for the reproduction of the human species, for pleasures of vision, for a happy sex life, whether by sensuality, romance, philandering, courtship, for the approval of others, for the sense of personal worth, for dominance, for the welfare of others. We ask similar questions concerning the nation's laundry bill, funeral expenses, and insurance payments.

It may be admitted at once that nobody can answer such questions accurately save by an enormous amount of careful and impartial observation of a representative sampling of what they buy, what they do with it and what desires seem to be operating in the case of their purchasing and use. On the other hand, economists, business men, sociologists, psychologists and intelligent people in general are observing pertinent behavior constantly, and have a fund of facts which are far above zero knowledge and, we may hope, fairly free from constant errors of prejudice. It may be very useful to collect and organize samples from this fund.

This we have done, using as our retrospective observers eight psychologists (six men and two women), five women (including experts in nutrition, home economics and the family), three economists, and a small miscellaneous group of intelligent persons (used only in part or occasionally as a check).

Table 5 presents the average opinion of the two juries (psychologists and others) concerning what we spend our money for. The reader will note that purchases of *food* are judged to contribute appreciably to every one of the twenty-four satisfactions except protection against bad people, that purchases of *clothing* are judged to contribute appreciably to every one except the pleasures of taste and smell, and that *rent* is judged to contribute to all without exception. The reader will perhaps think that some of these allotments should be reduced to zero, because he himself gets no such gratifications from his payments, but he is probably wrong.

The table shows that the two juries agree rather closely.[1] The psychologists tend to break away oftener and further from the conventional overemphasis on food for hunger, clothing for warmth, rent for shelter, and insurance for security.

Table 6 may be called a budget in terms of wants or satisfactions. The allotments by the two juries agree rather closely, the correlation (omitting

[1] The closeness of agreement between the two juries is measured by the following correlation coefficients: food, .85; rent, .89; clothing, .85; laundry, etc., .79; life insurance, .71; death and burial, .84.

Table 5 Average allotment (I) by psychologists and (II) by others of 1,700 units spent for food, 800 units spent for clothing, 800 units spent for rent, 400 units spent for home furnishings, 480 units spent for fuel and light, 350 units spent for life-insurance, 150 units spent for laundry, cleaning and dyeing and 75 units spent for death and burial (the unit being 10 million dollars). Amounts are to the nearest unit, less than 5 million dollars being entered as 0

	A. Hunger	B. Protection against cold, heat, wet	C. Exercise	D. Sleep, rest	E. Sex relief	F. Reproduce species	G. Protection against animals and diseases	H. Protection against bad people	I. Reduce or avoid pain	J. Pleasures of taste and smell	K. Pleasures of sight and sound	L. Sex entertainment	M. Security	N. Affection (to get it)	O. Companionship	P. Approval of others	Q. Approval of one's self	R. Mastery over others	S. The welfare of others	T. Mental activity	U. Curiosity and exploration	V. Social entertainment	W. Physical entertainment	X. Comfort not in A to W
Food:																								
I	876	27	0	3	3	21	50	0	26	275	62	45	8	15	48	71	5	4	53	1	4	74	3	46
II	931	20	12	2	5	7	48	0	5	202	15	64	2	25	37	53	10	0	53	1	10	170	3	20
Clothing:																								
I	1	302	2	1	6	7	57	4	13	0	42	69	29	21	14	101	47	42	8	1	4	14	3	16
II	0	309	5	5	13	1	35	0	6	0	58	67	1	20	7	123	64	25	21	0	0	39	4	12
Rent:																								
I	15	235	4	94	22	20	37	36	3	4	21	21	80	16	18	48	28	13	28	3	1	31	3	17
II	8	250	1	66	9	17	36	30	2	3	40	25	35	13	10	78	44	6	31	2	2	48	6	39
Life Insurance:																								
I	0	0	0	0	0	17	3	0	3	0	0	2	73	23	5	29	48	2	143	0	1	0	0	0
II	0	0	0	0	0	10	8	6	3	0	0	2	166	12	0	3	8	1	124	0	0	0	0	7
Laundry:																								
I	1	6	1	5	1	2	26	0	1	9	14	13	1	0	1	25	18	3	8	0	0	4	0	15
II	1	3	1	0	0	1	12	0	3	9	21	5	0	4	1	32	20	1	9	0	0	8	3	11
Death and burial:																								
I	0	0	0	0	0	0	6	0	1	0	0	0	4	5	0	28	13	1	4	0	0	3	0	10
II	0	0	0	0	0	0	5	1	0	2	0	0	9	4	0	28	6	0	8	0	0	4	0	8

Table 6 The totals of the 33 items of expenditures after allotment (I) by the psychologists and (II) by the group of economists. experts in home economics. etc.

		I		II	
		In units of $10 million	In percentages of the total	In units of $10 million	In percentages of the total
A.	Hunger	1.018	11.2	1026	11.3
B.	Protection against cold. heat, wet	925	10.2	889	9.8
C.	Exercise	39	.4	63	.7
D.	Sleep, rest	239	2.6	184	2.0
E.	Sex relief	77	.8	81	.9
F.	Reproduce species	172	1.9	73	.8
G.	Protection against animals and diseases	404	4.4	377	4.1
H.	Protection against bad people	227	2.5	140	1.5
I.	Reduce or avoid pain	322	3.5	209	2.3
J.	Pleasures of taste and smell	414	4.6	434	4.8
K.	Pleasures of sight and sound	359	3.9	471	5.2
L.	Sex entertainment	356	3.9	374	4.1
M.	Security	959	10.5	1015	11.2
N.	Affection (to get it)	163	1.8	169	1.9
O.	Companionship	210	2.3	211	2.3
P.	Approval of others	657	7.2	653	7.2
Q.	Approval of one's self	367	4.0	347	3.8
R.	Mastery over others	276	3.0	164	1.8
S.	The welfare of others	656	7.2	786	8.6
T.	Mental activity	175	1.9	210	2.3
U.	Curiosity and exploration	168	1.8	211	2.3
V.	Social entertainment	380	4.2	613	6.7
W.	Physical entertainment	104	1.1	115	1.3
X.	Comfort not in A to W	411	4.5	273	3.0

X, miscellaneous satisfaction or comfort), being .92.[1] Table 6 states that we spend about one ninth of our money to ward off hunger, about one tenth to keep warm (or cool) and dry, that our payments for games and sports are for entertainment rather than exercise, that we spend much time but little money for rest, that the mental features of sex life cost us about five times as much as the physical, that the reproduction of the species comes chiefly as a by-product, that we pay twice as much for protection against diseases as for protection against bad men.

Some Freudian psychiatrists say that what human beings want above all else is love and security, but in Table 6 security averages under 11

[1] It would probably be higher if each person's X could be distributed among A to W.

percent and affection under 2 percent. We pay more to get companion-ship than to get affection. Approval of others and of one's own self (conscience, self-respect, pride, etc.) rival hunger and security. A cynic may say that the percentages for Item S (the welfare of others) show modern civilized man to be only one twelfth altruist and that the percentages for item T show him to be only 2 percent intellectual. This is harsh, neglecting the *time* that persons (mothers especially) spend for the welfare of others, and the fact that a fine intellectual life can now be lived at almost no pecuniary expense. But Table 6 does fall far below the ideals set by moralists. For entertainment (L, V, and W) we spent more than for mental activity and the welfare of others combined. Less than a third of the expenditures are allotted to keeping the population alive, well, and able to reproduce itself. The pleasures of the senses take a tenth; the pleasures of the intellect less than half that. The selfish satisfactions which depend rather directly upon our fellow men take over a fifth. This becomes over a third if the satisfactions of the love-life and benevolence are included. *Homo* (of U. S. A. 1929) seems much more sociable than *sapiens*. He seems to be mainly a hedonist, but most of the pleasure he seeks is not of the senses.

"What we spend our money for" may be translated into "What we spend our waking time for," and then combined with the facts reported in the earlier section about our uses of leisure. The combination will give some idea of the gratifications for which all our days are spent. I conjecture that the 16 hours of the working day of adults in the United States are spent roughly as follows:

25 percent for subsistence and perpetuation.
 2   ,,   to avoid or reduce sensory pain.
 7   ,,   for security.
 8   ,,   for the welfare of others.[1]
30   ,,   for entertainment.
10   ,,   for companionship and affection.
10   ,,   for approval.
 4   ,,   for intellectual activity.
 2   ,,   for dominance over others.
 2   ,,   for other wants.

Man does not put first those wants the satisfaction of which ensures survival, the production of offspring and their survival, and attend to others only after these have been satiated. His craving for social

[1] This estimate is specially insecure because the budgets of time include none for mothers. I have had to guess what allotment to make for them.

intercourse and the approval of self and others is for greater amounts and different sorts than are needed for survival; his craving for sex pleasures is out of all proportion to what is needed for the production of offspring; his craving for entertainment may even operate against the nourishment of the young and the protection of the community.

This seems to have been true of all peoples and times so far as their histories have been recorded, and of the so-called primitive peoples of the present. The peasants of China and India who live on a few cents a day and do not save enough to carry themselves through a year of bad crops none the less spend time in social intercourse and such entertainments as comes their way and in rites and ceremonies which increase their peace of mind and self respect. The savages of Central and Northern Australia have almost no clothing to protect them from cold, wet, or insects, but they have many ornaments; they have dogs as companions rather than as aids in hunting; they spend an enormous amount of time in ceremonies which have little or no utility other than to minister to self-approval and social approval, gratify the desire for sociability and entertainment, and perhaps maintain the authority of the old men.[1]

Human Wants in Detail

Almost every human want deserves more study than has been given to it. Terms like hunger, craving for sexual activity, ambition, love of distinction, present us with questions as well as facts. We say that John Doe wants alcohol which is true and useful as far as it goes, but we need greatly to know also what inner stimuli or clues tell him to take a drink and what the drink does for him.

To illustrate and enforce the principle, I present here some of the facts concerning two of the simpler sensory wants, and one notably imaginative or ideational want.

The Desire for Food   Hunger and thirst are identifiable not only by the fact that the intake of certain substances normally reduces the strength of the want, but also by certain fairly definite feelings. A person who is dehydrated feels thirsty, and does not mistake this feeling for any other. The feeling of desire for food is not quite so simple. There are the so-called hunger-pangs due to the contractions of an empty stomach, and there is the very different hunger (or "appetite" as Maslow prefers to call

[1] The natives, of course, impute to these magic ceremonies efficacy in maintaining the supply of animals, plants, and other features useful for living. Consequently their performances give peace of mind, but if they felt no need of magic control of nature there would be no anxieties to be quieted. In this case magic cures only what magic causes, leaving sociability and entertainment as its net contributions.

it to distinguish it from the aforesaid pangs) which a healthy person feels after a certain abstinence from food. The latter is the ordinary signal and stimulus for eating.

Hunger does not act logically as a symptom of the need of food or a motive to ingest it. Psychologists who have starved themselves report that after a rise to notable intensity the hunger weakens so that after a time as the need for food becomes greater the craving for it becomes less. This being true of one of the most fundamental natural wants, where the correspondence with need has a clear survival value, what can we expect of wants in general? Wants are very inadequate symptoms and measures of needs even when they are the best symptoms available.

Hunger is instructive also in that it becomes the base for an enormous edifice of derived and specialized wants. The human race could doubtless be entirely healthy, and moderately happy, on some cereal and a modicum of fruits, vegetables, roots, animal flesh, and salt. This could be eaten casually and without ceremony. But man in satisfying his hunger satisfies the desire of the palate, experiments with new foods and combinations, prepares these in many ways, attaches imaginary potencies among them, and sets up rules for who should eat what. He invents tools, containers, and cooking utensils. He transforms certain meals into feasts and ceremonies, and makes the satisfaction of hunger an occasion and excuse for vicarious consumption, conspicuous waste, and display calculated to secure self-respect and social admiration.

The Desire to Smoke Tobacco   The desire for tobacco is interesting in several respects. The human genes have no specific power to make man like absorbing nicotine, or sucking in tobacco smoke, or manipulating a pipe. It is rarely or never fostered in infancy. It develops in spite of the absence of pleasure from the early occurrences of smoking. Smoking was outlandish in origin and had little prestige value. Yet the craving spread over the world with extreme rapidity. Tobacco has probably more followers than any one deity, and a large number of slaves. The inhabitants of this country spent for tobacco in a recent year a fifth as much as they spent for clothing.

Any habitual smoker knows when he wants a smoke, and rarely mistakes this want for any other. But just what the inner state, condition, or stimulus is that makes him light his pipe or cigarette, he finds hard to determine. Five of seven well-known psychologists who are habitual smokers (they would want from $25 to $500 as compensation for abstaining for two weeks) when asked "What is the stimulus or combination of stimuli which makes you want to smoke? replied as follows:— "A craving at the midriff." "Feel uncomfortable without it, particularly when there is some tension in the situation." "Malaise, akin to thirst in mouth-roof and esophagus." "I wish I knew." "Physiological discomfort if I don't." The other two had even more indefinite ideas about the state provocative of the craving.

Any one person's experiences are likely to provide him with a stock of resources which act or are supposed to act in stimulating, relaxing, sedative, hypnotic, or more vaguely comforting ways. They range from foods and drugs with important intrinsic potencies to things which influence him only through the associations they have had in his experience. But most of them have some intrinsic potency. For example, a cup of tea has some of the drug, a good deal of heat and liquid, some quickly absorbed nourishment if it contains sugar, and usually a few minutes of relative relaxation of the muscles, as well as whatever personal consequences have been attached to it by associative habit. Even the most potent drug may have a yet stronger effect by such associative processes. One who buys any article for personal consumption buys not only the materials constituting that article, but whatever has been attached to the consumption of such articles by his experience. The identical constituents disguised or distorted might fail to give the desired result.

The Desire for Life after Death   The desire for a good life after death has been widespread and often powerful. The first question is how and why mankind, creatures born of nature and bred in nature, fit by their anatomy and physiology to deal with natural objects, invented so many super- or extra-natural objects to respond to. Why, for example, did men not respond to a dead man as a corpse, adapting their thought and acts about dead men to what corpses actually do as natural objects? Why invent a life after death for dead men?

The important general principles are two: First, the ideas, notions, or representative conceptual thoughts of men are a superstructure which, though constructed out of things which are like natural objects, can transcend nature fantastically as dreams do, inconsistently as wishes often do, abstractly as in the geometer's planes with zero thickness, in fact, in any ways that one can think of. Man's ideational life can be as much at home with the ghosts it has imagined as with the men it sees. The power of reorganizing experience in thought is so great that man can easily disregard or distort natural facts so as to believe that there are somewhere animals that talk or weapons that always hit the mark, so as to think of the dead as more powerful on earth than the living. The wonder is not that mankind has entertained so many superstitions, but that it has not entertained many more.

Second, until rather recently and exceptionally men have not distinguished between ideas which operate well in predicting events and ideas which operate well in making one comfortable. We now know that sowing a certain sort of seed in certain places at certain times will under certain conditions produce a crop, and that the incantations one pronounces or the libations one pours will, in and of themselves, do nothing to the crop, though they may add to the hope and peace of mind of the farmer. But that is a late discovery.

As a consequence of the first principle we may expect a practically infinite number of beliefs to have occurred. As a consequence of the first and second principles we may expect that an enormous number of beliefs will be retained by one or more persons; namely, all those which are not displaced by some belief which was more comfortable. From those retained certain ones will die a natural psychological death from disuse; others will be selected for permanent survival in the individual; a few will become fixed traditions of the family, community, or entire population.

Beliefs may obviously also spread or perish because the acts based upon them are so beneficial as to favor the perpetuation of the believers and their offspring or so harmful as to reduce it. After a belief is once established in a community, new members of the community will usually acquire and retain the belief because the social environment causes the belief to occur in them and strengthens it by a diffuse approval.

The belief in life after death was then, one may say, sure to occur in men who did not attach the feelings or abilities of living men to their living bodies in any absolute way. So long as he did not think about it at all, a man could treat a human corpse as a dog treats one, being triumphant, miserable, curious, or cannibalistic according to the circumstances, but if he thought about it at all, there was certainly little in his experience until a few hundred years ago to make him conclude that the person whom he knew had been annihilated simply because his body was now cold and motionless. That would have been a far harder belief to invent and make popular.

As another general principle we may note the general weakness of beliefs founded on ideas in comparison with beliefs founded on repeated habits or memory of repeatedly perceived events or repeatedly experienced acts. A man may believe in the heaven described by the New Testament and by the pronouncements of his church in the sense that he has no conscious doubts about it and would emphatically reject any view contrary to it, and yet not believe it nearly as strongly as he believes that the shoes he is wearing are black or that certain movements of his arm will put food into his mouth.

Among theories all arrived at via ideas, supernatural theories and superstitions may be even more acceptable than scientific theories, but between expectations rooted directly in perception and action and expectations derived from thought, the former have superior power to compel belief.

Science is a hybrid from this direct knowledge gained from perception and action mated to imaginative and abstract thinking as subtle and daring as that of poets or theologians. Using a different metaphor, we may say that by its procedure of verification it keeps anchored to the former so that it may risk any hypothesis; and that (changing the metaphor again) it makes all its hypotheses out of stuff that is of the same flesh and blood as what one senses, sees and touches and what our muscles act with and upon. Science is thus adapted to the world of nature to a degree of intimacy, thoroughness, and certainty which philosophy, theology, poetry, and religion have hitherto not attained. It thus commands a belief more like the plain man's belief in what he sees, and less like his belief in what is comfortable for him to think.

It is in a supernatural world, which never (or only occasionally by a miracle) disturbs the course of the natural world, that men do live after their bodies are dead, according to the religions which are acceptable to intelligent people of recent times. What is the value to mankind of a belief in this sort of life? Its value science cannot profitably discuss since it has no information about the nature of such a supernatural world. Its value to men as inhabitants of the natural world will depend chiefly upon other concrete particulars. A belief that whoever dies fighting for Mahomet will after death cohabit with houris *ad lib* was probably demoralizing to human welfare in the natural world. A belief that whoever fulfills certain obligations of ceremonial and penance will be made happy in the supernatural world can hardly be other than an unmitigated nuisance to the welfare of natural men. A belief, on the other hand, that the injustices of the natural world will be counterbalanced in some supernatural world may do good by supporting the decent behavior of men with the hope of eventual justice elsewhere. It may, of course, do harm by causing good men to relax their efforts to attain justice for themselves and others in the natural world.

If, in the hundred or thousand years to come, men over the world should retain unchanged their present beliefs about life after death and its rewards and punishments, or if they should increasingly believe that the fate of all men rested entirely with nature, including themselves and other men, and that what justice and mercy is done will be done by us in this world—which would be better? It is a hard question.

Five facts may be noted, two well-known, two where common opinion is ignorant or in error, and one where knowledge is lacking: (1) We should not use the supernatural as an excuse for doing less well than we can. It was bad to let people suffer from smallpox, typhus, tuberculosis, septic operations, and useless pain, assuming that supernatural forces would compensate them.

(2) The churches have been urging good works in this life more, and preparation for a supernatural life less. They have presented stimuli to men's good natural impulses more and relied on promises and threats relating to life after death less. They are increasingly favoring the improvement of the natural world by the virtuous use of natural forces.

(3) Some persons of mean natures living selfish and depraved lives assert disbelief in a supernatural world and have no affiliations with bodies of religious believers. But they seem to be exceptional. Criminals in general, according to the investigations of Havelock Ellis and others, are as often believers and communicants as non-criminals. The village drunkard, rake, or crook who avoids the churches may do so partly because his character is so well-known that he would be made uncomfortable there, partly because, by a perverted logic, his disbelief serves him as an excuse for not being a decent man, and partly because the avoidance permits him to respect himself as not a hypocrite.

(4) Intellectuals who are agnostics, in spite of resulting difficulties with friends and risk of general unpopularity, have probably deserved extremely high ratings for private and public virtues. These, whom we may call "conscientious objectors" to immortality, are men and women whom all the world except the ignorant or bigoted honors.

(5) Certain people in recent years have accepted the denial of supernaturalism and life after death as a dogma in much the same way that their grandparents accepted its affirmation. Many of them are followers of Marx or Lenin. What net effect, if any, this has had and will have upon their contribution to the good and ill of the world is as yet unknown. Their so-called "scientific materialism" and their economic and social doctrines seem in combination to induce a spirit of self-sacrifice and loyalty to their fellows combined with a calculating, ferocious, and bigoted hate toward others. But this seeming may be illusory in respect to both the nature of their behavior and its causes.

Another general problem concerns the proper use of hope versus resignation. Whatever the total effect on welfare of belief in life after death may be, its help to worthy souls in enduring injustice, calamity, and bereavement can hardly be doubted. Just as, in the natural world, we gain comfort at a present injustice by the hope that the future years of life will atone, or at the present absence of loved ones by the hope that in time we shall have them with us again, so when the injustice is beyond this world's power to cure and when the absence is caused by death, comfort comes from hopes for supernatural compensation. It seems cruel to lessen either hope merely because the probabilities do not fully justify it.

How far shall we tolerate hopes that the *natural* world will be better, kinder, and more just, and when shall we shift from hope for the best to resignation to the probable? One essential feature of the problem is the fact that the person's hopes are themselves creative forces in the natural world; being part of him they help to determine his behavior. A patient may live because he expects to live, and die if he expects to die. Hope, more than probabilities warrant, is probably also on the whole favorable to experimentation, creative work, and forward-looking activities, as contrasted with playing safe, preserving past gains, and living for the present.

On the other hand, unwarranted hopes obviously will, in the end, bring disappointment and consequent discouragement, and they will lead to imprudent and wasteful activities. Moreover, it is easy to overestimate the satisfyingness of hope in comparison with that of resignation when both deal with the natural world.

Hopes for supernatural events, being themselves natural forces, vary in their concrete details and accompaniments and consequences according to the persons who entertain them. The natural value of the belief in life after death will then vary enormously with persons and conditions. Some may be bettered by having the belief destroyed. To destroy or weaken it in some others would be like killing all the animal pets of little children to make fertilizer. To destroy it in certain others might even be like teaching mothers to hate their children or thinkers to hate the truth. Whatever is done to the belief in any person should be done, as always, with the consequences of the action in view.

Chapter 5
The Measurement of Wants and Satisfactions

The measurement of wants, satisfactions, aversions, misery, and the like suffers from certain special difficulties. The only system of measurement which has been widely used for them is, of course, money. Opinions concerning the possibility and practicability of measurements of a person's wants and satisfactions more direct and more widely applicable than by the money would vary widely. At one extreme would be a few who would in general eschew efforts to put the different wants of a person into any exact order of magnitude, or to put the similar wants of different persons into any such scale. At the opposite extreme would be a few who would insist that any want or satisfaction which exists at all exists in some amount and is therefore measurable, how exactly and how commensurably with others, we cannot tell until we have tried. This small group, with whom the writer sympathizes, points to the successes of physical science in measuring the subtleties of electrical phenomena and making various forms of energy commensurate.

Before considering what is possible, it will be profitable to note what is actually done now. For any one person any two wants or preferences, W_1 and W_2, may be compared in respect of "strength." Judgments are made in the forms: "$W_1 > W_2$"; "$W_1 \simeq W_2$"; "$W_1 < W_2$"; "W_1 and W_2 are both so great that I have no opinion concerning which is greater."

Nobody doubts this in the case of varying amounts or intensities of the same sort of want, such as hunger, desire to stop work, or homesickness. So we may pass to the case of two wants that are qualitatively different but in the same person. An observer with adequate data can reasonably assert that to John Doe at 10 A.M., January 1, 1940, the desire to intermit work and smoke a cigar for 10 minutes was approximately equal to the desire to intermit the work and smoke a pipe, and less than the desire to intermit work and telephone his girl friend.

We may conclude that, for any one organism in any one condition, all possible wants can be put in an order of magnitude, save that, toward the extremes of desire and aversion, there may be and probably will be undiscriminated imperatives of demand and rejection.

A certain point in this order of magnitude is a true and absolute zero in the sense that the fact in the person has approximately no strength or intensity, being properly called indifference, or 0 preference. We often define degrees of strength at various points along this order of magnitude as we define degrees of temperature by the freezing point of alcohol, the melting point of lead, etc. So the reader knows roughly on different occasions that he wants a drink of water enough to drink it when offered, enough to walk a mile to get it, or enough to pay a dollar for it, that he wants the thrill and memories of a certain game enough to spend an afternoon and five dollars therefor. Rightly or wrongly, the reader may define his aversion to being blind as so great that he would prefer death.

To have an adequate system of measurement is to equate the difference between the zero or indifference point and some definable degree of preference, with the difference between that and some definable greater degree or strength, and so on. Since the zero of the scale is just not any of it, we can use the "times as much" judgment and the full arithmetic of multiplication, division, and percentage.

The most important available means of trying to obtain such equal units of difference in the strength of wants is *via* the monetary units used in the exchange of commodities, services, etc. But it will be instructive to consider first two other possibilities. Suppose electrodes to be so adjusted to John Doe and suppose that he pays for this, that, and the other satisfaction by receiving 1, 2, 3, etc. shocks, all physically equal, and far enough apart so that late ones in a lot produce the same physiological effect as early ones. John Doe will very quickly be familiar with the shocks and competent to bargain in terms of them.

If John Doe in condition A would bid just 2 shocks to eat a gram of chocolate, 6 shocks to smoke a cigarette, 10 shocks for a bath, and 20 shocks to be freed from an hour of work, we can meaningfully and probably usefully say that his want for a bath was as much greater than his want for a cigarette as that was greater than his want for the chocolate, and that he wanted freedom from an hour of work more than chocolate, smoke, and bath combined.

Moss ['24], Warner ['27 and '28], Warden ['28], and others, have used standard shocks, though not in just the way described above, to measure the strength in animals of hunger, thirst, sex-longing, and the desire of the female to be with her young, and have obtained important results.

A different way of attaining equal units of a sort would be by experimentally equating so many satisfactions of want A against so many of want B, and against so many of want C, and so on, either directly or by using shocks and their avoidance, sums of money, foods, drinks, amusements, applause, and anything convenient. Suppose that John Doe is in condition A during enough thousands of experiments to give data as follows:

He wants 1 occurrence of B as much as 2 occurrences of A,
He wants 1 occurrence of C as much as 2 occurrences of B,
He wants 1 occurrence of D as much as 2 occurrences of C,
He wants 1 occurrence of E as much as 2 occurrences of D,
He wants 1 occurrence of F as much as 2 occurrences of E.

Where a barter of n occurrences of the satisfaction of one want against $n \pm N$ occurrences of the satisfaction of another is direct, we have an unimpeachable method of scaling wants provided only that the sum of n satisfactions of a want is the same regardless of the sequence in which they are taken. Since, by hypothesis, the person is in the same condition at all occurrences, this condition is fulfilled.

Consider now the money bids made by John Doe in condition A for the gratification of the wants point by point along the order of magnitude determined for him. Concretely, suppose that he is in condition A on a hundred occasions, and on each is given $1.00 to spend, and that he spends it on one occasion for $10W_1$, on another for $8W_1$ and $1W_2$, on another for $2W_5$, on another for $1W_1$ and $3W_3$, on another for an installment of one tenth of W_{100} for future delivery, in what sense can we use the resulting equations to infer that the quantitative relations of the intensities of the wants in question correspond to the quantitative relations of the monetary payments? If the amount of preference represented by each 10 cents is the same regardless of the position in which it appears in the order of payment, the correspondence may be regarded as complete.

In a scale for amounts of preference the steps from 1 to 2, 2 to 3, 3 to 4, 4 to 5, etc. are, of course, not equal in the sense that the smoking of a cigarette *is* eating two grams of chocolate or one tenth of seeing a movie. No more does the scale for volume mean that a 50-foot steel tape *is* 50 wooden foot-rules or $16\frac{2}{3}$ linen yard-measures. It is the abstract feature of intensity or amount of want, gratification, or preference that we are concerned with.

I venture to remind the reader of two obvious limitations upon scaling. All scaling fails when the person's wants are so imperative or "infinite" that they cannot be rated as multiples of other wants, or even be put in an order of magnitude. All scaling for any given person in any given condition will suffer in precision from failures to keep him in that condition during the observations and experimentation, and will depend for its precision upon the impartiality and precision of the observations.

In strict logic, the order or amounts found for a certain man in one condition give no certitude concerning the order or amount for that man in different conditions, or for other men. It is this variation, not any essential immeasurable quality in human preferences, which hinders quantitative studies of wants. To discover whether, over a ten-year period, John Doe's desires to have friendly companionship (or his satisfactions from having friendly companionship) were $1\frac{1}{2}$, 2, 3, 4, or 5 times as strong as his desires to hear music, might be a long and difficult job. To discover whether these desires in R. Roe were .1, .2, .3, .4, etc. as strong as in J. Doe might be an even longer and more difficult job. To use measurements in units of money, shock, avoidance, etc. in such comparisons we need to know changes in the value of money, shock, avoidance to the person from one condition to another and differences in their value to different persons.

Nobody has scaled accurately any considerable number of wants of the same person in the same conditions, partly because the information is not in and of itself of sufficient importance. Nobody has scaled the wants of the human species because the difficulties are appalling. Thinkers realize the importance of such measurements, but lack the facilities to make them.

They therefore do the best they can in the case of problems in psychology, ethics, government, sociology, penology, and the like, using judgments which seem probable, such as that the average prudent modern European adult from 60 to 70 wants security more than excitement, or that the youth of 1940 want security in respect of the avoidance of hell and purgatory less than the youth of 1540 did, or that the average American family wants a $3,000-a-year home plus an automobile more than a $5,000-a-year home and no automobile. But Veblen's belief that the leisure classes want self-approval and the admiration of others so much that they spend most of their surplus in "vicarious consumption" and "conspicuous waste" has not been accepted by all. And the assumption made by high-minded rationalists that all normal men and women have a strong desire to think out a logical, consistent plan of life and pursue it at least so far as it does not interfere with other wants, seems fantastic to the working politician, advertising man, or psychiatrist.

Units and scales would be valuable as a language in which to discuss human nature and behavior even if practical difficulties prevented any wide use of them. Our opinions about amounts of preference might become more useful if they could be stated in terms of such units and scales, even though they remained as subjective as before. It was advantageous to express opinions about the age of the earth in terms of years rather than as old, very old, and extremely old, even when such opinions were very rough estimates.

Money Payments

If a person is willing to pay a dollar if necessary, but no more, for a certain book, for a certain concert, and for a certain added stylishness in a pair of shoes, and two dollars if necessary, but no more, for a certain added stylishness in a hat or for a hundred cigarettes, he may be said to have wanted the first three equally and to have wanted the added stylishness of the hat twice as much as that of the shoes. The added satisfaction from possessing and wearing the more stylish hat, if it lives up to its promise, may be said to approximate the satisfaction added by two cigarettes a week for a year. Such a person might learn to estimate his desire to take a day off from work, to feel that he had given a proper annual contribution to his church, to spend a Sunday at the beach, to have cream in his coffee for a year, or to stop a certain toothache, by the limit he would pay.

But such estimatings may give different results from those which would be found by confining the person in an experimental environment where the prices of things could be shifted at the experimenter's will. So a person who is sure that he would never pay five cents for a cigarette might do so if he could not have one otherwise, and some other person who is sure that he would go barefoot rather than lack tobacco might in reality suffer the craving rather than the ignominy. The money unit can, I think, be useful in measuring wants over a wide range of phenomena. In a sense any satisfaction that can be bought with money is measurable in money units, and workers in other sciences than economics should recognize and make use of this fact.

The Use of Intrinsic Units of Satisfaction, Discomfort, Desire, and Aversion

Consider first the want for water of a person in a specified state (say 24 hours after satiation with water, all spent resting in a temperature of 70° F., eating at will of plain white bread), the annoyance of that state during its last hour, and the satisfaction from the ingestion of so much water as reduces the want to zero.

If we should use this amount of want or this amount of satisfaction as a unit to which to refer other amounts of want and of satisfaction, and should assume that it was the same amount whether John was richer or poorer, more virtuous or more vicious, wiser or less wise, how large an error would we make?

We do not know. The way to find out would be to identify the physiological facts in the man and the changes in them produced by the water. If these were the same on the different occasions, there would be no reason to suppose that the want, annoyance, and satisfaction were not the same on the different occasions. These physiological facts are at present inaccessible. On general biological grounds, we may expect that the differences would be small.

How large errors would we make if we assumed that the amounts for Richard Roe subjected to the same experience would be equal to those for John Doe? The way to find out would be the same, by comparing the physiological facts in Richard and in John. If all men show the same patterns for the thirst and its abolition, their amounts of want, annoyance, and satisfaction may be treated as equal.

Ordinary businessmen, statesmen, teachers, physicians, or clergymen explicitly or implicitly compare the amounts of the aversions, satisfactions, discomforts and pleasures and of different persons, putting them on scales running from indifference to extreme amounts. They act on the basis of such judgments as "A wants that block of stock or piece of land much more than B does"; "Mrs. C. is satisfied by flattery a little more than Mrs. D."; "G dislikes mathematics more than any other pupil I ever had." "In intensity of desire to help their fellow men, I would rank the five men in the order K, H, L, J, I." We all use such judgments unhesitatingly unless we are made critical by the difficulty of proving the judgments valid, or by the difference between them and judgments of physical magnitudes, or by scruples about knowledge of other minds than one's own.

They, and we, judge the direction and amount of a difference in the wants of two persons by the behavior of the persons and by any other observable facts about them. A's want for X is judged to be great, and greater than B's, because A keeps watch of the prices on X, responds differently when X is mentioned, has a special need for X. C's enjoyment of flattery is judged to be more than D's because C shows more emphatic signs of enjoyment and is moved to buy, consent or grant favors more by flattery than D is. The facts which lead us to judge that A wants X, also lead us to an estimate of the intensity of his want for it. Whatever facts lead us to think that a person has a preference are able to lead us to some rough estimate of the amount of the preference.

Two facts support these practices. The first is that the judgments are not chaotic and futile, but reasonable (in the sense that competent judges agree far above chance in such judgments) and profitable (in the sense that we keep alive and happy better by accepting them than by accepting their opposites or by making no such judgments at all). This is a sufficient justification for science to proceed to refine and extend and safeguard such judgments.

The second fact is that fundamentally our comparisons of length, volume, mass, temperature, and other physical magnitudes, too, rest upon human judgments; only the agreement here is very much closer, and the measurements are simpler and more direct. We know and measure men's wants, pleasures, etc. as we know and measure their heights and weights and body temperatures, by data of our senses treated by our intellects. We know that the voltage in circuit A is 1.4 higher than in circuit B with great certainty; we may hope to know that the satisfaction in person A is .4 thirstads greater than in person B, but much less surely. This second fact may serve as an antidote to squeamishness about efforts to measure what is alleged to be inaccessible.

"Infinite" Desires and Aversions

The desires of man vary in strength from mild preferences to absolute categorical imperatives which exclude self-denial. The latter may be called "infinite" in the sense of immeasurably great to the person who possesses them.

They occur more or less normally in extreme hunger and thirst, in sex desire, in cravings for the relief given by drugs, and in the body's demand for sleep.

Specially rational minds may reduce these immeasurable desires to measured amounts and put them in comparison with the sums of lesser wants. But the drunkard who in his actions prefers his want for alcohol to the sum of his wants for the welfare of his family, the approval of his friends, the self-respect of his better moments, probably does not make the calculation and choose the alcohol. He simply at the time of temptation acts upon an absolute, unrestrained, obsessional desire.

In an experiment, persons were asked to state the number of days they would spend in jail at hard labor (but with no disgrace to them) in order to gratify various wants, one of which was "to spend a year with Byrd at the South Pole." One person, who seemed entirely sincere, reported that he would spend ten years in jail for that privilege! And in fact that item was included in the experiment because a boy among a thousand who were tested by my staff at about age 14 and followed thereafter made three desperate attempts to hide on Byrd's ship. Such cases probably mean that the wants in question are almost immeasurably great.

The case is even clearer for aversions. Let the reader consider what sum of measurable benefits to himself (or to himself and all others, for that matter) would induce him to be blinded and have both legs and both arms cut off.

To many persons, even a minor mutilation of one's body, or insult to one's nature, or a deprivation from some customary enjoyment, seems intolerable, as in the experiment reported in Table 7 in the case of (A) 60 students and teachers of psychology and (B) 39 persons under 30 years of age, mostly college graduates, all of whom were destitute recipients of public relief, and so presumably very sensitive to the value of money. The 39 persons of group B were all used to psychological tests and question-naires and cooperative and sincere in their replies.[1]

The instructions were: For how much money, paid in cash, would you do or suffer the following? Write the amounts on the dotted lines. You must suppose that the money can be spent on yourself only and that whatever you buy with it is destroyed when you die. You cannot use any of it for your friends, relatives, or charity.

Doubtless actual cash offers lower than the amounts stated would have been accepted, if made. But many of these statements of "no sum" would, I think, have been duplicated as responses to real offers. At all events they and also the absurdly high demands expressed in dollars, testify to a strong tendency of human beings to consider some of these events as immeasurably repugnant.

---

[1] Data from Thorndike ['37].

Table 7   Valuations of certain mutilations, deprivations, etc.

Item	Median amount demanded		Percentage reporting that no sum would suffice	
	By students and teachers of psychology	By young recipients of relief	Students and teachers of psychology	Young recipients of relief
Have one upper front tooth pulled out	$ 5,000	$ 4,500	23.3	20.5
Have your left arm cut off at the elbow (right arm if you prefer)	No sum	2,500,000	70.0	41.6
Have a little finger of one hand cut off	75,000	200,000	35.0	30.8
Have the little toe of one foot cut off	10,000	57,000	25.0	25.6
Become entirely bald	750,000	75,000	43.3	28.2
Have smallpox, recover perfectly, except for about 20 large pockmarks on your cheeks and forehead	No sum	1,000,000	50.0	33.3
Become totally blind	No sum	No sum	76.7	53.8
Become unable to speak, so that you can communicate only by writing, signs, etc.	No sum	15,000,000	71.7	46.2
Become unable to taste	1,000,000	5,000,000	45.0	41.0
Become unable to smell	300,000	150,000	36.7	33.3
Have to live all the rest of your life outside of U.S.A.	200,000	150,000	16.7	5.1
Have to live all the rest of your life on a farm in Kansas, ten miles from any town	1,000,000	300,000	40.0	15.4
Eat a dead beetle one inch long	5,000	5,000	21.7	15.4
Eat a live beetle one inch long	25,000	50,000	35.0	30.8
Eat a live earthworm 6 inches long	10,000	100,000	31.7	33.3
Eat a quarter of a pound of cooked human flesh (supposing that nobody but the person who pays you to do so will ever know it)	1,000,000	100,000	45.0	25.6
Drink enough to become thoroughly intoxicated	100	50	6.7	7.7
Choke a stray cat to death	10,000	10,000	35.0	30.8
Attend Sunday morning service in St. Patrick's Cathedral, and in the middle of the ser-				

TABLE 7 (*Continued*)

Item	Median amount demanded		Percentage reporting that no sum would suffice	
	By students and teachers of psychology	By young recipients of relief	Students and teachers of psychology	Young recipients of relief
vice run down the aisle to the altar, yelling "The time has come, the time has come" as loud as you can until you are dragged out	100,000	1,000	31.7	10.2
Spit on a crucifix	300	5	23.3	20.5
Have nothing to eat but bread, milk, spinach and yeast cakes for a year	10,000	25,000	15.0	7.7

The Use of Equally Often Noticed Differences

One of the hopes of psychology was to obtain equal units of sensation, and one of the proposed methods of doing so was by treating any difference in, say, sweetness which one could just barely perceive as equal to any other barely perceptible difference in sweetness. If these just perceptible or least noticeable differences can be treated as equal, it is possible to form a scale for any one person in any one condition running from 0 to that which is so sweet that no sweeter sensation can be had. The physical stimuli causing 1, 2, 3, 4, 5, 6, etc. units of sweetness, or sensed pressure, or sensed heat, or sensed length, could be used to produce and define them.

In the actual determination of equal units of sensation for any person by this assumption it becomes desirable to shift from the least noticeable or barely perceptible differences to very small differences that are equally often noticed or perceived, for the person's variability of response to any external difference is very great. Two lines 1 and $1+k$ in length being presented a hundred times, $1+k$ may sometimes seem much longer than 1, sometimes barely longer, sometimes equal to 1, and sometimes even shorter. Moreover, the mind does not make its sensation or perception by the addition of so many tiny sensations of length. A person's judgment of the difference between $1+k$ and 1 is not based on a direct comparison of them, but is a response to the two stimuli $1+k$ and 1 which is mediated by complex and hidden cerebral processes. In the case of preferences, wants, satisfactions, annoyances, pleasures, and pains it is equally often noticed differences that concern us, not least noticeable differences.

I shall give a very incomplete account of this matter for the following reasons: (1) The logic of measurement and comparison by the percentages of differences that are observed is subtle and not adequately explored. (2) The facts concerning actual cases of such measurement and comparison are numerous but disturbed by accidental variations and are often not relevant to our present problem. (3) What most readers of this book will desire and need is a general notion of what may be expected from such measurements made by scientists who understand their theory and technique, not an understanding of that theory and technique themselves.[1]

If the same person in the same condition prefers A to B in 75 percent of his choices between them, and B to C in 75 percent of his choices between them, we know at least two things about his preferences. (1) In neither case is the preference very great, since it is so often reversed; (2) the order of preference is almost certainly A B C. This latter has been found again and again by experimental comparisons of A and C in such cases. We also know (3) that the preference of A over B is equal to that of B over C in the sense that it occurs equally often.

The method of comparing the magnitude of differences by such percentages is flexible and applicable in a great variety of cases. We may, if we do not misunderstand what we are doing, profitably compare things which seem to ordinary opinion incomparable. For example, if 80 percent of college seniors get more enjoyment per hour from reading Galsworthy's novels than from reading Thackeray's, and if 80 percent of them get more enjoyment per hour from swimming than from tennis, the difference being moderate in all individuals, then in a certain real though limited sense the two differences are equal. Access to Galsworthy's novels rather than Thackeray's and to a swimming place rather than a tennis court will be in a certain sense equal boons to the college seniors. If I get more pleasure from coffee than from tea, and from salted butter than from unsalted, and from *The Times* than from *The Herald-Tribune,* in each case in 73 percent of the trials, the differences in pleasure all being of moderate

---

[1] The method of treating as equal differences which are equally often noticed by a specified observer or group of observers was used early by Cattell and others. A simple account of the procedures will be found in Thorndike ['13, Chapter VIII, especially pp. 122f.]. A more refined technique is presented by Thurstone ['27] and elaborated by Horst ['32]. The treatment when not all of the *n* differences are judged by all of the N judges has been described by Thorndike ['16]. For results obtained by the use of this method in the measurement of degrees of value or merit and preferences of various sorts, see Thorndike ['10, '11, and '13A] and Horst ['32].

amount, then in a sense, the three differences are equal and my loss of pleasure would be as great from restriction to tea as from restriction to unsalted butter or to the *The Herald-Tribune.*

The method is specially suited to differences which are small and dubious, such as differences in the preferences among certain foods, articles of clothing of equal price, poems, or minor discomforts. It can, however, be made applicable to differences of any magnitude, by inserting intermediate steps.

Its acme of utility is reached where we can assume that the real magnitudes of the difference if we knew them, would be distributed symmetrically and approximately as shown in Fig. 3, the bell-shaped surface of frequency which is characteristic of so many living phenomena, individual and social. For example, there would be only a small risk

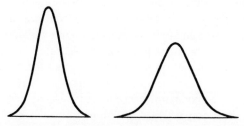

Fig. 3. Type of distribution to which variable traits in individuals often roughly approximate. The two diagrams represent the same "normal" form of surface, the only difference being in the variability.

in assuming that the greater satisfaction from 11 cc of water than from 10 cc to a man on a thousand occasions of equal dehydration would approximate such a distribution; or that the greater satisfaction to a thousand men equally dehydrated on one occasion would do so. Similarly for other cases where the causes of variation in each of the two sets of wants, satisfactions, etc. are numerous, independent, and not greatly different in the magnitude of their effects.

It would, on the contrary, be very imprudent to assume that the greater preference for the Christian than for the Jewish religion, or for the Republican rather than the Democratic party was so distributed in a thousand men. These differences are due to a few causes, often inter-correlated, and differing greatly in the magnitude of their effects, such as parentage and friends in the former case, and geographical location, parentage and occupation in the latter. We may have faith that behavior parallels and reveals the strength of desires and aversions, satisfactions and annoyances, and that science can learn to use facts of behavior better and better.

Criticisms of Measurement

One important criticism is to the effect that one pleasure (say, of eating) is qualitatively different from another (say, of hearing music), that one aversion (say, against being beaten) is qualitatively different from another (say, of being ridiculed); that each qualitatively different sort requires a quantity scale of its own; and that the amounts on one scale are not comparable with those on another, just as amounts of length are not comparable with amounts of electrical resistance.

Both parties must agree that there are qualitative differences, and that for a complete inventory of, say, the reader's pleasures from eating an apple and from hearing an opera, at least two different scales must be used. When we say that the reader's pleasure from hearing an opera is n times that from eating an apple, we must not imply that it is identical. But the two may be comparable in *amount* of pleasure. And they certainly are comparable in amount of preference, if in fact the reader does make identical sacrifices to hear one opera and to have n apples to eat.

Whether they are comparable in amount of some general quality of pleasure depends upon whether a common element exists in the two "pleasures." The usage of language suggests that there is, but language may mislead. We cannot tell in advance. Man could not have told in advance that the motions of men and the heat of their bodies could properly be put on one same scale, or that lightning and loadstone were quantitatively comparable, but that lightning and Jove's wrath were not. Nobody has yet found any convenient way to isolate one quality common to many experiences and reasonably called pleasure. But physiology and biochemistry may isolate such a quality in the near future.

The real force of the criticism is as a warning against providing too few scales, and especially by presuming to measure a certain quality in things none of which possess any of it. An error of this sort was made by those in the past who treated the scale for amounts of pain as a negative continuation of the scale for amounts of pleasure. On the whole, we may conclude that one scale will be applicable to all amounts of preference, though it will, of course, no more describe all preferences fully than one scale of length describes fully all the characteristics of all men, light rays, and planetary orbits.

If it is desired to reproduce in measurement such particular qualities as most of us have in mind at the words contentment, enjoyment, gladness, irritation, discomfort, and misery, they may need more than two separate scales for the amount of pleasure and the amount of pain. Moreover, there are biological facts in favor of making one scale for sensory or "bodily" pains and another for the "mental" pains of fear, shame, remorse, nostalgia. When a person rates certain pangs of hunger and certain pangs of regret as equally painful, he may be doing little more than calling them equally objectionable, that is equally contra-preferred.

The psychology of pleasures has been so little studied that it would be rash to guess whether all of them have any common strand. The pleasures of taste and sex, of bodily play, hunting and victory, of color and rhythm, of thought and expression, of relaxation and peace, of giving and receiving affection, of public approval and self-respect—all these are alike in that they ordinarily cause satisfaction and are preferred above zero, and may be alike in some further unitary element or feature. But this last is certainly not obvious and emphatic.

I venture another criticism of the scales of preference, satisfaction and annoyance, which, so far as I know, has not been put forward hitherto. It is that no fundamental, natural, biological unity parallels any one of them. A person's amount of preference for and against may be shown now by approach and retreat, now by reaching and withdrawing, now by swallowing and spitting out, now by laughing and weeping, and so on for scores of instinctive and acquired behaviors. His amount of preference often has to be inferred from an elaborate survey of many diverse courses of action. For some simple sessile animal that ingests or discards what the environment presents preference is a unity, and variations in the vigor of its sucking in or waving away may be a scale for its amounts of preference. But in man the scale has to be constructed by ingenious study; it seems too much imposed on nature and too little derived from it.

The best answer to the criticism will be the pragmatic one of what good comes from the use of the scale. Provisionally we may note two facts: (1) For treatment of the life of man in the state of present civilization, any adequate preference scale will probably have no simple natural unit back of it. The scale is imposed on nature only to the extent that man has imposed business, government, and other features of civilization upon nature.

(2) The contrast with demonstrably valid and useful measurements is not so great. The scales of electrical resistance, conductivity, and impedance, for example, are not so simple as the scale of length; few, if any, scales of purchasing power have been in natural units; very

important work was done in measurements of electrical currents and atoms before their "natural" units were discovered.

The Measurement of Needs

The measurement of needs is in certain respects easier than the measurement of wants. Men are much more alike, though far from identical, in what they require in order to have normal health and growth and to do specified amounts of work, than in what they enjoy.

The bad results of a given deficiency in water, carbohydrates, vitamins, iodine, sleep, or exercise, can be estimated more or less well from loss in weight, failure to gain in size, weight, or strength, atrophy, lowered resistance to certain diseases, etc. Needs for sleep, muscular exercise and sex indulgence are not so well measured, the criteria for mental health, growth, and efficiency being less well established and defined than that for physique, but science may be trusted to make progress here.

Adequate criteria for mental health and efficiency will involve satisfactions and avoidance of annoyers and so re-introduce the problems of measuring wants. An expert in nutrition can measure the food needs of an army or a college, but only from somewhat narrow criteria. The morale and fighting power of the army and the work and spirit of the college may depend on the satisfyingness of flavors as well as the number of calories. The body will absorb a vile hash of food and ashes, but no sane dietitian would serve food so. A certain degree of contentment is needed as truly as a certain intake of chemicals.

Experts now consider that babies need fondling and human play as truly as food and sleep. Psychiatrists teach that mental health requires affection, romance, and restraint. Sociologists consider that a person who does not feel that he belongs to some human group and that the group belongs to him is maimed as truly as if he had lost a limb. These and other alleged needs can be measured with enough inventiveness and care. For any defined standard from mere survival and production of viable offspring to an nth degree of health, happiness, and usefulness, it is theoretically possible for science to find out what things are needed and to measure the amount.

Chapter 6
Mental Dynamics

In thinking about human nature we use many terms: emotions, interests, propensities, thought, feeling, action, intellect, character, temperament, sensation, imagination, memory, reasoning, suggestion, obsession. This chapter will add certain facts and principles concerning the physiology of abilities, wants, and propensities, their evolution, the influence of rewards and punishments and of custom.

The Physiology of Abilities, Wants, and Propensities

If we had perfect knowledge of a human body including the workings of the billions of cells (called neurones) which compose a man's nervous system, we should presumably have nearly perfect knowledge of him. His abilities, wants, and ideas are presumably events in time and space which a physiologist could read in the structure and activities of his neurones more completely and accurately than a psychologist or historian can read them in his words and acts—more completely and accurately even than the person himself can report them from his introspections. If we wish to change the person by natural means, we must use physiological avenues. If the person's abilities and wants are to change the world, they can do so only by taking shape in the man's body, especially his brain, and so influencing his speech, acts, and ideas.

89

Present knowledge of the workings of the neurones is however so scanty that we cannot now tell from examining a man's brain whether he spoke English or French, whether he knew as much physics and mathematics as Einstein or as little as Bernard Shaw, whether he was a general in the army or a private. We do not know fully how a neurone differs from other cells in structure. About its activities we know still less; and about the detailed relations of these to so-called mental facts we know next to nothing. The facts and principles of sociology, economics, government and other sciences of man in the main have to be derived from external behavior, and will for long years to come.

The help that is given by biological science may be roughly inventoried as follows:

1. It lends strong support to arguments from the external behavior of men. For example, a population instructed in the development of the brain could probably not be persuaded to believe in the transmigration of souls and to act accordingly. Nor could physiologists of today believe that the soul ruled the mind from its seat in the pineal gland, or that mathematical ability, love of children, and desire for approval are localized each in a separate part of the brain. Education and business theories about personnel assumed the existence of faculties which operated like machines, regardless of the content upon which they operated, and which could be strengthened equally for work with all by work with any one sort. Experimental and correlational psychology finds that such training of such faculties does not occur, and present knowledge of brain anatomy and physiology strongly suggests that it could not occur.

2. Biological science of the brain warns us against exaggerating logical consistency as a force in human life. The brain in general seems an organ to maximize comfort rather than consistency. The dog seizing another's bone may think "It is his" and also "It is mine." A child's doll is both a thing of rags and a person to love. A man may feel the sanctity of life so strongly that he will not permit physicians to administer euthanasia to wretched incurables and so weakly that he votes for the wholesale murder of war. The biology of the brain warns us against "logical" doctrines of the causation of human affairs, such as the doctrine of the social contract, or the doctrine of a progress from promiscuity through group marriage to historical forms of marriage.

3. Biological science prepares us to expect and accept queer events in a man's history and queer appetites or prejudices in him. Why do we go more or less insane every time we go to sleep and get cured by waking up? These are explainable, if at all, as consequences of brain physiology.

4. Biology encourages us to operate on man not only by economic incentives, laws, education, rewards, example, persuasion, and other social agents, but also by direct physical and chemical agents. In certain circumstances, a quarter of a grain of morphine is better than a vast amount of sympathy. The population of certain areas will probably be more benefited by putting a little iodine in their salt than by giving each of them ten dollars a year. We should appreciate and support honest and competent work along these lines as a most productive long-time investment for welfare.

5. Biology reminds us that the harmony of action of the cells in the body is far from perfect. We may think of many cells in the body as acting primarily to keep themselves alive and unimpaired, and only secondarily to preserve man. We may go so far as to assert that all the knowledge, wisdom, art, music, games, and sports in the world are in a sense by-products of action taken fundamentally to maintain neurones and groups of neurones in the standard of living to which they are accustomed! In persons suffering from certain dissociative diseases one part of the person sacrifices the whole to itself, and something of the sort may occur in all of us to some extent. Freud's speculations concerning the Ego or organized person and what he calls the Ids, which are dramatizations of fragmentary and elemental parts of human nature, have at least some basis in biology.

6. Finally, the facts of neurology help to protect the sciences of man from mystical doctrines. They inform us more or less well concerning the improbability of certain doctrines. For example, doctrines about instincts, learning, senility, and suggestion, which can be translated into terms of sensitivity, conductivity, connection, facilitation, and other known activities of neurones are, other things being equal, preferable to doctrines which rely upon fields of force, tensions, equilibria, valences, barriers, libido, specialized energies, and other activities not as yet demonstrated in the neurones.

It is known that some abilities and wants depend normally upon the action of particular groups of neurones. Injuries which interfere with the transmission of activity along these strands and chains of neurones weaken or destroy the ability or want in question. The abilities and wants whose biological bases are thus known are in general relatively humble matters of sense perception, movement, and bodily appetites. Such abilities as intelligence, self-control, statesmanship, ability at law or medicine, and such wants as for companionship, approval, mastery, truth or beauty are unknown as to location, except that the cerebral cortex has much to do with all of them.

Lashley has argued that location in the cerebral cortex counts for very little, any one part of it being able to do more or less well the work of any ability. This seems extreme. Very few neurologists would expect the neurones that were most active in a man's musical activities to be identical with those most active in his work as a lawyer. Probably Lashley himself would not. But it is almost certainly true that one same cerebral neurone plays a part in hundreds of abilities to which we give different names, and that much the same end result may be produced by many different activities in the human cortex. There are three possible exceptions. The hypothesis has been advanced that the degree of intelligence depends upon the *number* of possible axone to dendrite connections in the cerebrum. It could be argued that the ability to keep sane was a function of the health of the cerebral associative neurones. It can be argued that the so-called speech center has an important relation to linguistic ability as a whole as well as to the mechanisms of making articulate sounds.

The Evolution of Abilities, Wants, and Propensities

The original nature of man, and such features of his behavior as are caused by his genes acting in the environments are products of evolution. His intellect is probably a variation from the general mammalian type, caused by a great increase in the number and complexity of the associative neurones. The forebears of many human propensities and wants can be seen in most mammals. They make love, care for their offspring, fear strange noises, are stimulated to mastery and to submission, and often indulge in entertainment, that is, non-utilitarian activities.

General statements about mental evolution are not of much use in the sciences of man or the work of human engineering. But if they are particularized into natural histories of the details of maternal care, mastery and submission, courtship, fighting, etc., they become more so. The evolutionary link between mastery in cattle and mastery in man is not between enjoyment of and indulgence in dominance in general, but between such particulars as enjoyment of leading the procession or indulgence in poking a fellow cow out of your way in cattle and similar particulars in children and men. A particularized evolutionary psychology helps us to understand why the same person who will attack you if you run away from him may run away from you if you attack him, why the voice of love is low while that of hatred is loud. It perhaps helps us to understand why the perceived misery of one sufferer arouses more emotion than a printed report of the misery of a thousand. Laughter can, I think, be shown to be two distinct things, one part the chuckle of enjoyment, the other the cry of triumph. But the evolution of behavior is, in the main, still to be written.

The historian, James Harvey Robinson, observing some of the traits which man shares with the primates, asserts that "Problems of economics, government, law, ethics and the like would be vastly illuminated by a comprehension of our simian nature. And if we viewed our neighbors and ourselves as big monkeys, trying to do our best under the limitations imposed by our simian heritage, we would not only have vastly more understanding of human behavior and its frailties, but would also be far more full of understanding, tolerance, patience, and, perhaps, hopefulness." ['37, p. 176].

This is, I fear, rather optimistic. The study of man will be supplemented by study of his simian heritage rather moderately. One great difficulty is that science has not yet found out what our simian heritage of ten million years ago was—for example how much of it was like that of the brutal baboon, and how much like that of the kindly chimpanzee.

The coordinated behavior of mastery and submission has been studied by Maslow and by Yerkes and his associates, but the details of the evolutionary changes in it have not been worked out. The maternal behavior of the chimpanzee, as reported by Yerkes ['37], is like that of the human mother in kindliness and in stimulation to bodily exercise and learning, but perhaps not much more so than is that of the mother cat. A common and striking form of mutual aid in the primates is grooming, and this would possibly manifest itself in man if adequate stimulation were provided by the conditions of life.

The evolution of mind is complicated by the fact that man is essentially a self-domesticated animal, so that selection is for survival under the special conditions of domestication. He has been selected to live in a family or tribe of hunters, or pastoral or agricultural community, with interests and ideals, fears and glories which may deviate from the original human patterns as truly (though not as much) as a man's ideals for his horses and cows differ from the "natural" ideals which horses and cows have for themselves.

Some competent thinkers take the hand of evolution more or less for the hand of God, arguing that evolution works on the whole for welfare. Such a creed is a fairly good one, as moral creeds go. But it should be accepted with full awareness of the errors and inadequacies of evolution. It may be instructive to note a few samples of these:

The human eye is not a very good optical instrument. Man has bettered evolution's work greatly by microscopes, telescopes, and corrective glasses.

Man has many useless or harmful vestiges like the vermiform appendix.

Evolution has no partiality for man, and is now busily developing viruses which may exterminate him.

That it has more preference for the civilized and humane parts of man than for his baser wants, is doubtful. Evolution did not select for survival the versatile and sensitive abilities of the Athenian Greeks, or the solid administrative and legal abilities of the Romans.

Inspecting the body surface of a fellow primate, and eating the vermin discovered thereby is a quaint form of early mutual aid. If this had been preserved as an act of refined politeness, the ravages of typhus fever might have been much reduced! A tendency to eat rats, which was presumably a part of a general omnivorousness of early man, has disappeared except from a few cultures. This is a beautiful case of how misguided evolution and civilization can be. Some of his most dangerous enemies are certain rat-borne diseases. Man should have continued to eat rats, cooking them thoroughly, making their flesh a more and more fashionable food, the rarer it became, until they became extinct like the wild pigeon! Suppose that the energy spent in hounding heretics, Jews, Mormons, suffragettes, and harmless eccentrics had been put into crusades against rats!

An outstanding change from the other mammals to the primates in the matter of social behavior is the shift from the decent periodic indulgence in sex to the possibility of an almost incessant preoccupation with it. Man has also the unenviable distinction of being able to commit rape, sex union in most animals being impossible without the consent of the female. The false doctrine that the original nature of man is right is especially false in the case of sex. The substitution of other interests for a large percentage of the typical primate's sex activities (often called sublimation) is evidence of superiority in men. A large part of the work of civilization has consisted in remedying nature's mistake.

Most of the lower animals for most of their lives respond to situations with few or no ideas about them. Man on the contrary has a large fund of ideas, by which he reviews the past, foresees the future, makes models of events, finds entertainment, works out conclusions, and expresses truth. This life of ideas is man's glory, but it is not an unmixed blessing. Ideas can perpetuate the follies of the past. They also subject him to hopes which can never be realized, to harmful fears of things which do not exist and events which cannot occur. They provide entertainment that is sometimes mean, degrading, and demoralizing, as the simple plays of the lower animals rarely are. They help man to find and keep not only the truth, but also superstitions and delusions.

Slowly the world has found the way to distinguish good from bad and indifferent ideas. The way is the way of science. It was a series of wonderful triumphs when he learned that spring would follow winter, that the seed would germinate, that all this happened by no deity's caprice, that no sacrifices were required, that the revolving years were functions of the number of days and nights.

His success in working with ideas has had extreme ups and downs. Egypt won much and lost much of it. Ancient Greece won more and lost it. The way of science seemed a few years ago to have been adopted by all civilized nations, but great nations are now seeking to deform science into a slave of prejudices. Good ideas can be killed by bad; the fittest need not survive.

Rewards and Punishments

The word reward may be used to name any satisfying thing or event which is considered by the person to be the consequence of certain behavior. The word punishment may be used to name any annoying or unwelcome thing or event which is considered by the person whom it annoys to be the consequence of certain behavior.

The tradition of common sense and of the sciences of man was that rewards and punishments were the positive and negative halves of one gradient, closely alike in potency. Recent experiments with men and animals prove this false. A reward accompanying or immediately following a modifiable $S \rightarrow R$ connection, strengthens it; and this action is direct, inevitable, uniform, and ubiquitous. A punishment under the same conditions exerts no corresponding weakening force, except when it causes the person to shift to the right behavior and receive a reward; punishment has no beneficial effect comparable to reward. Man has no inhibiting reaction comparable to the confirming reaction.[1]

Certain punishments can attach fear, shame, or other attitudes to certain things, places, conditions, and acts, and so cause them to be more avoided, in the same way that certain rewards can attach security, pride, joy, or voluptuous sensation to them. Even in remote and indirect

---

[1] A punishment may be useful by counterbalancing the satisfyingness of consequences, and so preventing the confirming reaction. For example, if a child is caught in the act of grabbing and eating his sister's candy and is punished then and there, the total consequences may fail to evoke the confirming reaction which the taste of the candy alone would have evoked. But to be effective in this way the punishment must be administered before, or along with, or only an instant later than, the pleasant consequences. Immediate retaliation, as in returning blow for a blow, has certain merits which are lacking in delayed vengeance, as in returning a raid by a counter-raid, or a blow by action in a law court.

effects, however, punishment is inferior. The reward leads from the wrong to the right; the punishment only leads from the wrong. The reward stimulates to active and possibly progressive life; the punishment is discouraging. The remote effects of rewards and punishments need much more study, but it is highly probable that investigation will demonstrate a substantial balance in favor of rewards. Certainly when both the immediate and remote effects are considered together psychology now offers a strong argument in favor of rewards rather than punishments.

Although the sciences of practical life have not altered their theory of reward and punishment, they have in practice more and more favored the former. Reformation is set over punishment; restrictive legislation is deprecated; bonuses replace fines; corporal punishment has almost disappeared from schools. A general growth of humanitarianism has been in their favor.

In the case of government, psychology emphasizes the importance of making a community attractive to the able and good rather than unpleasant for the incompetent or vicious, and of encouraging the good in each person rather than discouraging his evil traits. Governments should work by education, persuasion, example, and other forces of encouragement and reward.

A man may be coerced into abstaining from the use of heroin by threats of punishment supported by actual punishment as occasion requires. Or he may be coerced into abstaining by the fact that he can nowhere buy it. A man may be coerced into loyal behavior by threats, or by such experiences that the idea of doing anything rebellious never occurs to him. The second method has been used profitably in the relation between policemen and children. Transfer to another environment in which good behavior will be rewarded has been found a useful form of coercion in the government of a school. Of a bonus for superior quality of work compared with a fine for inferior quality, the former is psychologically better.

We have no benefactor law as a counterpart for criminal law. Personal freedom and community respect are rewards for good behavior and confirm decent, law-abiding conduct more than we think. But the law does little to encourage this. Its voice is threatening and its acts are punitive. Not the law, but Mr. Carnegie, rewards heroes. Not the law, but Mr. Nobel, rewards benefactors.

In civil suits damages are both a punishment of the wrong-doer and reward of the wronged, but the picture is blurred by notions of compensation. The fact that virtue has as a reward a low probability of being successfully sued for damages probably never enters the head of ninety-nine good men out of a hundred, the rewards of the business virtues lie more in the esteem of other men.

Economics has paid little attention to punishments. Its explanations of wealth have used chiefly rewards. Economists would admit as forms of economic "friction" vengeful acts to ruin a competitor, and other punitive behavior. They would be suspicious of permanently forced labor as in slavery, serfdom, or convict camps; but they have not, to my knowledge, demonstrated the causes of the inferiority or made detailed comparisons of work motivated largely by reward (as under piece-work and bonus systems) with work motivated largely by punishment (as in the case of child labor where the parents take the entire wage). I conjecture that historical inquiries and experiments would show a substantial advantage for motivation by reward.

Business, in contrast to government, has operated largely by rewards. The shift from feudalism to the contract of the modern world was a shift from support by threats and punishment to support by hopes and rewards. The business man who organized and managed natural resources, capital, and labor to produce and market something people wanted did so for reward under no threats. Each successful transaction was validated by reward. Pecuniary punishments either led the entrepreneur to do something which was rewarded, or quickly put him out of business. The workmen labored as a rule for rewards.

Piece-work payments are pro-rata rewards for regular work; there are bonuses as rewards for extra performance; there are special rewards for high scores in attendance and punctuality, for length of service, for useful suggestions. The reward of promotion comes to those who are competent. The reward of a chance to start a rival business was once common for those who could amass a little capital.[1] Employees should encourage the use of rewards since it is probably greatly to their advantage. If they have any childish yearnings for the older regime, where a boss was esteemed because he could lick any workman, they should restrain them.

The public should use the principle of reward in dealing with business. Other things being equal, we should trade and buy where we get the best service. If we reward those who cheat us we will be increasingly cheated. If we reward those who entice and flatter us, it will be useless to complain

[1] This is now relatively rare, the average employee of General Motors having about as good a chance of succeeding with a rival company as a peasant in 1400 had of becoming lord of a manor. But there may be new lines of business ready to reward the entrepreneur with small capital, as the moving-picture business did.

that business is dishonest. In most cases if we take the trouble to find out what a just price is, and go without it rather than pay more, we will have only just prices to pay.

The treatment of the blind, deaf, crippled, insane, feeble-minded, and other victims of misfortune has had a very varied history in which punishment has played no small part. Provision for them became confused with provision for paupers. Treatment in poorhouses was considered partly a punishment for unwillingness to work and as a threat to those outside. Such stupid punishing is now universally condemned by experts, but the use of punishment in the case of idlers, drunkards, and bums is still common. But the means of curing an idler is to somehow get him to work and reward him therefor. Similarly the best means of curing a drunkard is to reward him when he is sober. But the practical difficulties in rewarding the rare good impulses of persons who are on the whole worthless are very great; the doctrine is sound but hard to put in force.

It would not be difficult to compute for each person a quotient of deservingness which would be essentially his achievement divided by a composite of his abilities and good fortune. Persons with higher merit quotients could properly be rewarded by society, whether they were rich or poor, the rewards both honorific and pecuniary. The deserving rich would on the whole use the pecuniary parts of their rewards well and the deserving poor would probably prize the honorific parts of theirs dearly. A somewhat similar measure, the accomplishment quotient, has done good service in schools, and would do more, except for the folly of parents who would rather have their children labeled intelligent but shiftless than dull but hard-working!

A change in the theory and practice of living to the effect that all good tendencies should be rewarded and no bad tendencies should be, leaving punishments as a secondary and relatively unimportant matter, has much to recommend it. It is not only ungrateful and unjust to leave intelligence, industry, and virtue to be their own rewards; it is foolish, and, for the world as a whole, suicidal. By any reasonable view of human nature and history, society's primary duty to itself is to favor and encourage its better elements. Next in order is to cease paying bonuses to bad tendencies, to quit admiring ostentation, supporting indolence, paying money for flattery, submitting to brutal force, and conniving at injustice.

There doubtless will always be need for punishments and threats, but the extent to which they have been reduced in intelligent families and in schools during the last two or three generations gives promise that much can be accomplished in government, law, and religion. Punishment is in general not only inefficient but expensive; it may debauch the persons who inflict it, and give a much-desired notoriety to those receiving it.

Familiarity and Novelty

Each nation likes its own customs, though others abhor them. Many persons feel an observable satisfaction in being in their own beds, in hanging their hat on the same hook, or filling their pipe in the same way, though they would have enjoyed equally a different sort had they used it. These are samples of facts which have led students of human nature to think that familiarity breeds enjoyment rather than contempt.

In many cases it *must* tend to do so because the familiar experience has been frequently and intimately associated with some satisfier. The sight and feel of one's accustomed spot becomes imbued with the relaxation, rest, and security with which it is associated. The frequent performance of any custom which is validated by the approval of parents and friends and by the inner consciousness that one is doing and being what is proper *must* become satisfying. Moreover, the frequent evoking of a response by a situation also associates with that situation an impulse to make the response; not to make the response involves a certain annoyance.

There may be also an intrinsic tendency for mental connections which frequent occurrence has caused to operate readily to become satisfying thereby. Maslow arranged that a group of fifteen young women should have certain experiences frequently during ten two-hour periods and make certain choices indicative of preference after these experiences. All was under the guise of learning and work. No subject was aware of the real purpose of the experiment. On the whole, what had been experienced or done frequently was preferred. For example, subjects used fountain pens throughout the experiment, being warned of fines if they used pencil. On day 9, pencils were piled on the table along with paper, etc. The experimenter waited until someone noticed. "Oh, yes! The experiment's about finished now. If you wish you may use pencil or pen. It makes no difference to us. Only if you use pencil, keep on using it; if you use pen, stick to that."

At the moment they were working with mimeographed material for which ink is undesirable, since it tends to run and blot. Eight subjects used pencil, seven continuing to use pen in spite of the inconvenience and inefficiency.

After 30 minutes of this, they began to copy sentences on the glazed white cards which take ink well. For this all but 4 subjects switched back to pen and ink, in spite of the fact that instructions had been to choose either pen or pencil, and then not change. In the control experiment 0 percent used pen in any of the tasks. ['37, p. 177]

Not enough is yet known to enable a psychologist to predict when the attractions of novelty, curiosity, adventure and the like will outweigh the attraction of the familiar and habitual. The following principles are of some help:

(1) There must be enough familiarity in the novelty to enable the mind to grasp it.

(2) Novelties of perception have a wider appeal than novel ideas or acts. For example, new shades and combinations of colors in clothes, flowers, etc., are commonly liked.

(3) Novelties of action have a wider appeal than novel ideas. Learning to ride a bicycle or drive a car is liked better than learning to understand a ball-bearing, chain-drive, or internal-combustion engine.

The craving for novelty has much resemblance to the craving for certain habit-forming drugs; and its strength in modern man seems out of all proportion to its utility and to any demand in man's genetic constitution. Whole civilizations have lived happily with far less novel experiences as Americans today have. What then are reasonable amounts of novelty and what novelties shall they be? I will give as good answers as I can, but cannot guarantee that they are right.

By the nature of his genes and the laws of his learning, a man repeats what he has done, especially if it has profited him, and enjoys these repetitions when they are unforced and fluent. But he has also certain instincts of visual, manual, and oral exploration of objects to which he has no habitual response. He has further a tendency to be pleased at harmless surprises such as the unexpected happenings in a tale that he hears told. We may conceive of events in the neurone apparatus in his brain as including habitual functionings, which as a rule give moderate peaceful satisfactions allied to the pleasures of eating, digestion, or rest; and novel stimulations, which as a rule give exciting satisfactions allied to the pleasures of pursuit, hunting, or fighting (real or mock). A man eating unknown food in a foreign restaurant, and having something suddenly swell in size in his mouth, may exemplify the latter.

In the life of the chimpanzee the former would make up perhaps 999 parts in a thousand, and the novelties would be mostly rather gentle, like finding a nut in a queer place or encountering a new hold in a wrestling match. In the life of an English village community five hundred years ago, the former would make up not much less. But in the life of a village of today, novelties abound. The child sees them on the billboards as he rides to school in the bus and hears them in the classroom and on the playground. A single copy of a magazine has hundreds. The factory work of the father may be repetitive, but he has a greater variety of experiences in reading his tabloid newspaper than his great-grandfather had in all his work. We may have more than is needed for entertainment and recreation, more than is good for health and efficiency. Qualitatively, many of the novelties are too stimulating, likely to spoil the taste for simpler pleasures and dull the sensibility to more intellectual pleasures. They also in my opinion are likely to dull the enjoyment of even their own sort, and cause people to require stronger and stronger doses.

The original exploratory tendencies of man and his enjoyment of thought for thought's sake have borne wonderful fruit in technology and science, and the novelties of science have in general great social utility. The passion for novelty in facts, principles and powers of prediction and control can hardly become excessive, although two-hundred-inch tele-scopes, atom-splitters, measurements of the movement of the universe, fishing up incredible monsters from the sub-conscious, improving society by eugenics should not cause scientists to lose their ability to work happily with less exciting ones.

In art, music, literature, philanthropy, and government the passion for novelty seems to need restraint. Joyce's *Ulysses* contains over 1500 new words; does any one book need so many? Roosevelt's government has produced scores of new governmental agencies; were they all improve-ments?

Custom

In spite of the claims of novelty, everybody from psychologists to poets agrees that men are bound by custom. In spite of the apparent superabundance of facts about the potency of tribal, community, and personal customs, not all the needed facts are available. The following facts seem fairly well established, however.

The Customs of Groups   For a "closed society" the maintenance of a custom has certain psychological utilities. (1) Other things being equal one law, custom, or habit is more satisfactory than two or more, since it gives a person less trouble to learn and operate. (2) Customs are in general forces contrary to the immediate indulgence of individual wants. (3) An established custom represents the learning of the members of the group living and dead in some opposition to its unlearned tendencies. It is a transmitting of the culture which acts as a check on instinct. (4) A society's customs are to some extent a part of the self of each of its members. They enhance his personality as compared with that of a person's in a different society. (5) The shift of a society from an old custom to a new and better custom is often laborious and insecure, whereas its shift to original instincts which are worse for it is easy.

When a group having a certain custom comes in contact with another group which responds in a different way, there will be a substantial tendency for each to retain its own. So the world is full of different customs of treating the same situation. Even when a custom is acknowledged by a group to be better than theirs, they may not adopt it.

But some customs become established widely in a few generations. Europe adopted tobacco smoking from the American Indians, in exchange for the use of whisky. More usefully, the Europeans adopted the cultivation of the potato and of maize, and the Indians the use of horses and firearms. The Japanese quickly absorbed Europe's technology and science, but were little influenced by its religion. Many Negro tribes in Africa quickly absorbed the Moslem religion though they were little influenced by their science.

The spread of customs from one society to another is determined by psychological and economic forces. A custom attached to some material object will spread faster than an equally advantageous custom attached to an idea or theory. It is easier to learn because the situations and responses involved are more available and its advantages more obvious. A custom that requires a shift of feeling or emotion is especially slow to spread, because men's feelings are particularly unavailable and hard to connect with the situation in question. A custom of esteemed persons will spread faster than an equally advantageous custom which is characteristic of a "lower" class. It is more rewarded by social approval.

The Customs of Individuals   An individual takes on and maintains customs when he is too young and too weak to resist. He will rarely even think of responding in any other way. He will, according to most anthropologists and psychologists, feel a strong aversion for persons who do otherwise.

Chief among strong contrary forces are (1) instinctive cravings, as when sex craving is directed to an object forbidden by custom, (2) insanity or disorganization of the self which upsets or distorts a person's desires and inhibitions, and (3) rational thought which learns what seems to it a better way of thought, feeling, or action than the customary one.

The group will often be at a loss to distinguish between the products of insanity, of divine inspiration, and of rational thought. Even modern civilized groups find it hard to distinguish the eccentricities of genius from those of madmen, and the reforms that are products of impersonal thought from those which are cooked up to glorify some charlatan.

As the methods of science extend further we may expect greater accuracy in distinguishing valuable from worthless attacks upon custom. There is a popular misconception to the effect that the scientific mind is ready to entertain any idea and willing to try any plan. It is true that science has little reverence for customs as such, and is not repelled by ideas because they conflict with what one learned at his mother's knee. But science entertains ideas and tests plans in the order of their probable merit and has no time to try those which have nothing to support them.

Before the liberalism of the eighteenth and nineteenth centuries, the most impressive danger was that all people would be discouraged from trying to alter customs. The impressive danger of the future may be that many changes will be brought about either to satisfy the desire of certain men for profits or for power. The misguided success of missionaries in putting clothes on Africans and South Sea islanders may be a trifle compared to a campaign of some cosmetic trust to make them use lipstick. The stifling of the civilization of the Roman Empire by barbarians may be equaled by fanatics who captivate enough man-power to put disastrous changes in operation.

Short-Lived Customs A person desiring attention and approval may use what power he has to start a custom of a certain sort. His self-esteem thrives upon imitation in such matters and upon being heralded as a leader in them. Only by accident is there any merit in the changes. Much time and useful property are wasted and much unhappiness caused in those who are unable to keep up with a fashion. Industry based on fashions has always been essentially unstable for planned economical production and distribution, but a business expert's account of the present state of affairs reads like a nightmare.

The merchant buys from hand to mouth watching to see which way the fashion cat will jump. There are hundreds of thousands of Mah Jong sets hopelessly awaiting a resurrection of that game.

The waste of time and property is to a psychologist not so irritating as the needless misery of women and young people who have to be out of the fashion. Louisa May Alcott was as immune to false pride and shame as anybody can be expected to be, yet her books show wearing unfashionable clothes as the tragedy of girlhood.

The custom of purchasing approval by money deserves further notice. When a person uses his earnings to buy a productive enterprise which he has the ability to operate well and gains the approval of solid men, he deserves it, but it is really his ability which they approve in his ownership. When he buys land to acquire approval from social status, he deserves it much less. When he buys a peerage or a senatorship by political contributions, he deserves little or none, but we may be partly consoled by the fact that he had great ability to make money and whatever other abilities are correlated therewith. But when he buys clothes which are thrown away almost before they are worn, or beds that will never be slept in, we approve those because we are ignorant.

Chapter 7
Individual Differences

Common observation shows that persons differ in every one of the abilities which man has. In intellect there are Aristotles and idiots, in art Rembrandts and persons whose drawings decrease the value of paper. If a thousand six-year-old children taken at random spend equal time and effort in learning to read or spell, some will make more than twice the progress made by others.

Common observation shows also that persons differ in what they want and enjoy. One man will go without a meal and stand on his feet through an evening to hear an opera which another man would not listen to if it were performed outside his window. One woman will minister to the weak and unfortunate for no reward beyond seeing their happiness; another will heed their welfare no more than the dirt under her feet. Most of us prefer society to solitude, but there are hermits.

Science studies the nature, causation, and consequences of the differences found among individuals in all traits which are important for theory or practice.

Qualitative and Quantitative Differences

Some differences we call qualitative. Such are differences in blood type, in finger prints, in sex, or in one's profession. Some we call quantitative, such as differences in stature, intellect, enjoyment of praise, or income. The clearest cases of so-called qualitative differences are those where there are certain conditions (call them A, B, C, . . . N) which are distinguishable, and where no conditions intermediate between A and B or B and C or A and C, exist, and where A, B, C cannot usefully be thought of as consisting of the same thing in different amounts; and where there is little or no variation in A or B or C, wherever it occurs.

The difference between qualitative and quantitative may be less misused by considering some facts about scales for measuring human traits. A man's stature is measurable on a continuous scale beginning with a true absolute zero (meaning just not any distance), and so also is the difference between the statures of any two men.

Suppose now that all human beings were either just 20 inches tall, or just 30 inches, or just 40 inches, or just 70, and that infants born 20 inches tall expanded to 30 inches in the twinkling of an eye a year later, passed from 30 inches to 40 with equal suddenness at age 6 yr. 0 day, and from 60 to 70 with equal suddenness on their twenty-first birthday. We could use our old method of measuring and expressing differences in stature, but it would seem rather pedantic; and the difference of 10 inches in stature between a newborn of 20 and a yearling of 30 would not seem the same difference as the difference of 10 inches in stature between youths of 60 and adults of 70. We should be tempted to think that the differences in stature between a new-born, a yearling, a child, a youth, and an adult were qualitative, and to describe a person's stature as (A) new-born's, (B) yearling's, (C) child's, (D) youth's, or (E) adult's, and to refuse to add, subtract, multiply, divide these. Being impressed by such facts as that an adult does not equal $3\frac{1}{2}$ newborn babies, we might fail to see that the length of one adult from head to foot does precisely and absolutely equal $3\frac{1}{2}$ times the length of one new-born.

Suppose that a continuously extending scale was represented in nature at only one point. Suppose that instead of gradations in curliness of hair from perfectly straight through mild degrees of waviness to the most extreme kinkiness, nature provided only hair of a certain moderate curliness or none at all. Then it would seem utterly pedantic to specify the amount of curliness of any person's hair. If nature provided two amounts of curliness, as in lank hair *à la* Chinese and moderately curly *à la* the heroine in North European stories, we could state the facts about the curliness of any person's hair by saying whether a person had any hair, and if so whether it was curly.

A world of continuous quantities could be treated like a world of qualities if the continua did not show themselves in nature. The universe could then really be all quantitative (it probably is) and yet appear as qualitative in spots. Abilities, wants, and proclivities are, with few or no exceptions, quantitative. Such statements as "A is a statesman; B is only a politician; C is a genius; D is not; E is sane; F is insane; G is a miser; H is a spendthrift, are qualitative only in the sense that they do not direct attention to the quantities which they really imply and roughly measure.

Most of the nouns and adjectives by which we describe persons have the merit of calling to mind concrete examples of persons with all their quantitative traits, and so giving a sort of rough composite picture or bill of specifications of the amounts of various traits of the person in question. They have the demerits of depending too much upon the hearer's experience, of arousing attitudes rather than analyzing facts, and of concealing their quantities by a verbal mask. They are not qualitative in the way that the following are: A is a dog; B is a crocodile; C is a sun; D is a planet; E has malaria; F has smallpox; G is a picture; H is a song.

In the social sciences a statement that two persons differ qualitatively with nothing added about magnitude is usually a sign of ignorance and inaccuracy. Many such statements mean little or nothing more than that: One person has much and the other little of a certain ability, want, proclivity, or the like; e.g., "A is brave; B is a hero." One person is above and the other below the average or common status; e.g., "A is good; B is bad." One person has much (or little) of something of which the other person has less (or none); e.g., "A is a hero; B is not. A is an idiot; B is not." One person has a certain amount of something of which the other person possesses an unspecified amount, and the other person has a certain amount of something of which the former possesses an unspecified amount; e.g., "A had artistic ability; B had scientific ability." One person has on the average much and the other person has on the average little of a group of related abilities; e.g., "A likes mathematics; B does not."

Single and Compound Differences

A statement about differences between two individuals often concerns their differences in several traits. When John and Richard are said to differ in A, A may be as unitary as the ability to add integers or as manifold as ability to add or ability in arithmetic. It may be the desire to hear a certain story, or a certain kind of stories, or to be entertained. It may be honesty in school examinations or honesty in general.

Any compound difference implies that several amounts have been assigned relative "weights" or "importances" and combined. The assignment of weights and method of combination may be objective, deliberate, and explicit or it may be subjective, casual, and impressionistic, but it always occurs. A large amount of work is required to make a satisfactory choice of the quantities to be combined to measure intelligence, honesty, love of praise, or the like, and to devise a reasonable system of weights to be used in combining them. This work is still to be done in most cases.

Simple and Complex Differences

At or near the extreme of simplicity are differences in stature and the like. At or near the other extreme are differences in executive ability, or the desire for security. The latter are compounds in which the presence of certain components may influence the action of other components in subtle and complex ways. The amount of one component may act as a multiplier to certain others as in the case of energy with abilities, or sensitiveness with certain satisfactions and annoyances. Some components may act somewhat as hormones or enzymes do.

Differences Known Only by Their Results

As a consequence of facts stated above, the great majority of individual differences are known and measured only by their results. Differences in intelligence may really be differences in the number or complexity of connections in the brain, but that is only an hypothesis. Our actual knowledge of them is all by differences in the products produced. It is as if we knew a difference in two men's statures only by differences in how high they could reach, how often they bumped their heads, how well they could see the stage in theaters, and the like. For many purposes of the social sciences this does little harm, since they are often concerned with the consequences of abilities or wants rather than with their internal constitution. But it makes the measurement and comparison of individuals indirect and difficult.

The Measurement of Individual Differences

In Chapter 5 difficulties in measurement of wants, so as to compare persons, were described, as well as certain ways of overcoming them. The measurement of abilities is free from some of these and has been carried further toward success, but has its special difficulties.

Measurements in Units of Time

Almost the only mental measurements where the way is easy and the sailing smooth are those made in units of time. If individuals I, II, III, and IV are measured as having done the same task equally well in 100 sec., 110 sec., 150 sec., and 200 sec., respectively, there is no difficulty so far as the facts go. II takes 10 sec. more or 10 percent more time than I; III takes 50 sec. more or 50 percent more time than I. IV takes twice as long as I.

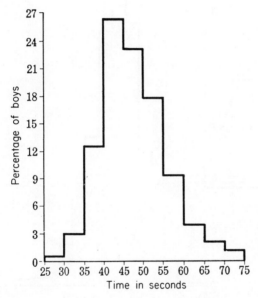

Fig. 4. Time to sort 48 cards by color. [Data from Woolley, '26, p. 72.]

If the same task is repeated over and over, the number of achievements within a given time is similarly an easy score by which to differentiate individuals. The same is true of different tasks which are equal in difficulty. The number done per unit of time is transferable into the time per task.

Figures 4 and 5, which present the scores of 14-year-olds in a card-sorting test and in a tapping test, illustrate measurements in terms of time per achievement, and number of achievements of the same task per unit of time.

Such measurements in terms of time are valuable. Ways of using time to measure wants and satisfactions are conceivable, as if we should observe how long each person looked at a certain picture, or read a certain collection of jokes or stories, or played a certain game.

In the case of abilities time serves to compare only those persons who accomplish the task perfectly, or to the same degree of imperfection. If a person cannot accomplish it, his differences from the others are measured

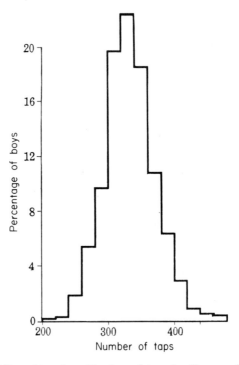

Fig. 5. Rapidity of tapping: Number of taps in 60 sec. with right hand. [Data from Wooley, '26, p. 70.]

only very crudely. It is very hard to get tests of important abilities that all who accomplish them will accomplish them equally well. Allowance often has to be made for defects or errors (most suitably by estimating the time the person would have needed to attain the perfect, or acceptable, or standard, accomplishment).

It is also the case that with most abilities we are much more concerned with how hard things the person can do or how well he can do certain things. It is relatively unimportant how quickly a physician can diagnose clear cases of measles, or how quickly a musician can play a certain piece. Similarly in the case of wants and satisfactions we are likely to be more concerned with how much a person will sacrifice to gratify the desire than with how long it will take for the enjoyment of it to give place to indifference.

Measurement by Amount of Difficulty Overcome and Sacrifice Made

The level of a person's ability is usefully measured by the difficulty of the hardest task at which he can succeed. The CAVD intelligence examination (C for completion, A for arithmetic, V for vocabulary, D for directions or comprehension of sentences) consists of sixteen sets of 40 tasks each, equally difficult (approximately) within each set and progressing from sets with which all save low-grade imbeciles succeed to sets with which only one or two percent of adults succeed. Success at any level is defined arbitrarily as performing perfectly 50 percent or more of the tasks at that level. (60 or 75 or any other percent could be used instead.)

Hartshorne and May measured honesty in school children by giving them certain opportunities to cheat, lie, and steal. These ranged from those to which fairly honest children would succumb without great shock to conscience to some which only a habitual cheat, liar, or thief would embrace. An honesty score by levels comparable to the CAVD intelligence score could have been given to each child who took these honesty tests. The facts for 2443 school children are shown in Figure 6.

Hartshorne and May also gave children five opportunities to work or sacrifice for the welfare of others. One was by giving each child a kit containing an eraser, a double pencil in two colors, a drinking cup, a ruler, a sharpener, etc. and then later providing an opportunity for each child as follows:

Pass the kits and give time (10 minutes) for them to be examined.

"Now I want to pass on a suggestion from the principal. He says there are many schools even in our own country where the children have no pencils or interesting things such as these in these kits. He thought possibly some of you might like to help make up some kits for other children. You might put in one of these little things, or two, or three, or all ten, or the whole thing, box and all, or just the box, keeping the articles for yourself. If you want to help make up some kits for other children, just put whatever of these things you want to give in the red envelope. You may put it all in, or just the empty

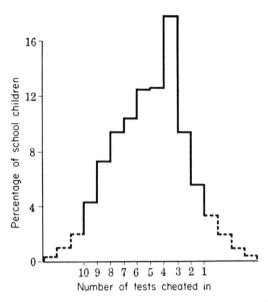

Fig. 6. Resistance to temptations to cheat. Percentages of school children who cheated in every test, in nine out of ten, in eight out of ten, etc. The frequencies of the dotted-line columns to the left of 10 are estimates of the percentages that would have succumbed to slighter temptations than those furnished by any of the tests given. Those of the dash-line columns to the right of 1 are estimates of the percentages that would have resisted even more tempting opportunities than those furnished by any of the tests. [Data from Hartshorne and May, '28, Book two, p. 220.]

box, or just one or more of the things, or nothing at all. Tie up the envelope and drop it into the basket whenever you want to before you leave to-day. Please put in the envelope in any case. It is *quite* all right for you to keep any or all of the kit if you would rather. The kit belongs to you." ['29, p. 62] The child received a score ranging from 0 if he kept all, to 36 if he gave away all. In another test he had a chance to collect jokes, stories, and pictures to send to sick children. He received a score running up from 0, according to what he cut out or copied, the pains he took to mount pictures, etc. In two other tests he had a chance to work in the class for himself or for others.

The distribution of the total scores for 728 children was as shown in Fig. 7. The high scores could be attained only by giving away some of the most cherished objects as well as the least, and acting for the welfare of others when to do so was least attractive.

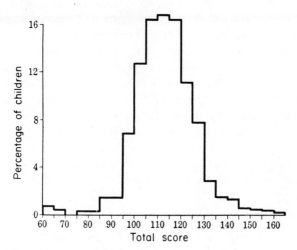

Fig. 7. Scores of 728 school children in tests of service. [Data from Hartshorne and May, '29, Book one, p. 108.]

Measurement by a Miscellany of Behaviors Indicative of Certain Interests

There are scores of such tests and questionnaires. Often the same test or questionnaire is designed to measure many features of a person. A test in which a person gives, for each of several hundred words, the word he thinks of may be used to give him scores for his interest in music, in art, in science, in the opposite sex, etc. If four boys respond to *white* respectively by "piano key," "high lights," "zinc oxide," and "girl" they might receive credits respectively for those four interests. All such tests are revealing, but that no one of them reveals very much very surely. Moreover, the person can often deliberately misrepresent his nature by his responses. However, a thousand situations chosen carefully as specially revealing will be better than a random thousand, and they may conceivably be built into test series which, though artificial, will show a person's real nature.

The Form of Distribution of Mental Traits

In Figs. 4 to 7 three characteristics are notable: (A) From the smallest to the largest amounts there is a practically continuous series. All intermediate amounts occur (save for occasional gaps which would surely be filled if the number of individuals measured had been larger). (B) There is little evidence of any separation of the persons into two or more groups or species; there is one mode or common condition. (C) This commonest condition is at or near mediocrity.

Continuity is well-nigh universal in mental traits. Unimodality is somewhat less so. The tendency toward symmetry as in Fig. 8, rather than toward skewness as in Fig. 9, is very common, though not universal.

It may be noted here that the forms of distribution of economic, governmental, legal, and theological facts about persons may be very different from those for abilities and propensities. Income is enormously skewed. Union wages in a trade rarely show a tailing out up or down. Political power was until recently distributed in most cultures with a mode near zero for slaves, serfs, and most women. The law scores a

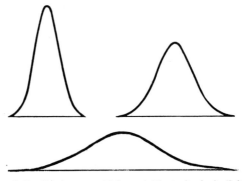

Fig. 8. Type of distribution to which variable traits in individuals are often roughly approximate. The three diagrams represent the same geometrical form of surface, the only difference being in the variability.

person as a minor or not a minor, and operates with the two modes of 'responsible' and 'not responsible.' Theology has its grades of sainthood and of sin, its heaven and hell, its hierarchies in the transmigration of souls.

The common approximation to Fig. 8, the so-called normal distribution, is not compelled by any tendency of nature to abhor skewed or other irregular distributions; perfectly normal distributions are rare. The strength of many wants, as for food, drink, freedom, vision, movement, may be expected to have a mode at a very high amount and to fall off at the low (left) side in a very long skew. The same in probable for many aversions.

Fiction and popular science are full of suggestions that the distribution of wants and proclivities is multimodal (usually bimodal), that men split into warlike and peaceful, musical and non-musical, introverts and extraverts, efficient and predatory, "rentiers" and speculators, conservatives and radicals. The evidence does not support this. It is much safer to expect that the distributions will be unimodal and continuous. Again and again in human abilities and propensities the form of the surface of frequency approximates to the bell shapes of Fig. 8, the so-called "Normal" distribution, bounded by the probability curve.

Consider the use of the form of distribution of a trait in predicting the rate of progress of a political change. Let the amount of aversion to the change have always the same average, 100, and the same variability, namely, an average deviation from 100 of 20, and consider the rate of change in annual votes when certain arguments or events overcome each year 10 units of aversion. Consider this rate for the four cases of a

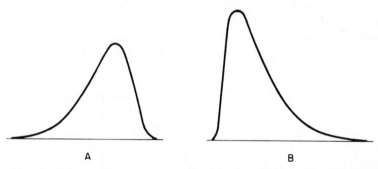

A   B

Fig. 9. Two distributions: A, with moderate skewness; B, with much skewness.

rectangular distribution as in Fig. 10, of a normal distribution as in Fig. 11, of an extreme skewness toward the low amounts of aversion as in Fig. 12, and of an extreme skewness toward the high amounts of aversion as in Fig. 13. Suppose that at the time of prophecy, the change received only 1 affirmative vote in a million, practically 0 percent. In Fig. 10, the overcoming of 10 units of aversion each year will put the vote just past $12\frac{1}{2}$ percent, 25 percent, $37\frac{1}{2}$ percent, and 50 percent in four successive years. In Fig. 11, the overcoming of 10 units of aversion each year will put the vote up only to about a quarter of one percent in the first year, and only to $5\frac{1}{2}$ percent in five years, but in the next two years it will pass 21 percent and in two more years it will reach 50 percent. In Fig. 12, the vote will rise to about one half of one percent the first year and to about 14 percent in 4 years and will gain increasingly each year thereafter until a majority is reached at the end of eight years. In Fig. 13, there will be a large gain in the first year, and victory in the third. In the case of Figs. 10

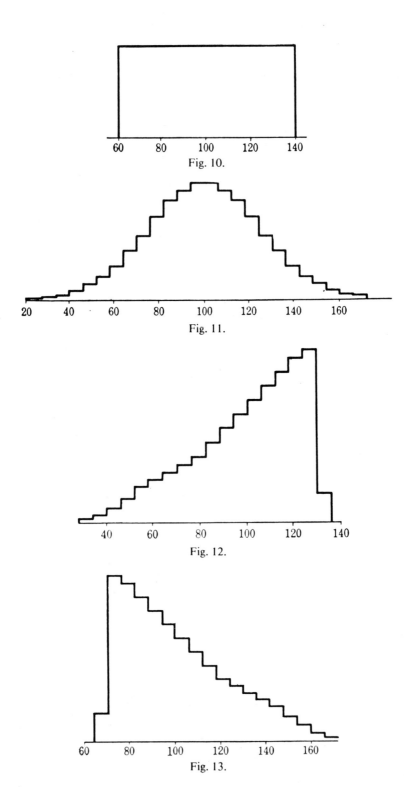

Fig. 10.

Fig. 11.

Fig. 12.

Fig. 13.

and 12 the progress from a majority to unanimity would need only four and three years respectively, but in the case of Fig. 11 and Fig. 13, nine and eight would be required.

Consider finally the difference in consequences between continuous unimodal distributions of ability like Figs. 4 to 9 and 11 to 13, and distributions with a secondary mode as in Figs. 14, 15, and 16. If the distribution is thought to be like Fig. 14, man can hope to find natural leaders, experts, and superiors easily. If it is like Fig. 15, the imbeciles, defectives, perverts, unemployables exist as classes to be found and dealt with as such; they can be described in words and legislated for without subtlety or mistake.

The Apparent and the Real Form of Distribution

The real form of distribution of a mental trait may be obscured or falsified. The following examples illustrate chiefly ignorance:

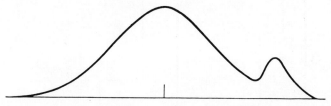

Fig. 14. A distribution with a second mode near the highest ability.

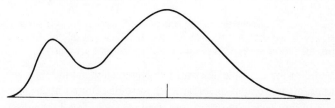

Fig. 15. A distribution with a second mode near the lowest ability.

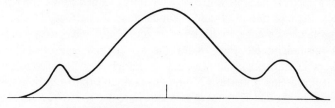

Fig. 16. A distribution with two secondary modes.

The score obtained by a person in the well-known intelligence test Army Alpha used with literate recruits in the United States Army during World War I was the number of items done correctly within a specified time, each being multiplied by a credit number. The distribution of scores does not tail out as much as it should at the high end because the experts who analyzed the scoring did not give large enough credits for the hardest of the items; later investigations showed that the successful performance of one of these represented a greater increment of intelligence than the success with the average item of the same sort. Fig. 17 shows the upper tail of the distribution of pupils in grade 9 by one well-known test when the scores are taken at their face value (A) and when they are transformed into terms of units that are equal or nearly so (B).

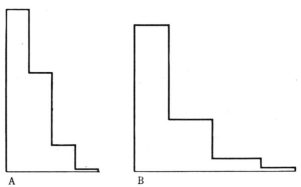

Fig. 17. A: The upper tail of the scores of 9th-grade pupils in an intelligence test, taking the scores at their face value. B: The upper tail for the same group when the scores are expressed on a scale whose units are equal.

The following example illustrates chiefly misunderstanding.

Suppose the population of age 50 were distributed according to the number of times each had been convicted of crime. The distribution would consist chiefly of zero scores. But these zero scores would represent a very wide range from persons who had just barely escaped conviction to saintly heroes. Perhaps nobody would misunderstand the surface of frequency in this particular case, but in subtler cases zero scores and perfect scores have been misunderstood. Fig. 18 for the age at marriage of skilled male workers might cause misunderstanding in anybody who failed to consider that it represents a mixture of first, second, and third marriages. Many flattened or skewed surfaces of frequency are due to the mixture of things that would be better kept separate.

The following illustrates chiefly misuse. The annual wages of males aged fifty would be very greatly skewed toward the high end. With a mode near $1000 the upper extreme would exceed $200,000. Does this mean that the ability for which employees are paid has really a range upward from its most common amount that is over two hundred times its range downward? Yes, in the sense that the men in question may well have earned them in the sense that their services added 200 times as much to the general welfare or to the profits of their employers as did the services of the $1000 men. But in the sense that these men have two hundred times as much of an intellectual or moral trait or combination of traits as the average man, the answer is probably "No." We may have a very high opinion of the genius and expert in industry and trade, but deny

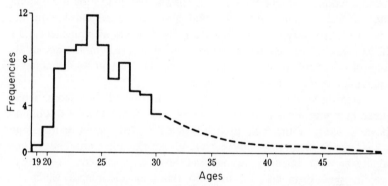

Fig. 18. Age at marriage of the skilled male workers who were married in York, England, in 1898 and 1899. [Data from Rowntree, '01, p. 400.]

that he has two hundred times as much managerial ability, or organizing ability, or planning ability, or business foresight, as the average man. We may think that the world could well afford to pay a certain man of affairs even a million dollars a year rather than go without his services, and yet insist that, though his services were worth five hundred times those of the average man, he did not have five hundred times as much of any conceivable mental ability.

In the case of wants, satisfactions, and services, the money scale is much more likely to represent reality. Data are scanty since people very rarely have to pay what they would be willing to pay in money. We should, in my opinion, not be very skeptical if the distribution of the strength of wants for jewels, morphine, popularity, power, beauty, or whatnot shows very great skewness when expressed in terms of the gross amount or the percentage of one's income that one will pay to gratify the want. But there can be extreme intensities of wants such as do not occur in abilities, in the sense that it seems utterly intolerable to the person to lack the desired satisfaction or endure the hated aversion.

As a final example consider the following: Children from a little under 2 years to a little over 4 years were observed, with respect to how often they came into conflict during ten sample periods of 15 minutes each in the nursery school or day nursery which they attended. The scores for number of conflicts by way of aggression showed a range from 0 to 42 around an average of 13.4. The zero scores here *do* represent a general pacifism in the sense that the child did nothing aggressive in a general environment which led other members to average 13 aggressive acts and some members to engage in over 40 such. A count of *one,* however, may mean anything from merely reaching for another child's toy to knocking the child down and urinating upon him! Those responsible for the observations wisely refrain from using the numbers as equivalent units. If, as is probable, the more extreme aggressions are common among the acts of the more frequent aggressors, the skewness in total amount of aggression is even greater than appears.

Special heed should be paid to (1) undistributed zero scores which mean in reality not a true zero, but only not enough thereof to obtain a positive score by the scale used; (2) undistributed perfect or maximum scores which mean in reality not the greatest possible amount of some ability or want, but only so much as tops the scale used; (3) scales on which equal distances are used to represent differences which are unknown or are known *not* to be equal.

The form of distribution is the consequence of the causes of the amounts of the trait possessed. If there are many uncorrelated causes of about equal influence and if each person is approximately a random sampling therefrom, the distribution will be closely like the "normal." If there is in addition one very influential cause or group of closely correlated causes, the distribution will show two clusterings around two modes. For example, certain causes give ten thousand babies varying capacities for vision clustering around the ordinary human status, and gonorrhoeal infection acts as a large cause to make a few of them blind; certain causes give them varying degrees of "general intelligence," and disease of the thyroid or hydrocephaly acts to bring some of them far down.

There are more complicated cases of the influence of large causes. There are those where attaining a certain amount of a trait makes further attainments easier. So knowledge of one foreign language may make the acquisition of others easier, or possessing $1000 may make it easier to acquire the next thousand. A skewness toward the high end of the scale will result. There are those where reaching a certain standard brings important benefits so that time and energy are spent abundantly until that point is reached. Thus there are humps in the distribution of school grade reached at the end of graduation from a high school and from college, at the cost of the steps of the scale just below these points.

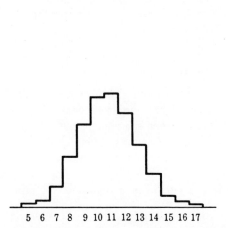

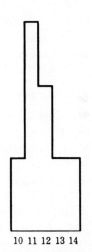

Fig. 19. The distribution of Trait C when the measurements are affected by a large chance error.

Fig. 19T. The true distribution of Trait C from adequate measurements.

The measurement of any individual in most traits is his true status plus the influence of various errors of measurement. If a thousand persons were really identical in the trait, their actual obtained measurements would still differ, the errors of measurement alone usually being continuous, unimodal, and symmetrical, following closely the "normal" form. If the errors of measurement are large compared with the real differences, the obtained form of distribution will have a spuriously large variation, and will be coerced considerably toward "normality," as shown in Fig. 19. If knowledge of the exact form of distribution is a matter of importance, reducing these errors by repeated and varied measurements should be studied.

Manufacturers had the facts of individual differences among workingmen thrust upon them by Taylor and his followers. That the first-class man can do in most cases two to four times as much as is done on an average is realized only by those who have made a thorough scientific study. If an economist does not base his theories upon the existence of an almost infinite number of different human factors, his problems will not concern the real world. The law makes sharp divisions between sane and insane, responsible and not responsible, and the like where none exist. It may be advisable to do this, but it should be done with full awareness of essential falsity. Theories and practices of government have erred both by neglecting certain important differences and by assuming that differences (in sex, race, color, noble birth) involved other differences which were in fact only loosely correlated with them.

The Amount of Variation in Human Traits

Common sense judgments find that men differ more in weight than in stature, more in intelligence than in weight, more in musical ability than in intelligence. Science supports our common-sense judgments.

Wechsler has computed the range of human differences in many physical and mental traits. He uses the ratio which the amount possessed by the next-to-the-highest person in a thousand is to the amount possessed by the next-to-the-lowest person in a thousand. He reports ['35, pp. 139 to 146] ratios as follows:

Normal body temperature	1.03
Calcium per unit of volume in the special fluid of adults	1.16
Stature at birth	1.21 (English males) and 1.25 (English females)
Stature, length of leg, length of femur, sitting height, height of sternal notch, length of foot, and span of arms, in various groups from	1.26 to 1.32
Acidity of the blood, hemoglobin content, calcium in the blood of children, urea in the urine, and heat production (calories per square inch in adults) from	1.21 to 1.32

Various intellectual traits showed ratios of 2.30 to 2.85, viz.:

Number of digits repeated correctly after a single hearing in 236 male adults	2.50
Mental age in years of children chronologically 9 to 9.9 years old	2.30
Time required to place certain simple blocks correctly in a board with holes to fit them	2.42
Time required to perform an easy substitution test	2.85

Wechsler included no wants in his study because careful measurements are not available, but it is common knowledge that the variation is probably greater in many of them than in the traits of Wechsler's list. For example, the desire for alcohol varies so greatly that by any reasonable scale of units the persons who are Number 2 and Number 999 in a thousand vary by more than 10 to 1.

In estimating the amount or intensity of a want, science is commonly concerned with its average strength over a long period, and in a normal variety of conditions. The ups and downs from day to day or minute to minute are a different problem. Wants are supposed to be measured adequately in each person over a long enough time to be characteristic of him, not of any more particular part or condition of him.

This requirement of combining more observations under more conditions is one reason for the scarcity of measurements of wants, in large groups of persons. Other reasons are the absence of convenient scales, the costliness of providing individuals with money so as to observe what they spend it for, and the general backwardness of the psychology of character and temperament, in comparison with the psychology of intellect and skill.

The ratio in many knowledge functions will be well above a hundred. The number of German vernacular words known by the 99.9 percentile American will be over twenty times that known by the 0.2 percentile American. In ready knowledge, as measured by the number of correct answers which a person could give to the millions of sensible questions which could be put to him, the score for adults will run from near zero for some idiots to over a million and probably to over ten million.

In economic value to the world as a worker, the ratio for adults is theoretically infinite, since the 0.2 percentile man surely cannot earn his keep in a modern civilized community. In morality, in the customary sense of a tendency to have good will toward men and control bodily lusts in favor of truth, beauty, and welfare, the ratio is again extremely high. In esthetic appreciation or good taste in matters of form and color, in the McAdory art test for example, an appreciable number of persons agree with the consensus of experts only by chance. In the Abbott-Trabue test of good taste in poetry the same is true.

In the intensity of the hunger pangs caused by a stomach empty too long, the ratio is low, probably somewhere near $1\frac{1}{2}$. In appetite, the desire for food after abstinence, the ratio is probably higher. There are one or two persons in a thousand whose appetite is so weak that they forget to eat lunch when deeply interested in some activity, and others who forget all other duties and pleasures at the smell of food.

The craving for the voluptuous sensation of sex after abstinence probably varies very widely, with a ratio approaching infinity. But as in many other cases, the intensity of the desire cannot be truly measured by the intensity of the indulgence, indulgence being a result of weakness of control as well as strength of desire.

The Interrelations of Mental Traits

Many of the important questions in the sciences of man concern the relations of some one mental trait to some other. Does insanity go with genius? Is virtue antagonistic to health, so that the good die young? Is ability to make money a sign of greed and predacity? Does nature compensate individuals for weakness in one ability by strength in another? What is the relation between the popularity which causes a man to get votes and the traits which cause him to be a good representative? Such questions require a description of the correlation of two traits in the way and degree to which the status of an individual in the one is linked with his status in the other. Table 8 estimates the morality of each of 269 male members of European royal families in relation to his estimated intellectual ability. Each little line represents one person.

There is a positive correlation: the abler intellects are the more moral persons. But it is far from close: r=.56.

Table 9 shows in a similar manner the relation for 197 girls between intelligence score at age 14.0 and earnings at clerical work 8 to 10 years later. Computing reveals that the average yearly pay is $32 greater for the 96 girls who scored 75 or higher in the test than for the 101 who scored below 75. About 56 percent of the girls are above average in both test score and earnings or below average in both; r is in fact .23.

Negative correlations among desirable abilities are exceedingly rare. The notions that quick learners retain less than slow learners, that wide knowledge goes with little depth of understanding, that ability in science implies insensitivity to beauty are disproved by the facts.

Among desirable wants and propensities there is more chance of finding a negative correlation because a person who obtains all the satisfaction he needs from a few wants may fail to develop or retain others, and a person who is sufficiently superior in a few estimable qualities to win approval may fail to develop other virtues. What facts there are make it probable that positive relations are the rule with desirable traits of character as with abilities. The correlations are, however, often very low for abilities, and are probably even lower for traits of character.

Table 8   The relation between estimated intellect and estimated morality in male members of European royal families

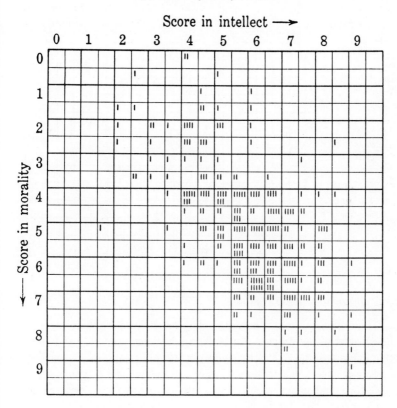

Correlations may have very great significance for the world's affairs, even though they are very low. A treatment of cancer which correlated only .20 with prevention and cure would fail often; yet it could save thousands of lives. A correlation of .30 between a certain form of municipal government and the welfare of cities would mean that ninety-one percent of the welfare of cities would be due to other causes than having this form of government. Yet to adopt it would be a distinct advance. In the prediction of the future success of a person in a certain vocation, a dozen components, no one of which alone showed a correlation of more than .30, could together provide a perfect prediction.[1]

[1] If each was independent of all the rest they would do so, but they are likely to have positive correlations *inter se*, which reduces their combined value.

Table 9   The relation between score in an intelligence test at age 14 and earnings at clerical work at age 20–22

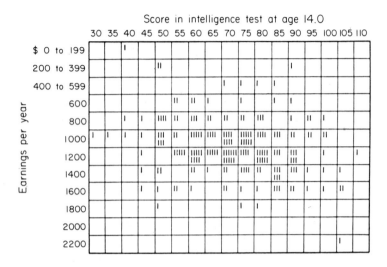

Score in intelligence test at age 14.0

Earnings per year	30	35	40	45	50	55	60	65	70	75	80	85	90	95	100	105	110
$ 0 to 199		I															
200 to 399					II								I				
400 to 599								I	I	I	I						
600						II	II	I			I		I	I			
800			I	I	IIII	II	III	II	II	II	III		I	II	I		
1000	I	I	I	I	III III	II	IIIII	IIII	IIII IIII	IIIII IIIII	IIII	III	II	II	II		
1200					I		IIIII IIII	IIIII IIII	IIIII	IIIII IIIII	IIII	IIIII IIIII	III	III III		I	I
1400					I	II		II	I	II	IIII	II	III III	III	I	I	I
1600					I	I	II	I		II	I	I	III	II	I	I	II
1800					I				I	I							
2000																	
2200																I	

The Organization of a Person

The organization of a person is almost unbelievably complex. If exact inventories of the natures of a million adult men taken at random from the United States were made, probably no two of them would be indistinguishable. Correlations surveyed to find traits which are self-contained and independent of the rest, correlating zero with all other traits, are very hard to find.

As one feature of the complexity there is specialization almost everywhere. Characters are not good or bad, strong or weak, but chock full of specificity. Helpfulness is partly allied to a general, over-all decency, but partly to separate and distinct tendencies. Honesty is not unitary: cheating in school is not the same as in games, and neither is the same as dishonesty with money. It is the rule rather than the exception that when mechanical skill, appreciation of beauty, strength of bodily appetites, sociability, curiosity, or openmindedness, is measured by careful observations and tests, its verbal unity conceals a factual variety and specificity. Most of such words and phrases really refer to statistical totals or averages.

Any simple classification of persons into physical types is probably misleading. The most reasonable classification into bodily types is probably into lanky and stocky, but these "types" mix and overlap. There are no reasonable simple classifications into mental types. E. Spranger lists the theoretical man, the economic man, the esthetic man, the social man, the man of power, and the religious man, as fundamental types. Of the adult population of New York City probably not one in ten would be put in the same Spranger category by five experts who knew all their thoughts and behavior for five years. His list would work much better as a classification of buildings!

A student of psychiatry suggests that "human behavior phenomena are ultimately organizations of four psychological processes varying in quantity from individual to individual, and of a fifth force, the environment. The psychological processes are form recognition, organizing energy, affective drive, creative activity." [S. J. Beck, '33, p. 374f.]. By this doctrine Napoleon, Einstein, Shakespeare, and probably Al Capone, would be classed together as having similar mental constitutions! No system of mental types has ever been validated. The system of Kretschmer classifying by body into pyknic, athletic, leptosome, and dysplastic, and supposed to be indicative of deep-seated mental constitution, has been carefully tried and found wanting by Klineberg and his associates ['34] and by Cabot ['38].

Especially misleading are classifications into two opposite types. All such systems that have been proposed misrepresent the two ends of a continuous distribution as descriptive of the bulk of the population, when they really describe only the status of one small part of a person who happens to be extreme in respect of it. One of the least objectionable is the division into introverts and extraverts, but the great majority of people are neither; and if one is sure that a person is at one or the other extreme that does not tell much more about him. If all at the introvert extreme were thoughtful, sensitive, shy, rather melancholy, desirous of a few intimate friends, disliking general sociability, and careless of food and drink, and if all the extraverts were active, thick-skinned, forward, uninterested in themselves, joyous mixers, not averse to gluttony, the classification would not be so bad; but they are not.

Any good system of types will recognize that intermediate conditions will be very common, and make free use of them as descriptions. But it will be still better to use only one type, the common ordinary man, and describe individuals by the features in which they differ and the amount of difference in each such feature. These facts have to be known in order to make a valid selection of the type to which he belongs, no matter what the typological system is.

With few or no exceptions superiority in one desirable trait implies superiority in any other. The various sorts of intelligence (with abstractions, with things and mechanisms, with people and their motives) are positively related; intelligence in general is correlated with virtue and goodwill toward men; both are correlated with skill in control of hand, eye, voice, etc.; all these are correlated with health, poise, sanity, and sensitiveness to beauty. Some of the intercorrelations are low, as in the case of intellect and musical ability, artistic appreciation and athletic ability, health and scholarship, but there is, I think, no demonstrated case of a negative correlation in all the work so far done.

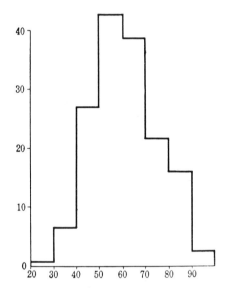

Fig. 20. Percentage of persons 16 or 17 years old attending school, 310 cities.

The existence of positive correlations among all or nearly all desirable traits may be caused in part by differences in the environments as it seems probable that an environment which increases one desirable trait will tend to increase others. The existence of positive correlations among the gene determiners of desirable traits need not be a mysterious ultimate law of mental constitution, but may have developed as a consequence of like mating with like.

If the relative importances of all these desirables were known, they could be given appropriate weights in the composite so that it would be a true index of the total desirability of the person. Its application would lessen the injustice of damning individuals in general just because they are dull (as teachers have done), of damning them because they are shy (as psychiatrists now do), of damning them because they are not cheerful mixers (as sales managers often do). Its application would also prevent the fantastic notion entertained by some sociologists that when the entire make-up and history of each man is considered, one man is as good as another.[1]

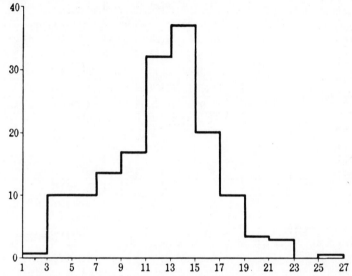

Fig. 21. Number of radios per hundred population, 310 cities.

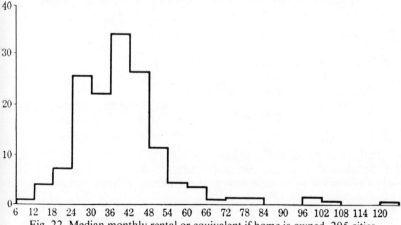

Fig. 22. Median monthly rental or equivalent if home is owned, 295 cities.

[1] The treatment of human mental variations in this chapter may be supplemented conveniently by Part II of Volume III of the author's *Educational Psychology* |'14| and Anastasi's *Differential Psychology* |'37|.

Table 10   Intercorrelations of 23 traits in 295 cities

	2	3	4	5	6	7	8	9	10	11	12	13	14	15	16	17	18	19	20	21	22	23
1	77	56	59	55	37	70	47	42	44	22	25	41	46	24	54	74	30	43	59	64	53	17
2		53	54	31	30	66	51	24	18	14	09	25	40	-05	15	63	09	-05	63	66	42	12
3			51	46	41	46	52	39	20	19	22	40	51	23	24	60	04	29	39	45	63	31
4				34	46	48	37	36	17	17	29	39	23	34	56	63	34	32	32	33	44	06
5					32	32	50	79	58	-05	35	38	37	56	66	52	67	50	20	23	47	25
6						36	31	22	06	-06	34	17	23	08	33	44	26	25	18	24	54	02
7							59	27	26	39	-07	33	59	14	16	75	08	10	44	57	57	25
8								70	38	-01	14	25	40	11	21	50	30	04	43	37	46	32
9									70	08	18	35	27	54	57	54	71	31	27	07	41	37
10										9	19	53	25	70	64	59	74	49	30	22	27	52
11											27	33	16	15	21	26	03	33	13	21	09	-06
12												28	21	34	61	13	37	51	-03	29	30	06
13													64	60	54	61	48	44	25	22	43	13
14														36	45	65	33	32	30	38	47	10
15															61	47	69	68	-08	03	26	26
16																66	75	69	20	32	36	09
17																	54	48	47	56	62	33
18																		61	17	13	27	29
19																			-04	16	46	20
20																				62	23	24
21																					46	17
22																						45
23																						

1. Infant death rate reversed
2. Typhoid death rate reversed
3. Per capita public expenditures for schools
4. Per capita public expenditures for libraries and museums
5. Percentage of persons sixteen to seventeen attending schools
6. Per capita public expenditures for recreation
7. Rarity of extreme poverty
8. Infrequency of gainful employment for boys 10–14
9. Infrequency of gainful employment for girls 10–14
10. Frequency of home ownership (per capita number of homes owned)
11. Per capita support of the Y. M. C. A.
12. Excess of physicians, nurses, and teachers over male domestic servants
13. Per capita domestic installations of electricity
14. Per capita domestic installations of gas
15. Per capita number of automobiles
16. Per capita domestic installations of telephones

17. Per capita domestic installations of radios
18. Percent of literacy in the total population
19. Per capita circulation of *Better Homes and Gardens, Good House-keeping,* and the *National Geographic Magazine*
20. Death rate from syphilis (reversed)
21. Death rate from homicide (reversed)
22. Per capita value of asylums, schools, libraries, museums, and parks owned by the public
23. Per capita public property minus public debt.

Individual Differences in Communities

It is obvious that villages, cities, and nations differ widely in almost every trait which a community can have. In the case of the three hundred and ten cities of the United States having 30,000 or more population in 1930, the variation in each of several hundred traits at or near that date has been measured. Figs. 20 to 22 show samples taken at random.

In these cities the variation is usually continuous. The residential suburbs are not set off sharply from the rest in wealth, creature comforts, or amount of manufacturing; manufacturing cities are not set off from commercial cities and trading centers for agricultural districts. The variations typically cluster around a single mode, as they do in individual persons. Skewness is common, however.

The fact of positive correlation between desirable traits generally holds true of these cities. Table 10 presents the intercorrelations of the twenty-three traits listed below it in 295 cities. The cities which do most for education also have most creature comforts; the cities which read the most also have the best parks; the cities which avoid child-labor also pay high wages. But there is notable specialization as there is in persons; no city is equally superior in all desirable traits; even so similar traits as average salary of high-school teacher and average salary of elementary-school teacher correlate only .78; the frequency of telephones and the frequency of radios correlate only .66.

Chapter 8
The Causation of Abilities,
Wants and Propensities

The genes are not speculative constructions. invented to be carriers of hereditary traits. As an outcome of the brilliant work of T. H. Morgan and others they are being counted. located on chromosome maps, and credited with definite achievements.

It is a customary, convenient and useful procedure to study the causation of the abilities and wants of the general human type, *homo sapiens*, separately from the causation of the individual differences of persons from that general human type. Let us follow this procedure and deal first with the question: "How much and what in *homo sapiens* is caused by the genes of the human type?"

The Genes and the Mind of Man

The great majority of hereditarians take it for granted that what is universal in all men of all times is caused by the genes. neglecting the fact that certain features of the environment. such as companionship with and care by human beings, were also universal in all men of all times. Logically this is a serious error. but factually it is hardly an error at all. Given the world as it is, the genes of a male human join with the genes of a female human. or die. The union of the two sets of genes selects a human uterus to grow in, or dies. The child that is born attracts a certain minimum of care in its tender years, or dies. The child manifests certain abilities and wants which are tolerated by the culture, seeks out a different culture more hospitable to its nature, or dies without leaving offspring. The hereditarian needs only to restate his position in this form: "The genes *and such experiences as the genes select by their own nature if they live at all* cause so and so."

Another instructive question is to ask how great the differences between the abilities and wants of man and those of other animals would be if the paraphernalia of human culture and tradition were wiped out and man were left with no language, no tools, no transmitted customs. Suppose the ten thousand babies born last week in America or Europe were put in the place of ten thousand born a quarter of a million years ago. What abilities and wants they then had would be given by their genes aided by a most meager environment.

Another desired answer would be in the form of measurements of the variation of some ability if all the different animals were given identical training. For example, if all the creatures had identical exposures to trees and rubber balls proportional to their sizes and identical experiences of immersion in water, would the abilities to climb and swim, and play with the ball be less alike or more alike than they now are in men, monkeys, dogs, and rats? It may be surmised that the differences in motor apparatus, themselves largely due to the genes, would cause large differences in the abilities.

Most observers think of the inherent nature of mankind as a rich endowment of abilities and propensities which parallel the rich variety of human achievements, virtues, and vices. A man is, they think, quite irrespective of the circumstances of life, a collection or organization of qualities, capacities, and tendencies, some possessed also by the lower animals, others distinctively human.

This view has, however, been challenged by certain psychologists and especially sociologists, who regard it as a gross exaggeration of the part played by the inherited qualities of *homo sapiens*. The great bulk of what man is today, what and how he thinks, does, wants, fears, loves, hates, etc.—he is, they would say, by reason of the environment that acts upon him. He does not by inherited nature enjoy dominating over others, but mastery has been associated with his getting the lion's share of food and fondling. Human nature is largely manufactured by human training; man is to a large extent neutral, clay in the hand of the family and community, ready to be "conditioned" to moderation or greed, modesty or display, curiosity or dullness. So they say.

The Influence of the Genes on the Abilities of Man   The genes decide what sense organs and sensory neurones man has, and what ranges of stimuli he is sensitive to. No training will make man see the ultra-violet or infra-red rays, or hear pitches which mice hear.

Perceptual abilities (to see a triangle or a diamond as it is, or to hear and distinguish words) work with patterns and combinations of sensory data, rest upon sensory abilities proper and upon ability to make mental connections, and upon certain aspects of "intelligence." They are largely influenced by the genes, because all their components are. What the environment does for men in general is to improve the abilities to perceive words, space forms common in human constructions, number, and other widespread objects in human culture.

Man's ability to be sensitive and to respond, including what used to be called attention, and his ability to form and retain mental connections are caused by the genes and such environments as the genes select. There are great differences among human individuals, and possibly the rich and varied life of modern man increases those powers for the species over what they would be in a meager and monotonous life. But the superiority of a man over a dog or a chimpanzee is probably over ninety-five percent due to his genes.

Much the same is true of the ability to have ideas free from immediate attachments to sensed objects. The number which the typical man *can* have depends upon his genes, and the number that he *does* have depends much more upon them than upon the circumstances of life, though opportunity and habit count somewhat.

The ability which has been most studied is intellect. Until after the middle of the nineteenth century the respectable solution was that the animals had the faculty of instinct whereas man had the faculty of reason. Neither the alleged "Instinct" of animals nor the alleged "Reason" of man could be identified, and nobody even conjectured what the physiological cause of either might be.

With the process of biology and psychology Instinct as a single mystical faculty was replaced by instincts, each an unlearned tendency to respond, irrespective of experience. It was shown that the associations made by chicks, dogs, cats, and monkeys were mainly not of ideas, but of motor responses to directly perceived situations. It was also shown that the reasoning of man in solving novel problems was not a new ability, sui generis, which worked apart from and against ordinary associative habits.

It is true that animals do not reason in the sense in which that word was used in 1900, but neither does man. We need not account for that difference between man and the chimpanzee by differences in their genes because that difference itself is largely unreal. As a result of nearly forty years of experimental study of animal intellect and the contemporaneous advances in knowledge of human thinking it now appears that no clear, general, qualitative distinction between the intellectual possibilities of the genes of man and those of the lower animals can be made. The ability to reason is now known not to be a primary quality or essence—a force over and above the laws of mental habit or association—but a secondary consequence of them. Man forms mental connections just as the animals do; but he forms an enormously greater number of such. As a by-product of this multiplicity of connections his powers of abstraction, generalization, and reasoning are developed.

So-called reasoning consists of representing experiences by ideas and symbols, analyzing things into elements, responding to these elements instead of to gross totals, and organizing a number of tendencies into a weighted total tendency. Some extremely dull men show little or nothing of this sort. Chimpanzees using sticks, and rats using topographical experience, have at least convinced Köhler and others that they do something of this sort. In general, if the facts interest animals and if there is a rich and varied behavior toward the facts, the animals seem somewhat like man. Animals make many unreasonable blunders. So Sturman-Hulbe and Calvin Stone ['29, p. 209] note that a white rat making a nest by picking up things and piling them there will often pick up her own tail, carry it to the nest and deposit it there. One of Köhler's chimpanzees, in the course of learning to put a box under a banana which hung from the ceiling, mount the box, and jump to obtain the banana, got the box, put it far from the banana, went to the spot beneath the banana and jumped! But you and I make the same sorts of mistake as those at harder levels.

The human species has an extremely varied repertory of responses and it enjoys these achievements for their own sakes. There is no gene for making or using tools, as such, nor, probably, any gene for making or using language, but there is a quantity and variety of play with things and sounds which has made man the creator of tools and speech.

Speech in a certain sense each human being has to create anew. As a ubiquitous feature of his social environment speech will not, in and of itself, impart speech to him unless he himself experiments extensively with making sounds in relation to his experiences. If the experiment of the Kelloggs, who brought up a chimpanzee with their own child for a year with scrupulous scientific care to treat the two alike so far as possible, had been continued for three or four years more, it is certain that the chimpanzee would have failed to learn to talk and to think in words. His failure would not be for lack of an impulse to express himself nor for lack of the custom of using voice to obtain certain desired treatment from his social environment; the chimpanzee would have both. But his brain does not cause him, even in a human environment, to indulge in multiplicity of connections of vocal play.

Man has a brain that can form an enormous number of connections, and a long life in which to form them. The chimpanzee's total life may be roughly estimated as about half that of man. He has time enough to acquire ideas, words, abstractions, if he were able, but still suffers a substantial handicap.

A simple but momentous quantitative extension of abilities already well developed in the primate stock and a long life may then conceivably be all that human heredity contributes directly to human intellect. The rest of its triumphs may require the cooperation of the environment which has preserved the earnings of this ability generation after generation in language, knowledge, customs, and tools.[1]

One is tempted to make a distinction between what a man *can* do and what he *does* do, and to say that what man can do is caused solely by what the human genes are, whereas what he does do is caused by what the genes are plus what the environment is. Ability defined otherwise than by achievement is however too ambiguous and too little understood. What man can do in this sense of *can* nobody knows. The only way to estimate it is precisely by such evidence and arguments from achievements as have been presented.

The above account of the causation of human achievements may be summarized as follows: Human genes are necessary; they are primary, leading the way, and receiving in most cases only moderate increases from one environment rather than another. In the case of intellect, motor skills, communication, and special abilities derived from these, the

---

[1] Not only may a very simple gene variation have given man his distinctive richness in associative neurone-connections; this variation may have been caused, facilitated, or permitted by a still simpler one, the stopping of the development of the head at a fetal stage. Stockard writes:—"What seems to be the most plausible possibility yet offered involves two developmental inhibitions. The first of these is uniquely human and results in the retention of head proportions comparable to those found in the fetal stages of the higher mammals. This gives the disproportionately large cranium and big brain with the small facial region, as compared with the reverse adult proportions of small cranium and excessive facial development among the other mammals. And still further, as Huxley remarked, the higher races of men have a larger brain and a smaller jaw than their lower 'big-jawed brothers.' The highest apes failed to retain this large-brained fetal proportion. The mutation which brought about the large brain was limited to ancestral man." [Stockard, '31, p. 300f.]

increases are much greater. The genes of an Aristotle in 100,000 B.C. would perhaps have done well to have used a thousand words and made a drum. The same genes growing up from 1930 to 1990 would easily acquire a vocabulary of a hundred thousand words, find safe ways of utilizing atomic energy, or perhaps a cure for cancer.

The practical consequences are that any deterioration in the environment is dangerous, but not irremediable. What the genes of man have done they could presumably do again. Any deterioration in the genes may be not only deplorable and dangerous, but irremediable. Whether the genes could be got to recover the loss by new mutations is very doubtful.

The Influence of the Genes upon Character, Propensities, Wants   In the case of likes and dislikes, proclivities to feel and act in certain ways, and other features of action, emotions, and preference, even the most extreme environmentalists credit man with certain inherited bodily wants and tendencies to act. There will be a wide difference of opinion about such questions as: Do men by nature hit back when they are hit, grab whatever they want, fight to retain possession of it, fabricate a lair in which to rest, collect miscellaneous and useless oddments, look in the direction in which others are looking, conduct love-affairs in the dark, etc.?

Extreme environmentalists rely upon training chiefly in the form of associative shifting or conditioning, to do what the hereditarians attribute mainly to the genes. They would assert that the human being by heredity smiles only at food and stimulation of the erogenous zones, not at the smiles of others, nor at soft and gentle sounds. But since he is smiled at and spoken to gently while he is being fed, he learns to smile at smiles and cooing sounds. Man, they say, has no inherited fear of snakes, but acquires these via the behavior of parents or nursemaids. Their screams or sudden jerks of him cause shock which causes fear in him which then shifts to the sight of the snake.

This parsimonious doctrine has the merit of being parsimonious. The process of associative shifting is real and important, and does account for many features of what we like, approve, scorn, fear, laugh at, eat, drink, and make love to. Yet infants near the end of the first year object to solitude, though solitude up till then has been connected with security from shock, amusing toys, and happy play. The ordinary home and school of a hundred years ago exerted great pressure toward submissive behavior by the young, but adults manifested attempts at mastery none the less. Conditioning or associative shifting from the satisfactions of food and sex or fear at shock do not easily account for responses to situations which are rarely or never connected with food, sex, shock, etc. The patterns of behavior referred to by the words, jealousy, shame, display, shyness, and rivalry, for example, seem underivable by shifts from the simpler repertory.

Moreover, even in cases such as the fear of snakes, where the shift is verbally plausible, its adequacy may be doubted. The scream or jerk which seems to produce fear of a snake is rather impotent to produce fear of a mud-puddle, a newly painted post, or a revolver. The widely quoted experiments reported by Watson and Rayner ['20] have probably been very misleading. Dr. Bregman ['34] repeated the Watson experiment with 15 infants, and with a variety of stimuli. Her results are diametrically opposed to the conclusion that a score, or even a hundred, connections of a stimulus originally neutral with shock will cause the mental stimulus itself to produce emphatic shock and fear, or any considerable degree of fear. I venture to prophesy that investigation will show Man's repertory of inherited propensities or dispositions to be not poor, but rich and varied. It will, however, be limited in certain important ways.

Let us consider some of these limitations. (1) The genes do not come out of a dictionary! The words which sophisticated civilized man uses to describe large segments of behavior or important qualities of behavior will seldom describe accurately the inherited components of human nature. Man's unlearned propensities are in particular often more or less specialized than the words would indicate. He has, for example, no general instincts of self-preservation. The realities are certain tendencies to avoid large missiles, etc., by jumping; attacks by dodging; falling by clutching; to suck, bite, chew, and swallow; to push away objects that interfere with breathing, etc. The realities of the "instinct" for constructiveness are the enjoyment of doing anything to anything which causes something interesting to happen. Whether the result is constructive or destructive is irrelevant. It is from specific behavior and with cooperation from other instincts, that rivalry in games, scholarship, or politics develops, not from a general passion to outdo others. Imagine a party for five-year-olds at which the games were to see who could sit still longest with his eyes closed, and who could say the most verses from the Bible!

On the other hand the genes are sometimes less specific than we think. For example, man has no particular instincts to love one's real mother rather than foster mother, to crave alcohol, paddle in the water, be excited by fire, be curious about machines, hoard money, or worship the sun.

(2) By heredity alone man is not frightened by the *idea* of solitude nor made angry by *thoughts* of insults. Ideas and thoughts, memories and expectations have no dynamic power save what they acquire by their connections with perceived facts or by their likenesses to perceived facts. The power which ideas acquire varies greatly with the idea and with the person who has it. Memories of past dangers do not often fill men with fear but memories of past insults often rouse anger anew. The imagination of delectable viands rarely gives enjoyment, but the imagination of a beautiful scene often does.

We can probably rely on inherited propensities to mutual aid in the form of liking to see people rejoicing rather than complaining, giving bits of food to children, protecting the weak who appeal submissively, and joining in attacks and certain other group enterprises. But any considerable reliance upon the genes to respond favorably to rational appeals and statistical evidence so as to further peace on earth and good will toward man is probably misplaced.

(3) Since acquired tendencies to respond are not transmitted to offspring, we may conclude that there will be few instincts of response to the creations of civilization as such, with their meanings. For example, if there is an unlearned interest in jewels, it will be irrespective of their exchange value. The so-called culture-epoch theory, a doctrine popular in the nineties, that children by original nature passed through a hunting stage, a pastoral stage, an agricultural stage, etc. was nonsense. If Mary likes her little lamb, it is not because of any inheritance from the pastoral experiences of her forebears.

There remains a rich and varied repertory of gene-caused propensities. They include, in my opinion, the whole range of sensitivities and a wide range of quasi-sensitivities. The genes provide man with the capacity to have many of the states of mind and brain which we call internal sensations, emotions, moods, and the like. Fear and anger are the best known, but there are many others for which training is equally unnecessary. Among them are hunger-pangs proper, repletion, restlessness, voluptuous sexual sensations, startle, nostalgia, disgust, feelings of competence, elation, feelings of inferiority and shame.

The genes have so made human brains that certain situations not only evoke certain muscular and glandular responses, but also these states of mind. A sudden loud sound not only makes a child tremble and cry but also have this inner fear component. By the genes' arrangements these states of mind tend to be evoked by certain experiences and to evoke certain responses. But they can acquire attachments to anything which has been connected with them. So some persons come to feel panic at even the thought of a robber breaking in, or voluptuous sensation at the mere sight of the loved object. The existence of an unlearned tendency does not prevent the situation involved from occasionally becoming linked with responses very different from those to which the genes have linked it.

Shrinking from clammy and creepy touches with fear and disgust, startling at strange loud sounds, fear when alone or in the dark, many sorts of angry behavior at being restrained, smiling in comfort, embracing, open-mouthed interest in certain sorts of novelties, envy when another receives what one craves, and dozens of other tendencies—all seem gene-caused. So do smiles and pats for what is gently satisfying, respectful stares and encouraging shouts at gorgeous display or natural acts of daring, hoots and sneers at deformity, physical meanness and cowardice, swaggering, being abashed in the presence of one who can outyell and outstare us, and many other forms of behavior which operate mainly in courtship, family life, and other human relations, and are the original roots of gregariousness, approval, display, rivalry, mastery, submission, teasing, self-consciousness, modesty, courtship, kindliness, and other so-called "social instincts."

The preceding inventory of the contributions of the genes to human propensities will be unsatisfactory to some because of its omissions. It has no religious instinct, no "instinct of workmanship," only a few fragments of the "instinct of the herd," and little of the Freudian equipment of polymorphic perverse sexuality, death instinct, hatred of old men by young, etc. It reduces sweeping, almost omnipotent potencies to specific tendencies. It omits or minimizes the scope of Kline's migratory tendencies, James's "fear of the supernatural," McDougall's instincts of self-abasement and of self-assertion, the "slavish instincts" of Galton, Royce's "social opposition," Henry Marshall's "blind impulse leading man to create" and Alfred Marshall's "desire for excellence for its own sake," and many less plausible candidates.

My inventory will be unsatisfactory to some psychologists because it includes too much, they will think. Can we expect the genes to provide connections between a hundred situation-patterns and a hundred or more response-patterns? Can we expect them to provide a thousand such?

So far as the mere number and variety of the connections is concerned, there should be no difficulty. The genes provide tens of thousands of specific details in making the sizes and shapes and colors of the parts of a man's body, details which we can count up in showing how closely alike two twins are. Let nobody think that the elaborateness and complexity of some of these tendencies, for example the tendency to enjoy "humble approval by admiring glances," is an insuperable barrier to their development. The extremely elaborate and complex patterns of the songs of roller canaries, which everybody supposed needed careful training by imitation, have been found by Metfessel to be due to the canaries' genes; kept in sound-proof compartments they produce their characteristic songs.

Many behavioral tendencies are only slight variations from tendencies possessed by many mammals, so that many millions of years are available for them to have originated. Others started with the pre-human primates. If the human stock started on its course as a genus distinct from other primates a hundred thousand generations ago, and accumulated one such tendency every thousand generations, there would be a hundred post-primate tendencies. It is known that mutations are occurring in man, and it is not unbelievable that in a thousand generations such a tendency developed and spread as to smile at a smile, or manifest approval at gorgeous display.

Those who for any reason wish to minimize gene contributions to human behavior emphasize the recent findings of anthropologists that certain cultures show notable departures from any such inventory as that presented here. For example, among the Arapesh, according to Margaret Mead ['35], approval is given not to gorgeous display or victory, but to being modest and inconspicuous; among the Manus the children dominate their fathers. [Mead, '30]. Such facts are valuable as evidence that men with a special ancestry and special training may show eccentricities, and that training can cause the facts of human behavior to be enormously different from what they would be with a different training. But they are not very important for a general estimate of the contributions of the genes because the criterion of universality has been overworked in arguments pro and con about the contribution of the genes. That the typical *homo* has a certain equipment of genes does not imply that this identical equipment is present in every man, much less that it will produce its ordinary consequences when the environment is extraordinary. The genes may cause a tendency which does not show itself at all universally, being inhibited by the circumstances of life or denied the stimuli adequate to evoke it, or modified to unrecognizable form. On the other hand, that all men manifest a certain behavior does not imply that the behavior is caused by the genes. If a certain environmental force is universal, its consequences will be universal also. So language is universal, though it may be prepared for in the genes only by a proclivity to move the mouth in a great variety of ways.

The best criterion *pro* gene causation is the existence of behavior *against* training but likely by the genes. Almost equally good is the existence of behavior toward which training is neutral, but which is likely by the genes. The best criterion *con* is perfect or very close correlation between the amount of training and the strength of the tendency. Thus nothing in the genes has any influence in causing the verbal forms by which a person expresses past time, plurality, or the difference between motion and rest.

The Environment and the Mind of Homo Sapiens

What the general human type is now we say is the result of what the general type was a hundred thousand years ago plus a little caused by the changes in its genes during that time plus more caused by the environmental changes by which the general run of the men of today have profited. Until very recently, one generation did little or nothing more than maintain the rude culture of its parents.

It is instructive to take away one after another feature of the environment and inquire from history and anthropology what man was without them. Radio, telephone, electricity, steam power, steel, clocks, printing, writing, wheels, iron, textiles, pottery, levers, wedges, domestic animals, agriculture, fire, schools, religions, mythologies, parliaments, kings, police, armies, laws, ceremonies—if these and the other demonstrably environmental facts were not at man's disposal he would not look like the man of our history and geography books.

This is all true and important, but it does not controvert the earlier contributions of this chapter. Man a hundred thousand years ago probably hated and feared and loved, dominated and submitted, approved and disapproved, was curious, greedy, jealous, and even modest, as described herein. And, after all, man's genes made the environment which now fashions him.

Environments as Forces Selecting Certain Gene Constitutions for Survival   The man-made environment changed very slowly until about ten thousand years ago. Beginning with the domestication of animals and the cultivation of plants it has assumed the forms of civilization. There was presumably no appreciable change in the genes of man during this ten thousand or more years by mutation, but they may have changed by the elimination of individuals and groups which had certain genes disabling them from surviving in the changing world. Each change in the environment might thus select certain qualities in man. It is easy to argue that when concerted fighting by a group against alien groups was invented, groups that could not learn to cooperate in war would not survive as well, or that when the cultivation of plants was invented, groups that could not learn when to plant and preserve the harvest would not survive as well. The man-made environment would thus be steadily molding man into adaptations to it. But such speculation is risky. The brutal marauder might conquer the agriculturalists and compel them to feed him and his offspring. Living in a walled city may have killed more by spreading contagious diseases than it kept alive by security from outside attack. The qualities inducing man to sacrifice for his tribe may have negative correlations with the qualities inducing fertility.

There is not enough evidence concerning what qualities various environments select for survival. Does war preserve the brave or the cowardly? Does the establishment of ownership of land cause the land owners to have more children or fewer than landless men? Does universal education favor the survival of those who enjoy schooling over the survival of those who dislike it? An environment which esteems holy men may associate holiness with celibacy and thus eliminate holy men as fast as it can. An environment which cares for culture and refinement may disappear in degradation if it cannot protect itself against brutal force.

Environments as Forces Modifying Man's Acquired Nature   Any universal feature of the environment may modify all men, and so the average man. For example, if all infants are fed at the mother's breast the satisfyingness of a filling stomach may become attached to the movements they make and they may then enjoy sucking a thumb, rag, or "pacifier" more than they otherwise would. But the environment in such cases does not act magically. If children are taught to prostrate themselves when a majority of the group do so, they will have on the average a stronger feeling of submission and reverence toward the king or idol in question, but any increment of general submissiveness and reverence will be almost negligible. Soldiers trained to unquestioning obedience to their superiors are not characterized by notable obedience to law, conscience, or civil authorities.

What is required is careful specification of the detailed stimuli involved and of the consequences to human behavior in detail. Thus the anthropologist tries to determine in detail how the introduction of the horse into America by early settlers from Europe modified the behavior and nature of the American Indians. As to the more impressive industrial and social changes, history and sociology have hardly begun their tasks. Just what the change from status to contract did to man, nobody knows. Just what the change from superstition to science is doing to man, nobody knows.

The Veneer Theory

There is a well-known theory that civilization suppresses the old Adam of man, covers it with a veneer of customs, or is, in Bergson's simile, "a thick humus which covers today the bed-rock of original nature" but does not really replace it; and that animal nature still exists ready to overcome the suppressing forces if something excites it to action, or to operate if the veneer wears off or is removed by some shock. Such imagery does not represent adequately either man's gene nature or the relation between it and his acquired nature.

Man's gene nature lacks many of the virtues and amenities of present civilizations, but it is probably not so horrid as literary scientists imagine it. The baboons are certainly very unpleasant; but the chimpanzees are rather decent creatures, and their life is more like a human family picnic than like an orgy of demons. Early humans may have been rather inoffensive family men. Civilization does not so much suppress gene nature as use it under the conditions of civilization.

The veneer theory does however contain an important truth, which is that civilization's treatment of gene nature modifies it for use in ordinary and conventional circumstances, caring little of what they will do in extraordinary ones such as mobs, burning buildings, sudden accessions of power, or attacks of insanity.

Consider two examples,—honesty about property and taking pains to discover truth. They are not virtues of the genes. The former is inculcated (within certain limits) by capitalistic civilizations as a habit of great advantage for the common good and of even greater to business men and all who save against need. The latter (though of enormous advantage to the common good) is as yet inculcated emphatically only by courts, moralists, and men of science.

Chapter 9

The Causation of Individual Differences
in Achievements, Wants and Propensities

It is important to know the causes which make persons differ from the average human being, in some ways more important than to know the causes of typical humanity. Economics and business need to know them in order to utilize each person to the greatest advantage to maximize human enjoyments. Government needs to know them in order to prevent and cure criminals, loafers, meddlers, and fools. Even more important is the need to know the limitations set by human nature to the attainment of liberty, equality, fraternity, and other goals of idealistic humanitarianism.

Education has been finding that the efficacy of going to school depends largely upon who goes, and is busy in devising means of selecting for any given sort of education those whose education will benefit the community, and in devising varieties of schools to make education profitable in the case of those for whom existing types of training do little or no good. Its compass in this is knowledge of the causation of individual differences.

We cannot ever be sure of identity in the genes of any two persons, but we approximate it in twins formed by the splitting of the same fertilized egg. Newman, Freeman, and Holzinger have been sedulously investigating cases of such twins brought up in different homes. Their main findings to date are as follows: Nineteen twins judged to be "identical"

145

brought up in separate homes from a very early age show an average difference in I.Q. of 8.2 points. Fifty twins judged to be "identical" brought up in the same home show an average difference in I.Q. of 5.4 points. If the twins had been measured on various occasions with alternative forms of the best test, the 8.2 and 5.4 would have shrunk, probably to about 3 and $\frac{1}{2}$ respectively.

The variation in intelligence of twins is greatly reduced thus from the variation in unrelated persons brought up in the same home or in the same orphanage (these will differ one from the other by about 18 on the average).

We cannot ever be sure of identity in the environments of any two persons, but we approximate toward it in children brought up from infancy in an orphan asylum. Kate Gordon ('19), Hildreth ('25), Davis ('28), and Lawrence ('31) found that children who have lived from half to all of their lives in the same institution differ nearly or quite as much as children reared in different homes and become no more alike the longer they stay in the same institution.

A certain fraction of the environment can be made approximately equal for different persons. Thus a hundred persons may be given equal instruction and equal practice periods at typewriting, or learning the meanings of German words, or estimating the lengths of lines. In such experiments, great differences are found in spite of the approximate identity of the training. The ordinary arguments to the effect that going to college greatly increases a person's influence in the world, or that the longer one stays in school the more he will earn in after-life, or that studying Latin and mathematics will improve one's mind enormously more than studying stenography and cooking, are worthless because of neglect of selective forces.

The sound procedure in investigating the influence of difference in training upon any ability is to measure the person's status in that ability before the training begins, and compare individuals or groups who were equal at the start. When this is done the causal efficacy of training upon intelligence as measured by standard intelligence tests is very slight. For example, about 14,000 pupils in high school were carefully measured by a battery of dependable intellectual tasks with verbal, numerical, and spatial content, before and after a year of study. Consider the gains for two groups of pupils, of equal intellectual ability whose studies were the same except that those in LAGT group had Latin, Algebra, Geometry or Trigonometry, whereas those in BCSP group had Bookkeeping, Arithmetic, Cooking, Sewing, Stenography, or Physical Training. The gain for the LAGT group averaged 25, whereas the gain for the BCSP group averaged

24. The average gain for a group which stayed out of school for a year and worked at mechanical or clerical work is estimated at 18. The difference of 1.0 between the LAGT group and the BCSP group is then about one eighteenth of the gain due to a year's growth and the experience of taking the test. Being the brightest pupil of a thousand rather than the dullest will cause twenty times as great a difference in the gain as taking a course in Latin, or Algebra instead of one in Stenography or Physical Training.[1]

The Environment

Differences in the genes and differences in the environment tend to go together. If a person, A, has more of trait X than the average human by reason of his genes, he tends to have parents who are + in X, and so to live in a home which tends to favor X. He tends also to select an extra-home environment favorable to X. The environmental difference then acts to maintain and accentuate the inherent differences due to original nature. So neurotic children tend to live with neurotic relatives; child criminals may be taught crime by their parents; gifted children often are subject to stimulation by able parents.

There are cases where training acts against a difference caused by the genes. If a child born in a decent respectable family has specially strong tendency to quarrel, appropriate the possessions of others, demand approval, the family provides contrary training, with as much skill as it has. Such home training to correct bad tendencies in the very young is often ineffective. A psychologist noted for his faith in training had great difficulty in curing his child of such tendencies! Moreover, if home training is very influential in causing the resemblances of sibs one to another, the resemblances of children to the mother should be closer than resemblances to the father, since they are with her much more. There is, so far as I know, no such evidence.

Differences caused by training tend to be more specific than those caused by the genes. Training in language is always by way of some particular languages. Certain features of this training spread their influence beyond a particular language, but many features do not. The genes probably provide nothing characteristic of only one language, but much for an interest in and ability with symbol-making and using relations potent in learning any language.

There is then no one answer to the problem of nature *versus* nurture in causing the differences found among men. At one extreme are things like color blindness for which training can do very little. At the other extreme

---

[1] The facts are reported in Thorndike '24, and Brolyer, Thorndike, and Woodyard, '27.

are things like whether the person knows what a certain doctor's telephone number is; probably 99.9 percent of the variance in this is attributable to environment.

Toward the former extreme we have such things as intelligence, the variation in which may be allotted roughly as follows: To the genes, 80%; To training, 17%; To "accident," 3%.

Toward the other extreme we have such things as food-preferences and dress, the variation in which may be allotted roughly as follows: To the genes, 10%; To training, 85%; To "accident," 5%.

Most of what has been said here about individual mental differences is applicable to the mental differences of families and races. Such exist as a consequence of differences between the genes or training or both, of one family from another, one race from another. But it is easy to overestimate these family and racial differences, and in the interest of one or another theory or prejudice this has often been done. The popular notion that all the persons of each race are closely alike mentally and very different from all the persons of any other race is sheer nonsense. There is usually great variation within the race and great overlapping between races. The case about which most is known is intelligence in American Negroes, including Negro-white hybrids, and Whites mostly of English and North European descent. The overlapping here of persons who have had equal numbers of years of schooling is estimated by the writer to be that shown in Fig. 23.

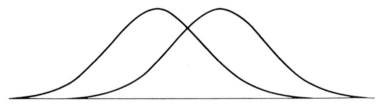

Fig. 23.

We must now consider again the objection that too much variety and complexity is required of the genes, this time of the differences between the genes of one person or family or race and those of another. A complete defense against this objection is furnished by the recent work of Loeb on the responses of animal genera, species, races, and individuals to grafts of foreign tissues. He has shown that each individual's tissues have a unique constitution in this respect, and that this is due to the individual's genes.

Causation by the Environment

Individual men owe much of their natures to the circumstances of their lives. The environment may maintain or increase abilities by giving them adequate exercise, and by making their exercise satisfying. Abilities are correspondingly weakened by disease, lack of exercise, and interfering abilities. Other things being equal, the ability to "reason" becomes less in alcoholic dementia, in persons who are never stimulated to reason or rewarded for doing so, and in persons who are taught to be entertaining at all costs.

Wants and propensities are influenced by general hygiene and special drugs and hormones, more than knowledge, habits, and abilities are. In general, however, repetition and reward form and strengthen wants and propensities as in the spheres of ideas and skill. The same forces of lack of exercise and interference weaken them.[1] There are, however, certain special difficulties in changing wants and propensities. It is harder to get these connections to occur, and to attach adequate rewards to them. The desired response is less available than ideas and acts are. It cannot so easily be summoned by the learner at will or aroused in him by stimulation from without. There is likely to be a certain incompleteness about the desires or emotions which are evoked. They are likely to be less rich and thrilling, less emotional. A person may learn to hate false logic or misleading advertisements, but not quite as he hates his mother-in-law. He may learn to be calm in conflict, but the calmness is not the enfolding calmness which he feels when the conflict is over, the victory won, and repose is earned. Wants and propensities which are not inherent in man's genetic constitution are much harder to put into him than ideas which can be introduced through sensations. The detachment of desire from certain objects and its attachment to others is usually much harder than with ideas and bodily acts.

Besides modifying the natures of men, the environment furnishes new tools to work with. Skates, skis, camels, bicycles, locomotives, and airplanes are all alike supplements to man's legs. Crowbars, wedges, wheels, mills, and dynamos are new arms and fingers. Microscopes, telescopes, and television are improvements on his eyes. His brain uses all these much as it does his own bodily organs. Written language extends speech and aids memory. Laws extend and refine customs. The accumulated discoveries of science facilitate the work of his mind even more than machines facilitate the work of his hands.

Limitations to the Action of Environments

The features of a person are made up of connections between

---

[1] The evidence is given in Chapters 13, 14, and 15 of the author's *Psychology of Wants, Interests and Attitudes* ['35B].

situations and responses. Abilities or wants are modifiable by training in so far as these connections are. If the eyes and brain of a person do not respond differently to red light and green light of the same intensity, it will do no good to shoot red and green rays at them a million times. Some of the reflexes used to be regarded as absolutely unmodifiable by training. Psychologists have found that man can by training be taught to contract or dilate the pupil, manifest the psychogalvanic reflex, and the like. A few persons by diligent trial and self-reward at success have learned to weep, to wag their ears, and the like, at will. In certain tribes everybody acquires some such ability. Klineberg ['35] writes that among the Maori of New Zealand it is not etiquette to make any demonstration at the departure of a friend; tears are reserved for his return, and it is real weeping; a man wails or howls, the tears streaming down his face.

Some situation-response connections cannot be made perfectly. So nobody can hold a rifle absolutely still or keep it aimed at absolutely the same point; nobody can draw free hand a perfect circle. When a person has practiced long under optimal conditions and in hundreds of further trials makes no improvement we assume that he has reached what is called his "physiological limit." Further training may make the trait less likely to weaken with disuse, or less wearying, but will not bring it nearer perfection.

There are for any given person such "physiological limits" to how fast he can learn, how angry he can be, how ecstatic his delight at music can become, how big a business he can manage, how great temptations of certain sorts he can overcome—in short, to the extent to which he can carry almost any ability or propensity one can think of. Common opinion judges these limits by what it observes and hears. It consequently underestimates what men can do because they happen never to have done it, and it overestimates what they can do by ignorance of individual differences and the consequent fallacious argument that what one man has done, most or all men can do again.

It is also erroneous to suppose that any environment, no matter how favorable, can bring a person to his physiological limit and keep him there in many traits. Even unremitting devotion soon meets limitations of time and loss from disuse and interference which prevent any more abilities from being perfected. And the same is almost certainly true of the traits of character called propensities or proclivities. If a man is as cheerful, cooperative, and kind as it is in his nature to be, he will find it hard to be also as honorable, industrious, and just as it is in his nature to be. The perfectibility of human nature is wisely put by religions in a heaven, with an optimal environment and infinite time. No environment on earth will make men perfect.

Most men live below their physiological limits in everything. They are not even as happy as their natures and environments permit, misunderstanding their own interests. Still less do they achieve as much in health, knowledge, skill, or virtue as they might. They really do not want to; they prefer to be as they are. This is as true of persons who have had the advantages of political freedom, sufficient wealth, kind and intelligent parents, access to science and art and other features of the most beneficial environment available as of the underprivileged. So, in order to do its perfect work environment must change people's wants as well as their opportunities.

The Method of Action of the Environment

Suppose that by a miracle the thousand best poems, philosophies, sonatas, statues, and paintings of the last fifty years, and the thousand best laboratories, medical schools, engineering schools and factories, and the thousand best laws and moral gospels had been set on earth in 938. Some of them would have been promptly destroyed as works of the devil. If any forward-looking alchemist had tried to use the laboratories he would probably have been executed.

The social and intellectual environment has been supposed to operate by a potent tendency of mankind to imitate. The evidence for such a general tendency is scanty, the fact being rather that only in special cases and special conditions do men or children duplicate in themselves what they observe in others. If ten thousand intellectual and moral super-men were dropped, a few in each county of the United States, I fear that in any case they and their very few imitators would be derided as crazy, undemocratic, and incomprehensible. If they had an inveterate habit of forgetting the names of all the persons they met and falling asleep whenever we tried our best to entertain them, I fear that they would have neither imitators, wives, children, or friends. If they tried to rule the world for its own good they would surely be put out of the way as traitors. We might say what they said but would not mean what they meant.

Imitation is surely limited by the repertory of the imitator and is weak except when driven by admiration. *Example is stronger than precept mainly because precept has a strength near zero.* Many hopes are founded on the power of the environment by way of suggestion. Suggestion is often better than coercion and sometimes better than persuasion because it does not arouse opposition or rely upon threats, and also lets the person have the satisfaction of feeling that he is master. For a suggestion to be potent it is usually necessary that its acceptance by a person shall not involve any annoying associations. So the advertisers who suggest to us that we buy ABC toothpaste or XYZ gargle try to link the idea with success in love and business. Suggestion is in fact a sort of trick to get a certain mental tendency to occur and to reward its occurrence.

It may be deduced that the human environment exerts an extremely powerful force by approval. From early infancy a person is permitted, stimulated, and encouraged to do what the mores of his family and neighborhood approve. Such acts on his part are often definitely rewarded by his environment. He comes to think of them as proper and so rewards them himself by the inner satisfactions of self-respect and a good conscience. Whether we eat with fingers, chopsticks, or forks, whether we believe in the divine right of kings or in the divine right of mobs, whether we bow toward a superior or turn our backs and bow away from him, as some South African Negroes do—all such matters are easily amenable to environmental control by social approval and scorn.

We should examine history, biography, and case-studies as well as mass experiments and statistics. We have not found published cases where differences in the environment account for a large fraction of the variance in behavior partly because we have not looked in all the important places. For example, Bliss Perry, a man of notable charm and influence as a college teacher, was at the age of twelve captain of a successful baseball nine composed of boys in a small New England town. Of his team one became captain of the famous Negro team, the Cuban Giants, another became an infielder of the Buffalo professional team. It is fantastic to suppose that inborn fitness for baseball caused this. The cause was probably environmental in the shape of Bliss Perry's zeal and magnetism. If he had started a missionary society, or a gang of bandits, he would perhaps have two or three saints or famous crooks to his credit.

I have failed to present the Freudian doctrines of the causation of human behavior in great measure by occurrences during infancy and life in the mother's womb. I have neither accepted nor denied the doctrine that a craving to return to the safe parasitism of life as a foetus is a prime factor in human toil and trouble; or the doctrine that reluctance to discharge the feces, which the infant is alleged to esteem as a part of himself, will cause a general miserliness all through life if it is not properly outgrown or "sublimated"; or the doctrine that auto-erotic practices are the cause of neurasthenia; or any other of the Freudian causal hypotheses. First, it would take too long to separate the facts from the fancies. Second, the facts are applicable mainly to disorganized hysterical minds, and a sound way to treat such in government, business, law, education, and religion is to proceed with the world's work as if they were sensible persons or troublesome children. For medicine the case is somewhat different; psychiatrists have to deal with such minds and should be taught the truth about Freudian doctrines, in full detail.

Chapter 10
Values

A person's desire of the moment may conflict with his long-time plans; his bodily passions may be antagonistic to his esthetic ambitions. The wants of one person often conflict with those of others. The wants of men have been supposed by various theologies to conflict with those of the tribal god. If the conflict is within a person, the conflicting wants may be overruled by the prudence, reason, or conscience of the person. If the conflict is between persons, law, custom, or public opinion may compromise or coerce the parties.

Various mechanisms have been supposed to exist in man to help him to choose the right, when the conflict is between a right and a wrong. A favorite doctrine of philosophical moralists has been that the right was ordered by natural or divine law, revealed to man by his reason, conscience producing in him guilt and remorse. Freud invented a Super Ego to do this.

The science of psychology finds no identifiable realities corresponding to Ids, Ego, Super Ego, evil spirits, conscience, spiritual nature, but rather continuous gradations from unorganized to organized, bad to good, carnal to spiritual, anti-social to socialized, prudential to conscientious. Neither psychology nor anthropology has confidence in conscience as a judge which settles conflicts within a man or between men. Men's consciences seem rather the products of their careers and the

154

representatives of tribal prejudices. The sciences of man are suspicious of philosophies and theologies of values, but deeply interested in the facts of valuation.

Judgments About Values

Astronomy, physics, and physiography are rarely distracted from their inquiries concerning what is and what will happen by questions of what is desirable. But psychologists cannot easily avoid good and bad. In fact, psychological scales for abilities are often scales of merit, rather than mere amount; and certain wants, as for beauty, truth, or justice, are distinguished as "higher" or "nobler."

Just where psychology leaves off and ethics begins is of no consequence for our purpose, which is to get and report facts and principles regardless of where they should be classified.

The first important fact is that all things which can be experienced or thought of by man can be valued by him. Situations are valued; sunshine is in general better than inky darkness; sweets are better than intense bitters. Responses are valued; chewing is better than hiccuping; rhythmic dancing is better than writhing. Persons are valued; Jane Addams and Madame Curie were better than the average woman. Abilities and proclivities are valued; honesty is better than thievery; much intelligence is better than little. Wants are valued; a passion for justice is better than a passion for mastery. Objects are valued; an ounce of gold is better than an ounce of sand, even if the prices were the same. Values to men may approximate a neutral zone between good and bad. But the number of things which are really neither good nor bad in the slightest degree is small.

A second important fact is that judgments of values antedate judgments of existence or "mere fact". Such judgments as "That is good to lie on" or "It is good to run away from that," are more fundamental than such as "That is black" or "This is longer than that." The latter are the servants of the former.

A third important fact about human valuations is that they usually refer to and depend upon satisfactions and annoyances, desires for and against. Things are good because God wants them, or men want them, or would want them if they were wise. A man's judgment of a value is, obviously, not the same as his judgment that he wants it. It is rather a judgment that he approves it, or ought to esteem it. So the reader may want to smoke another cigar, but disapprove that act. But moral and prudential judgments are in the end justified by wants.

Serious students judge values by their consequences or their affiliations. The majority want to see people happy rather than miserable. The moralist (and each of us, also) has a rough schedule of persons, and perhaps deities, whom he esteems; wearing clothes, avoiding cannibalism, and being loyal to the government are rated as good, partly because these esteemed persons are rarely nudists, cannibals, or traitors.

In assigning values on the basis of consequences, we attach various weights to the consequences for ourselves, our friends, white men, black men, and yellow men, sane, insane, and idiotic men, dogs or snakes, living men, the spirits of dead men, and men yet to be, the God of our fathers and other Gods.

We can choose whose satisfactions we shall give weight to, and what sort of persons we shall esteem; the two amount to essentially the same. But if sane and intelligent, we rarely attach value to something which makes no difference, directly or indirectly, to the satisfactions and annoyances of any sentient being. When certain moralists and theorists assert that certain qualities and acts have an absolute, intrinsic value regardless of any satisfaction or annoyance to any sentient being, they are probably confused by analogies or verbal subtleties. It can be observed that the qualities and acts alleged to be thus justified by their mere nature are easily justifiable as ministrants to real desires and aversions. When the plain man values certain qualities as intrinsically noble or beautiful, though he can see no good that they do and does not regard them as more characteristic of God and good people than of the Devil and bad people, he usually is accepting at second-hand a valuation which did originate in an expectation of good consequences or good affiliations. Thus when I regard a painting by Picasso as a better gift to the world than one by Watts, I am reflecting a valuation of artists; those who made it got more satisfaction from Picasso and were confident that a wise God of art would also.

Values are rarely transcendental, beyond explanation in terms of wants, but they are often hard to agree upon. Judgments about values are obviously not *just* like judgments about time, distance, volume, mass, temperature, dreams, knowledge. The actual values attached by even the most expert and rigorous seem to be more arbitrary, more dependent on prejudice, than most facts concerning mere existence.

Much of it is due to the fact that there is a conditional factor at the very basis of values in that what will satisfy and annoy John Smith and the God he worships is in each case a brute fact depending upon their natures. But facts about values are in this respect no more arbitrary than facts about diseases, hormones, customs, or beliefs. The action of each of them depends upon the nature of the organism on which it acts.

There is a further element in the process of weighting satisfactions. The saint may weight the satisfactions of any other Christian as equal to his own, but the average man does not. The abstract thinker may give substantial weight to the satisfactions of the human species in A.D. 3000, but these vanish in the valuations of most of us. Habits and attitudes acquired in ordinary life are hard to exclude when one tries to judge impartially. It does not, however, make valuation futile. If a hundred moralists set values upon the courses of conduct which a given person in a given situation might pursue, there would be very substantial agreement; if every ignorant person accepted the valuations of this hundred, the world as a whole would profit.

If we knew the exact difference which any event made to the satisfactions and annoyances of all sentient beings, and agreed about the weights to attach to these, we could determine values in the same sense that we can determine the probable age of life upon the earth. But our agreement upon values would not be forced by reality as is our agreement upon the diameter of the sun. It would be attained in part by compromise and pressure and will still be dependent on the states of mind of persons, changing if different men take their places. A science of values will not be *just* like the sciences of atoms, digestion, diseases, abilities, wants, or communities. But it will be true and useful in its own way.

The concrete valuations of reputable transcendental systems of valuations are in so close agreement with any reputable scientific system of weighting wants that it is not necessary to argue about them. When philosophers seem to assert that qualities and acts have value regardless of any satisfaction to anybody, their inferences about goods and bads commonly agree very closely with what any well-informed and benevolent trustee for the human species would decide on factual grounds. The commonest cases of alleged absolute values are truth, beauty, the perfection of human powers, and the will of God.

Truth is a pure good. Anyone can possess it at no cost to any one else, and often to their enrichment; an increase in the amount of it possessed by any individual, is an aid in the satisfaction of other wants and interferes with none of them. Whatever is in essential conflict with it is bad.

Beauty (in the sense of that which causes unselfish, impersonal, and noble enjoyment) also ranks very high in any reasonable scheme of values. Creating and enjoying truth and beauty are samples of the class of satisfiers which involve positive satisfactions for some without sub-traction from, and often with addition to, those of others. Enjoyment of the happiness of others is a third, and good health is a fourth.

The doctrine that the perfection of human powers furnishes a general rule for valuation was probably invented because of the belief that there must be some one adequate universal criterion, and the fact that to be the best of a certain sort is very often good. Since some powers, such as to defraud, terrify and torment, are obviously better restrained than devel-oped, the limitation "harmonious" is often inserted.

The will of God, whether the personal God of various religious systems or the Absolute power responsible for the universe in various philosophies, is unknown to science. Descriptions of it vary from items repugnant to both good sense and common decency to items which have supported some of the most beneficial activities of mankind. The historic religions are admittedly projections of man's own ideals, and the ethics of absolutist philosophical systems are disappointingly barren in the settle-ment of the values of actual experience and conduct. The whole matter seems most reasonably treated by assigning to the wants of whatever supernatural beings one believes to exist, whatever weights seem reason-able, along with the wants of the natural beings which science estimates by systematic study.

We have the possibility and desirability of a natural science of values, which will progress from the best present opinions about what is good and what is bad by studying the consequences for the satisfaction of wants present and future. This science will also study affiliations, using the general theorem that what is affiliated with things known to be good (or bad) will probably be good (or bad).

Much of the work done in the sciences of man concerns facts of mere existence with no reference to their values.[1] It is possible to argue that this is proper and that all statements about values should be relegated to a separate science of ethics, or to the common-sense judgments of men. But it is foolish to erect barriers between the study of biology and the study of health, between the study of poverty and of its goods and evils, when the barriers do not improve progress on either side.

The notion that the physical and natural sciences have rigorously excluded valuation has been exaggerated. Scientific work is directed more by curiosity than by compassion; but it is not antagonistic to it. The

---

[1] This discussion is limited to a factual science of the consequences to the wants, satisfactions and discomforts of sentient beings. The reader who wishes to know the general body of philosophical opinion about valuation might read *The General Theory of Value*, by R. B. Perry ['26]. *Comparative Value and Human Behavior*, by Joseph Mayer ['36], and *Economic Motives*, by Z. C. Dickinson ['22].

astronomer or paleontologist is never a mere observer or analyst: the stars and fossils are his playthings, or his tools to construct an hypothesis, or the forces by which in creating truth he hopes to create a better world. Usually they are all of these.

The natural sciences have not become scientific by eschewing valuation. They have no more hesitation in stating that morphine does good by stopping pain and may do harm by forming a drug-habit than in stating its chemical composition or its derivation from the poppy. They are as ready to learn and teach that sunshine is good for children as that unprotected steel will rust. Students of man should do at least as much. If they have proved that monogamy is better for the present generation in Europe than polygamy they should consider that fact as much a part of science as the fact that x percent of marriages now end in divorce.

In the sciences of man it is possible to separate certain judgments which are valid regardless of what values are set. 2 and 2 are 4; the earth will revolve around the sun; most children enjoy sweet tastes—these are independent of any valuations (except the preference for truth rather than error). In another class we may put judgments of value with their assumptions explicit such as, "If you prefer the comfort of people to their misery, it is better not to put typhoid germs in their milk." In still another class we may put judgments of value whose assumptions are left to be inferred, such as, "It is better to be temperate with alcohol than to get intoxicated frequently." "It is better to be very abstemious than to be merely temperate." The advantages of such separations are obvious, but they do not require that the sciences of man should turn over all in the third class to experts in ethics. On the contrary it is desirable that experts in the consequences of behavior should have influence in deciding the values of any acts.

Science will begin modestly. Suppose that it is the values of municipal ownership of gas works, or of a certain parole system. Science would begin with the facts and opinions of able engineers, city managers, and business men, of able penologists, educators, and social workers.

Two inferior procedures may be mentioned. One is to try to discover what God's will is, as revealed by holy books, oracles, official heads of churches. The second is to put it to a vote of all citizens, each being given equal weight. Whatever merits these procedures may have, they will not be used by science. Science will be democratic not in form but in spirit by choosing men as intelligent, wise, and impartial as may be and trusting them to decide as best they can what the "true" values are.

A science of values tries to make use of the insights of the sages and seers of the past and present, but it is forewarned against their prejudices and certain inferior methods of deriving values. It does not rely upon revelations, marvelous events, and mental eccentricities. Science expects truths about values to be *worked out* in the same general ways by which truths of mathematics, physics, geology, and anthropology, have been worked out. There will be a few accidental discoveries, but science attaches relatively little importance to having new ideas about morals and values and much importance to the discovery of ways and means of testing and verifying them.

Efforts to devise general theories of the good and the beautiful or of what men ought not to enjoy have been unsatisfactory to philosophers as a whole, and rather mystifying or empty to men of science. Nor do they seem to profit by the general advancement of knowledge; Aristotle's solutions seem as good as Hegel's. In cases where such ideas concern matters of observable fact, the observations and experiments of working scientists have often disproved brilliant conjectures.

Just what is the important and operative distinction between judgments of worth and judgments of existence? The naturalist's answer is that judgments of value are simply one sort of judgments of fact, distinguished from the rest by two characteristics: they concern consequences, and these are consequences to the wants of sentient beings. If the occurrence of X can have no influence on the satisfaction or discomfort of anyone (present or future), X has no value, is neither desirable nor undesirable.

Competent students judge the existence of things by observations of them; they judge the values of things by observations of their consequences. Values appear in the world when certain forms of preference appear, when certain animals like or dislike, are contented or unhappy. They apparently precede learning and knowledge. Chicks or rats are indeed in a sense more confirmed moralists than civilized men; they pursue what is good, fit, and proper to their minds with a wholehearted devotion.

In civilized man there are many scales of merit. One thing may have a score of different positive values and a dozen negative ones. The inborn values of sweet tastes, exercise after rest, courtship and love, etc., are worked over into an enormous structure by man-made forces. Man acquires multifarious customs and traditions about values. Opinions about values become diverse and conflicting.

The Analysis of Consequences

The total effect of an event, institution, etc. may be to produce a clear balance of satisfaction of good wants of good persons, but it may include some bad consequences. By analysis some of the elements which are responsible for the bad consequences may be detected and a still greater balance of good obtained. Similarly a thing may be clearly bad on the whole but include some precious elements.

As an illustration of many good with some bad consequences consider the organization of teachers. Graham Wallas wrote ['21, p. 144]:

> Anyone ... who has studied the position of English teachers for the last century, must recognize the enormous benefits which the teachers and the community have gained from the recent growth of professional organization. The private school 'usher,' clinging to the rags of his gentility with the wages ... of a footman has a chance of becoming a man when he joins the Association of Assistant Masters; the sweated schoolmistresses have successfully claimed the wages of a skilled occupation; some 'public school' masters have been drawn out of their atmosphere of elderly boyhood; the whole profession has gained in intellectual independence.... But the vocational organization of teachers brings with it the same dangers as the organization of other vocations.... Teachers, like bricklayers, cling with passionate loyalty to their existing methods of work; they personify the subjects ... which they teach and the institutions in which they teach, and stimulate with regard to them their primitive instincts of corporate defense.

Suppose that the founders of the teachers' association had written into its constitution, as one of its main aims, the improvement of methods of teaching by research and experimentation, had charged a regular committee to work on this, and had set aside a certain percentage of the dues for it. It would be desirable for somebody to study the different organizations of professional workers in various countries to discover what sorts of organization have produced what sorts of consequences.

The history of experiments in government, education, charity, the treatment of criminals and other social changes includes many which had the desirable consequences which were claimed for them but had also other consequences (usually unexpected) which caused the change to fall into disrepute and be abandoned. The monitorial system of instruction of Lancaster and Bell, solitary confinement for criminals, and Puritanism are more or less apposite illustrations.

Affiliations

If knowledge of consequences is lacking it is better to trust what is affiliated with good things than to merely guess. I conjecture that a custom, law, or institution, that is beneficial by attaining the purpose it was designed to attain, is likely to have more beneficial than harmful by-products, though there are notable contrary cases.

A general case of affiliation is that of good and bad intentions. The value of either depends upon the correlation of intentions with acts. Bad intentions are regarded as bad on the assumption that if good comes from them it is by mishap. If there is a high positive correlation between what men seek to produce and what they do produce, and a low correlation between our estimates of what they are producing and what they really do produce, we may reach truer valuations by considering intent as well as achievement or even instead of it. But the best procedure is obviously to attain more accurate and adequate estimates of the achievements themselves. Incompetent demagogues easily put on an appearance of aiming at valuable ends. Any one of us, lacking some small but vital item of knowledge, may do enormous harm with the best will in the world. So a kindly visitor of the sick may spread disease through a community and a benevolent missionary may undermine the morality and happiness of a heathen tribe.

From correlations or affiliations we may argue that the practices of the intelligent, humane, and cooperative are likely to be better than the practices of the dull, selfish, and trouble-making. Also that the practices of healthy and virtuous cities are likely to be better than those of communities conspicuous for disease, misery, and vice, even though no superiority in consequences can be demonstrated. So we argue that it is better to read Robert Louis Stevenson than B. E. Stevenson, to listen to Beethoven than to Charlie McCarthy, to wash our bodies daily rather than weekly, to incarcerate imbeciles rather than drown them.

This argument from correlation gives some support to practices which seem to have nothing but custom in their favor, but which are the customs of superior persons and communities oftener than of inferior. Still the argument should be replaced by facts about consequences. From little matters like the alleged superiority of linen over oilcloth for the table and of collars over no collars, to great matters like trial by jury and representative government, the affiliations of the practices are not enough to know.

If all the consequences of an act were known to the smallest detail and for the entire universe, there would still be individual differences among men in the values credited to that act. Some of these differences would be due to attaching different weights to consequences. One judge may assign no weight to the alleged satisfactions of angels because he does not believe that such exist. Another may assign very little weight to the wants of dead people, considering that if they have any they should be satisfied by what benefits the living. Another may scrupulously regard the interests of all living things. Wise and foolish, old and young, men and women, blind and seeing, all tend to adopt schemes of weights under the influence of their respective natures.

Science tries to assign such weights, its main criterion always being the consequences. If the satisfaction of a certain want in A bids fair to cause great benefit to all men, whereas the satisfaction of the same want in B bids fair to cause little, it will weight A's wants more heavily. Science will do well to weight the wants of the men of today above the same wants in men of 2050, unless it has reason to suppose that the latter will be better men for there may be no men in 2050 or they may lack the want in question. Science will, however, give far more weight to future men than statesmen or most philanthropists have done.

Ethics, politics, and philanthropy have been guilty of neglecting individual differences, partly because of prejudices in favor of the equality of man. No egalitarian system of weights can be just or wise. More weight should be given to the wants of superior men than to the wants of inferior men. What able men want is much more likely to be better for their community or race or the world than what stupid men want. Providing for their wants will presumably enable them to do more of what will improve the world.

It is of special importance to attach great weight to the wants of those individuals who have eminent abilities in the impersonal activities of art, science, and the management of men. What such persons want will be largely time and freedom and conditions enabling them to do their best. It seems possible that the ruthlessness of some men of genius in business and government would have been reduced if they had been *given* power more and been less required to extort it by force. The world's greatest folly has been its treatment of those who are most superior. One good clue to what they need is what they themselves desire.

Systems of Weights

In default of anything better, I present a rough scheme of the weights which determine my own judgments, to illustrate the general theory and practice of weighting according to the nature and status of the person who has it, and also to expose the personal equation which may operate in later chapters. In this scheme 100 is used as the ordinary weight attached to a living person.

My weights for the unborn grade down in a curve such that a person 200 years from now has half the normal weight, one 400 years from now has a quarter, one 600 years an eighth, and so on.

Zero weight is attached to the satisfactions of the spirits of the dead.

This does not relieve us from the duties of gratitude to the dead, or of fulfilling whatever agreements were made with them when they were alive, but the performance of these is considered as a matter of decency and self-respect in us rather than a favor to them. My weights for the dead are far less than most societies have made; theirs may, however, conceal expectations of help or harm from the dead, and so be made in the interest of the living.

A weight averaging about one five-hundredth that for a man is attached to the satisfaction of a useful domestic animal or pet, a variation up and down for special merit and deficiency. Since we manage the lives of these animals in our interest, we have a special responsibility for them. A weight averaging about one ten-thousandth that for a man is attached to the satisfaction of other animals capable of feeling. This recognizes the value of conscious life wherever it is found, and a certain responsibility to creatures less powerful. But it assumes that in general each animal species must take care of itself, avoids undue deprivation of human beings, and outlaws perverse sentimentalities.

Any person's wants receive weight according to his known or esti- mated score in a composite of intelligence and other desirable abilities. The ordinary man counting as 100, a man of the average ability of Newton, Pasteur, Darwin, Dante, Milton, Bach, Leonardo da Vinci, and Rembrandt will count as 2000, and a vegetative idiot as about 1.[1]

Any person's wants also receive weight according to his known or estimated score in a composite of traits which indicate that his life will be directed toward the welfare of mankind. A plus will be added up to 500 for the average of, say, Jane Addams, Madame Curie, Sidney and Beatrice Webb, and Pasteur. An amount will be subtracted ranging from zero to something like 200 for perverted monsters of meanness and cruelty. Credits plus and minus are given for special good sense and balance on the one hand and for instability and insanities on the other.

A person's credit will vary from birth to death because of the variations in his behavior which go with mental growth, maturity, and old age. In addition I add ten points of weight for ages 0 to 3, eight points for ages 4 to 6, six points for ages 7 to 9, four points for ages 10 to 12, and two points for ages 13 to 15 on the ground that the younger children are, the more innocent they are and the less able to make their wants understood and gratified.

No difference in weight is attached to one or the other sex, or to race or family, to wealth, or to creed. But twenty-five percent of the plus or

[1] The idiot's happiness will, however, be provided for better than this ratio suggests: for the wants of his parents for him will have their proper weight also.

minus difference of his parents' average weight from 100 is combined with each child's intrinsic credit until the age of twenty-five. After that age he derives weight only from his own merits and defects.

I have in mind other provisions for attaching weight to persons' satisfactions according to the burden they carry (as in the case of pregnant women), the undeserved misfortunes they suffer, and other features of their natures, ideals, achievements, and sufferings. But these may be left undescribed.

Tracing Consequences

Some events and acts are almost pure goods. The discovery of truth by a man of science, the painting of a beautiful picture,—such make the creator happy and enrich mankind. Some, like gnawing envy, sheer malevolence, or fear of bad luck, are almost pure bads, making the person who has them miserable, ineffective, and a nuisance. At these extremes there is no difficulty, and no need of estimating weights.

Going in further from the extremes, activities which are "productive" in the ordinary senses of these words and which exhibit Veblen's "workmanship" are presumptively good because they at least aim to produce satisfaction in all concerned. The "selfish" activities, as in ordinary eating and drinking, ownership, self-adornment, and the use of the services of others, are under a certain suspicion, because the satisfying consequences to the person indulging in them are commonly at some cost to others. In a court of morals he may have to justify them by the secondary consequences which come from his use of them.

We thus come to the edge of an enormous area of debatable conduct, including much of what most men do, some of what the best and the worst men do, where valuation requires careful tracing of consequences and assignment of weights. By sufficient ingenuity, unsatisfied wants may be fulfilled and conflicting wants may be harmonized at no cost to anybody. The simplest case is where A wants x, and our ingenuity consists in showing him how to get it at no cost (or even a gain) of y also. Education and hygiene furnish many cases. A very important case is where A wants x which he has not and wants to get rid of y, whereas B wants to have y and get rid of x. The inventions of barter, money, and trade remove the difficulty. Consider what a blessing it would be if undesired bodily and mental traits could be exchanged in this way between the fat and the thin, the over-confident and the over-cautious, the excitable and the apathetic!

A direct cause of satisfaction is better than an indirect, other things being equal, things good in themselves being better than instrumental goods. The reason is, of course, that the attainment of a consequence is better than even the best promise of it. Definite, specified consequences are better than vague general consequences. Assured rights to think what is true, say what is true, buy what you can pay for, are better than a promise of "liberty."

A great temptation in valuation is to cherish doctrines that make us contented with ourselves, and to blame their errors and failures upon something else. The national prohibition of alcohol did not have the consequences which millions of people expected who worked to attain it; who knows what its consequences would have been if the work that attained it had been quadrupled to secure its enforcement? Preventives against syphilis and gonorrhea were deplored as a good that would do great harm by causing unlimited male lust; the effect was inappreciable. Coeducation was viewed as a sure stimulus to both sensual and romantic love, but its actual consequences seem to have been the opposite. Among all the consequences, beneficial and ruinous, which were expected from the granting of votes to women, which were real? People follow the unconscious logic of hope and fear in estimating consequences, perhaps because they feel that good intentions are the important requirements!

People also naïvely expect that everything will stay the same except what is changed by direct action upon it. Nine persons out of ten assume that the general features of civilization which are stable in their experience will remain so. Roads, schools, policemen, houses, payment for work, a chance to buy what you want if you have the price, and a hundred other commonplaces of our social order will continue like the sunshine or rain. To think anything else is almost a psychological impossibility for the ordinary man. He has no more fear that any act of his will stop railroad trains from running than that it will stop the sun from shining. Laying a tax on incomes is to him like digging a ditch that diverts the rain from one place to another. He does not have the slightest fear that it will have any effect on the amount of income. To do so he must reason against habit and experience, and only exceptional minds do that.

In tracing the consequences of ideas, acts, laws, inventions, etc., both the biological and the social sciences have somewhat neglected the inner or mental wants of men. Nourishing foods, hygienic housing, medical care, relief from bodily pain have, quite naturally, been emphasized. But inner peace, contentment, a sense of personal worth, surety of friendship and affection, the absence of fear, the presence of a good conscience, and other states of mind are also real and important.

Many features in religions and other folkways which seem undesirable to us did have the merit of satisfying some of these deep inner needs. If we abandon such we should replace them by something true and just which gives equal comfort, dignity and flavor to the inner lives of men. Doubtless it is better to be a dissatisfied Socrates than a satisfied pig; but also it is worse to be a dissatisfied coolie than a satisfied coolie. Most discontent is not divine. Not once in ten thousand times will becoming dissatisfied cause a coolie to become a Socrates.

The beginnings of Ethics as a natural science have not got so far as to produce a system of valuations to compare with the present customary valuations of Western civilization or any other. So I must resort to a notation which seem to me to be probably justified by what is now known about consequences. For one person to do this is unscientific, not to say foolish, except that it may stimulate investigation, and that the merits of the method may outweigh the weaknesses of my ignorance.

The Value of the Civilizations of the Past

Many thinkers today have a bias toward expecting that any plausible change will be for the better. This disvaluation of the past is not confined to eccentric, disappointed, and doctrinaire persons. We may agree that the triumphs of civilization outside the physical and biological sciences have been dubious and insecure, full of mistakes and inadequacies. The civilizations of the past were at least tolerable by the men living in them, however, and perhaps suited to them in unsuspected ways. The liberal civilization of 1850–1910 had the special merit of being fairly well suited to specially good and able men. It did not so often stone its prophets. It is reasonable, therefore, to attach a positive value to the civilization that has been bequeathed to us, and to require evidence that proposed changes will have beneficial consequences.

Freedom

The familiar arguments for setting a high value upon freedom are strengthened rather than weakened by the consequences of recent governmental interference with them in various parts of the world, so far as these can be appraised impartially. The value would probably be even higher if more scientific criteria could be adopted for the limits which even the most liberal societies have set.

Some dull persons should be supervised in their thinking, any truly free thought on their part being valueless to them and others. The most valuable consequence of freedom of thought for people in general is the product produced by the top tenth of one percent of thinkers. Rather than lose it we tolerate much worthless eccentricity. Rather than stifle or delay it by the tyranny of age and custom we may profitably tolerate and even reward independence, rebellion, and extravagance in young people of great ability.

Two Sorts of Sympathy

Sympathy in the sense of enjoyment of the welfare of others has high value, but in the sense of misery at suffering its value is negative except as it stimulates beneficial acts of relief. This it often does, but relief may be given without it, as by the nurse, physician, or social worker who has had to learn not to feel miserable at pain and distress. By original nature sympathy tends to produce comforting sounds and gestures, physical protection and perhaps gifts, which are often inadequate under the conditions of modern life. The behavior of the nurse, physician, and social worker seems the best general solution,—to help the suffering but without suffering with them.

Race Mixture

Miscegenation has been the object of two extremes of misvaluation. On the one hand, it has been supposed that racial "purity" has some value in itself, and that half-breeds are inevitably inferior. On the other hand it has been supposed that miscegenation has some value by its introduction of new blood. The truth is that whether the genetic consequences are good or bad depends entirely upon what genes enter into the mixture. Since unit characters are small and multiple for most features of intellect and character, the average hereditary status of the half-breed in these is likely to be midway between the two parental strains. Since the mating of the two stocks brings in a greater variety of genes, the half-breeds are likely to vary more widely than either parental stock, unless some of the genes neutralize each other.

On Man's Place in the Universe

Various moral lessons have been drawn from the fact that man and his works are a very late and small part of a long and extensive development of life on a planet that is a very tiny part of a universe. One lesson is that man should not expect the universe to be specially mindful of him. This is undoubtedly a reasonable and healthy view, in the sense that weeds will not commit suicide to please us and meteors will not avoid dwelling houses. But at least a *modus vivendi* does exist between man and the universe, since he is a part of it and is getting on well in it to date.

A second moral lesson is that man should consider his life and works an unimportant thing in comparison with the whole business of the universe. This suggestion seems likely to have undesirable consequences. Shall the painter throw down his brushes because there are probably a thousand better painters elsewhere? Should men temper their pride at discoveries, inventions, masterpieces, and reforms by the solemn thought that it is all being done better in a billion or more other planets? Whatever the bad points of life on this planet may be, it is not unimportant unless everything is. And it is exceedingly bad policy to teach man that his work is not important—to man. That is bad for his mental health, happiness, and achievement.

On the Great Value of Certain Small Social Changes

The time saved by the change from fire-places, wood, and tinder to stoves, matches, and modern fuels is doubtless enough to cover a year's schooling for everybody. Small physical changes have enormous consequences when they operate nearly all the time for nearly all people. The same may be expected of small psychological and social changes. If the satisfaction of men at the welfare of others could be shifted upward by one third of its range, the sight of any child happily at play would, I estimate, produce about as much satisfaction as the sight of one's own child happily at play does now. Our pleasure at the welfare of men of other races and creeds would as a rule triumph over our prejudices against them. In the sciences of man it is folly to disdain small items of fact about him and his institutions.

On Repetitive Work in Factories

Repetitive work in factories is commonly supposed by writers about labor and welfare to have bad consequences for body, mind, and morals. This may be partly a conclusion due to the dislike of such writers for everything about factories from their appearance to their owners: the repetitive work of the agricultural laborer is much less often decried. But most of the criticism is sincere. When Lewis Mumford writes that "uniformity of performance in human beings, pushed beyond a certain point, deadens initiative and lowers the whole tone of the organism" ['34,

p. 278], he really thinks so. What are the real consequences of such repetitive work as is done in factories for any given sort of person? How do the real consequences of such repetitive work compare with the work which they would otherwise do?

Repetitive activity which does not require close attention may "deaden initiative," but it does not "lower the whole tone of the organism." On the contrary, it is rather restful, so that walking or the "sedentary routine" of knitting is a pleasure and recreation for many.

Repetitive activity which *does* require close attention and prevents a person from doing anything else at the time is unpleasant because of the feelings of strain at the time and of fatigue after, but it has the great merit of being free from anxiety and worry. Changing activities with their emergencies, new difficulties, and risks of failure are more annoying, fatiguing, and nerve-wracking for most persons than repetitive activities where one has mastery. Worry is in general much more wearing on the organism than any sort of work.

Repetitive activity tends to be monotonous. We may contrast the work of a man in the automobile assembly line with that of a taxi driver. If the former craves excitement he must get it in his leisure time. The amount needed for general mental health is probably small, the function of excitement in nature being to prepare the body for violent muscular action. By nature we do not fight in order to get a pleasant excitement, but become excited when there is need to fight. There is little need for it in a pastoral, agricultural, or industrial life, and a psychologist views the life of gamblers and speculators with more alarm than that of repetitive factory workers.

The consequences of repetitive factory work also vary with the nature of the worker. My friend Sullivan, an elevator man, got more satisfaction of achievement, mastery, excitement, pride, and sense of duties well done from running his elevator, I think, than I did from my work as a psychologist. Doubtless most writers about labor would be miserable if compelled to do repetitive factory work for a living, but most factory workers would be miserable if compelled to study, teach, and write for a living.

If the repetitive workers were not in factories they would in general be unskilled outdoor laborers, farmers' helpers, domestic servants, proprietors of one-man farms, or wives of such. The sorts of persons who in medieval times were skilled craftsmen making clothes, jewelry, and cathedrals, or even designing these, are not doing repetitive factory work today. They are surgeons, dentists, engineers, inventors, surveyors, or skilled craftsmen as before. The present incumbents of posts at repetitive factory work have chosen it in preference to such work as is available for them. Doubtless many of them have chosen unwisely. The owner of a one-man farm may do well to stay on it if he does not mind isolation, likes domestic animals, cannot endure taking orders, and dislikes indoor work. But his son, who wants sociability, likes machinery, is miserable at having no cash to spend, and is in love with a girl who has gone to the city is probably wise to choose the assembly line. It is likely that the majority of those who have chosen factory work in preference to what else the world offered them do not regret their choice and would make it again.

Neither the writers of the past, nor the moralists of the present can dictate values. Nobody is compelled to consult or obey them. The valuations made by individuals or implied by their behavior are, however, more or less sensitive to the valuations recommended by the thought and customs of the times, including the thoughts of ethical theorists and literary enthusiasts. The Bible does influence men, though very few rich men sell all they have and give the proceeds to the poor, and perhaps no Christian has ever loved his neighbor, the blatant atheist, quite as himself.

The considerations of this chapter will, I hope, not only guide valuations to a better adaptation to reality, but also appeal to what philosophers call reason, and theologians the divine element in man, which acts in the interest of all the good in all men.

Chapter 11

Living by Science

Many humanists, statesmen, and men of affairs distrust the methods of science, thinking that science makes men mere puppets in a fatalistic world. Some think that the world of science is a sort of squirrel cage, enormously complicated but fundamentally repetitive; such a world seems to them objectionable and false. Some find little or no room in science for teleological forces, in the sense of powers of human purposes to control events; since their daily business consists largely in trying to control events, they resent doctrines which seem to assert that they are deluding themselves.

If thorough-going use of science means a denial of human freedom, progress, and power, much of this book is misleading. If, on the contrary, it can be shown that the views described above are caused by misapprehensions and errors, we shall be rid of a serious barrier to the advancement of science for welfare.

It is true that science deals mainly with oft repeated events. The movements of masses, the pulls of lines of electric force, and the growth of plants from seeds are the subjects of its ordinary triumphs. Indeed it searches for repetition and rejoices when it finds it. But science would not sacrifice reality to get it into repetitive form. Astronomers are studying the movement of the stellar universe as a whole as well as the revolutions of satellites around their suns. Biologists are concerned not only with events that occur in cells billions of billions of times, but also in the evolution of the vertebrates from invertebrates which, to the best of our knowledge, never will occur again.

Science does not destroy anything by finding out what elements compose it. Alcohol loses nothing of its peculiar individuality by knowledge that it is made out of the same elements that make sugar. Dante is no less Dante by being made of protoplasm. Moreover, science itself adds novelties to the world at the same time that it finds repetitions in it. By "reducing" a host of natural events to certain simple electromagnetic repetitions, it creates dynamos, transformers, self-starters, trolley cars, refrigerators, razorless razors. By "reducing" the facts of hybrid plants to the simple law of Mendel, it has created new flowers of surpassing beauty.

Nobody need feel that he is just one of a million squirrels treading a well-worn path in a gigantic squirrel cage. The number of persons duplicating him as an adult is probably less than five in a million million. If he travels exactly the same path that any other person has traveled since the world began, it is by his choice.

For the objection against science that it leaves human ideals powerless, science is in part to blame. Physiology and psychology have neglected human purposes in comparison with sensori-motor mechanisms. Their standard treatises gave over ten times as much attention to how man's muscles or memories work as to how his purposes work. Human purposes exercise a control over human behavior minute by minute and in what one thinks as well as what he does. The brain has the power to modify itself in favor of the person's purposes, and is busily engaged in doing so. Psychology teaches that human purposes control events which are modifiable connections in the brain, which the confirming reaction can reach and reinforce. Indirectly they determine what ideas and acts he shall repeat, what habits he shall form, and consequently how he shall influence the things and persons in his environment. What science does to the freedom of the will, the creative elements in human life, and the control of events by human purposes is not to deny or limit them, but to show how they exist and operate in the natural world of reality.

In proportion as we treat the world as regular and resistant to outside influences we influence it. If science in the next hundred years should describe the ways of human nature and behavior as accurately as it has by now described the planets and stars, every immutable "law" of human physiology and psychology would turn into an instrument to change human life. By the same token, if, by science, I could prophesy exactly what I would think, feel, or do in every conceivable situation that life could offer, and knew that my thoughts, feelings, and actions were as inevitable as the pull of the magnet on steel, I would thereby enormously increase my power to change my fate. In Marett's fine words, "Freedom is the preperception of destiny." Every fact which science takes from the realm of fortuity, miracle, and caprice, and puts under the rule of the regular ways of nature, means one more addition to control over nature. The more the world is determined, the more man can work his will upon it.

Men and women who are disturbed because the march of science seems to reduce the world to a mere machine, have thought that one must choose between science and freedom. Science does not necessitate fatalism, however. The uniformity of nature is consistent with changes in nature made by human thought and action. This is possible because science is a part of nature, because knowledge is a natural force, because human ideas, wants, and purposes are part of the stream of natural events. Your consideration of whether to say Yes or No in certain situations is an event in nature. Your "No" of yesterday may have changed the world by the death of a prisoner whom you refused to pardon, and your "Yes" of today may have changed you from a bachelor to a husband and been a link in a chain of causation resulting in the birth of a child who in 1983 will discover a cure for cancer.[1]

The essential facts are as follows: The course of nature is partly cyclical, as in the movements of the planets or the turn of a motor, and partly creative, as in the development of a new species of animals, or the construction of the Panama Canal. Parts of the world change other parts. Changes in the moon cause changes in the tides; the birth of a baby changes the habits of a household. Notable among changes are those initiated by changes in human brains. To them are due all the material paraphernalia of civilization—on the whole serviceable in satisfying human wants. Those which are outcomes of scientific observation and inference have been specially successful in satisfying human wants. They operate by changing man's own behavior better to obtain satisfaction from the rest of nature, and by changing the rest of nature into forms that suit man's needs better.

If the world is a great self-contained machine whose operation no god or devil can alter, it is a peculiar sort of machine which has produced the

---

[1] Professor A. B. Wolfe wrote, "One may be a determinist and a behaviorist and still not a fatalist. . . . The future of society and the fate of human welfare will be determined. in part at least, through human attitudes, human motives, and human intelligence. . . . Will, attitudes, are themselves a part of the causal nexus of things." |'31, p. 221|

Divine Comedy, Paradise Lost, Beethoven's symphonies, and all the truth, goodness, and beauty that man knows. The zest of life does not consist in fortuity and ignorance of what will happen. It would not be increased if days and nights come by chance like the red and black of a roulette series.

The freedom of the will means different things, some of which are of no consequence whatever to human welfare, and some of which are highly undesirable. It sometimes means simply that there is a small margin of sheer chance in the universe, so that electrons might vary slightly one from another in unpredictable ways, but the average behavior of any atom composed of them might be perfectly regular and dependable. The doctrines of theology and of intelligent people are wisely not concerned with margins of unpredictability, but with the freedom of a person from domination by circumstances. Others would mean by the freedom of the will the power of a man's deeper self to direct his life with or against the pull of external influences, superficial motives, or casual enticements. "I am the captain of my fate, I am the master of my soul." Nothing in science denies this. On the contrary, the more fully man knows the ways of nature, including human nature, the better able will his deeper self be to rule the external, casual, and superficial.

PART II
SPECIAL FACTS, PRINCIPLES, AND APPLICATIONS

Chapter 12
Human Nature and Philanthropy

The term philanthropy is out of fashion, but I retain it in order to cover the broad problems of human welfare as well as the narrower problems of alleviating and preventing poverty, delinquency, and other social ills. Welfare work is one of the main goals of man at the present time. Good government is supposed to be in the interest of the governed. The law is concerned largely with "social legislation." Economics is becoming more a science of using natural resources, labor, and capital to maximize welfare.

The Good Life

Let the reader regard himself as a scientific trustee for the human species, making a rough bill of specifications which (1) will include the satisfactions possible for men today without imperiling the satisfactions of other men now or in the future, (2) will approximate to a reasonable compromise among wants, (3) would be approved by a substantial majority of humans if each were omniscient, chose wisely in his own self interest, and in the interest of others. As a scientific trustee he will avoid putting in items so alien to the original nature of man that they can be realized only with tremendous coercion. He will attach great weight to items which promise to make the social order attractive to the good

179

rather than the bad in men. He will, however, hope to have a social order in which undesirable tendencies are redirected or weakened by disuse. And he will be democratic in the sense that he will consider the wants of every person on their merits, and catholic in the sense that he will try to realize and appreciate the wants of all persons in all lands, creeds, and cultures.

Desirable Provisions to Be Made for Man

1. Maintenance of the inner causes of the joy of living at or above their present average.
2. Food when hungry, and drink when thirsty.
3. A diet that is physiologically adequate.
4. Protection against pain-causing animals.
5. Protection against the causes of disease.
6. Protection or insurance against accidents and disasters for which the person in question is not responsible.
7. Protection against extreme shocks, fear, and strains.
8. Some place where he can rest undisturbed, protected from the elements and from uncongenial men.
9. Enjoyable bodily activity, especially when young.
10. Enjoyable mental activity, including esthetic pleasures.
11. Opportunity for human society.
12. Opportunity for courtship, love, and life with one's mate.
13. Opportunity to care for children and to be kind to human beings and animals.
14. The approval of one's community, or at least the absence of scorn.
15. The approval of one's self, self-respect, the absence of remorse.
16. Opportunity to have friends and affection, if deserving.
17. Opportunity to be a friend and give affection.
18a. Opportunity to exercise power over some persons, things, or ideas, making them do one's will.
18b. Opportunity to serve a worthy master.
19. Membership in organized groups, and the right to participate in activities which are important.
20. Opportunity to compete with one's peers, winning in about 50 percent of the trials.
21. Opportunity to compete with one's past record, and, if deserving, to have the pleasures of achievement.
22. Occasional opportunities for adventure, risk, and danger.
23. Something to be angry at and attack.

24. Protection by society (via customs and government) in what is regarded by the existing moral code as a good life.
25. Freedom to discover and publish verifiable truth.
26. Enjoyment of the happiness of others.

I make no claim that my specifications of a good life are the best possible. They do, I hope, have the merits of being impartial and definite, of fitting human nature better, and of being more easily maintained, than the general run of such recommendations.

It is obvious from the items that the intention is not to provide each and every person with all the items, or each person with an equal amount of each; any such identity would be unjust in view of the individual differences among men. Each person should have a larger provision of certain items that satisfy him more than others would.

Item 1 is of great importance, though the biological sciences must increase their knowledge of these inner causes of enjoyment before government, education, or philanthropy can act intelligently in the matter. If some baleful miracle reduced its level in the population by a substantial amount we should be a sorry collection of neurasthenic, puritanical, weepy grouchers, with suicides an everyday occurrence. If science could give all as much as the most favored one percent now have, shaving oneself, washing dishes, typing letters, milking cows, and teaching school would be quite as much enjoyed as our recreations are now.

This tendency, which we may call Gen. Like, seems to be determined in part by the genes; the Negro races, for example, seem to have more than North Europeans. It is strong in youth, weakens in old age, has extreme ups and downs in the same person, often without any obvious cause.

Item 6 points to the fact that if present-day beliefs take from God the responsibility for floods, pestilences, senility, and the like, our practices should not leave their sufferers to be requited in heaven, but should insure them on earth. A word may be added of the beneficence of coercion, and control. Man's gain from the extermination of yellow fever mosquitoes, from the addition of iodine to his salt, from inoculations against smallpox, from the inspection and treatment of water supplies, probably far outweighs his gain from all the activities of his elected political representatives for the past twenty-five years.

Items 9 and 10 provide for the satisfaction of the tendencies to physical and mental play, vocalization, manipulation, "being a cause," and whatever leads man to jump, climb, hunt, see, hear, tinker, dance, think, write, though no profit is his as the outcome; such will satisfy men unless they have been spoiled by fond parents or commercial stimulation. Productive labor has often provided interesting bodily and mental exercise. The same activity is work for some and play for others.

Item 11 is available without special care on anybody's part. The love life has not been so much prevented as burdened with restrictions, ceremonial observances, and confusion with mere erotic gratifications.

Item 12 might be restated as: "Opportunity for courtship, love, and life with one's mate, or for some better arrangements for love and the production and rearing of offspring when discovered." But on the whole I prefer to leave it. Modern psychiatry favors the more romantic and ideal forms of love between the sexes as the more healthy.

Item 13 does not require any mystical bond between a mother and children. Some good men and women would perhaps be happier in a world devoid of any creatures needing relief, comfort, and consolation; but most would not.

Items 14 and 15 are potent satisfiers whose nature is somewhat misunderstood by moralists and sociologists. Item 15 means what it says, without idealization, and is differently caused in different persons. It need not be logical, moral, or refined; a selfish moron may have it as well as a saint.

The satisfactions of domination and submission are deliberately bracketed as Item 18, to suggest that there need be no conflict between them, because each in its place and to a suitable stimulus is part of the good life for man.

Item 20 recognizes the zest of rivalry and victory, purging the competition of schools, sports, and business from conditions under which the majority are doomed to depressing failure or demoralizing success. A person who wins in 50 percent of the trials may well have in memory the sense of having won in 60 percent or more.

Item 23 will be objectionable to many pacific idealists who do not themselves desire it and think it harmful. They may be right; I hope they are. But on the whole, it probably is better to let men hate poisonous snakes, loathsome diseases, and their human counterparts.

Item 24 is defective in that it leaves the person in advance of his times unprotected in his eccentricities, permits prophets to be stoned, and probably would not have saved Socrates or Jesus from execution. Item 25 would have saved Galileo and will save many a reformer who limits himself to statements which can be verified or disproved by prediction, observation, and experiment.

Item 26 is deliberately limited to the positive side of good will, because I am doubtful of the value of being miserable at the misery of others.

Concessions to Human Weaknesses or Irrationalities   Items 19, 20, 22, and 23 may seem unworthy to intellectualists, for philanthropists should not cater to childish or vulgar tastes. They may be right, but I think that desires for innocent ceremonial, rivalry, and adventure are intrinsically good, and, second, that it is risky to starve them.

Cost   In many cases the better a man's wants are, the less they cost. In many other cases sheer habituation decides whether the costly or the cheap satisfies.

Items 3 and 5 require allotments for research and preventive medicine and hygiene, but what is so spent may be saved in increased health and efficiency.

Item 8 would require the reduction of overcrowding, but many of the refinements we must, as psychologists, admit are not essential to human happiness. Bad housing, misery, disease, and vice are associated, but the causal relations are not clear.

Items 14 to 23 and Item 26 require little expense, being attainable, if at all, chiefly by changed attitudes of men in respect to themselves and their fellow-men, and other forms of social engineering.

Certain Criticisms and Amendments   The worthy satisfactions of religion have not been rejected but the term religion seemed too vague. Items 6, 7, 10, and 13 to 19 specify the satisfactions to which religion (minus superstition and efforts to purchase favors from supernatural agencies) ministers.

For our purpose, it seems that liberty is valuable to men in so far as it means relief from needless pressure to suffer the disliked, and freedom to do what one likes. Our list includes the best fruits of liberty. Such liberty as helps to secure these fruits is all that we should require. Some coercion there must be. Parts of an individual are coercing other parts of him; and until the breed of men is very radically changed, it will be for the common good that some individuals should coerce others. Liberty of religious belief and of conscience, liberty to think and learn, equality of opportunity to those equally deserving, careers open in accordance with merit, freedom from coercion by lies, are specified or assumed by our list.

There is a more special sort of liberty, namely liberty in the sense of self-regulation and freedom of choice. All of us who are oppressed by physiological, financial, moral, and other coercions might hope for a life free from them. Our heavens and Utopias are often glorified vacations. Benevolent reformers often aim to turn the world into a minimum of obedience, work, and responsibility with a maximum of self-expression, play, and entertainment. This is wrong in that it tends to disregard attainability and to regard superficial goods at the expense of more fundamental ones. Men should not be misled into making a fetish of enjoying only what they choose for themselves. If the meat someone orders for you is good, it is folly to poison it by the thought that you wanted fish.

As with liberty, so with fraternity: seek the desirable consequences rather than the thing itself. To have the general good will from all humans will not do the work of actual close friends and kindly neighbors. To have a sense of kinship with all men causes a noble pleasure, but it requires a high degree of abstract ability to keep from becoming mere verbalisms or cheap sentimentalities. What is desired is a good will toward men which will operate vigorously in our thoughts and actions.

Wars between nations are great disasters which man creates for himself. The satisfactions which they produce in the way of group activity, rivalry, adventure, and attack are producible in healthier forms by other means. War is hell, and our trustee should get it outlawed as far and as fast as he can.

The desire for equality may refer to many different desires, satisfiable by different states of affairs. We may conceive states in which all human beings are equal in some one or in all respects. Communities have approximated such in the right to vote, access to various religious privileges, and protection by the courts.

There is no evidence that the genes of man give him either a desire for, or an enjoyment of equality. The craving for an egalitarian society, is, on the contrary, a late product of extreme cultivation. So far as original nature provides anything relevant it provides a logically inconsistent set of tendencies to enjoy being superior, to pity certain sorts of distressed persons, to be kind to certain sorts of weakness, to admire or envy those who are better off, to exult at the downfall of others, especially the mighty. The desire for an equalized world is derived, in superior persons, from pity, kindness, and certain intellectual processes, and, in inferior persons, from envy, self-esteem, and the general tendency to accept any belief which is comforting.

Equality is a false and useless God for philanthropy. Benevolence and mercy are better. Justice is much better. If the world made equality its sole aim after subsistence was provided for, it often could not attain it by any methods short of a disastrous reduction of all to a level much below the present average, or by wholesale murder, because the abilities and virtues of men are intercorrelated positively. It is easier to equalize in happiness. We can give the imbecile food and toys and the gifted child food and higher education.

It is better to expend the time and energy in increasing goods than in equalizing them. This is obvious in the case of health, strength, knowledge, peace, happiness, where an addition to any one person rarely involves decreases for others. It is almost certainly also true in the case of wealth. If a person receives less wealth than he deserves, justice should provide remedies, but if he receives less than some others, the matter is of very little importance.

Ways and Means of Attaining and Maintaining the Good Life

The Family   A wise and competent family may provide its children with most of the opportunities of our list. This does not require great wealth, though it is very hard to manage in poverty. There are, however, few such families. Some parents seem to have a positive genius for putting their children in the way of happiness. On the other hand, man's cruelty to man often begins in the family.

There is a general feeling that the family is the strategic place for improving personal habits and traits. It has the first chance; it is a "natural" group to which man is adapted; its situations and responses are real; its authority and example work at deeper levels than do the church or state. It may consequently be well to put on the family as much responsibility for the welfare of its members as it can carry, and help it when it needs help.

Government   It is a well-recognized function of government to provide water at a fair price, but such provision of food is much rarer. Protection against germ diseases and accidents is accepted as a duty by all civilized governments, but protection against inadequacies of vitamins and essential salts in the diet has barely begun.

What government does is a mixture of reason and custom. Protection against a foreign attack is obviously reasonable for the governing classes, since to be conquered is for them to lose approval, power, and property. At the present time its logical value is less certain; in some cases the populace of A might be better off to surrender to B, and exchange the ruling class of A for the ruling class of B.[1] The customary part is

[1]This matter has been treated acutely and entertainingly, though somewhat one-sidedly, by Veblen, in *The Nature of Peace*. He says, for example, "Any passably dispassionate consideration of the projected regime will come unavoidably to the conclusion that the prospectively subject peoples should have no legitimate apprehension

illustrated by the existence of laws forbidding marriage within certain degrees of relationship, a matter which might well be left to public opinion guided by science.

What government *should* do is not known. It may be asserted, however, that we should not assign responsibility for an adequate diet entirely to the family, or responsibility for inner peace entirely to the church, or responsibility for security against foreign attacks entirely to the government. A coordination of forces to favor the good life is usually required.

The Church   Almost every church, even those that confine themselves most strictly to supernatural affairs and the preparation of men for a life after death, contributes to several items of our list. Membership gives opportunity for human society. It adds a measurable amount of approval. It may add enormously to the inner sense of being worthy.

Probably neither worldly success nor philosophic acceptance of life equals the triumphs of religious habit in freeing men from regret, discontent and shame. The church offers a worthy master not only for the daily needs of the humble, but also to the occasional needs for submission of proud and ruthless masters of men who feel a genuine pleasure in humbling themselves before their Lord.

Industry   Productive labor, including the care of children, absorbs a large fraction of the time and energy, and provides food, drink, protection, security, entertainment, and power so far as these are purchasable. These goods may come from unskilled and menial work. A feeble-minded girl may have psychologically the same satisfaction in making beds that a prima donna has from singing songs.

Everything goes to show that activity of body or of mind, in and of itself, is more desirable than inactivity. Much of our dissatisfaction with labor is due not to what it makes us do, but to what it deprives us of. So it would be an evil to be forced to lie in bed when one wanted exercise, or to go to a party when one wanted to be alone. If we were good observers we would often express our feelings of fatigue from labor as the child in school did who said, "I am tired of not playing."

Apart from debarring men from certain other craved activities,

---

of loss or disadvantage in the material respect. It is, of course, easy for an unreflecting person to jump to the conclusion that subjection to an alien power must bring grievous burdens, in the way of taxes and similar impositions. But reflection will immediately show that no appreciable increase, over the economic burdens already carried by the populace under their several national establishments, could come of such a move." ['17, p. 145] productive labor is often bad by being too meaningless. Meaninglessness is bad. In fact, anything that is true and adds dignity to work is good. A factory manager who was notably successful attributed his success to such simple measures as requiring every foreman to learn to pronounce a worker's name properly and call him by it!

Schools There are literally thousands of varieties of schools contributing differently to the various items of our list. Schools also offer interesting illustrations of unintentional cruelty, of inept failure, of silly adherence to stupid or outworn custom, such as too often characterize institutions and activities conceived in good will and nurtured by intelligence and idealism. The free common school was cruel when it made six-year-olds sit motionless; it has often stimulated the harmful envy and discontent which wise governments and churches try to reduce; it has maintained a forced competition among unequals.

Schools also illustrate the appearance in human institutions of beneficent by-products not expected by the planners. The common school was not invented to provide affection or friendship, but many a child of ill, harassed, or neurotic parents gets his first healthy love and friendship from a teacher. And many teachers have had their lives enriched by giving and receiving affection or friendship in schools.

Public Opinion and Custom Opinions about what is are potent, and opinions about what is valuable are still more so, because less easily checked by facts. When enacted into laws, opinions determine what activities are permissible and forbidden and where governmental protection and coercion will be applied. A person cannot easily lead the life which would be best for him and for the world unless opinion approves it as a life for him. Families, rulers, churches, schools, industry—all are sensitive to, and interact with, public and class opinions.

Attempts to make people accept any particular truth are undesirable if such attempts cause aversion toward science and scientific institutions. Truth is mighty and ought to prevail, but any sagacious reader of history and observer of human nature can think of conditions in which the science of today might have to fight political and physical force, and might perish in the fight.

The effort to convert the truth known to a few into the opinion of many may be given up or postponed if it is likely to be misunderstood or misapplied. If the Einstein equations as finally mutilated in the popular mind became a belief that "the surest things in science may be insecure; we may be living on the inside of this planet instead of its outside; I may really be you; right may really be wrong" they would better have been left to the sole possession of the mathematicians and physicists. Consideration of these exceptions should not, however, in any way lessen the importance of the rule that, in general, public opinion should follow science, thinking what is true rather than what is habitual or comforting or consistent with human hopes.

The Welfare of Communities

The welfare of a community in the sense of the goodness of life for good people can be measured fairly well by a weighted average score of its status in the following items:

Items of Health

Infant death rate reversed
General death rate reversed
Typhoid death rate reversed
Appendicitis death rate reversed
Puerperal diseases death rate reversed

Items of Education

Per capita public expenditures for schools
Per capita public expenditures for teachers' salaries
Per capita public expenditures for text-books and supplies
Per capita public expenditures for libraries and museums
Percentage of persons sixteen to seventeen attending schools
Percentage of persons eighteen to twenty attending schools
Average salary of high-school and elementary-school teachers

Items of Recreation

Per capita public expenditures for recreation
Per capita acreage of public parks

Economic and "Social" Items

Rarity of extreme poverty
Rarity of less extreme poverty
Infrequency of gainful employment for boys and girls 10–14
Average wage of workers in factories
Frequency of home ownership
Per capita support of the Y. M. C. A.
Excess of physicians and teachers over male domestic servants

Creature Comforts

Per capita domestic installations of electricity and gas
Per capita number of automobiles
Per capita domestic installations of telephones and radios

Other Items

Percent of literacy in the total population
Per capita circulation of Better Homes and Gardens and National Geographic Magazine
Per capita circulation of the Literary Digest
Death rate from syphilis (reversed)
Death rate from homicide (reversed)
Death rate from automobile accidents (reversed)
Per capita value of asylums, schools, libraries, museums, and parks owned by the public
Ratio of value of schools, etc., to value of jails, etc.
Per capita public property minus public debt

A weighted composite of a city's score in these items we may call its General Goodness score (or G); I have computed for each of 310 cities a score, P, representing more or less well its residents' intelligence, morality, and devotion to home; and also a score, I, representing more or less well the per capita income of its residents.[1] I have also as an approximate measure of the wealth of each city, the per capita value of the taxable property; call this W. By the use of the technique of path coefficients the causation of the differences among the cities in G can be found.

Differences in the personal qualities of the population are much more important as causes of differences in the goodness of life for good people than differences in per capita wealth and income. There is evidence that the I and P scores have as a common cause certain qualities of intelligence, competence, industry, sobriety, and thrift.

Cities are made better than others in this country primarily and chiefly by getting able and good people as residents—people who, for example, are intelligent, read books, do not contract syphilis, or commit murder, or allow others to do so, own their own homes, have telephones, and support doctors, nurses, dentists, and teachers rather than lawyers and domestic servants. The second important cause of welfare is income. Good people, rich or poor, earning much or earning little, are a good thing for a city, but the more they have and earn the better. They and their incomes account for at least three fourths, and probably more, of the differences of American cities in the goodness of life for good people.... The safe and prudent cause for any city to pursue is to improve its population and increase its incomes. [Thorndike, '39C, p. 67f.]

[1] Thorndike. E. L.. *Your City*, '39C.

Chapter 13
The Welfare of Man

Long-time provisions are likely to be neglected relatively to the care for the present generation. Individuals often sacrifice their future to immediate cravings, except for the natural ties causing parents to work for the welfare of their offspring, and for a rare abstract general benevolence in a few. Gortner notes that "in spite of the fact that the world's resources of tin are exceedingly limited, we still demand tinfoil around candy and cigarettes, and the world's available sulfur supply is being rapidly exhausted in the demand for cellulose products which have a silken sheen. . . . Viewing our wastage of natural resources, I sometimes wonder if we are civilized." ['33, p. 442]

A Meager Life for Many Versus a Good Life for Few

The number of persons has long been enormously in excess of what is needed to guarantee the protection of the species from destruction by other animals. The questions (I) "How long do we wish the human race to be perpetuated?" (II) "How many persons do we wish to have on the earth from now till the end of time?" and (III) "How many do we wish to have in the generation of 1971 to 2000, and so on?" are not unimportant, though questions concerning the quality of the persons are much more important.

In so far as it is good to be alive, it is good for more men to be alive. It would, however, be more reasonable to weight numbers by welfare and to prefer a population of half a billion with an average welfare of 10 to a population of a billion with an average welfare of 5. This is reasonable for the extremely simple reason that the second half-billion by delaying their lives would have the welfare of 10 instead of 5.

There are certain minor advantages to sheer numbers. Life in families seems to average better than life single; and life in families with two or more children seems to average better than life in families with one or none. Other things being equal, the greater the number of persons, the greater the number of those persons of very great ability whose work will contribute to the good life for all.

The Dependence of the Good Life Upon the Quality of People

All matters of the size of the world's population are of little consequence in comparison with its quality. If the best third of the population had eight children per pair who lived to bear children, and if the best third of these repeated the process and so on with the result of increasing the world's population steadily up to twice its present size in fourteen generations, it is practically certain that the world could then support this doubled population in a much better life than we have now. It would have more than made up for the loss in certain natural resources by the discovery of others; and it would have accumulated man-made resources much more rapidly than the past has done.

Whether the present apparatus of material equipment, knowledge, institutions. etc. could be kept as a going concern if the world did not continually replace its top five percent in intellect and in managerial ability is very doubtful.

The population should probably not include many who can do nothing which machines cannot do better. As science and technology spread persons who now earn subsistence by brute strength will be unable to earn that which is necessary for a good life. Such persons may be given good care out of benevolence, but that will not provide the good life for their children.

Eugenics and the Good Life

Philanthropists and reformers have suffered from extreme ignorance of human inheritance. Some of their proposals seem to be valid only if traits acquired by a person are perpetuated in his genes and offspring; but they are not. Some are valid only if the original unborn individual differences among men are very slight; but they are very great. Some of the hopes of the devotees of eugenics also seem to assume a simplicity in the gene determination of important human qualities which is quite out of harmony with the evidence.

We cannot choose and arrange genes directly; we can choose them only by the persons who carry them. Those carried by any person in each of his germ cells are not identical lots. John Doe mated with Mary Roe produces children whose variation is about 87 percent as great as the variation of the general stock of the country of which John and Mary are citizens.

Suppose that every person in the world were given an accurate score based on some reasonable composite of health, sanity, ability, morality, and other traits beneficial to the good life.[1] Suppose that the thousand men and the thousand women scoring highest were used as new Adams and Eves to people the earth. The scores of these two thousands would be very closely alike, and would be in the neighborhood of $A+.99K$ on the composite scale where A is the present average and $A+K$ is the average of the genetically best. But the scores of a thousand children born from the thousand pairs would not average near $A+.99K$ but at a much lower score, near $A+.5K$, and would not be closely alike but would vary from $A+.99K$ to as low as the average, K, and perhaps much lower because the genes which the Adams and Eves produce include many less favorable variations. This great variation in the genes produced by the same person, which seems not to have been fully appreciated by even specialists in genetics and eugenics, explains why so many extreme deviates are the children of rather ordinary parents.

Eugenic progress toward a race optimally equipped in its genes for the good life is slow and insecure. Certain particular qualities caused by the presence or absence of single genes can be bred in or out with surety in a few generations. Certain others caused by the presence of certain known combinations of two or three genes can be bred in or out with surety though much more slowly.[2] But when the trait is caused by unknown

[1] A reasonable composite would be one which made sure of not losing from the world any desirable gene. It would be arranged so as to include persons with certain harmful traits if there was any risk that by excluding them some desirable gene might be lost. For example, a person of supreme achievement in poetry would not be excluded even if he were a deep-dyed villain, unless the thousand already included enough persons gifted at poetry to ensure that the genetic basis of poetic achievement was included. Indeed the ablest person in every important sort of activity would probably be put on the list regardless of his score in other sorts of activities.

[2] Mendel's discovery and the important experiments and studies of pedigrees by students of genetics during the past generation are of paramount importance to the

genes in unknown combinations, or when many genes are involved even if they are known, the reduction in the variation in one breeding becomes only 13.4 percent.

The Elimination of "Bad" Men and "Bad" Genes

Certain combinations of genes are favorable to the production of those who do the world more harm than good. Selective breeding against them is advantageous though probably not so advantageous as breeding for excellence, since idiots and delinquents probably do much less harm than their opposites do good. Intelligent social workers have in general accepted the practice of segregation or compulsory sterilization for certain sorts of habitual criminals and of voluntary sterilization for the feeble-minded, insane, and others burdened with some grave heritable defect.

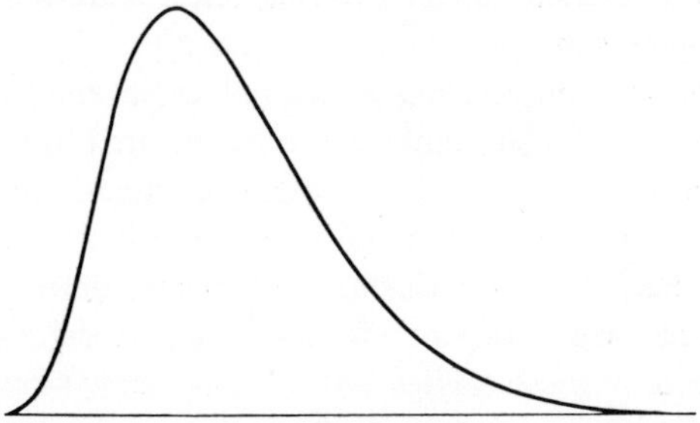

Fig. 24.

The zero line below which a person does more harm than good will probably rise with the increased complexity of civilized life. As heavy and repetitive work is given over to machines and closely supervised work is eliminated by a better organization, more of the dull will be unemployable. As the prudent conduct of life comes to depend more upon following abstract rules set by science and less upon concrete habits, fewer of the dull will be able to keep healthy, get fair value for their money, and avoid making public nuisances of themselves. As economic, legal, and social relations become more complex, more of those with psychopathic tendencies will break out into harmful eccentricities, become insane, regress into childish evasions of reality.

---

understanding of the biology of inheritance, but the early hopes that abilities and interests would be found to be "unit-characters" caused by the presence of a single or double dose of a certain gene were doomed to disappointment. Some genes have been discovered which do cause idiocy, but over ninety-five percent of idiocy is not caused by them. Not a single case of the causation of some highly desirable human trait by one gene has yet been found.

Since the regression of offspring toward the mean of the population makes their average "values" plus even when those of the parents are minus and since the reduction in the variance of children of the same parents is only 13.4 percent from that of the general population, the elimination of harmful genes will progress only slowly by restraining the lowest levels from reproducing. If, as is possible, the low end of the distribution of mankind for general excellence tails out less than the high, as shown in Fig. 24, it will be still slower.

Eugenic Practices

Improvement of the human genes produces indirectly better customs and institutions; it is an insurance against the deterioration of good customs and institutions. It is in conflict with only the desire to have offspring and the aversion against having one's body tampered with by anybody for any reason.

No well-informed and sensible persons object to the general principle of eugenics, but some able thinkers are fearful that any control of the next generation will be worse than present practices, and not nearly so good as some form of education and moral suasion. MacIver objects to the law which permits the sterilization of mental defectives, epileptics, habitual criminals, moral degenerates and sex perverts, saying "Only in respect of the first of these classes is there reasonable biological evidence to justify compulsion in the name of the welfare of the race. As Bertrand Russell observes, 'such laws would have justified the sterilization of Socrates, Plato, Julius Caesar, and St. Paul.' . . . Compulsion cannot, without serious risk, do more than obviate the more extreme social dangers. Beyond that, it is necessary to rely on social education." ['36, p. 151][1]

Much in the legislation concerning sterilization is doubtless misguided, but on the whole its operations seem more beneficent than those spent in "social education." Indeed the first lesson in social education for a habitual criminal or a moral degenerate might well be to teach him to submit voluntarily to an operation which would leave his sex life unaltered but eliminate his genes from the world.

The principle of eliminating bad genes is so thoroughly sound that

[1] The brilliancy of Bertrand Russell's comment are admirable as entertainment but in my opinion that law would not justify him in the case of any of the four except Julius Caesar. Socrates was not a "habitual criminal" or "moral degenerate" in his own time in the sense of the law. Neither Socrates nor Plato was a sex pervert in his own time. St. Paul probably did not have epileptic fits but cataleptic trances like those of some modern mediums.

almost any practice based on it is likely to do more good than harm. Add to it (1) the facts of correlation whereby defects and delinquencies imply one another so that moral degenerates tend to be dull, imbeciles to be degraded, etc. (2) the facts of homogamy, that like tends to mate with like, and (3) the fact that genes which make able and good people also tend to make competent and helpful homes.

In the case of efforts to increase the birth rate among superior persons, some thinkers are fearful lest our wisdom be insufficient to prevent a bigoted or at least narrow selection of the superior according to notions which would defeat the real purpose of genetic control. Boas, for example, writes:

> If it is a question of breeding chickens or Indian corn, we know what we want. . . . But what do we want in man? Is it physical excellence, mental ability, creative power, or artistic genius? . . . Considering the fundamental differences in ideals of distinct types of civilization, have we a right to give to our modern ideals the stamp of finality, and suppress what does not fit into our life? . . .
>
> Such a deliberate choice of qualities which would modify the character of nations implies an overestimation of the standards that we have reached, which to my mind appears intolerable. ['28, pp. 113 f.]

No competent geneticist would make such blunders as Boas implies. But the general warning should be kept in mind.

If a narrow selection of parents were made universal, certain good genes might become too scant to supply the world with enough of certain sorts of abilities. However, the danger that breeding for high levels of ability A will reduce the percentage of genes productive of high ability B in mankind is very slight. The result is almost certain to be the great increase in the percentage of high-A genes directly sought and a substantial increase in the percentage of high-B genes. There will for example be more "high-ability-in-music" genes in a thousand gifted men of science than in a thousand men taken at random, and more high-ability-in-logic genes in a thousand gifted musicians than in a thousand men taken at random.

The possibility that legislators, schools, or churches will establish customs in this respect is estimated as zero by some. Raymond Pearl, for example, says:

> The efforts of the eugenists to correct the evils of the differential birth rate, by endeavoring to induce the socially, economically, and in some part biologically, superior classes to reproduce more freely, as a sort of transcendental social duty, have not met with any discernible success, and in my opinion are not likely to. When the issue is drawn between the present comfort, happiness and well-being of the reproducers on the one hand, and the indefinitely future welfare of society in general, or the race or state, on the other hand, he would seem indeed a

simple-minded, not to say fatuous optimist who supposes that the latter will outweigh the former. It will do nothing of the kind. ['25, p. 176]

In my opinion a moderate expenditure of money and ingenuity should enable any nation to discover what prevents some of the able and good from having children and what causes others to have many, and to influence these causes in the public interest. One change is to provide allowances for children to men of very high intelligence and achievement during the period from 21 to 30. Such men now work some years as internes in hospitals, assistants in the great law firms, instructors in colleges, apprentices in engineering concerns, with low pay. Many of them would be glad to get married if an allowance for each child were made; the experience of the post-doctoral fellowships in science where allowances for wife and children were made shows this. The moral qualities of such men average very high, the home environments which they will provide will average very high, and their tendency to choose wives of superior ability is very strong. To extend full maintenance scholarships for able boys and girls for the four college years is a prudent expenditure quite apart from any eugenic influence it may have. It would probably cause a considerable number of promising babies to be born, by removing the fear of the very definite and large costs of college education. A world that has pushed the number of children of the able and good down from to below two per married pair ought to be ingenious enough to put it back up. If it can maintain so biologically perverse a custom as the celibacy of the clergy, it ought to be able, in the interest of human welfare, to make a four-child family as respectable as a four-car garage.

Trustees for man should consider the welfare of men in the distant future and even attach some weight to it when it conflicts with the welfare of the present and near future. But what they will be permitted to do will depend on what can be shown to be in the interest of the persons now living and their children.

The Improvement of the Environment

Our psychology has included a naive confidence that if we make the environment better for ourselves we are doing our children and children's children a service. A more enlightened benevolence is leading men to inspect the accounts and make it clear just how much of the world's natural resources we are using up, how much we are transmuting into more or less durable goods, and how much, if any, we are putting into a sort of reserve against depreciation for the benefit of the future.

The reaction of the first generation to mine coal or pump oil was pride in the discovery and utilization, with never a thought that they were robbing future men. If anybody had suggested that, they could have retorted, "Except for us, future men would not even have known there was any. Let them discover something for themselves as we did." This same attitude still holds among many. Gratitude is rare, and gratitude for what past generations have done is especially rare.

My maxims for maintaining and increasing material and immaterial wealth are:

1. Increase the production of what aids the good life.
2. Use consumption both to provide the good life for now and to enable people to maintain and increase production.
3. Save in distribution and consumption, and invest the savings in durable goods.
4. Favor the forms of production and distribution which least impair limited natural resources.
5. Other things being equal, increase the amount of wealth that is held in trust for the welfare of man, at the expense of wealth held at the disposal of individuals.[1]

These maxims mix ethics with economics to the extent of insisting that what is produced and saved aid the good life. They distinguish emphatically between a billion dollars worth of flour, cows, telephone lines and good books and a billion dollars worth of hashish, foxes, billboards, and prostitutes.

Private and Public Improvement of the Environment   About three quarters of the adults dying in the United States do not leave estates large enough to be probated. A few of these, possibly one in five thousand, do leave appreciable immaterial wealth in science, the arts, memorable deeds, or other forms.[2] It is possible to argue that some of them were paid less than their labor contributed and that this balance represents a forced saving by them, although economists will deny this. Some of them may have contributed toward the improvement of the environment by gifts made or taxes paid during their lives which were so used.

Certainly nearly three quarters of American men and women give

---

[1] The "other things being equal" is important. In some cases it may be better for mankind to have a parent leave his property to his children rather than in trust for mankind. On the whole, however, the endowments of universities, hospitals, libraries, and philanthropic foundations do more good dollar for dollar than the same amounts in private hands.

[2] For example, the material estates of Poe, Whitman, Walter Reed, Edward Mac-Dowell, Lincoln, and Grant were small or nonexistent.

back to the environment little or no more than they have received from it. Such contributions as they have made are via their children and in their friends and neighbors. The percentage of testators leaving anything to anybody except relatives is small. Nobody should scorn them. They have paid their own way and have insured the world to some extent against having to support their children.

Lastly there are the persons, few in number but important in welfare, who usually, after providing enough to guarantee their children support in the sort of life to which they are accustomed, leave their estates to serve welfare. If some foolish dictator should seize the funds in question and spend them on armies and doles, the loss to welfare by the decrease in the production of immaterial wealth would be calamitous.

Public improvement of the environment is characteristic of all civilizations. In primitive communities it is concerned mainly with placating spirits and deities and constructing communal shelter and protection. The work has often been saddled with nepotism, favoritism, and corruption; Herbert Spencer's famous diatribes against public action are more or less justifiable. It is significant that benevolent men who make gifts to the public almost never give to a government. They do not trust either the public or its elected representatives to act for its welfare; they put the power in the hands of appointed trustees.

Yet in spite of inefficiency, folly, and graft, the schools, parks, and hospitals made by the public are probably a blessing. A museum can be worth only half what it cost and still be better for welfare than a graveyard. A state road can be badly designed and still be a good public investment. The principle that the public can tax and spend to make life better for the future is itself worth something, as is the principle that the selfish should do something to improve the environment which the past has improved for them.

The able and good ordinarily contribute from private funds to establish a library, museum, park, college or the like, and after it has proved its worth, ask public funds to maintain or improve it. In so far as this forces a selfish public to give for welfare, and accustoms the public and government to using public funds wisely, it probably is a forward step. There is, however, the psychological danger that the public will be encouraged in its fatuous belief that if the government pays, we are getting something at no cost and will vote for appropriations against its real interest. It is then conceivable that the real triumph might be for the able and good to serve the public's real interests in entire independence of government. It may be that putting welfare into the hands of politicians and voters is a backward step.

Pareto has pointed out that a capital investment of one centime at the time of Christ's birth would by now have produced houses, roads, buildings, bridges, etc. to the value of billions of billions of dollars, if it had been undisturbed by wars, crusades, speculations, and the like.[1] The achievements of the Romans were lost to the world because they did not keep the barbarians out nor teach them to use the good environment properly. Fanatical Christians destroyed thousands of beautiful temples. The Parthenon was razed by shells; the trade of honest men is ruined by pirates; thrift has been stabbed in the back by gambling rulers who debase the currency. Coercion or cajolery must support a good environment unless men can be made better.

The Improvement of People

Many of our present afflictions are caused by man himself, not by adverse forces in the environment. Such include envy, greed, injustice, ostentation, war, and unemployment.

The remedies and preventives are to be found largely in genetics and education. Eugenics is sure but slow, whereas education is rapid but extremely variable. It has performed wonders, but not always those hoped for. The sciences of government, law, economics, and sociology also provide suggestions for the improvement of people. The improvement of the population by reducing the numbers of defectives, delinquents, and dependents presents problems, some of which may be discussed now.

Defectives

The burden of physical and mental defects is obvious. The genes share directly or indirectly in the causation of most of them, the share varying from probably 70 percent or more in defective intelligence to 3 percent or less in the case of broken legs where the only genetic influence is by greater clumsiness, carelessness, and stupidity. Important environmental causes include diseases, war, industrial accidents, falls, intoxication. Psychological factors in persons are influential in all of these, and still more so in the psychic injuries, from terrifying shocks, premature sexual experiences, and bad habits.

An important question is what sort of persons are being maimed. If only reckless drivers were hurt, traffic accidents would be less bad. If only unorganized, hysterical, infantile persons were upset by psychic

---

[1] *The Mind and Society,* '23, English translation of '35. Vol. IV, pp. 1664–1667.

shocks in childhood, we could be less worried by Freudian discoveries. But if the accidents fall like rain upon the just and unjust alike, the calamity is unmitigated; and if healthy, good, and able are preferred victims, as in modern wars, the calamity is multiplied.

Once the harm has been done, defectives must be adapted to their condition and the world adapted to them. Where the victim prefers death it would often be humane to let him have it, as many cultures have done. But where the victim can manage a good and useful life, it is prudent to minimize the defect. Defectives are made miserable and resentful by being treated as inferior, even in the most kindly spirit.

Productive labor fitted to a person's abilities and interests is better than idleness for most persons, and the progress of the last generation in adapting tasks, machines, and working conditions to important varieties of defect is beneficent. These are good rules, but must not be made into fetiches. There are cases where the expense of arranging for the defective to earn is so much greater than the amount he will earn that the possible improvement to his morale and self-esteem is not worth it.

Assuming that a certain fraction of the national income is to be spent to care for defectives, the reasonable allotment of it would be to spend little or none in prolonging the life of suffering incurables, or of dangerous defectives, such as imbeciles who may set fire to buildings, or of utterly worthless and repulsive defectives, such as certain insane whose death will be a blessing to their relatives and friends. Many defectives are victims of misfortunes for which the neighborhood, or city, or nation is more responsible than they or their families. Money contributed to their care is reasonably considered a fine which society imposes on itself for its shortcomings.

Popular ideas of what is fit and proper are influenced by certain instinctive and traditional tendencies, such as to relieve, comfort, and console the perceptibly miserable rather than those who conceal their suffering, and the frail and weak rather than the fat and lusty.

Criminals

Persons guilty of breaking the criminal law present an almost infinite variety in what they do, why they do it, what sort of persons they are, how they came to be so, and how they respond to treatment. Casual criminal offenses are extremely rare, as of a man who under great stress steals food, or stabs a tormentor, and would be of little consequence, except that the absolutism of the law may brand them and the public may treat them as regular criminals.

Habitual criminals include those who make it their business—thieves, killers, con-men, counterfeiters; those who fail to control their passions—rapists, wife-beaters, drunk, and disorderly; those who are moved by obsessions and strange quirks such as some kleptomaniacs; and rebels against the established order—anarchists, atheists, pacifists in war time, deserters, revolutionaries.

If the obsessional and morbid cases are turned over to psychiatry and the rebels against orthodoxy are treated as cranks, martyrs, or notoriety seekers, and if all genuine first offenders and rare offenders are given such individual treatment as seems best for the welfare of all concerned, there will be left a great body called vicious criminals. If they are decent to their families and friends, they indulge themselves by stealing their living instead of earning it. If they earn an honest living they are likely to spend it on themselves, or to be mean to others. When they seem to be weak rather than vicious, it will usually be found that they resist opportunities to work hard or to help their wives and neighbors. They are easily led into crime, but social workers find it extremely hard to lead them to industry and decency.

The Affiliations of Criminality

Criminal parents have much more than their share of criminal children and the sib of a criminal is much more likely to be a criminal than is the sib of an unconvicted person. How much this family resemblance in criminality is caused by resemblances in the genes is not known. The best way to approach the problem is rather by measuring the variation in criminality of unrelated persons, the variation of sibs brought up apart, and the variation of sibs brought up together. The causation of the variation could then be analyzed. And such an analysis will, I prophesy, give allotments near the following:—Genetic factors, .15; Home training, .15; Common to genes and home, .40; All other, .30. In the facts available at present these four sorts of forces are confused. Crime runs in families, but so does home training, overcrowding, poverty, and many other things. Crime is correlated with homes broken by death, divorce, or desertion, but these may in part mean inferior genes. Crime is more prevalent in certain "races," but these show also inferior homes and inferior surroundings. Crime is usually prevalent in certain parts of a city but these districts may select bad people as well as make them bad.

This much greater frequency of crime in certain neighborhoods is the favorite cause of those who trust that some one major environmental cause of crime can be found to explain it. Cyril Burt ['25] found it in

London. Shaw and his co-workers ['29] found it in Chicago, and Maller ['37] found it in New York City. The districts are characterized by "congestion, poor housing and lack of recreational facilities." [Maller, '37, p. 25] But this effect should not be exaggerated. Those who would assign 50 percent or more of the causation to a complex of "economic, social and cultural factors" exaggerate. Bad genes select a bad environment, and make its economic, social, and cultural factors worse.

Poverty is doubtless a genuine cause, but the expectation that if all children were well housed, fed, and clothed, few or none of them would get into trouble is a notable exaggeration. In her important studies of the business cycle Dorothy Thomas ['25] found that the correlations of pauperism and crime with good times were definitely opposed. Maller ['37] found that the number of persons brought before the Children's Court in New York during the five boom years 1925–1929 was increased by only six percent in the five depression years 1930–1934.

The clearest affiliation of criminality is with sex, crime being so far in history a male characteristic. Of the children brought before the New York City Children's Court as delinquents from 1903 to 1936, nearly 17 times as many were boys as girls. The explanation may be found to lie partly in sheer custom, partly in the fact that girls and women stay in the home more, and partly in the stronger original bent of men toward violent action.

A strange apparent affiliation of crime is with religion.[1] The figures showing this may be caused by lying in answering questions, but it has not been denied by those intimate with criminals. Bartlett and Harris ['36, p. 655] found that delinquent boys "were definitely superior in

Table 11[2]   Percentages violating parole

More likely to violate parole		Less likely to violate parole	
Hoboes	40	Irish	31
Ne'er-do-wells	46.4	Farm boys	15.1
Paroled to rooming house community	54	Criminals by accident	17.7
		Paroled to farm	17
Habitual criminals	58.8	First offenders	12.9
Never employed	38.5	Skilled laborers regularly employed	5.6
Sexual psychopaths	40		
Neuropaths and psychotics	38.1	Emotionally unstable	16.6
Feeble-minded	37	Sex offenders	8.0
"Lone wolves"	33.1	Eleven months' sentence or less	13.7
Negroes	35.7	Prior recommendation of leniency	12.9

[1] See, for example, Havelock Ellis, *The Criminal*, pp. 156–161.
[2] The facts of Table 11 are from Glueck and Glueck ['30], but the table is quoted from Michael and Adler, '32, p. 199.

ability to identify biblical and religious names and terms." The reform-school boys had religious instruction on Sundays, which may have accounted for all their superiority, but this seems doubtful.

The Gluecks made an intensive study of the careers of 500 young men sentenced to a Massachusetts reformatory, to find correlations between engaging in crime after being discharged on parole and various features of their careers before entering the reformatory. Among criminals the amount of crime and idleness give the best prophecy of further crime; nothing else has much predictive value. Percentages of violation of parole among those of the 500 who were habitual criminals, first offenders, ne'er-do-wells, skilled laborers, etc., is shown in Table 11.

Treatment

A very little wise treatment may reform those who are criminals by accident or misfortune. The writer was once consulted about a child of wealthy parents in a boarding school who was stealing repeatedly. Inquiring what he did with the money, I was told that he apparently spent every penny of it for candy. Yet it had not occurred to the parents to supply the boy with candy or with money. So far as I know he never stole after this was done.

Arthur Woods writes concerning some of his experiments as Police Commissioner of New York City:

The experiment was tried ... of assigning Crime Prevention Patrolmen to some of the more busy precincts for the purpose of having them ferret out conditions in the precinct which seemed to be ... leading boys and girls astray.... Many temptations to petty stealing were discovered.... This was regarded by them purely as play, but led soon to the genuine article, and the thoughtless playful boy found himself, often before he at all realized it, a law-breaker. Conditions ... seemed made to order to lead boys into crime. In fact, it has often seemed to me that in some parts of the city it is practically impossible for a growing, healthy boy to play at all without doing something against the law. ['17, p. 78 f.]

Reformatories do not reform. To make the person as miserable as possible, to keep him in solitude that he might reflect on his iniquity, and to ply him with religious admonitions were favorite treatments of bygone days; they failed. To provide routine work and a simple life with bonuses in the shape of shortened sentences for good behavior is a standard present method; it fails.

Teaching trades and wholesome recreations to those who know none, providing adventure for adventurous youth, work for those who will work, taking the profit out of crimes so far as is possible, and permitting men in prisons to earn money for their dependents will perhaps do better. But the time and labor cost of changing the habits and personality of one of the vicious criminals into those of an honest citizen would be very great, and much better spent in doing something for the worthy poor and suffering.

Dependents

A person is economically dependent when he uses up more natural resources and wealth than he produces. It is customary to leave out those who are provided for by the work of relatives, living or dead; children supported by their parents and adults supported by inherited property are then not thought of as dependents. There are many other sorts of dependency. If a person receives more affection than he bestows he is a pauper in affection. Some gloomy souls are paupers in cheer. Some boring persons are paupers in respect of entertainment. This section will however, be restricted to dependency as ordinarily considered, with pauperism its most characteristic form.

The form of distribution of income in a modern state differs greatly from the form of distribution of any of the abilities that have been measured. The income curve for adults is like Fig. 25.

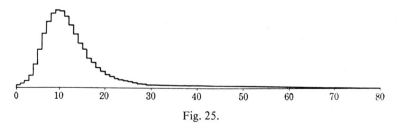

Fig. 25.

The incomes of the business managers, lawyers, surgeons, and entertainers whose services are most desired will run up to two hundred or more times the income of the common man. The long tail is important because most of the funds for both charitable and public relief come directly or indirectly from those having incomes three or more times that of the common man.

The standing army of dependents are the true unemployables, the persons whose services are worth nothing or less than nothing, so that prudent employers will not hire them at any price. Next come a larger group of persons whose services are worth a little when business is booming, or when crops must be harvested, or when needed labor is reduced by war, pestilence, etc.

Next come a group of persons whose services are worth substantial amounts, but not so much as the price they set, collectively as in unions, or individually. They accept charity rather than a wage lower than what they think is their right or is needed to uphold the cause of labor. Many employers discharge old men whom they might be glad to keep at reduced wages, knowing that many men would aggravate the inefficiency which old age brings.

There are some dependents with hitherto valuable services which they offer at rates below the ordinary market price, but with no takers, because some advance of technology has made their skill useless or because business is so disorganized that who gets work is partly a matter of chance.

Dependency in the age of machinery and power is very different from dependency in the feudal age of agriculture and household crafts. One who was not crippled or bedridden could then at least gather sticks for fuel, pick berries, or dig roots. Calamities came by ravages of lord by lord, and by failure of crops. The unfortunate could look to their neighbors, their lord, and the church.

Things are now interlocked in a productive "structure" so intricate that almost nothing adverse happens which does not make a sizable crop of paupers. A village community managed itself after some fashion; but no modern city or village does. If the present population of the United States were put back on the virgin land as it was in 1620, each having only such equipment as the settlers at Plymouth had, most of them would die before the first winter was over. We need our farm machinery, power plants, mines, oil wells, water-works, etc. to keep us alive, but we do not know how to keep them fully at work.

Many people have no ideas or utterly fantastic ideas about how much the national income is, how much each person would get if it were divided equally, how many persons there are working or trying to get work, how much return the owners of railroads get per year per dollar invested. The total income for the good and bad years 1920 to 1940, if divided equally, would give less than $500 per year per person. A large part of it, however, probably over half, is earned by our material equipment, and much of this must be spent to keep that equipment in fit condition to continue earning for us.

People do not know this. Skilled laborers who are now getting more than they would from such an even division think they would get double. Families with incomes of $4000 often have the notion that if incomes were divided equally they would be better off than now! Workingmen and many professional men have fantastic notions of the return which comes from money invested in business, setting it at 10 or 25 or $33\frac{1}{3}$ percent. They contrast this easy road to wealth with what they can get from the savings bank. They do not know that the returns with equal safety are the same on money put in business, in land, in labor, or in the savings bank (subject to a small premium for the conveniences offered by the bank). So many do not think it worth while to save.

The combined action of ignorance, lack of intelligence and of foresight is beautifully illustrated by the payment for warmth in winter. The cheapest way to get warmth is by clothing. Yet families will burn their furniture when from ten to a thousand times the heat value could be obtained by pawning the furniture and buying woolen clothes. They will pawn their overcoats to buy food, most of the energy of which is then dissipated in heating all outdoors. A man will buy a drink of whiskey which has less power to warm him than a newspaper worn under his coat would have.

Pauperism has roots not only in ignorance and improvidence, but also in habits, physical, intellectual, moral and social. James McKeen Cattell relates that when a magnate was asked whether he got most gratification from his steam yacht or private railway car, he replied that he did not see how anyone could get on without either. The depth of humiliation was reached by one of Edith Wharton's heroines when she had to wear a pair of ready-made shoes! But we are all tarred with the same brush. Mechanics and farmers cannot get on without a car and a radio. Whatever standard of living men get used to they will feel they cannot get on without.

Workingmen in this country two generations ago were grateful to anybody who would give them a decent job. Their gratitude was perhaps somewhat misplaced, since it was the application of science as well as the enterprise of employers that gave them decent jobs. But it had the merit of appreciating the reality that jobs were not a prerogative of anybody willing to work, but a gift from something or somebody. This seems to have been replaced by a bad habit of being grateful to nothing, not even to the man's union. It is a bad habit because it avoids reality in favor of self-esteem.

There is a percentage of persons to whom the work of the modern world is so distasteful that they will steal, beg, and suffer to avoid it. Most men share an intolerance of regular work, but workers overcome it in favor of the satisfactions of a home, friends, a community life, security, certain comforts and luxuries. They satisfy their cravings for irresponsibility, wandering, hunting, or combat in their vacations and leisure time.

The preventive of dependency is productive employment. Given a certain status of science, the key to productive employment is peace, capital, and entrepreneurial ability. The psychology of the ability to manage things and men together in producing goods which men want and to market the goods for enough to pay for raw materials, usage of plant, equipment, and labor, has been insufficiently explored. Some of its notable possessors, like Andrew Carnegie, would have won success in almost any occupation. In others it seems to be highly specialized: the senior Rockefeller could hardly have become a great man of letters, artist, military leader, or surgeon. Ability as an executive runs in families to an extent greater than home-training can account for. Its possessors have often lacked personal winsomeness, magnifice, and general benevolence. They can easily be made the butts of literary men, but they are rarely geese, and if they are, they lay the golden eggs of employment.

Kindly Behavior

To raise the general level of health, ability, morals and taste of a population is more important than to reduce the number of defectives: to increase kindly behavior in all is more important than to handle criminals better. In this section we study the qualities and behavior referred to as good will, the "social attitude," altruism, and kindly behavior.

Kindly acts and desires for the welfare of others are the results of the combination of forces resident in heredity and environment. Just what the genes of a typical human being contribute is not fully known. Man as a species is by original nature more disposed to kindly behavior than the baboon, but it would be possible to argue that the original nature of the chimpanzee is kindlier. Man has a repertory of smiles, pats, fondlings, coos, offerings of food and the like which seem to be unlearned. Yet it would be folly to rely upon a tendency to kindness in the form of encouragement to the awkward and shy, or forgiveness to persons who step on our feet, or support for a man of genius whose work we do not understand. Such provisions as the genes make for kindly behavior are specialized along lines of feeding and fondling those who whimper and wail, picking up the fallen, holding those who cling, and the like. They cause responses to sensed situations only. If we feel pity as a result of ideas caused by hearing of misery it is only by a secondary, derived attachment.

Individual differences in original dispositions to kindly behavior and feeling would be expected on general grounds to be as great as individual differences in stature, strength, intellect, or cheerfulness; and inferences from observation confirm this.

The sex difference has perhaps been exaggerated by poets and proverb-makers, but it surely exists. It is by no accident or environmental favoritism that women so quickly put men out of the profession of nursing, figured so numerously among social workers, and monopolized the kindergarten. They are better fitted to relieve, comfort, and console.

Kindly behavior is very amenable to training, both in its general amount and the situations which evoke it. Repetition and reward strengthen the connections between observable need and kindly acts and attitudes. Such kindliness is evoked less by those less often seen and dealt with, and becomes weak toward those who are strange in shape, color, language and manners.

The treatment of children has included harshness from sheer custom and from a high sense of duty (as in the denial of childish pleasures by the Puritans) but also extreme indulgence. Within hardly a generation the primary schools of the United States shifted from a militaristic regime in the interest of the teacher, enforced by corporal punishment and fear, to a regime of instructive play. But, on the whole, the trend has been toward greater benevolence to a greater number of fellow-creatures. The British planters in Africa may be callous toward the natives in comparison with certain humanitarian ideals, but kind compared with the Pharaohs.

It would be valuable to devise measures of the intensity of kindness to one's family, friends, neighbors, fellow citizens, one's race, all sentient beings, and to discover the correlations among individuals between kindly behavior in one and another of these widening spheres. I am strongly of the opinion that these correlations will be positive in any community under ordinary conditions. There are two exceptions which are rather proofs than disproofs of the rule. The first is the extremes of kindness toward offspring combined with callousness toward almost all others. The second is the occasional cases of general humanitarians who grossly neglect their wives, children, and neighbors.

It is reasonable to suppose that any given individual has a certain fund of kindly behavior to expend and that if he spends much on dogs and horses there will be less for women and children. If he spends much on his family there will be less for his neighbors. But it is also reasonable to suppose that many causes which stimulate kindly behavior to any will increase it somewhat toward all. A child who is taught to smell the flowers in his mother's garden instead of pulling them to pieces, to feed his kitten instead of mauling it, to pat baby sister instead of glowering at her, and the like, should get a certain broader gain in his treatment of other people's flowers, other pets, other infants, and so on. One's fund is maintained and increased by spending it.

The persons in whom kindliness toward all good people is a potent force are so few that Helvetius could write that he mentioned them "only for the honor of humanity." By my computation eight percent of human activity in the United States is spent for the welfare of others; but probably not over five seconds per day per person is spent for the welfare of mankind. It is significant that a very common reaction of even the most benevolent people to reading the specifications of twenty-six items for the good life presented in Chapter 16, is to ask, "How many of these do *I* have?"

By the nature of the genes and the deep-rooted traditions from ancient community life we tend to feed our hungry, comfort our obvious sufferers, rejoice with our fellows who rejoice, protect them when attacked, and the like. This natural-traditional philanthropy is provincial, temporary, and opportunistic. By the Christian doctrine we tend to broaden the meaning of 'our', to even to all mankind. We tend, however, to minimize the happiness and misery of this life in comparison with that of life after death; welfare in things temporal becomes of minor importance. The Christian set of mind did not, however, decrease the absolute amounts of worldly kindness. The brutalities of Christian conquerors were due to their general human nature rather than to their Christian set of mind. At its worst the Christian mind has caused men to distrust natural benevolence, deny innocent means of happiness, and endure unnecessary remorse and fear. At its best it has endorsed the brotherhood of man, the duty of cooperating with a God who is the supporter of all good in all men, and of a kingdom of heaven free from bigotry.

The scientific set of mind in philanthropy eschews reliance upon any other world than that known to our senses. The very person who as a Christian most devoutly believes in life everlasting will, as a physicist or physiologist, exclude that life from his postulates and conclusions. The scientific set of mind also pays more heed to the consequences of kindly action. Not brotherly love as a duty so much as brotherly love as a satisfier and harmonizer of wants; not the relief of the beggars but the abolition of poverty. Science in philanthropy as elsewhere seeks control through comprehension rather than comfort. Whether a belief will cause comfort or distress is minor in comparison with whether it is effective in predicting the course of nature and in controlling nature or ourselves in relation to the rest of nature. The scientific attitude toward philanthropy stresses action to the relative neglect of feeling; it is chiefly through action that feelings produce their consequences.

There is between science and the essentials of natural humanity a substantial positive correlation. Facing the facts will involve no net loss in instinctive kindliness. We may hope that the scientific student of human nature and social activities will extend kindly behavior to include the welfare of men's minds, will cure rather than palliate, will prevent rather than cure, will weigh future consequences as well as present relief, and will protect the interests of the able and good against a too sentimental indulgence of the weak or worthless.

Almost every advance in knowledge and change in human nature or customs acts on welfare. Certain facts about wealth and income, knowledge of the sciences of man, harmony among human wants, and the extraordinary complexity of many problems of welfare will be presented here.

Wealth

Wealth can, in Soddy's words, "build up a type of civilization nobler and more humane than was possible in a world held in the grip of, and limited by, want." ['35, p. 12] Other things being equal the greater the income of a community the greater its welfare should be. But other things are rarely equal.

As was seen in Chapter 17, income which is saved and put into improvements in the environment usually benefits welfare. Modern individuals and communities are, in general, less considerate of welfare in their use of current income than in their use of savings. Men who would spend their salaries in drink or ostentation will not so readily borrow on their life-insurance to do so. Communities which will endure the waste of current taxes by graft or inefficiency would probably be aroused by a capital levy to be spent similarly.

From the view of welfare a considerable amount of income is spent harmfully and an enormous amount is wasted; consider the waste (1) from the use of fashion-goods, (2) from small-quantity purchases which a little foresight could prevent, (3) from advertising which is not informative or entertaining or productive of economies in production, (4) from expenditures to demonstrate one's social rank.

Bowly writes, in connection with the general rise in the standard of living in England, "A very great deal of the improvement in all classes has been wasted by a continual straining after what I may call conventional uselessnesses, by which one group tries to mark itself off as superior to another group." ['15, p. 159] Veblen risks a quantitative statement: "I believe it is within the mark to suppose that the struggle to keep up appearances is chargeable, directly and indirectly, with one-half the aggregate labor, and abstinence from labor—for the standard of respectability requires us to shun labor as well as to enjoy the fruits of it—on the part of the American people." ['19, p. 399 f.]

The rich are abetted in wasteful expenditures by people who admire them for it and who scorn a rich person with frugal habits. There seems to be preserved by oral tradition a genuine belief that it is the duty of persons of rank or wealth not to economize in anything. There are probably more complaints against the rich for making so much money than for spending so much on luxury and display.

The Distribution of Wealth and Income

A body of impartial trustees for the welfare of mankind would rate proposals for the distribution of wealth and income according to their probable effects in satisfying all human wants, each want being weighted reasonably.

The present distribution is obviously defective in many particulars. Each reader can point to some person who has income which he misuses, and to some other who lacks wealth which he would use to benefit himself or others. A certain percentage of those inhabitants of India and China who live on a few pennies a day are as meritorious as unskilled American laborers who have twenty times as much. A community where thieving and graft are profitable is distributing its income badly.

Proposals which theorists make or which governments are now adopting seem likely to get welfare out of the frying-pan into the fire. Consider first the famous, "From each according to his ability; to each according to his need." If this is interpreted as, "Let each do his best for mankind; then mankind will provide him with what he needs in order to have a good life," it is an attractive idealistic doctrine. But it is very inadequate for it provides no means of getting each to do his best except the promise that such action will be rewarded in so far as the world's products when divided up are able to supply all needs. Nor does it provide any means of deciding what the needs of each person are. Whether each person takes what he thinks he needs, or each nation takes what it thinks its nationals need, or some super-government distributes the world's property and income—if the persons are then left to produce each according to his inclination, the result will be disaster; the habits of useful production will have been disorganized and the motives for it greatly weakened.

A second proposal is that the wealth and income of the great human family of the world be shared as in a single family. The meaning of this, if ninety-nine out of a hundred families are the model, will be a distribution caused by autocracy, affection, wheedling, and guile, tempered by a host of customs good and bad. Some agency must decide whose turn it is to mind the baby, wash the dishes, feed the pig, eat the chicken's neck. Only a small amount of the production or distribution of wealth can be entrusted to anarchistic benevolence. If elected governments do anything to distribute wealth and income, it is almost inevitably to take it from their opponents or from the innocent bystanders and give it to themselves or their supporters. A representative government represents its nationals, but it represents especially those whose votes it hopes to have.

There is, naturally, a tendency for a government to get taxes to support it from persons who will cause it little trouble. Thus the old monarchies taxed the peasants. Thus democracies today tax the rich who have few votes and the dead who have none. The government of a democracy is thus strongly moved to tax the few rich to benefit the many poor. At first the benefits took mainly the shape of free schools, parks, libraries and museums, and public health enterprises, felt by many, both rich and poor, to be a fit and proper contribution to welfare via government. Recently the benefits are largely in the shape of doles, consumed by the poor regardless of merit with no cultural gains.

Neither the wealth nor the income of the families or individuals of even a single city in this country has ever been recorded. But the 1930 census does report the value of the family home if owned and the amount paid for rent by families living in rented houses or apartments. These amounts (especially in the lower brackets) are presumably in fairly close correspondence with family incomes. Better estimates could be had by first multiplying these amounts by successively higher amounts, in accordance with the well-known fact that the greater the income the less the fraction of it that is spent for rent.

I compute for each city the 5 percentile rental (i.e., the rental less than which is paid by 5 percent of the city's families and more than which is paid by 95 per cent of them), the 10 percentile rental, the 25 percentile, the 50, 75, 90, and the 95 percentile. The results in the case of 12 cities are shown in Table 12. I compute also for each city various differences and various ratios (such as 95 percentile divided by 5 percentile, etc.), each measuring a certain feature of the variability of the city's families in amount paid for rent or its equivalent. They are shown for the twelve sample cities in Table 13.

I correlate these measures of disparity with a weighted index, G, of the general goodness of life for good people computed from the thirty-seven items listed in Chapter 12, including general death-rate (reversed); per capita expenditures for schools, libraries, and museums; average wage of workers in manufacturing plants, etc.

Table 12   Rental percentiles for 12 cities, 1930 (in dollars)

Cities	5	10	25	50	75	90	95
Augusta, Ga.	5.1	5.9	8.4	14.0	29.2	58.2	85.2
Meridian, Miss.	5.1	5.9	8.3	15.0	34.6	61.3	83.2
Paducah, Ky.	5.8	7.2	11.3	17.7	33.2	60.9	79.5
Kansas City, Kan.	7.4	10.3	15.2	23.8	38.1	51.4	67.8
Bay City, Mich.	8.5	11.1	16.3	25.2	40.1	55.3	70.3
Tacoma, Wash.	10.3	13.0	19.2	28.5	43.2	60.3	72.8
Yonkers, N.Y.	20.6	24.4	37.2	60.8	102.5	175.6	225.2
Syracuse, N.Y.	20.1	24.1	35.4	54.7	78.3	140.3	181.7
Dearborn, Mich.	23.3	30.4	40.9	59.6	84.9	123.5	146.4
Brookline, Mass.	25.2	35.6	64.9	105.5	161.7	235.9	279.5
Evanston, Ill.	34.0	45.1	66.4	99.0	160.2	234.5	278.1
Montclair, N.J.	28.2	36.7	62.6	124.3	200.7	262.1	301.1

Parity (the disparity score reversed) is a good symptom for a city, accounting for six percent of its variation from the American mean in G, the general goodness score. We can discover that parity in incomes as indicated by rentals was beneficial in these cities. There are three possibilities: parity selected better people, made people better, or was itself a by-product of a better population.

The proof that these are the only possibilities lies in the facts that for cities identical in P (a composite index of the quality of the population) parity *does not correlate with G* and that consequently *the percentage of the variation determined by P alone is as great as the percentage determined by P together with a parity score.*

As one feature of study of 295 cities, an index (P) of the personal qualities of the population was computed for each city, using the items

Table 13　Measures of disparity: differences and ratios of rental percentiles in the twelve cities of table 12.

Cities	Differences				Ratios	
	Unit = 1 Dollar					
	95–5*	95–50†	50–5‡	90–10§	95÷5‖	90÷10¶
Augusta, Ga.	80	71	9	52	16.7	9.9
Meridian, Miss.	78	68	10	55	16.4	10.5
Paducah, Ky.	74	62	12	53	13.8	8.4
Kansas City, Kan.	60	44	16	41	9.2	5.0
Bay City, Mich.	61	45	17	44	8.3	5.0
Tacoma, Wash.	62	44	18	47	7.2	4.6
Yonkers, N.Y.	204	164	40	151	11.0	7.2
Syracuse, N.Y.	161	127	35	116	9.0	5.8
Dearborn, Mich.	123	87	36	93	6.2	2.8
Brookline, Mass.	254	174	80	200	11.1	6.6
Evanston, Ill.	244	179	65	189	8.1	5.1
Montclair, N.J.	272	177	96	225	10.6	7.1

*The 95 percentile rental *minus* the 5 percentile rental.
†The 95 percentile rental *minus* the 50 percentile rental.
‡The 50 percentile rental *minus* the 5 percentile rental.
§The 90 percentile rental *minus* the 10 percentile rental.
‖The 95 percentile rental *divided by* the 5 percentile rental.
¶The 90 percentile rental *divided by* the 10 percentile rental.

shown in Table 14, with the approximate relative weights noted after each.[1]

Whatever good parity does is by its association with P. The influence of P together with that of parity accounts for no more of the variation of the cities in G than the influence of P alone. A population high in P creates parity and selects for parity by making its city unattractive to defectives, delinquents, and bums.

In so far as the causes which make some cities better than others can be trusted as guides to making all cities better than now, parity for

[1] The P score is of course not a perfect measure of the intelligence, character, interests, etc., of a city's population, but it would probably correlate over .85 with such a perfect measure. Details of the correlations and determinations are available in the *American Journal of Sociology*, Vol. 44, pp. 25–35. [Thorndike, '38]

Table 14   Constituents of index P of personal qualities of a population

	Approximate Weight
Per capita number of graduates from public high schools in 1934	1.50
Percentage which public expenditures for the maintenance of libraries was of the total public expenditures	.75
Percentage of illiteracy (reversed)	.87
Percentage of illiteracy among those ages 15–24 (reversed)	1.00
Per capita circulation of public libraries	1.66
Per capita number of homes owned	1.50
Per capita number of physicians. nurses. and teachers *minus* domestic servants	1.25
Per capita number of telephones	1.00
Number of male dentists *divided by* number of male lawyers	.66
Per capita number of deaths from syphilis (reversed)	1.00
Per capita number of deaths from homicide (reversed)	1.00

parity's sake is a false god. Philanthropy should then try to make the rich richer, but still more to make the poor richer, and still more to make people abler and better. As the people of a community become abler and better they will probably become less disparate in income, but if not, no harm will be done. Philanthropy and government need spend no more effort on the disparity of people's incomes than on the disparity of their toenails.

Knowledge

Increases in welfare require enough knowledge in the experts to ensure sound plans, and enough knowledge in the public to permit the experts to operate. Addressing college graduates a few years ago, Owen Young said: "It will not do for you merely to determine what you would like human relations to be. It will be necessary for you to find out what human behavior is, and then fashion the social machinery which will make for human happiness, and the sensitive controls which will be so necessary to keep such fragile mechanisms from running to their own destruction." ['34, p. 17] In so far as the last sentence is true, students of welfare are in a different position from the students of physics or physiology, or the inventors of dynamos or surgical operations. The public knows little about what the physical and biological sciences are doing, and except for occasional threats of fundamentalist religious interference lets them alone. How much the public needs to know of the sciences of man is not certain. People should know at least enough to trust the experts, whether there are any experts, and how to find them.

There are experts of the highest type in regard to what the law is and how it applies but what we are concerned with here is experts to inform us of the consequences of legislation, and what legislation should be enacted to produce such and such results. There are experts in history and government, but we need experts who know who will start wars and how they will turn out, how to harmonize conflicting interests within a nation, etc.

These sciences have not advanced so far that the most inferior expert is superior to the wisest layman. In the case of the treatment of delinquents and dependents, for example, there is no large body of demonstrated principles, based upon many thousands of instructive, often crucial, experiments, which no layman can understand without special study. There are important principles, the psychological ones among which have been noted in this volume. There have been important inventions such as the profession of nursing, the organized management of private charity, the social settlement, the children's court, the probation system, and national parks; but these have been fewer than one would wish, and have come more from trial and success and less from principles.

Social workers, teachers, vocational counselors, psychiatrists, economists, and others may aid welfare by the knowledge and advice they give as truly as by their own acts. Many thousands of dollars that would have been spent on the musical education of those with inadequate musical capacity are now saved by such consultation.

Reconciliation and Harmony of Wants

Man sometimes works against himself when sufficient genius can find ways and means to reconcile the conflict at no cost. The sex cravings of the male and the female are harmonized by courtship and union. Dogs want to have human masters as much as boys and men want dogs to attend and serve them. The bard and his hearers, the artist and those who view his products, the natural leader and his willing followers—these are samples of activities which are satisfactory to all concerned.

Along with his discoveries of ways to utilize natural objects and forces to satisfy his wants, man has made social discoveries and inventions, some of which operate largely by reconciliation and harmony. The invention of barter was a great step forward for welfare. The invention of each early step in the division of labor not only increased production but enabled persons to do more of certain work that they wanted and less of the work that they wanted to avoid. It was often a gain in happiness as well as efficiency when one daughter could specialize in caring for small animals, one for the garden, and one for spinning.

The discovery that the person who kept money safe could lend money to those who needed it harmonized the wants of owners, borrowers, and bankers. The invention of the savings bank, as a means to extend to small owners the privileges which large owners had, served a similar purpose. The inventions of insurance enabled individuals to buy security, companies to sell it, and actuaries to be paid for interesting computations. The invention of the cooperative store has probably saved people some money, given them business experience, and decreased unjust attacks on retail traders.

I will add two cases of harmonizing wants which may appear ludicrous, but not if one will divest himself of prejudices and realize the importance of preserving peaceful cooperation in a community in spite of the stresses and strains of theft, abduction, murder and the like. The first shows an Eskimo invention whereby an injured party gets revenge and preserves his self-respect, the injurer gets a chance to present his defense with a minimum of hard feeling, and the community gets free entertainment.

A Greenlander who has suffered some injury . . . will compose a satirical song in mockery of the culprit and challenge him to a public singing contest. Drumming and chanting, he throws his enemy's misdeeds into his teeth, exaggerating and deriding them and even rattling the family skeletons as well. The accused person receives the mockery with feigned composure and at the close of the challenger's charge returns in kind. Apart from the period of singing, no hostility whatsoever is displayed. The spectators follow proceedings with the greatest interest, egging on the performers to their utmost efforts. Such contests need not be settled in one evening but may be continued for a number of years, the litigants taking turns at inviting each other. [Lowie, '25, p. 413]

The second invention is the law or rule whereby a man who murders another must marry his wife. If shocking to our conventions, we must admire the simple perfection of its solution of the fundamental wants of a woman whose husband and supporter has been taken away, and of the community whose life and work must go on.

It is perhaps too much to expect that the disputes of employers and employees will be ended by some series of brilliant inventions which will give both parties what they really want; or that wars between nations will be ended by inventions to take care of all the ambitions, rivalries, loyalties, which cause or are gratified by wars. But I have hope that when man understands men as well as he understands the chemical elements he may control the explosions of the former as well as those of the latter.

The Complexity of Problems of Welfare

Human nature, though built on the simple plan of a system of connections, motivated by wants, and modified by satisfyingness, becomes enormously complicated under the conditions of modern life. Under one skin and inside one skull there are millions of connections, facilitating and interfering one with another. Within even a small city, there are thousands of social forces produced by various groupings and regroupings of its persons and features of its institutions.

Sometimes the forces one is using or opposing act together additively. Skill is a multiplier of time spent in much productive labor. Good will may be a multiplier of intelligence and knowledge in much welfare work. We may be suspicious of sweeping statements about welfare unless they are reached by a careful consideration of many facts, and fortified by observations, experiments, and analyses.

When the complexities of human affairs are aggravated by national ambitions and party politics the outcomes for welfare make strange reading. The passion of Rome for dominion gave Europe a peace and security greater in space and time than it has had since; but not the passion of the Goths, Vandals, and Huns. If the American colonies had been treated more wisely, or resisted less successfully, the United States might have been spared the Civil War. Most moralists would say that the British rule in India was conceived by private greed, born of injustice, and nurtured by misguided patriotism, but it presumably did better for the inhabitants of India than they would have done for themselves. The division, specialization, and cooperation of labor in producing goods is only one fraction, of the division, specialization and cooperation now required to produce welfare.

In so complex a task as increasing welfare, we should not expect too much. (1) Any man whose life and work satisfies some decent human wants and does violence to none may continue to mind his own business and leisure with a good conscience; he is probably more a benefactor than if he tried to serve all good causes. (2) Conflicts may arise and persist between agents each of which is on the whole beneficent; the church opposed science and there are quarrels within sociology and philanthropy. (3) Power will shift, as from warrior to medicine man to landlord to business man to party leaders. (4) Institutions will change; as production has left the household, entertainment and education are leaving it.

Guarantees that what seems best for welfare is best are not as safe as comparable guarantees in mechanics, or electrical engineering, or medical practice. The older moralists had an advantage over us, the courage of conviction being greater than that of critical knowledge.

Chapter 14
Economics

Economics and ethics

In the chapters on the psychology of economics and business, we shall
(1) study men as they are rather than as abstract entities each seeking to
maximize pecuniary advantage and minimize labor; (2) pay more
attention than has been customary to what they do to change wants
rather than to gratify them; (3) at times introduce ethical considerations
such as have usually been rigorously excluded from the sciences of
economics and business.

Economists themselves admit that the "buyer," "seller," "laborer,"
"entrepreneur" of economic theory have often been treated as too simple
economic forces, in particular as too rational, too insulated from habits
and prejuedices, too consistent. The second extension will also be
acceptable to realistic students of business and economics. The third,
however, will be criticized on the ground that it violates the established
custom in science of separating what is from what ought to be. When
ethics was a transcendental science allied to theology the criticism had
more force than it has in reference to ethics as a natural science of values
of all sorts. Any possible confusions caused by discussing some of the
consequences of economic facts to general welfare along with their
narrower consequences seem likely to be more than counterbalanced by
the advantages of seeing these wider relations.

Very few persons are influenced in their use of their capital and labor by purely economic considerations. Nor do many of them separate clearly their self-interest from the dictates of conscience or benevolence. At all events, I shall take the liberty of considering the consequences of the use of morphine to character as well as to productivity, the influence of a sale to others than the buyer and the seller, the general desirability of an industry as well as the additions it makes to income, and similar matters. It is relatively unimportant whether the psychology of a brigand who leaves us our life at the cost of our money or returns our child for a ransom is treated under crime or under business. The important requirement is that the psychology be true.

Utility and Disutility: Supply and Demand

Utilities and disutilities,[1] desirables and undesirables, satisfiers and annoyers are fundamentally facts of the effects of things on persons. In certain cases the utility or disutility of a thing can be equated into a simpler or wider or more instructive utility or disutility, where individual preferences and caprices are unimportant. So the utility of sugar as a source of bodily energy is measurable in calories; its utility as a sweetener could be measured along a suitable psychometric scale. When, as in diabetes, much sweetening with little carbohydrate bulk is required, sugar has disutility in comparison with saccharine. The common cereals in a raw state have utilities easier to estimate than those of the breakfast foods which certain persons have been taught to want.

In certain cases utility is determined chiefly by qualities by which it can contribute to the making of some other things or the performing of some service. So rubber, Portland cement, iron ore, wool, freight cars, and electric motors, are valued with little direct regard to the personal desires of individuals. At the other extreme are such things as women's hats, men's neckties, and certain novelties whose utilities are determined almost entirely by capricious personal wants.

By defining utility as desiredness or as satisfying potency, economics subtracts somewhat from the meaning which the word had in the minds of the early economists, who paid little heed to the eccentric, foolish, or perverse desires of ultimate consumers. Many human wants are little amenable to reason. France will not eat maize; America will not eat snails. Many of us retain a strong feeling that solid food is more strengthening than liquid.

[1] Irving Fisher has suggested that "wantability" be used in place of utility, and Pigou has suggested that "desiredness" be used.

Disutilities

In the main, disutilities are of two sorts: pains, including soreness, fatigue, nausea, fear, shame, disgust, or degradation; and deprivations, including such annoying lacks, as of customary eatables or drinkables, sex activity, entertainment, or ease of mind.

Some disutilities are regular features of certain forms of life and labor, but some are only greater or smaller probabilities of certain pains, diseases, and deprivations; a person's attitude of blissful ignorance or optimism may reduce these greatly. Systems of insurance are reasonable, especially where the probability is slight so that the cost of insurance is low.

The obvious pain or deprivation caused by an event may be a very poor measure of its total disutility. A short illness may cause a permanent defect. A slight insult may rankle for years. A single shock may cause a phobia.

The price paid to avoid a certain disutility is as inadequate a measure of the pain as the price paid for a utility is of its enjoyment. The natural tendency of a human mind is to regard emphatic utilities and disutilities as utterly desirable and abhorrent, and to refuse to bargain about them. Many persons honestly think that they want to read good books, who would not read them an hour a day if every duty was provided for. They think that they would not suffer certain infringements upon their prejudices for any money.

A man's satisfactions and discomforts are determined little by his absolute well-being; he rarely gets full value from security unless he has recently suffered anxiety. They are determined too little by what he possesses and too much by what other persons possess. Differences in the utility-disutility quality of the same thing with personal idiosyncracies are very great.

Scientific work in economics commonly makes a respectful bow to utilities and disutilities, and then shifts to the prices paid to obtain or avoid things. It acknowledges that certain persons on certain occasions would pay more than they do pay rather than go without. It acknowledges that certain utilities, such as health, friends, or a good conscience have no quoted prices in the market, but it leaves them as a vague lump of "psychic income." It excludes from study "free goods" like the air or the soul's salvation. The reason commonly given for doing so, that the only way to measure utilities and disutilities is by prices paid, is true in only a narrow and superficial sense. The fundamental truth is that money is a very convenient means of measuring indirectly on a very fine scale what can be measured more directly but less finely without it, and that the price a person does pay has certain obvious advantages over his estimate of what he would pay.

The satisfyingness or annoyingness of a state of affairs is an objective fact in nature. There is an inner subjective stream of being in a man to which he has access, which the world of scientific observers lacks. We must do as best we can without it; and we can do very well indeed.

That minds are insulated from one another is on a par with the difficulty for physicists due to the fact that two bodies cannot occupy the same space: the wise physicist never thinks of it. The real difficulty in studying human wants is that they vary so much with individuals, and with the same individual in different conditions; are so susceptible to change; and operate via a mechanism that comprises millions of neurones, each a very complex affair, and all shut up within a case of bone. The difficulties are thus of variability, modifiability, complexity, and access. Eye color and finger prints are extraordinarily variable, but we study them. Language is extremely modifiable, invertebrate zoology is extremely complex, and the structure within the atom is difficult of access. But we study all these. It may be desirable for economists to neglect the examination of human wants so far as they are not represented by money payments, but it is not necessary.

To a thousand babies, three months old, in varying conditions of health, sleepiness, hunger, ten drops of H_2O+ at $30°$ C in the mouth is for the time being more satisfying than the same $+ .1$ g. quinine sulphate and at $0°$ C, and less satisfying than the same at $30°$ C $+ .1$ g. of cane sugar. The three amounts of satisfyingness are measured roughly as primitive men measured the amount of light given by the stars without the sun and moon, by the moon and stars without the sun, and by the sun. Early astronomers measured the brightness of stars as of the first magnitude, second magnitude, etc., in much the same way. Certain impressions received from the babies' behavior produce competent estimates of the amount of satisfyingness just as certain impressions received from a star produce estimates of its brightness.

We go further and equate different states of affairs in respect to satisfyingness. We call the unit of satisfyingness that is produced in the average American male 25 years old by an average pleasant smile from an average male stranger 1 unit, and should estimate the number of units to represent the satisfyingness to an average member of the American Economic Association at seeing Adam Smith in the flesh; their estimates would vary widely, but they would be in numbers of the same order of magnitude. We would be equating the satisfyingness of a certain gratification in one group in terms of a unit of a different satisfaction in a different group. Nor would we have any essential logical difficulty in doing so.

States of affairs are incessantly rated and equated in terms of their satisfyingness and annoyingness by all of us to some extent. Just as we can have even very precise estimates of volume without any units of cubic measure, so we can, less precisely, sense the amount of satisfyingness or annoyingness which a certain afternoon of golf, or the bath and dinner following it, or a certain insult, will have for certain men. We advise our friends partly on the basis of such estimates. In this there is nothing subjective; nor is there necessarily any influence of money price.

This description of wants and their quantitative treatment may be contrasted with the orthodox view of economics that regards real wants and satisfiers as facts secluded in the inner life, and so to be abandoned entirely in favor of the money payments proportional to them. Taussig says that "Utility can be measured for the purposes of economic study in one way only: by the amount which a person will give to procure an article or service. Enjoyment or satisfaction is subjective. The objective test of it is willingness to pay." ['11, p. 124].

The attractiveness of money price as an indirect measure of satisfyingness is not that it is the only available measure, but that it is convenient, and consists of interchangeable units, related to a true zero point which means just not any purchasing power. These merits seem adequate to justify its use without recourse to claims that it is the only or best conceivable measure.

Teachers, reformers, religious workers, and physicians habitually measure wants and satisfactions in non-pecuniary ratios. Thus they desire to double A's thirst for knowledge, make the next generation crave peace among nations three times as much as the last, reduce the craving for sweets by twenty percent. Men of affairs often measure wants and satisfactions by living scales. They seek to make A want cleanliness as much as X does, or truth as much as Y does, or justice as much as Z does.

Somebody should study all utilities; and it seems wiser to have economists share in the work than to leave it all to psychologists, sociologists, and moralists. Among the reasons supporting this recommendation are the following:

(1) Purchasable and non-purchasable utilities intermingle. Persons who contribute money to support a church are giving to the Lord, providing insurance against hell, paying for the right to sit in a certain

pew. pleasing their wives, etc. Their prayers may have much the same utilities in view; and prayers were once as purchasable as shoes or sugar. Beautiful complexions are probably rarely purchasable, but millions are spent in the hope.

(2) Income is significant ultimately as a producer of satisfactions and preventive of annoyers which are essentially mental. In the last analysis a person does not exchange his labor or property for bread and meat, but for the enjoyment of tastes, the maintenance of health, relief from hunger, etc.

(3) Prices do not closely parallel utilities. (a) Consumers' surpluses may be enormous as in the case of a match, a needle and thread, an electric-light bulb: this magnitude may be more important than prices; (b) the world abounds in productive activities which have high utility as measured by prices and low utility in fact because one part of them cancels the other, such as when A pays for dainties which tempt him to overeat and then for a doctor to counteract the consequences. An important form of economic waste occurs when a person buys excitements which do not make him happy, cosmetics which do not make him beautiful, drugs which do not cure his ills. The economist by knowledge, interest, and training seems specially qualified to deal with such cases of utilities.

Observations of how people spend their leisure time should be as informative about utilities as observations of how they spend money received for their working time. An hour is an even better unit of measure than a dollar for the study of utilities, since it cannot be inflated or deflated, does not vary with the centuries, is being spent as fast as received, is comprehensible, and is divisible to any required fineness. Time is available in equal amounts for use by young and old, male and female, rich and poor, and leisure time is available for almost everybody in appreciable amounts. The expectation of future time differs relatively little for individuals of the same chronological age.

Economics as a rule eschews observations of utility and disutility but in two noteworthy cases it returns to them. The first concerns the common fact that, as a person receives unit after unit of an article or service, he receives ever smaller increments of satisfaction. This fact may be exalted into a law of "diminishing utility."

The second return to utilities concerns the fact that persons who have everything that they want cannot be satisfied further, that persons who have little that they want can be given satisfaction easily and cheaply, and that in between these is a continuous range of variation in the amount of satisfaction that can be provided. This has been elevated into the law that the increment of utility (i.e., satisfaction) is proportional to $\frac{\text{power added}}{\text{power possessed}}$. A million dollars to him who has a hundred million is then as one cent to him who has a dollar. Whether there is any one such law with wide applicability to persons is not known. No one relation can be applicable to all individuals because some satisfactions come from free goods and from goods not purchasable with money.

Desires and Satisfactions

There is a substantial correspondence between the strengths of a person's desires to have A or B and the amounts of satisfaction which he gets from having it. But nobody knows how close the correspondence is. Pigou argues that "For the most general purposes of economic analysis, not much harm is likely to be done by the current practice of regarding money demand-price indifferently as the measure of a desire and as the measure of the satisfaction felt when the desired thing is obtained." ['29, p. 24] He is probably not far wrong. The original nature of man links many desires to the corresponding satisfactions; and the experience of a thing's satisfaction-giving power is a suitable cause of desire for it in a reasonable person. But he is not entirely right. Many people on many occasions are not reasonable; and even reasonable people experiment to adjust desires with satisfactions.

Supply and Demand

In the broad sense of the two words, demand is determined by a study of human wants, has no important relation to supply, usually far exceeds it, and may often be considered indefinitely large. In the narrow sense, demand is related to the supply in so far as both are related to prices, one directly, the other inversely; elaborate experiments or observations are required to determine the demand for a certain commodity in this sense; it depends upon the wants of the group in question at each specified price for it and them, and probably also upon a complex set of forces of habit and prejudice. Economics consequently falls back upon the purchases actually made at various prices, as indications that there are effective demands at these prices.

Analysis of a sale from the supply and the demand points of view is not sterile psychologically. In customary usage, the supplier has a particular commodity or service to exchange, whereas the demander has purchasing power. The latter is in general the preferred status. The supplier tends to feel a certain insecurity as the residuum from experiences where he had things to sell, which is rarely fully counterbalanced by the brief triumphs of making the sales. The demander feels a certain confidence as the residuum of experiences of having power to get whatever he wanted that his money could buy.

Furthermore, the customary attitude of the supplier is one of request and submission whereas the customary attitude of the demander is allied to mastery. So the suppliers, who offers specific goods, and the demanders, who offers general purchasing power, are not psychologically equal in the exchange.

With supply and demand in connection with services, it is obvious that the supply of many is limited by the genes and by training. No stimulation could produce in the next decade ten thousand tenors equal to the ten best of the decade past, but this could be done rather easily in the case of electric welders, taxidermists, or interpreters. Contrariwise, the number of women willing to work as nurses in time of war, and able to do so after an adequate amount of training, is far above need.

Nothing like an inventory of the capacities of the genes to be trained to do the world's work is available. It is clear that the genes are very adaptable, maintaining life in jungle and desert, free and slave, antagonistic and cooperative. One is tempted to believe that they are almost indiscriminately adaptable to economic and social arrangements.

One is tempted to think that whatever modes of life and work the social order and industrial arts may prescribe, human nature will find tolerable and will supply any services demanded and properly rewarded. But this is not justifiable. The supply of great intelligence or great ability to rule is scanty; so is the supply of ability to understand, appreciate, and harmonize conflicting wants; so are many special capacities where no great improvement from wiser training can be expected.

The gene supply will vary slightly from decade to decade, but the training supply will vary greatly with changes in schools and lines of work. In the United States as large a percentage of boys and girls finish high school now as finished the grammar school about 1900. Many more farmers, probably, can drive a car than can milk a cow. Dressmakers are now much rarer than stenographers.

Scarcity

Scarcity of supply may mean a small number of units relatively to the number which are desired or needed. It may mean an absolutely small number of units. As a matter of strict reason, absolute scarcity is unimportant for economics, but psychologically it acquires importance by its affiliations. The greater an ability is the rarer it is: scarce articles are those which are very hard to produce; rare events are often celebrated; rare specimens often have a monopoly value. Consequently mere rarity, in and of itself, comes to be thought of as more of an asset than a liability. Such influence of scarcity of supply in and of itself is however very slight and operates probably from some faint hope that a demand may arise. A decrease in the supply of ragweed, crab grass, used razor blades, and amateur poetry, would not raise their prices until it reached the degree of scarcity which brought in a new demand from collectors of curios.

Natural Resources

Economics finds it convenient to distinguish between resources given by nature and additions made by man. Thus a river is a natural resource, but a canal or dams, levees, and sewage in the river are capital goods (or harms). The natural resources in man's nature are the genes and what they grow into; the modifications due to human institutions and training are mental capital.

It is conceivable that the genes have hidden powers to make men more intelligent, cheerful, and kindly, powers so buried by other components of man's genetic constitution that all the sages and psychologists from Solomon and Aristotle have failed to discover them; and that the psychology, biochemistry, and genetics of the future may bring them to light. But the more we learn the less probable it becomes.

It is certain that we can utilize the good elements in human nature better by directing and rewarding their activities. The curiosity of little children now largely runs to waste like an untamed colt or electric charge. The passion to exercise power often rages in destructive storms. The maternal tendency runs into vagaries of coddling or idolatry. It is doubtful whether employers and employees utilize their natures as persons better now than two hundred years ago; improvements in equipment, methods of work, accounting systems, laws regulating industry and trade, and the general conditions of city and country life may be enough to account for improved production without assuming that employers and employees have improved as such.

The utilization of a natural resource often uses it up, as in the case of coal, oil and plant foods, and almost never increases it; but a living resource, such as the "good" gene combinations of man, may be used over and over like a water power and multiplied in its descendants.

Theoretically the genes of a few males could be responsible for half the inborn qualities of the next generation. Actually the sphere of operation of a man's genes is usually very limited and localities have gained and lost greatly by the import and export of this natural resource, as in the migration of the Huguenots. The general theory for the economic utilization of human natural resources is much the same as for the utilization other resources, namely to have them work as much as possible.

The Psychology of Capital

A complete and accurate psychology of the creation of capital, its possession, and its use by workers must wait for many investigations and experiments and great talents to interpret them. These sections only present some of the facts and principles which appear when we examine man's economic activities in the light of the laws of the mind's working, so far as these are known.

The Creation of Capital

Almost everybody above the level where his maximum work just keeps him alive and able to work has the choice between more or less productivity. By more work he attains a margin of purchasing power which he may use to buy anything from theater tickets that have no value after three hours to a diamond ring or a farm or a share in a railroad which, except for accidents, represent an investment in perpetuity. Among his investments some are presumably non-productive, like the diamond ring, while some are presumably productive like the farm or the share in the railroad. When he uses his purchasing power for the latter he creates capital. Occasionally he creates it still more directly as in farm improvements with his own labor.

In choosing to create capital rather than work less or buy something non-productive, men are moved by many motives: to do less work at a later date; to secure protection for one's children; to have tools to make one's labor more effective; to have power in general; to win approval as a person of property; to satisfy one's conscience if it has been taught to esteem thrift for thrift's sake; to avoid the discomfort of not saving, if one has so formed the habit that he feels an unreasoned misery at not saving.

Saving and investing are appreciated in all discussions of thrift and capital. But the desire for ownership to make one's work more effective is not. Yet the musician saves for a violin, the scientist for books, the farmer to increase his holdings or build a barn, the manufacturer to extend his factory—in each case largely because the thing in question is needed to give fuller scope to abilities the man feels he has. The last thing a real carpenter will give up is his tools; they are psychologically a part of him. If the captain of industry is of such nature as to manage the factory or bank to public advantage, his saving to acquire it seems meritorious.

The next motives that require comment are the craving for power and approval. According to their inborn natures and training different men value power differently. Different forms of power are in part interchangeable, as when a man sells his political influence for money or spends his money to increase his popularity, but there is a strong tendency for a man to keep his power in the form in which he gained it. Many men create capital without caring much for it as a means to influence men. A politician may accumulate a large fortune without using it to gain his ends, his habit being to do that through politics alone. A great actor may use his personal influence to help his friends and annoy his enemies, but never think of using money so.

The satisfyingness of approval is especially potent as a motive for the creation of bodily and mental capital. The same general motive which makes one man throw dollars to the crowd makes another hoard them to invest. The difference is chiefly in the different weights that we attach to the admiration of different sorts of people. The scholar spends his energies for the admiration of scholars; the creator of material capital spends or saves his for the admiration of the "solid" men of the community.

Building factories and railroads often implies some general gift to the affected communities, though this may be retracted in their later operation. The case of new discoveries in science, technology, and business are of special importance in this regard. The man who uses time saved from self-indulgence to discover the cure for cancer, or more economical methods of bookkeeping, or even a better way to open mail, surely creates capital, in the broad sense of anything caused by man whereby labor and management can produce more. If he patents his discovery, it reverts to the public after a few years; if not, it almost always becomes public capital at once. Men of the ability to make such discoveries almost never hide them. They also want the satisfaction of seeing their ideas bear fruit, and of approval and power. Finally, all capital that is transferable as property is taxable, and the tax may be used for the public welfare.

Many of the valid arguments against the creation of capital are arguments against the creation of material capital at the cost of other capital. Thus we criticize the devotion to making and saving money which prevents a man from developing capital of body and mind which will be sources of satisfaction and efficient engines in public and private affairs.

Other arguments are against the creation of what turns out not to be capital. Thus we criticize the miser who hoards gold only to finger it, or the girl who toils to acquire a singing voice to which nobody will listen. The error here is obviously in creating non-capital. In some cases the capital is productive only for a short time and may not justify the sacrifice, as when a man accumulates a property but fails to educate his heirs in its use. But in general, the creating of capital is usually a good thing for those who do it, and better than what they would otherwise have done.

The soundest criticism of the creation of capital would seem to be that it tends to some extent to decrease the innocent pleasures of childhood, which are very cheap and very beneficial, in favor of the sophisticated comforts and luxuries of adult life, which are costly and often deleterious. The best time to invest in sheer non-productive play and pleasure is childhood. A pile of sand then may be worth a palace at sixty. A doll then may give more value than a fur coat later. Time is here worth little for production, but much for pleasure.

It is also sound to protest against a too one-sided devotion to productive labor preventing men from developing capacities for leisure. It would be a deplorable and grimy world if all men fitted by nature to be artists and scholars should be misled into the race for material wealth, but I for one would rather live there than in a world where all men fitted by nature to make material goods and manage commercial affairs had been misled into writing poetry. In any case the cure for excesses in productivity and thrift will not be found in negative treatment of men to reduce their appetites for the creation of capital, but in positive treatment to arouse love of and capacity for the impersonal pleasures of life.

One more moral reflection may suffice. If thrift in a small way by the creator of a savings bank account, or the maintainer of a modest insurance policy, is desirable, the creation of capital in a large way by the man who builds a railroad or a steel plant is more so. The inconsistency which praises the man for creating his first thousand and blames him for creating his hundredth million is explainable, but illogical and mischievous.

The Possession of Capital

The psychology of the possession of capital is much simpler than that of its creation. The possession of capital is a form of power, both directly by the habit of using it and indirectly by the treatment accorded to one who has such power by other men. This sense of one's importance is felt largely irrespective of how one came to possess that power. Men having power are ready to assume that they deserve it. This sense of importance tends to become generalized. The man who finds that he can work his will and that his opinions are reverenced by those who wish to get jobs or sell him something, tends to think that he should direct government or the local church, and that his opinions are authoritative in art, morals, and education.

All this is often very irritating, but is more suitably a subject for humorous reflection than for invidious comment. We are all tarred with the same brush. The schoolmaster, from being given power to teach his pupils, notoriously comes to feel that he has the right to teach the world (as I may be now illustrating!).

The Attitudes of Laborers Toward Capital

The capital with which one works—the farm, the cows, the machine, the desk or counter—receives a certain amount of regard and loyalty.[1] Sagacious employers know how to encourage this; and many a dingy factory is the recipient of love and loyalty.

The more usual attitude is, however, one of taking the existence of railroads, mines, factories, machines, and storehouses for granted, accepting them as facts like sunlight or rain. Just as the very little child accepts his meals or the lack of them as given facts of nature without tracing them back to the industry of his parents, so the ordinary workman does not trace back the shop he enters to the savings of generations present or past. If a new railroad or factory is built, the event appeals to him much as if a meteor fell from space. In this fallow soil of neglect, myths may be sown and nourished.

The myth of manual labor as the creator of all capital is like the story told to children of the beneficence of the cow as the sole cause of his

---

[1] Ordway Tead has given some striking instances: A book bindery in which work was seasonal undertook to distribute jobs by transferring the girls among the departments. The effort was met by a strong feeling that the particular process which the girl already knew was "her job;" she neither wanted anybody else's nor wanted any one to learn hers. In a large foundry facing a strike the men had all the forges numbered among themselves and each man was assigned by the group to one which he had grown accustomed to by years of use. The attempt of a new foreman to transfer the man at "number one forge" to a different workplace created a storm of resentment. Instances could be multiplied to show the strength of the feeling of "mine and thine," and the part it plays in the running of industry. ['18, p. 68 f.] See also Kipling's "McAndrew's Hymn."

milk; except for the direction of manual labor by non-manual planning,—by the intellect of the laborer or of someone else—the railroads
and bridges and homes would never have been built, any more than a
world of cows would organize the necessary arrangements to feed human
babies.

It is direction from the mind that has built granaries rather than
graves. The mere manual part of labor would as soon build a bridge in
the wrong place as in the right, or four-track the railroad from Peter's
Corners to Podunk as that from New York to Philadelphia. It is to those
early botanists who selected seed, those early zoologists who domesticated animals, those early engineers who invented the lever. those early
entrepreneurs who started manufacture and trade in arrow-heads, and to
their successors in intellectual and managerial leadership through hundreds of centuries. that we owe the capital of today.

The myth of capital as oppressor rests upon a verbal confusion of
capital with capitalists, a factual confusion of capitalists with managers.
and a misconception of managers. Material capital does temporarily
oppress certain forms of laborers when a new invention replaces their
skill by a machine. Such measurements as have been made of individual
differences in moral qualities do not indicate that those who own much
material wealth are inferior in sympathy or benevolence to those who
own little. And common observation seems to indicate that capitalists
and business men are less sharp and greedy in their dealings with their
workmen than with other capitalists, business men, and the purchasing
public. The purchasing and sales departments probably drive harder
bargains than the personnel department or the factory management.

Owners and Non-Owners

The attractiveness of these myths depends upon the inequalities in the
ownership of capital. A feeling of inferiority is common, and anything
that mitigates this feeling tends to be cherished. It is inspiring to think
that you and your like really created all the wealth in the world, that your
lack of worldly success is due to being held under the iron heel of monster
capital. Not one man in a hundred is honest with himself about himself.
Life devoid of the approval of one's world is dull and empty. but life
devoid also of the approval of one's own self is almost unendurable. A
man will accept any fantasy, and fabricate any delusion to retain inner
satisfaction.

There is a more sinister side to such myths. They are a standing excuse
for any worker who wishes to commit robbery without self-reproach.

Non-owners are probably as honest as men in general, but myths which make robbery respectable for anybody are dangerous.

It is extremely unlikely that the present customs by which ownership is attained and perpetuated customs made with little scientific knowledge of human nature or industry—are unimprovable. We may expect that nations could arrange conditions of education, industry, taxation, and inheritance so that power through ownership of material capital will be held by those who will increase its quantity and quality, and use it to serve the common good. But such matters of distribution are minor compared with the increase by the advancement of science and education and the decrease by war and folly. Largely as a result of the progress of science each family now owns a substantial property in his share in the roads, waterworks, parks, school-buildings, hospitals, and the like, and shares in the fruits of property held in trust for his welfare by foundations great and small. In war everybody receives his share in powder and ships which are all used up. Each family could, instead, have an automobile and a garage, or an excellent private library, or free admission to the movies for life, or a camp in the country.

In so far as the trouble lies in our institutions, laws, and customs, science should improve them as it has improved our material instruments. If it also lies in human nature itself, science should improve human nature.

Misleading Attitudes Toward Capital

There is too much interest in who owns capital and too little in what it is and what is done with it. For utility or welfare it may make a great difference whether savings are in the form of fruit trees, library books, and steel mills or in the form of marijuana, roulette wheels, and battleships; or whether a steel mill makes rails and girders, or cannon; or whether a battleship is used for justice or for greed. Who owns it is of no consequence save as an indication of how it will be used. It is relatively unimportant whether it is owned by ten thousand widows or by one, by Americans or by Hollanders.

When we aspire to increase public ownership of power-plants, railroads, certain school buildings, parks, we often believe that these are created by waving some magic social wand. But the public can acquire capital only by luck as in discovering a gold mine, or by working to produce it, or by taking it from somebody else. If the public took it from somebody, we did not create it; he did.

The public as public has hitherto produced very little. We may hope that in the future that community action may promote health, beneficial recreation, and desirable education, so that the doctors, dentists, clerks, factory workers, managers, and all others may produce a plus over what they would have produced otherwise. This plus could be taken as a tax which properly belonged to the public. That would be the nearest approach to public production in a modern state or city. If individuals have freedom to earn and save, the bulk of public capital will still probably be taken from private capital. It may be desirable for us to take it, but it is highly undesirable for us to think that we made it.

Many persons have no realizing sense of the importance for welfare of capital goods public or private. They understand after a fashion that railroads take people where they want to go, that sugar and soap come out of refineries and factories, and that almost everything they eat, drink, or wear is made by machinery. But the books they read in school tell little about factories; the movies they see are almost devoid of activities in production. Daily work may give one only partial knowledge of a very small sample. Books, newspapers, sermons, and political speeches are made by persons who are much more sensitive to the smoke, dirt, noise, and fatigue associated with production than with what capital does.

Persons of humanitarian temper, observing that a hundred thousand dollars worth of mortgages produces as much for its owner as the labor of a farm hand, coal miner, washwoman, and country school teacher produces for them, lament that the capital receives more than its due and the laborers less than theirs. Such humanitarians seem perverse in their ideas of how to change the ratio of the rewards to capital and labor. There are two sound methods, both consistent with general welfare—to encourage laborers to greater proficiency in their work, and to encourage people to save more and invest more in capital goods, so that the supply of the latter will increase faster than the population. Such creation will tend to cause a drop in the rate paid for the use of capital, and probably also a rise in real wages. Those who lament the high ratio of the wages of capital to the wages of labor seem unwilling to heed the fact that the cure for the evil they attribute to capital is to have more of it.

Property in the form of capital goods works for persons as truly as do doctors or schools. It is as truly in the public interest to keep shoe factories from being burned as to keep water or milk from being polluted. Action which maims capital goods in the hope of benefiting health and happiness may be like the action of a village which tears up and burns its railroad ties to keep its houses warm.

Mental Capital

Certain sorts of mental capital, particularly knowledge and ideals, are almost free goods. What were once trade secrets of shamans and priests are now public property; anybody who has certain intellectual abilities may possess them at moderate cost in time and effort. Sheer knowledge enables a farmer to grow more, a prospector to find more than he would without that knowledge. It enables us all to waste less (which is as good as to produce more) on foods, clothes, drugs, cosmetics, etc.

The applications of physics and chemistry to engineering and manufacturing, of biology and botany to agriculture and medicine, have been largely by-products of scientific curiosity and the love of intellectual achievement for its own sake. This is now changing; the bars are lowered between "pure" and "applied" science. The genes of a Darwin born again would not live as a country gentlemen, but as a worker in some institute of biology or eugenics. A Joseph Henry of today would very probably be working for the General Electric Company.

The Utilization of Capital

Much material capital is usable continuously except for periods of inspection, repair, and the like; its misuse and idleness are caused by human factors. We are to blame if ships and trains are motionless, if houses are tenantless, if factories make nothing two-thirds of the time, if churches are empty fifteen-sixteenths of the time. If people did not object to working at night, factories could run two shifts instead of being enlarged.

Pride, prejudice, and the enjoyment of ownership will eliminate the proposal that the Baptists, Congregationalists, Methodists, and Presbyterians should use the same church building, but what could be more Christian as well as reasonable? A nation-wide rental service of harvesting machinery which would be moved north with the season would meet strong opposition from the pride of possession of farmers, as well as from the irritation at dependence upon anybody for anything. Whatever causes the idleness of capital during the low swings of the so-called business cycle is psychological in that it is not a necessary characteristic of material capital.

The Utilization of Mental Resources and Capital

The waste from idleness of mental resources and capital is deplorably great. The placement of the world's n persons in the world's N jobs is far from perfect. By a perverse social inheritance men are taught that destructive sport and ceremonials are more reputable than productive labor. They are prevented from productive activities by business depressions, technological changes, strikes, and lock-outs. It is certainly far less however than it was a thousand years ago when the great ones so often wasted their talents in killing one another; the wise ones, in pedantry and sorcery; the kindly ones, in prayer and penance; the great majority, in dull and servile routines.

Chapter 15
The Psychology of Labor, Consumption, and Wages

The Psychology of Labor

Most of us think of labor as a necessary evil which men are bribed to carry on. Shorter hours and higher wages move the world's workers toward welfare. We may concede that labor has a value for health and morality, but intrinsically labor is a cloud whose only silver lining is wages. Labor is a suffering endured only because it prevents the greater suffering of lacking what wages or profits bring. Labor laws, labor disputes (at least on the surface), and welfare schemes for laborers reflect and in the main confirm this view. It is, however, an unsound view of the psychology of labor.

First of all, activity of body or mind is not intrinsically objectionable. We avoid labor nearly as often because we wish to do something else as because we wish to do nothing. Boys and men leave their chores to do more violent activity in hunting. The housewife abandons the family mending to do fancy embroidery.

Nor is productive labor more objectionable than is sport; human nature has no predilection for the useless as such. The child would prefer his mud-pies edible, the hunter would prefer a useful trophy. There is hardly a gainful occupation that is not used as a cherished pastime by some men or women. Rowing a boat, maintaining a garden, overhauling an automobile, and breeding livestock, are such cases.

238

Many men and women would continue productive labor even if they were wealthy. This is admittedly true of the eager inventor, the zealous musician, the captain of industry; the facts show that they work regardless of wage or the need of profit. The locomotive engineer may bewail his hardships, but his real longing may be for the work he is paid to do.

The economist will object that our illustrations are from highly skilled labor; most labor, he may assert, is objectionable to the laborer. Farm work, mining, factory work, routine clerical work, selling and domestic service are specimens of the great bulk of labor; and these, he will claim, are essentially unpleasant. Who would month after month milk cows or dig holes or hammer a drill or operate a punch press, or copy names, or scrub floors, except for a money reward?

Doubtless the economist would not. But he is not the one doing it. If the one doing it is a person strong in body, dull in mind, who hates being forced to decide, or step outside his routine, who enjoys the company of animals, and feels a certain sense of mastery and pride in being a good milker, to such a one milking cows and cleaning stalls may be no more objectionable than talking and writing is to the college professor.

Wages and profits are rarely the only reward for labor. Many work for love of the work. Still more are paid by the approval their achievements receive, by the sociability of the workers or the friendliness of the boss. We should not think of the laborer as leaving his human nature behind him when he goes to work, and becoming then a single-hearted devotee of money. We should consider all the instincts and habits that move him as truly when he works as when he rests or plays or fights or votes or marries.

There are five fundamental trends in human nature which deserve consideration. The first is the satisfyingness of activity at which one can succeed. Idleness is seductive when accompanied by sociability, or stimulation by novel sights, or a sense of superiority to those who cannot afford to be idle, but mere idleness *per se* is attractive only to exhausted bodies or minds. The labor problem is to induce men to be active in ways advantageous to the community.

Second is the satisfyingness of mastery. To have other human beings step out of the way, lower the glance and obey the command, is worth much. It would be an interesting study to ascertain whether a plumber has a helper, a farmer a hired man, or a waiter a bus-boy, more because these helpers increase efficiency, or because one thus has someone to gratify his craving for mastery.

There is also satisfyingness in submission—*to the right kind of man.* It is natural to submit to the person whose size, voice, prowess, and status make him an acceptable master. The same man who enjoys mastery almost to the point of tyranny over his employees may enjoy submission almost to the point of servility, to some business giant, baseball hero, or even to his wife. The strength of this tendency varies, being greater in some men than in others, and greater in general in women than in men. There may be too much need for submission and too little chance for mastery for the great majority today. But not all of submissiveness is annoying.

Next is the satisfyingness of company. Man is by nature gregarious, likes to have human beings around him, and to have them smiling rather than peevish and sad. The department store and factory are reliefs to many girls whose home life is a complaining mother and crying children. Many a young man gets enjoyment from the bustle of the office very similar to that for which he pays at the amusement park.

Most important is the satisfyingness of the feeling that one is of consequence, and should be treated respectfully. Man reacts to his own inner image of himself. If men neglect or scorn him, he may derive some satisfaction from concluding that they do not appreciate him properly. Religion may be a comfort by its assurance that in a future life he will have a higher station.

This hunger for consideration, approval, and eminence is one of the great moving forces in human life. It deserves to be ranked along with the primary motives of hunger, sex, the craving for physical safety, and the intolerance of bodily pain. The New England housewife did not relentlessly pursue dust beneath beds for wages; her husband would in most cases have paid her more to be less tidy! She cleaned her house so that it might force admiration from her friends and foes. Women devote an enormous amount of labor to personal adornment not as a matter of sex attraction but simply to win a general diffuse approval, chiefly from other women. We have the testimony of Carlton Parker that a miner will set up his blasts in such a way that other miners will admire his skill in using so few drill-holes, or the like.

The reward for labor is not only the power to buy whatever money will buy, but the degree of gratification given to every human craving by the job itself. The evil of work is not only that the worker labors so long for so little, but that he may have to work at what he is not fit for, submit to rule that is humiliating, and in general be thwarted in the fundamental impulses of his nature.

To understand a labor problem we must consider the total situation of which the job is a part. Human nature tends to attribute to any obvious external fact whatever feelings have been associated with it, regardless of their real cause. Thus a workman, really upset by the peevishness of his wife, may think his work is too hard, his machine not properly adjusted, or his foreman unfair. The behavior of the owner's family may soothe or irritate workers. If a worker has to go a long distance and stand up and travel in unpleasant company, he tends to figure this in on the job.

What is objectionable and attractive in each job will vary enormously with individuals. The postman's walk and burden would be a pastime to one and fatigue to another. The work of a clerk in an insurance company is as easy as knitting to certain young women with a passion for arranging items, but it would be a form of torture to others. Dirt, monotony, noise, and solitude vary in their annoyance to individuals. The conflict of personalities in trading varies from agony to joy. The politeness and winning persuasiveness required of salesmen would be ashes in the mouth of most miners, engineers, and cowboys.

Public opinion is a large factor in man's tolerance of his work. The opinion of Cedar Street that John Smith the barber has done very well counts more to John Smith than the opinion of all polite literature that the barber's is a rather servile trade. The man whose abilities qualify him to be a machine hand usually has been born and bred in a group who do not scorn him becauuse he is such; he is esteemed within his group as the tradesman is within his. Similarly a successful plumber usually feels no more degradation at not being a sanitary engineer than the average doctor feels at not being a Lister. The prize-fighter cares as little for the economist's scorn of his intellect or the moralist's scorn of his trade as they care for the prize-fighter's scorn of their puny blows; he lives in a prize-fighter's world.

By reducing what is really objectionable in labor—rather than by reducing labor indiscriminately—by attending to its immaterial as well as its material rewards, by considering the total situation as it influences the worker, and by studying men as complex individualities, we may hope to get more and better work done with more satisfaction to all concerned. Needless personal indignities inflicted by foremen, and others make work a misery and debauch the inflictors of the affront. It is not the actual infringement of personal rights and dignity that is the main trouble, but the rankling memory of them and the daily bitterness of expected tyranny.

The immaterial wages which the whole man receives in addition to the pay envelope which the "economic man" receives can be increased at little cost. How far business concerns should go is a matter for study and experiment. Other things being equal the worker will enjoy his work better in proportion as this is done, but the other things may not be equal. Here are a few sample problems: Should each job be given dignity by a title, so that the youth can say I am "Second assistant operator on No. 43" instead of "I am a machine hand"? Should each driver drive the same truck not only to place responsibility better and reduce accidents, but also to enlist loyalty and give room for his instincts of ownership and mastery? How far should the craving to "belong" be gratified by social and athletic clubs connected with the concern? Would it be silly to put the name and title of each clerk on his desk, so that he could be addressed by name by whoever cared to do so? What is the proper use of rivalry between individuals, and between departments?

Perhaps the greatest gains of all are to be expected from the adjustment of labor to individual differences. A perfect fit of work to workers cannot of course be guaranteed, but we can do much better than now, when vocational guidance is a mixture of casual reports of friends about their jobs, irrational prejudices, and fantastic expectations derived from story-books, all operating on ignorance both of the world's work and of one's own powers and temperament. Employers can realize that a job is never really filled until the employee is found who fits that job in the sense of being able to do it reasonably well and get reasonable satisfaction from it.

The Conditions of Work

A reasonable rule is that a person should, after a period of labor and its wages, be at least no worse off in mind and body than he would have been without both. The choice has sometimes been a cruel one for the worker. He has had to choose between death by exhaustion and death by starvation, or between the brutal customs of a factory and the degradation of an almshouse. A hundred years of advancement has improved the alternatives greatly. Moreover, investigations are being made both to discover improvements in the conditions of work which will benefit employees at no cost to employers and to prevent employers from causing injuries to laborers.

Besides improvement to lighten labor and reduce accidents, to reduce poisonings, respiratory diseases, and other physiological damage, and improvements by prompt medical and surgical care, psychological and social improvements are now being studied.

The optimum length of day to secure the maximum production per person will vary with the nature of the work. A bridge-tender or keeper of a small shop may suffer no harm from being on duty 12 hours a day since he may spend half of it in reading, seeing the sights, or conversing pleasurably; the disutility of longer hours to him may consist entirely in the other activities deprived him. For a worker on an assembly line or attending to an incessant flow of telephone calls or customers. even seven hours may mean discomfort during the work and a loss in enjoyment of the leisure following it.

All good observers will agree with Pareto's statement that "The best and most intense work is that of the man who works for his own profit: the worst is that of the man who is compelled by the fear of punishment." ['97. p. 189] Slave labor is notoriously inefficient. The more closely rewards are associated with, and belong to, the work for which they are given, the better; in piecework and bonus systems the arrangements should be made comprehensible by the worker so that he can be aware of what he is receiving.

The Psychological Specialization and Division of Labor

Besides the specialization and division of labor in the ordinary sense. there is a specialization in the bodily and mental qualities desirable for work and a division of the labor amongst persons in relation to these qualities. Jobs differ in their requirements of bodily strength. in its location in legs, back, arms, etc.. in the frequency of occurrence of exertion, in requirements of the sense-organs, in intelligence with things and their mechanisms, with persons and their feelings. with abstract symbols, in various forms or regularity, precision, and orderliness, in honesty with property. A man may fail as a truck driver because he (1) cannot handle heavy barrels, or (2) cannot read, or (3) cannot be polite to customers, or (4) cannot get on with a helper, or (5) cannot keep an exact schedule of appointments, or (6) indulges in petty cheating, or (7) is allergic to the substance he has to carry. Each of such terms as truck driver, salesman, foreman, stenographer, or cook covers a multitude of jobs, differing in the conditions for giving and getting satisfaction.

Even in one of the more definite fields of labor, as a railway engineer. telegrapher, or operator of a certain machine, there is not perfect uniformity. Even there certain qualities of decency and cooperativeness may count toward the satisfactions the workers give and get. It is well known that the social status of one's fellow-employees counts heavily, especially among women. Identical factory jobs may be considered "nice" in one town and degrading in another.

Educational and Vocational Guidance

Many schools and colleges try to inform pupils about various lines of study in advance to maximize the student's profit from what he studies. By tests and records they inform him of his academic achievements, and to some extent his other abilities. Schools also provide information about trades and professions. Educational and vocational guidance are not so surely beneficial as educational and vocational information, there being a possibility that the free play of interest and ambition will guide a boy or girl better than the prescriptions of counselors.

Vocational guidance can prevent obvious follies, such as the mistaking of an ordinary interest in construction for a special bent toward engineering, or an employer's confusion of verbal facility with intelligence, or the hoaxing of young people by fraudulent advertisements. It can measure so-called general intelligence (which, though not strictly general, is a *sine qua non* for graduation from certain professional schools) with a very small margin of error.

The adjustment of work to workers by the competition of employers to obtain the best services for their money and of workers to obtain the best rewards for their services is faulty, especially for beginners. But it is not so faulty as sometimes represented. It may seem a waste that gifted men should do brilliant work in law school only to become business executives. But it has not been proved that it is a waste, either for them or for the world. It seems a waste that men should take degrees in electrical engineering only to spend their lives in selling electrical apparatus, but many of them may thus be happier and more useful.

The only sound procedure in measuring dissatisfaction is to use a fair sample of all workers. Hoppock ['35] did this, interviewing every adult male resident of New Hope. He obtained replies that showed 15 percent of dislikes, 9 percent indifferent, and 77 percent of likes. Forty-eight percent reported that if they could have their choice of jobs they would remain in those they had. Sixty-six percent said they got more satisfaction from their jobs than from what they did in their leisure time. The writer ['35 A] found a little under 10 percent of dislike in 1140 young workers 18 to 22 years old. The percentage of dislike may be set near $12\frac{1}{2}$, the percentage of liking near 80, and the percentage of indifference or doubt near 10.

The Psychology of Management

The sciences of economics, business, and psychology have not yet discovered what abilities determine managerial ability of any sort used in industry and business. There are some grounds for distinguishing three varieties of intelligence—with ideas, with things, and with persons—and presumably the last is one important component in successful business or industrial management.

All would agree that sociability and persuasiveness are qualities useful in a manager, and more needed by him than by an inventor, literary man, scientist, surgeon, or farmer. Appreciation and tolerance of opponents, patience in getting one's way, and realism in one's hopes and fears also seem desirable.

In economic theory the entrepreneur often appears somewhat like a man with three bottles, of land, labor, and capital, who compounds a mixture which he thinks will maximize profit. This is, of course, only a small part of what he does. He does decide how much capital his enterprise needs, but chiefly in what machines, raw materials, etc. it is to take shape. He does decide how many employees are needed, but chiefly what they are to do, what sort they are to be, how they are to be treated, etc.

At least one economist has used the word "entrepreneurship" as if there were a real and fairly unitary behavior in business and a quality, or complex of qualities, in human nature corresponding to it. To a psychologist it seems extremely unlikely. Two things only can safely be asserted about entrepreneurial abilities; namely, that men differ widely in the amount possessed and that the great majority of men do not possess enough to make a decent living. Choose a thousand men of any age at random, give each of them $20,000, and persuade them to use it in industry or business for themselves. One or more of them will probably have made over $200,000 in business in ten years.[1] A considerable number will lose the entire $20,000 long before ten years. Over three-quarters of them will have failed in the sense that they did not make as much per year in business as their previous earnings plus what the $20,000 would have yielded if invested conservatively. These are dogmatic assertions, but probably no competent students of business will think them extravagant. Most of the persons who start in business with $20,000 of their own have saved it out of earnings as employees in business and are among the highest twentieth of the population in general business ability. Even among these the percentage of failure is high. Many of them can do well in a business run by others, but fail as entrepreneurs. About one out of eight retail-trade enterprises go out of business every year.

[1] Those making $200,000 or more are likely to be men who were already doing well in business before the experiment.

It would be instructive to study the psychology of hired managers, owner-managers, and originator-owner-managers. A common opinion among economists is that the first group will be less economically successful than the second and third, especially the third. Assuming that of two identical persons one is a hired manager and the other an owner-manager, the essential psychological differences due to their status are: (1) The pecuniary rewards for success and punishments for failure are much larger for the owner-manager; (2) These pecuniary rewards and punishments are inevitable and immediate for the owner-manager; but the rewards to the hired manager are more or less dependent on the whims of the owner, and punishment in the shape of dismissal or reduction in salary may be avoided or delayed, especially if his mistakes are not obvious; (3) The owner-manager is concerned about the total result of his behavior, one shrewd stroke balancing one bad blunder. The hired manager, unless he is an exceptional man, is more concerned to avoid blunders than to make hits; (4) The owner-manager has only himself to convince. The hired manager has to convince the owner or board of directors about certain matters; (5) The owner-manager more often dictates and competes with others. The hired manager must often adapt himself and cooperate.

The hired manager group will probably be somewhat less daring, masterful, and devoted to money-making, and somewhat more studious, cooperative, sensitive, and eager for approval than the owner-manager group. But these differences will probably be small. The men who work their way up as employees in an established industry with large units and the men who work their way up by ownership of small units which their ability expands will be much alike in fundamentals.

The Psychology of Trade

As a result of business experience a large part of the trade in civilized countries is freed from injustice, chicanery, and waste. Many products are standardized so that the buyer knows exactly what he gets; many prices are immovable by higgling, as in the mail-order houses or great department stores. The prices are fair in the sense that they are the same for any one as for any other at the same time and place. One is protected against his own inability to bargain as he is protected against his inability in physical combat by social customs. Trade is made more rational or logical instead of personal or psychological.

But its rationality is nowhere complete. A druggist buying from a dealer gets standard chemicals at fixed and published prices, but the reduction he gets by buying a pound instead of an ounce varies from $37\frac{1}{2}$ to 77 percent. The reductions made in price per unit by merchants when large quantities are bought abound in such irrationalities as this, and worse. [Thorndike, '39] The price-changes for stocks, bonds, metals, oil, rubber, etc. are surely partly psychological; if they were logical they would be narrower, varying more symmetrically around some reasonable trend.

Contrary to the trend toward rational trading is a tendency to confuse the issue by added services in the way of discounts, credit, delivery, privilege of return, trading stamps, care of babies, etc. These are often emphasized more than the adequacy of the stock and promptness of service. They are somewhat like the flattery and servility of the old-time shopkeeper.

Buyer and seller may derive other utilities from their bargaining than pecuniary gain. The pleasure in conflict, in argument, in victory may be considerable. Various amenities may be associated with the trading. The cooperatives of tobacco-growers found that their members contrasted the business-like methods of their buyers unfavorably with the cheerful sociability provided by the commercial buyers.

From the point of view of welfare, advertising causes a great waste of money by sellers and of time by buyers. Much of it is a series of attacks which neutralize one another. Most buyers will profit more from an hour spent in consulting some impartial expert than from a hundred hours reading of advertisements. Just as honest buyers pay part of the bills of defaulters, so buyers who never read advertisements pay part of the costs of printing them.

Advertising is not all waste. Some of it is informative. Some of it benefits both the seller and buyers, as when a peak load is spread out and a lower rate thereby given. Some of it is useful as entertainment. Idealists will reproach women for scanning advertisements to see the styles, but this mild entertainment may be better than the talking or day-dreaming it replaces. The waste in advertising is only part of the waste in buying and selling.

Among selling costs incurred largely in the buyers' actual economic interests are those which are largely due to the great number of assistants employed, the large stocks held, and the central sites required for display. The service of assembling and maintaining a stock so as to provide the buyer with whatever food, or drug, or tool, or article of clothing he wants has a high utility and is necessarily expensive. The general order of magnitude of a dealer's stock is often in the thousands. A distributor of chemicals, for example, lists about ten thousand of them and their accessories. A maker of types lists 860 varieties.

Inequality of Bargaining Power

A common view is that certain occupational classes suffer unjustly in the process of exchange. It seems improbable that the process of exchange should discriminate against farmers as such or unskilled laborers as such. Inequality of bargaining power afflicts those who cannot wait, who do not know, who transact their business with persons who outwit, out-trade, or victimize them. Pity is appropriate if the cause is sheer poverty or unfair prejudice, and permissible if the cause is ignorance. But it would be unjust to the dependable and careful if prices were no lower for them than for their opposites. A greedy farmer who tries to outwit a just middleman is no better than a greedy middleman who tries to outwit a just farmer.

The essential disutilities of poverty in buying and selling are the very strong temptation to go in debt and to buy in small quantities. The poor man's cash is as good as any, but his credit cannot be. The premium on small quantities is unavoidable except by mixing selling and charity. The best things to do for the poverty of the poor, short of enabling them to earn more, seem to be to make emergency gifts to them and to habituate them to purchase in quantity when that is desirable. A moderate amount of postponement of certain gratifications will permit a poor family always to buy milk by the quart, tea by the pound, sugar by the five pounds, soap in large cakes, etc.

The thing to do for the ignorance of the ignorant is to teach them to inform themselves. There are simple rules such as, "Salesmen who solicit your trade at your house or place of work are probably out to help themselves not you." "Learn what reputable dealers charge. Do not expect to buy for less." "Except for very important reasons wait till you can pay cash for it before you buy anything, except a productive property."

Non-Economic Influences Upon Buying and Selling

In my childhood it would have created a scandal if a clergyman had not bought his groceries from the grocer who was a member of his church. Even today one is expected to favor somewhat his friends, co-members of churches and clubs. Economics easily proves that freedom of trade from entangling alliances with race, religion, politics, friendship, etc. is good for trade and economic welfare; psychology could, I think, prove that it is good for people also. Evidence will probably show that an analytic and tolerant liberalism which rewards the good a man does and punishes the harm he does is better for mankind than a confused personalism which stamps certain men or groups as estimable and certain others as malefactors, to favor the one and disfavor the other.

The somewhat similar questions of national tariffs, quotas, and other systems of national preference and restraint have been argued fully by economists. It may be noted here that the divorce of buying and selling from like or dislike for nations seems likely to be good for mankind. It seems better to reward the good a nation does and punish the harm it does rather than reward or punish it *in toto*. For example, if we dislike a nation because it works too little and fights too much, why should we punish it for working by not buying the products of its work?

The Psychology of Consumption

We shall be concerned here with the so-called ultimate consumer, and with ultimate consumption, which transforms vendible goods and services into states of affairs in the human brain.

A person can absorb only a limited amount of food or wear only a limited amount of clothing at one time. He cannot attend to many entertainments or survey many possessions simultaneously. But he may derive satisfaction from the fact that things and services are reserved for his consumption. Since he thus causes certain things and services to perish or decay without being consumed by anybody else, he does, from the points of view of economics and of welfare, consume them.

In the case of food the amounts which any given population should consume can be stated with considerable exactitude. Somewhat similar knowledge exists concerning the good and harm to be expected from a given consumption of certain drugs. Standards for clothing to protect man, with minimum weight, impedance of movement, loss of ultra-violet rays, etc., could be established. In the case of shirts, stockings, shoes, silk hats, etc., nobody knows how many man should consume. His appetites for these vary so widely with custom and fashion that it is very hard to estimate the strength and range of such cravings. Savages may desire the shoes they see civilized men wear but use them as ornaments; civilized men may desire the tools of the savage, but use them as ornaments!

It is perhaps more important to learn the influence of certain games, books, movies, and radio programs on intellect and character than that of certain foods and drugs on the body. Reputable doctrines are that toys for children should be simple, to encourage free imaginative play rather than impressive operations, that participation in games is better than watching them, that intellectual entertainment is better than sensual, sociable than solitary. All these doctrines are qualified by an "other things being equal" clause. Actual consumption is influenced by these and other views expressed by leaders of thought or of fashion, just as the consumption of foods and drugs is. But in both cases consumers' own intrinsic satisfactions are dominant. More people live to eat than eat to live; and much more money is spent for sheer entertainment than for its recreational outcomes.

There seems to be less inborn protection against over-entertainment than against over-eating. Indeed, habituation to entertainment seems in some respects to act like habituation to certain drugs and require increasing amounts or stronger intensities to produce equal effects. It is a question of fact whether the genes supply controls preventing him from pursuing entertainment to the detriment of morals and health, and even of happiness. Apparently they do not.

The Producer-Consumer Relation

Some consumers have to take what goods the gods provide, being without power to cause anybody to produce for them. So birds hunt for worms, tigers for their prey, and human infants for the nipple. But most human beings consume in large measure what some other humans have produced. Some producers produce because their natures impel them to do so, regardless of whether anybody will ever consume the product. Music, paintings, poems, theories, proofs, science, and other things may be created so. Most men, however, long to have the work of their hands or minds appreciated and used, and most of it is produced for the satisfaction of consumers who will pay for it, with money, praise, or other valuables.

The deciding element in the production of goods for consumption by men is usually the consumer. A consumers' strike against wearing black would make an end of black-dye production; a similar strike against eating poultry and eggs would ruin the poultry industry. Consumers do not deliberately use this power except on very extraordinary occasions, but the same power put in action by widespread unpredictable whims of consumers causes frenzied production of Mah jong sets, midget golf courses, toeless shoes, and ruinous waste when the whim changes. Consumers obviously cannot now induce producers to make a cure for cancer, no matter how much they offer to pay, nor a pound of rubber to sell for a penny. Both must wait for science and invention to make them possible.

Some of the greatest goods to consumers were unwanted by them until they had them. There is a tendency for producers to try to lead. Having some by-product, they try to induce consumers to use it; being able to produce a surplus of some product, they try to get it consumed in some different form. But this reversal of leadership is dangerous: consumers may be wrong in following their natural inclinations, but they will presumably be wrong oftener if they buy what it is convenient for producers to sell. The reader probably has been deprived of the opportunity to buy some food, tobacco, or soap which he liked because some producer has abandoned its production in order to sell something more profitable. He probably also knows of some article which at a little higher cost could be made to give twice as much service.

Careful observation of any person would show that he had roughly measurable desires and aversions, preferences for and against. Some of them would be so strong as to be called infinite; some would be logically inconsistent; some would be against the person's real welfare. The wants which are normally satisfiable by money payments could almost certainly be arranged in such a rough want-scale.

The absolute and relative values of the items in a consumer's want-scale change with knowledge, experience, and influences, including advertising. These range from broad changes such as a strengthening of the desire to be attractive to the other sex to narrow ones such as to feel favorable to Dr. XYZ's toothbrush. They range from permanent changes to transitory ones. His want-scale is moreover influenced little by reason and much by habit and fashion.

Prices Paid by Ultimate Consumers

The cost of production in determining prices paid by ultimate consumers is much complicated by trade customs, ignorance, habit, accident, politics, and other factors. Moreover, the prices a consumer pays for a pound of coffee, a doctor's prescription, and a dozen towels will probably include parts of the cost of attention to customers who buy nothing, the bad debts of customers who buy but do not pay, other unprofitable sales, deliveries, and rest-rooms.

It is very hard for a customer to find out what just prices would be. Indeed the dealer does not know. He knows probably whether so and so is a very good customer or one causing more trouble than his trade is worth. He knows that cost price minus selling price on coffee is X cents a pound, and that the risk, waste, cost of stocking and handling of coffee are small.

The experiences of past retailing have established schedules of prices, by which fairly able and industrious retailers make a moderate living, and the past experiences of intelligent consumers have established habits of buying from reputable retailers. But to this there may be many exceptions.

Illustrations of the influence of politics upon prices are found at every turn. The retention of the 5-cent fare in New York City made a present of much of the property of certain transit companies to the consumers of transportation. The bonuses to wheat farmers of Franklin Roosevelt's administration for crop restriction made cuts in the price of bread impossible. The debasement of a currency robs consumers to enrich speculators. Tariffs are a tax on consumers.

Habit and Custom

Habits and customs rule ultimate consumption. We buy what we have bought in similar situations, especially if so doing was satisfying. We expect to have what we have had. It would be no defense for a landlady showing a bedroom containing only a bed, a cupboard, a stool, a pair of andirons and a small mirror, to state with truth that Henry the Eighth, King of England and lover of magnificence, had no more in his bedroom. Sudden changes of consumption with changes in fashion are only an apparent exception: repetitive habits are conquered by the habit of following certain models and by the intense craving for approval.

Waste

The impression of a psychologist is that fashion changes have been stimulated by producers and encouraged by dealers who expected to harvest larger profits by selling more goods. But, according to Nystrom, the changes of fashion so often leave the dealers with unmarketable stock that they would on the whole be nearly as well off with much slower changes of style: he also puts more responsibility on consumers.

Another cause of waste in consumption is ostentation, purchasing self-approval or the approval of the dull or misguided by "vicarious consumption" of retinues of servants who cause more annoyance than satisfaction, and by "conspicuous waste" in maintaining possessions and services. It is easier to mimic the vices and follies of an upper class than its virtues and wisdom: it is easier to duplicate its externals than its essentials. Customs which are intrinsically satisfying to the members of the class where they are natural may be much less so, or even annoying, to a class below or above it.

To make sure that this section is not misunderstood I note certain expenditures which may not be wasteful, although they seem at first thought to be. One such is expenditure for a parlor or "best room" in which nobody ever sits except to receive callers with whom the family are not on familiar terms. Though not much used, the best room produces not only self-respect, but a security against social disesteem and disturbance of family comfort. It stands there spotless, its chairs placed with dignity, permitting all else in the home to be disarranged and comfortable. It is a trap preventing the minister, nosey neighbors, casual callers, and all others from invading the family's sanctuaries.

Another is the grandeur of the entrances to moving-picture theaters, the outsides of savings banks, the trappings of bars and soda fountains, and other decorations apparently valueless to the users who pay for them. There is doubtless some waste in these apparently irrelevant magnificences, but most persons have an inveterate love of gorgeous display. From dreary workshops and modest homes we enter the movie palace, or take our places before the mahogany, onyx, and plateglass or the art nouveau of the soda fountain and become monarchs of all we survey. It is not a waste for us. The waste is rather with those ultra-rational souls who have analyzed themselves out of this naïve pleasure, and would as soon enter the theater through a second-hand store, and have their drink on a board covered with oil-cloth, saving a few cents to give to the poor.

The Organization of Consumers

Cooperative associations to sell at retail goods which they buy at wholesale and produce themselves began in Rochdale in 1844. Their psychological and educational influence has been probably more important than their influence on prices. They have prevented their members from buying unwisely, encouraged them to buy for cash, and given training in business management to a large number of idealists devoted to the welfare of working people. Except for the doubtful case of the chain-store, I know of no business inventions attributable to the co-operatives; but their staffs have been a very small minority of businessmen and could not be expected to contribute many.

The failure of the workers of the United States to establish consumer's cooperatives is rather a puzzle; the causes, economic and psychological, for this failure can only be surmised.

A second sort of organization of consumers, in which the United States did lead, aims to put needed information conveniently at the service of consumers, to provide subscribers with facts about the merits of various articles. If the impartiality and efficiency of this service is maintained, it will continue to be a great boon to consumers, and something of the sort should be set up in all countries. The ultimate consumer has too few such observation posts and defenses.

Payments for Human Factors

Payment for a person's inherited capacities is in a sense unjust, like payment to the persons whose farms happen to cover coal mines. It is also unnecessary in so far as the person obtains so much intrinsic satisfaction from the development and exercise of the capacity that he will use it regardless of what society pays him. Some poets, artists, mathematicians, philosophers, managers, preachers, reformers, teachers, and mothers would serve the world nearly as well (possibly even better) if the pecuniary and transpecuniary rewards for the services were reduced. But they will produce more with proper care.

Skill, knowledge, and good habits are active to some extent without reward, as human natural resources are. Much mental capital is owned by the public and requires no payment beyond what will keep it in proper repair; knowledge, customs, laws, and ideals are in this respect like roads, harbors, lighthouses, fire-engines, parks, and the like.

A laborer is paid for the natural capacities and capital of strength, skill, knowledge, and habits which he possesses as well as for his time and devotion. Most payments to persons for their services fall into three groups:—(1) payments to employees in accordance with some actual or implied contract, (2) payments of entrepreneurs to themselves by salary, profits or both, and (3) payments of allowances, food, lodging, etc. to wives and minor children in accordance with the will of the head of the family tempered by laws and customs.

Payment is never in money alone, and is never exactly described in the contract. There are always features of health, physical and human surroundings, social esteem, dignity, individual idiosyncrasies, and other things. Even when additional facts about the nature of the work could be known to both parties, they rarely are specified in the contract. Consider the probability of accident in different sorts of work. A worker on a ship has twice the chance of being killed at his work as a worker on a railway and fifty times the chance of a clerk. Consider the matter of tenure. In the Federal Civil Service from 1903 to 1917 the number discharged per year was only about $1\frac{1}{2}$ percent of the number on the rolls. [Florence, '24, p. 152 f.] In many school systems a teacher after a certain probationary period can be dismissed only for outrageous negligence or folly; few, if any, factories could give such a guarantee, being strongly tempted to replace workers of older ages. Certain health hazards are well known to experts in industrial hygiene. For example, Travers found stomach ulcers extremely common in a group of salesmen of a specialty the nature and price of which were such that only the most high-pressure attack could sell it.

Payment by employers should approximate the marginal utility of the service rendered, but in spite of cost accounting and industrial engineers an employer rarely knows how useful J. Doe and R. Roe are to him, or how much he would gain or lose if he paid more or less. I venture the assertion that in almost any factory or store having a hundred or more employees there is one employee worth to the employer more than twice what he gets and one worth less than half what he gets. Consumers and some employers act occasionally from unreasonable whims, and within the family such excesses are common.

Certain powerful labor unions attain a degree of monopoly and hold wages above what men of similar abilities and training receive in general, but this is usually temporary. Certain persons whose abilities can command a monopoly price may occasionally do so; but in general the greatest abilities are the most underpaid in money. Management in general acts as a multiplier of the services of those managed. Little is known about the relation of the payments for it to the product produced.

Entrepreneurs in the broad sense (including farmers, retailers, contractors, owner-managers of shoe-shine stands, professional men, and artists working for themselves, and certain piece-work operators in mines and factories take what is left after paying expenses. Their pecuniary and psychic incomes are caused by somewhat the same mixture of utility, custom, and accident which cause the incomes of employed workers of similar capacities and training, plus an amount caused by their willingness to take risks, their ability to choose which to take and how to treat them, and in particular their ability to treat them so as to make money for themselves.

The customs and ideals of farmers and professional workers place greater emphasis on the skill shown and the services rendered, and less on the pecuniary reward. Critics of business enterprise magnify this difference, however. They exaggerate the honor paid to money-makers as such, the extent to which making money dulls the mind to workmanship and utility, and the superiority of professional over business ways. They also glorify features of utility and workmanship which the public simply does not want—clothes which will wear for ten years, autos that will run for twenty, tools which father can hand on to children, furniture which will last for hundreds of years, and neglect such triumphs of workmanship as the electric-light bulb, the concrete highway, and the radio. They also fail to allot any of the blame to the inertia, dullness, and greed which lets us be outwitted and deceived.

Payments by companionship, entertainment, freedom from interference, applause, titles, and other forms of psychic income long antedated pecuniary rewards and may have antedated material rewards of any sort, except those received directly from nature. It is only within areas of work which are similar in transpecuniary rewards, that the order of human choice is determined by wage-rates. Business concerns now award degrees and honors, and so does Soviet Communism.

American civilization has the habit of rewarding those who provide material goods and entertainment, chiefly by money; those who provide order and security by a mixture of esteem, power, and opportunity to make money by graft; those who provide esthetic and spiritual goods, chiefly by reverent approval; and those who provide the fundamental advances in knowledge by the approval of the few who understand their work. This is rather a recent development. For thousands of years and in thousands of cultures the military and ruling classes and the priests or medicine men were highly paid in money or its equivalents as well as in esteem.

Partly because the old prejudice against handwork and trade still survives in the upper classes and in literature, and partly because those who are unable to make much money scorn it, there is a rather widespread feeling that approval is a more desirable reward than money. If one cannot have both, it doubtless is. But there is something to be said in favor of making the pecuniary rewards of legislators, the army and navy, magistrates and policemen, ministers of the gospel, philosophers, moralists, artists, and men of science more proportionate to our opinions of the value of their services. If they consider that poverty will be best for their work, they can give the money away as some Nobel prize-winners have done. It is somewhat demoralizing to people in general to be able to discharge their debts to their benefactors by applause and reverence only.

Attitudes Toward Wages

The notion, prevalent in the middle ages, that there is a certain fair price for any given service still survives in the popular mind. Many people think that farmers get too little and middle men too much, shop girls too little and movie actresses too much. Opinions about fair prices have been largely determined by customary prices. But moral considerations also play a part, and also one's natural aversion to considering the services of others as worth enormously more than his own. Human labor is commonly productive. hence we form the habit of attaching intrinsic merit to it. There results a feeling that if a person has worked faithfully his labor should be rewarded regardless of the utility of the product.

Another common opinion is that society or industry should provide any person aged 18 or over who is willing to work to the best of his ability with a living wage. The humane ideal of the first part of this opinion need not be disputed, but the wisdom of the second half depends upon many things. What is the probability that any given change of economic arrangements will lower rather than raise the national dividend or the share of it going to the persons now out of work? Is it so much easier to find work for men as long as they wish to work, than for machines as long as they can work?

Historically management has been the initiator of action in the employer-employee relation. It would be an interesting experiment to reverse this by having a group of workers hire a plant and a manager, contracting to work for, say, five years under his direction, dividing the proceeds among themselves according to some plan. They would own the business but not manage it: they would be exchanging their labor for a share of the product after paying for the use of the necessary capital and for management. There is no reason to believe that the earnings of persons of equal ability would on the average be much different in such an arrangement from what they are in the present hiring by managers. There would be losses due to internal dissension and surety of holding their jobs, and gains due to the knowledge that they were working for themselves. A psychologist would expect these nearly to balance in a hundred such enterprises.

Wage Ratios

The ratio of the wage of a locomotive engineer to the wage of the unskilled laborer working on the railroad was 3.6 to 1 in 1863 and remained near that until about 1890. But by 1925 it had dropped to below 1.6 to 1. These ratios of wages of skilled workers to those of unskilled, routine workers on railroads seem to have dropped in almost all countries during the last half-century.

It is certain that there has been no considerable change in the genes during this period in respect of fitness to do skilled labor or be responsible for work. Nor have the jobs changed greatly in their requirements. The change in the wage ratios must have been due to education, union tactics, government, or other environmental influences. It is instructive therefore to inquire what will happen to wage ratios in a world with its present genes but with all individuals having opportunity to be educated to the limits of their capacity.

Five hundred years ago, the ability to read and write commanded an appreciable premium. When there is free schooling to age twenty, the ability to typewrite and drive a car may well command no more premium. Whatever abilities education can give will become cheap relatively to those which are given or withheld by the genes. Nobody need be only an unskilled laborer unless he is by nature so lacking that he cannot be more. For those jobs which three persons out of four are able to learn to do, the ratio of the wage to the wage of the same person at unskilled labor will not be much above 1.00, if employers and employees are free, the minimum wage for any person being set by what it would cost to have a machine or some other person do the work, and the maximum by what the world will pay rather than go without the service. Human nature being such that men will nearly as willingly do skilled work as unskilled, independent work as supervised work, and responsible as routine work, when they are equally competent to do both, a very small premium will fill the jobs which once had a premium of 50 percent or more over the unskilled labor wage.

Extending educational opportunity not only reduces the inequalities of men in culture and refinement but also in wages if competition is free. Eugenic advance and what will presumably accompany it may carry this equalization to the point where most men are born nearly equal, and where, if competition is free, the pecuniary rewards are approximately the same for most sorts of labor for which there is any considerable demand.[1] At that point, whether a given person earns his living by designing houses or by cleaning them may be decided by his interest and society's need, the payment being a negligible factor.

---

[1] Since the upper limit of gene quality can be advanced very little and very slowly, selection not only raises the mean but also reduces the variability.

Chapter 16
The Psychology of Capitalism and Alternative Economic Systems

Money

A child's first lessons about money are that certain coins are what you transfer to some person or slot-machine to get certain objects and privileges. Through such experiences one attains a sense of varying amounts of money as potent to buy such and such. Even sophisticated economists have a much more vital and dynamic sense of a dollar or a thousand dollars as purchasing power than of sixty-seven billion dollars. or of $.00146.

The purchasing power of a given sum may change considerably without the fact being noticed. The increase in prices over time is not the same percentage for all commodities: and there may be no change in the general purchasing power of money. Consequently one is tempted to think of the value of money as constant and attribute changes in general price-level to the commodities rather than the money. If the change is slow and confused. a person may merely feel that somehow he does not get on as well as he used to.

The habit of multiplying money wages by a factor so as to estimate real wages was once rare. At least a large minority of persons do not know what their real wages are at any given time. While men are more likely to be logical with money than with most forms of wealth, it too is subject to sheer habit. For example, shopkeepers and other traders commonly dislike to pay money out for goods although doing this is nearly as essential to making a profit as taking money in. Children and sailors, whose direct associations with spending have been pleasurable, rather like to pay money out. In general people feel readier to spend if they have a large supply of coins and bills on their persons, other things being equal.

Money as a Medium of Exchange

Ordinary folk do not think of money as an invention to facilitate trade. They think rather of money as the most important, the best and safest, form of wealth, with universal purchasing power. They do not realize that the rate of circulation of money is in some respects as important as the amount of it, or that what is satisfactory as a medium of present exchange may be very unsatisfactory as a medium of long-delayed exchange via debts.

Money and Long-Delayed Exchange

The ordinary person in the United States who puts his money in a savings bank expects to get back approximately the same purchasing power that he handed over plus the specified interest. He expects the dollars promised from an insurance policy to be dollars closely like those he had when he made the contract. This expectation is often so strong that he does not think about the possibility of anything different.

Except for the brief period of the Civil War, his parents and grandparents had been subjected to no great sudden changes in the value of the dollar. From about 1815 to 1896 there had been a net rise of about 1 percent per year measured against wholesale commodities. Changes were thus on the whole a little in favor of the saver, counting the average experience of three generations. Farmers, workers, professional men, small business men, and trustees of institutions exchanged present dollars for future dollars with serene confidence. The experiences of nations since 1915 to a degree destroyed this confidence, but the old habits of action persist in many. The generation whose savings now buys only a fraction of what they once bought—the industrious, frugal, thrifty, and competent—have been robbed to enrich governments and other debtors.

A cynic may argue that if governments did not rob such by decreasing the purchasing power of money, they would do so in other ways. But no other way so far used is so temptingly convenient for governments and so disastrous for welfare. An advocate of debasement may argue that the reimbursement of debtors, for example, farmers who borrowed to buy property when it was dear, is a worthy act counterbalancing the harm done. This is of course nonsense. Rewarding persons who paid high prices for property is an inferior form of charity, and debasing the currency is a very inept way of accomplishing it.

If we are to have class legislation, there are much better classes to reward than either debtors or creditors, for example, babies suffering from malnutrition, gifted youths lacking education, members of trades outmoded by no fault of the members.

Stability of the Purchasing Power of Money

Psychologically a purchasing power that increases only by advances in science and management seems a suitable ideal. Stability would remove fluctuations caused by speculators: would make money as good a medium for delayed as for immediate exchange; and would prevent unforseen large shifts resulting from declining birth-rates, epoch-making inventions, or other potent economic forces. Suppose that a dollar was defined as power to purchase (when combined with 99,999 other dollars in a $100,000 certificate) the following:

a units of a specified grade of wheat delivered at Chicago
b units of a specified grade of beef delivered at New York
c units of a specified grade of coffee delivered at Cincinnati
d units of gold bars at Washington
e units of copper bars at Buffalo
f units of steel sheets of a specified sort at Detroit
g units of 2 x 4's of a specified grade at Boston
h units of gasoline of a specified grade at Kansas City (Mo.)
i units of rayon silk of a specified grade at Los Angeles

and a score or more commodities and services selected and weighted to represent what dollars now buy, and to be measured without error or ambiguity. The general purchasing power of such a "commodity" dollar would shift up and down not a hundredth as much as one based on gold. It would shift up very slightly and very steadily rewarding slightly those who sacrifice present for future goods. Such a dollar would not need to be "managed" by politicians. It would not be understood at first by most persons, but they do not understand now what a dollar or franc or pound is or is likely to be. Such a dollar would do for business and personal finance much the same service that exact physical units do for science and technology.

"Managed" Money

The writer is convinced that a money which is psychologically sound should have some stated physical equivalent which its owner can at will get for it, and not an economic equivalent dependent on the judgment of a government, bank, board, or person. It is largely because ordinary people do not care about the soundness of their money so long as it *seems* sound, that it should be exchangeable for a physical equivalent. It is no excuse for robbing people that shrewd ones among them could have avoided being robbed. A managed currency is a constant temptation to a government to punish good qualities in its citizens, and to bribe and to hide tricky operations.

Credit

It is often said that credit, i.e. delaying payment of money beyond the delivery of goods or services, is a necessity, in modern business. This is true where repayment is reasonably certain. So a borrower obtains a call loan in order to pay a bill at once and receive a discount for cash, or to make an advantageous purchase. So a lender obtains interest money for the use of purchasing power which he himself does not wish to purchase anything with.

Individuals, banks, and other concerns which make a business of lending money can be as beneficient as farmers who grow foods, or workmen who make houses, shoes, and books. The old-time church prohibitions against the taking of interest were foolish and wicked, supported by false psychology and vicious ethics.

Among borrowers those who pay interest and repay the loans are not injured as a rule. It is rather those who default, who may suffer from a guilty conscience, who find excuses for themselves, and form the deplorable habit of sponging upon others without shame.

A loan without interest should be regarded by both parties as a gift. The advantages of credit as a business convenience should not disguise the disadvantages of having weak-moraled persons misuse the kindness of friends and the ignorance of small tradesmen. Every interest rate is a rate for the use of money plus a rate for insurance against the risk of loss of the principal.

Whenever credit is given there is some expense of time and materials in necessary records of the transaction, the interest payments, and the safe return of the money. This may have a substantial influence on the interest rate. A man borrrowing $100,000 as a call loan with ample security pays 1 percent, or about three dollars a day, but he could not, though offering equally ample security, borrow $1000 for three cents a day. When the loans are small and for short periods, and the security is clothes, furniture, future wages or the like, the rate rises to 20 percent or more, even when the business is conducted on a non-profit basis by phil-anthropic agencies. The exaction of a rate of 20 or 30 percent is no proof that the loaner is a loan shark. He may be a benefactor, providing those who need it with services which nobody else will provide as cheaply.

Installment selling is subject to a strong temptation to deceive and to encourage persons to get credit who should not. By arranging to take certain risks which banks and ordinary retailers did not choose to take, certain concerns made a profit by selling to customers who had neither cash nor ability to borrow at a bank, nor even an unblemished record of paying their debts.

Persons who have not the imagination, foresight, and persistence to save for a radio, bicycle, automobile, or vacuum cleaner may work and save in order to retain one after it is in their possession. It is also true that there is a certain merit, or at least charm, in the carefree improvidence that buys what it wants and enjoys it while it can, leaving the future to be cared for as it arrives. But against these advantages there is the added expense, the misery of being work slaves of the collector, the loss of enjoyments to which one has become habituated, the dangerous habits of mortgaging the future, the loss of the anticipations which make planning and saving educative, and the probable failure to keep a reserve of purchasing power which can be applied to any purpose. Lending only to those who have adequate commodities, crop prospects, or negotiable securities to pledge is unsatisfactory. Even the most hard-boiled bankers think that ability and character should be considered along with the material collateral.

Some loans which might be entirely satisfactory to the lender may be unsatisfactory for general welfare. Loans for a great advertising cam-paign to induce people to drink more gin would not be desirable. Nor would loans to the Baptist and Methodist denominations to support a campaign to recruit members each from the other. But no simple general rule will serve. Some self-liquidating loans may be worse than some loans for teachers' salaries, for example, if the loan is paid off only by a municipal monopoly which sets prices far above market, or by some other pernicious form of indirect taxation.

Psychology as yet offers no important help. It is my opinion that when the psychology of lenders and borrowers has been studied certain ideas will seem probable: (1) that credit is neither the nourishment of business, nor its life blood, but one which has essential services to perform, but not something on a level with capital goods or scientific knowledge; (2) that there is far too much borrowing; (3) that an individual or company that wishes to buy something and has not enough money should ordinarily get the balance by selling something else; (4) that anybody building a house or a factory should plan to pay off about twice as fast as has been customary; (5) that insurance companies and other repositories of the small savings of the many should make it their aim to pay back equivalent purchasing power rather than equivalent monetary units, and should consequently hold relatively more real property and common stocks and fewer bonds; (6) that local governments should borrow less than in the past when an increasing population meant increasing needs and increasing future workers to pay the bills, and when the expenditures of the Federal government per capita were only a tiny fraction of what they are now; (7) that the Federal government should borrow nothing whatever for more than a few months; (8) least of all should it borrow in time of war when it will save enormously by paying in uninflated cash.

Ownership

It is obvious that present allotments of ownership are imperfect. Musically gifted children lack instruments, and musical dullards own them; able and industrious farmers lack land, and selfish sportsmen own it. But it is rarely certain how far a change in laws and customs of ownership will improve matters.

Principles Concerning Ownership Who should own a nation's capital goods—the instruments of production due to past human work? Other things being equal—(1) Those who are able to manage them to produce most at least cost of labor, depreciation, consumption of natural resources, etc., since those who have created capital goods by their ability are likely to be useful owners of it.

(2) Trusts devoted to welfare, especially by the advancement of knowledge.

(3) Those who are in general able and good and consequently will protect the welfare of others.

(4) As many decent people as possible, because material capital insures a person against ruin by accidents, and is educative.

(5) The public rather than any fraction of it. because it is thus secured against tyranny and extortion.

It is not known whether the railways should be owned by entrepreneurs with the genius to make them useful, by the federal government. or by some benevolent trust which might be set up to operate them on a non-profit basis somewhat as Harvard University is operated. No form of ownership is perfect, in the sense of guaranteeing that the property will be used to maximize the good life for good people. Psychology supports economics in its general emphasis on the advantages of having those own the instruments of production who can use them well; minor injustices and immoralities may be prudently left to the care of the law. Employees and consumers are likely to gain more from the ability than from the good will of owners.

There is a widespread opinion that the gifts of nature should be owned by all men to a greater extent than the products of the thought and work of particular individuals. Building a barn is certainly a different thing from finding that there is coal or oil under one's farm. The "rights" of future men to natural resources also are different from their rights to our factories and railroads.

Who should own the natural resources of ability and character resident in human genes? Other things being equal, those who are able and willing to use such ownership for the general welfare. This principle will sometimes oppose popular sentiments, which would regard it as an atrocity that a woman's bearing of a child should be in the interest of general human welfare, rather than in the interest of sexual enjoyment or the desire to possess a child. But the millions of women now bearing children to the misery of all concerned represent probably far more and greater atrocities than any regime of selective births which science recommends would entail.

Who should own goods used primarily for personal comforts? The principles are much the same as for the ownership of the more obvious productive instruments except for two facts.—(1) The enjoyment of possession has much importance in the case of these creature comforts. (2) The inconviences of ownership by the government or by boards of trustees are great. Intimacy of knowledge will make the owner of a property use it better. So farmers are advised for their own welfare and for the common good to invest in farm lands. and manufacturers to invest in factories. People in general are advised to invest in local enterprises (e.g. real estate in their town) which they can keep under observation.

These general principles are useful as checks against rash doctrines about natural rights, divine laws, the sanctity of the individual, of the state, of the proletariat, and the like. But they do not tell us forthwith who should own the oil-bearing shales, the steel mills, telephone wires, retail stores, churches, dangerous weapons, newspapers, rivers, medical schools, water mains, habit-forming drugs.

The choice between possible owners cannot be made solely by a consideration of general principles. Trustees for the welfare of *homo sapiens* can only experiment and be guided by accurate observations of the results.

As has been reiterated, human nature is extremely adaptable, and in the case of property many different arrangements will be tolerable. Most of us could have been fairly happy as tramps or mendicant friars if we had been bred to that life and successful in it. Indeed some persons who are able to own houses and factories, voluntarily live as glorified tramps going from hotels in New York to hotels in Palm Beach, owning only what is in their trunks and safe-deposit boxes.

Human Nature and Ownership   There is probably an original tendency in man to drive away animals, including persons, who intrude within striking distance of one's lair. There are probably original tendencies to resist the abstraction of objects which one is accustomed to have and use. There is probably an original tendency to respond to the abstraction by resistance, clutching the object, attacking the "robber," and anger. In general, however, the customs regarding ownership have been relatively recent human inventions to prevent or regulate robbery. Any workable system of ownership is much better than freedom for the powerful bully to take what he wants.

We may be proud of the systems operating in trade whereby a bushel of wheat or a ton of copper may change ownership a score of times to the advantage of all parties, with no risk of being abstracted by some strong-arm man in its course from farm or mine to bakery or factory. We may be proud of systems of public ownership and maintenance for the common good as the temples of Athens, the roads of the Roman Empire, the dykes of Holland, the schools of Scotland, the housing schemes of Sweden, and many other beneficent enterprises of government for public service. We may also be proud of such cases of public-spirited private ownership as the Mayo hospital, the Bell Laboratories, the Cadbury chocolate factories. The management of property held by trustees for universities and philanthropic foundations has been much better for welfare than the public's control of its public lands, oil deposits, and the like.

A common romantic argument in favor of some form of communistic ownership is that a nation should treat property as a group of parents and children treat what they own. This seems a very weak argument to a psychologist who has studied family life. He sees, it is true, certain happy-go-lucky families in which communism (or more exactly great freedom in borrowing) and a good life coexist, but he finds in families superior in respect of happiness and usefulness a stronger sense of individual property rights, but also a greater generosity in waiving these temporarily and transferring them permanently. The psychologist distrusts any argument that what is best for a mated pair and their offspring living under one roof will be best for the allotment of the properties of the residents of a state.

A common argument for ownership by an individual is that certain objects are the products of his physical or mental activities, belong to him alone, regardless of the consequences of his ownership. Socialists are justified in branding this as unsound. Any man's acts are made possible by his physical and social environment. This is not to deny that the distinctions between a man and the rest of nature, and between one man and another, are among the most important in human affairs.

Most questions about who shall own the world's wealth are relatively unimportant in comparison with questions of its per capita magnitude and rate of increase and of the elimination of violence and deception as means of acquiring or destroying it. If a thousand hours of unskilled labor could buy a well-built house; if five hours of unskilled labor could buy a radio; if a hundred hours could buy a car and four hundred gallons of gasoline—the question of who owned the houses, radios, or cars would lose interest. Anybody could own as much of them as he needed.

The misuses of ownership by the idle, the ignorant, and the hard-hearted are insignificant in comparison with misuses by the violence of whole tribes and nations. Two generations ago a mother in the United States was robbed of three or four times as many of her children by death before the age of five as she is now in our better states. War robbing us of children and friends is a worse enemy than the most predacious business practice. At trifling cost a man may possess almost limitless beauty in literature and music. Why then fuss about who owns the land and buildings, the ships and mines, the rails and cables? Why not make material goods so cheap that any man can own all that it is desirable he should own? Why not reward productivity and prudence and punish predacity and folly?

The Psychology of Various Economic Systems

To match this title there should be a long book written by a competent psychologist who has studied anthropological facts, historical and statistical records, and case histories that tell about man's work and welfare under various forms of free and controlled activity. There is no such book and I shall merely report very incomplete notes.

The adaptability of man makes it very risky to assert that "human nature can never prosper in" such and such an economic regime. But, the capitalistic system has the great merit that it operates on the whole in the interests of human wants. Its worst results are due to our vices rather than to its arrangements.

In it forces may give too much weight to the wants of inheritors of wealth, accidental discoverers of gold mines, and others ill-qualified to represent welfare. But they are at least the real wants of real people.

This system uses the distribution of wealth more as an economic force to increase its production than as an ethical force to direct its consumption. With capitalism Europe has attained a high level of goodness of life for good people. But along with its development there was the advancement of science and invention, which may deserve much of the credit.

Capitalism has the great merit of using rewards rather than punishments as its main motives, and contract seems superior to coercion by either custom or government. Capitalism has the merit of giving power over business to persons who have shown ability in business, and the demerit of giving them too much power over other human affairs.

Capitalism gives relatively too much power to wealth and business skill in comparison with other skills and knowledge; modern alternatives proposed for capitalism give too much power to persuasiveness, popularity, and political skill.

An economic system is good as it has each person do work which he is fitted to do. The difficulty of the work done under capitalism does not seem to fit the distribution of ability very well; there are not enough jobs for mediocre abilities, and too many at the lower level of unskilled labor. But there seems to be a worse fit in communistic Russia, and certainly it was worse in feudalism. Capitalism opened many careers to the talented. Probably any working socialism will also use material incentives to extract "from each according to his ability."

The doctrine of the equality of the genes of men is not a necessary feature of socialism, and it is very much stronger without it.

Capitalism is more closely affiliated with freedom and individualism than with restriction and cooperation. Present knowledge of human nature favors freedom, because it increases the probability that beneficent variations in the conduct of business will originate and survive, and the probability that power will come into the hands of the able. The elimination of undesirable and inferior behavior, though important, is far less important than stimulation to desirable and superior varieties. One Pasteur outweighs a million drug addicts. The invention of life insurance outweighs a million thieves.

As between cooperation and individualism, psychology favors cooperation which in general involves a richer life, a higher level of ability, increased production, and more stimulus to originality. Cooperation has historically meant co-working without too great differences in power, dignity, or reward, and it will be best to hold to these limitations. Such cooperation is hard, a human organization requiring leadership. Cooperative production or purchasing tends to be at least rivaled by individual profit makers. The California fruit-growers' cooperatives seem indistinguishable psychologically from a cartel of big capitalists. Early cooperative enterprises among workingmen, for example Powderley's Knights of Labor, were inspired by idealism, but it tends to lapse.

Proponents and opponents of capitalism alike lament the decrease in the opportunities for an able young man to "rise" from employee to employer. In 1901 Hadley wrote: "Certain it is that the prospect of becoming capitalists does not act as so powerful a motive on the laborers of to-day as it did on those of a generation ago. The opportunities to save are as great or greater; but the amount which has to be saved before a man can hope to become his own employer, has increased enormously. . . . We have a separation of the community into more and more rigidly defined groups, different in industrial condition, distinct in ideals, and oftentimes antagonistic in their ambitions and sympathies." ['01, p. 371].

What Hadley said seemed utterly true in 1900. But soon thereafter thousands of skilled laborers became employers in the automobile and automobile-parts business and any man who had accumulated a thousand dollars could set up in the garage; many tens of thousands have done so. It is not true that the percentage of manual workers who set up in business for themselves from 1800 to 1830 was much greater than the percentage of them who did so from 1900 to 1930. In 1920 the prospect for young women seemed worse than that for men. The dressmaking trade was declining; department stores were displacing specialty stores. But any able young woman who started a beauty parlor had a first-class chance to become an employer. We can today at least be sure that if new opportunities come the savers will have first choice.

The life of the small individual shopkeeper or manufacturer has value as training for larger entrepreneurial responsibilities. "Small businesses are on the whole the best educators of the initiative and versatility which are the chief sources of industrial progress." [Marshall, '20, p. 249] But in a capitalism of national railway systems, giant industries, power companies, chains of stores, etc., training as owner-manager of a small business may not be so good as the training of a subordinate in a large organization. And in a socialist economy training as a subordinate to meet the standards of the total enterprise should be much better. The abolition of the small farm and the small shop does not seem a vicious feature in a socialist or communist economy.

Socialists argue that many economic functions performed by private enterprise can be performed equally well and cheaper by government. So Mr. Hoan, the honest and competent Socialist Mayor of Milwaukee, writes that:

The average annual cost of police protection to a municipality runs from $4.00 to $7.00 per capita. This protection includes the patrolmen on the beat, detective service when needed, and, in short, all-year protection to both home and person. No one would argue that such service could be secured from a private agency for $7.00. The truth is, one could not hire a "tin-horn" detective to do much more than look through the keyhole for $7.00 and if you could, you would probably have to hire another person to watch him. . . . The usual charge of a doctor for vaccination was $2.00 to $3.00 a person. The Health Department performed the task and paid the salaries of the doctors and nurses who vaccinated 400,000 persons, . . . at a total average cost of seven cents a person. [Hoan, D. W., '36, p. 15].

The work of the United States Geological Survey, Public Health Service, and Bureau of Standards are similar examples on a national scale. No advocate of private enterprise should belittle such facts or exaggerate their dangers as precedents.

To leave to government only those services which private enterprise cannot or will not perform is unscientific and probably selfish. A wide variety of ingeniuous experimentation is desirable. For example, in certain states the population should have iodine to reduce certain diseases. Private enterprise might advertise the merits of salt to which iodine has been added. But it probably could not, except as a charity. So likely government will intervene.

Most of us want income, not managerial responsibility. Rebellion against capitalism is not like a rebellion of a district which really wishes to govern itself, or of a sect within a church wishing to conduct worship in its own way, or of teachers wishing to use a new method. Such rebels appreciate the importance of what they wish to change, but rebels against business enterprise usually minimize the importance of the entrepreneur and the business customs which he has established.

How the Russian system replaces the incentives and deterrents of capitalism may be judged from the sympathetic account of the Webbs ['36, vol. 1, p. 186 f.], which shows that "to each according to his need" has been "liquidated." Soviet Russia seems to rely on pecuniary incentives very extensively.

Veblen has asserted that modern capitalism loses sight of the forces of knowledge and skill which it uses and the wants of the ultimate consumers. Veblen's indictment would not be true of most of the business men dealing in potatoes or fish or automobiles, who would know and care about the catching of fish and the wants of buyers of automobiles. It would be true of the big financiers who buy control, merge, or take an industry "in hand," truer of the diminutive financiers who buy ten shares in the American Car and Foundry Company without knowing what it makes, or in the Union Carbide Company, thinking perhaps that it makes pencils.

Whatever Veblen's arguments show about the inadequacy of deductive economics, or about hedonistic theory in general, they do not demonstrate a weakness peculiar to capitalism. If financiers lose sight of human abilities and wants in their super-deals, and misuse economic forces for private gain, so do governors lose sight of them and misuse political forces to remain in office; so will top managers of socialist states in their super-deals.

A business man in a regime of capitalism, and equally a manager of production or distribution in a regime of state socialism, has to decide when to consider only business considerations, and when to consider both.

Adam Smith held the opinion that business men do more good by trying to make a lawful profit than by trying to do good. The great liberals from Bentham to Herbert Spencer favored letting business pursue its own advantage within the law, regulating it by added legislation when advisable. The elder Rockefeller, though a most benevolent man, wouldn't have mixed business and welfare work as his son did. Allport says:

Instead of calculating the wages and benefits to be given the employees upon the basis of the *profitableness* of such measures to the firm the basis must be the welfare of the human beings concerned. Interests of profit must be tempered by regard for the needs of the workers. This does not mean a socialistic control of industry: but merely a socialization of individual control.

To state the matter in another way, big business should be administered with two purposes instead of one. These two purposes are profit making and social adjustment. . . . Corporations, therefore, which control the livelihood and destinies of thousands must face the responsibility of so ordering that control as to satisfy the needs of human life and bring contentment to their workers. ['24, p. 414]

According to the Webbs the weakest spot in the Russian economy lies with subordinate officials, such as the inspectors, rate-fixers, foremen; shop assistants; chairmen of local soviets, directors and book-keepers of collective farms; station-masters, train conductors; men and women in charge of small posts who have not yet acquired the habits of punctuality, honesty, exactness, and fidelity to the trust given them. "At present the human links between the policy-makers and the primary workers are, as a whole, inferior in loyalty and efficiency both to the leaders and to the industrial wage-earners, and far behind those of Great Britain; and it is to this deficiency that the patent defects of soviet administration are very largely to be attributed." ['36, vol. 2, p. 797 f.]

This is somewhat puzzling. The workers in question would have approximately the same relative power, income, prestige and probability of doing the work they like in the Russian system as under capitalism. Brutzkus puts blame on those higher in the system: "Indeed, many of the failures of our socialist construction are obviously connected with the psychological weaknesses of our organisers. Many millions of pounds of potatoes were received from the peasants and were allowed to spoil; wood was stored only to be stolen, and so on. We may be sure that . . . a capitalist entrepreneur . . . will not be indifferent to the loss of the profit for which he is working, and he will vigorously defend himself against any attack upon his capital." ['35, p. 82] It may be taken as certain that the welfare of society will never be cared for by society acting by itself, but only by the acts of persons.

The merits of an economic system are not fully measured by its production and distribution of goods and services minus the discomforts endured in producing and distributing them. One test is to ask "What sort of person is rewarded by the system in question?" Under feudalism the brave and the faithful were specially rewarded, but also close servants, flatterers, and panderers. Under capitalism rewards come to the industrious, the thrifty, those who can manage machines, workers, and salespeople, those who can estimate costs, can learn to whom to give credit, can forsee business and industrial conditions, but also to those who are honest only when it is a good policy, who can hoodwink people into wanting what is of little good to them. Under state socialism the world's limited experience indicates that high government officials and those who, by merit or otherwise, please them are especially rewarded.

Another test is the behavior of people in neutral or indifferent matters, such as personal cleanliness, the disposal of litter, treatment of domestic animals, care of flowers, the use of leisure, the contents of popular newspapers, the general behavior of people on the streets, and the frequency of certain offenses against persons and property. It may be noted that these two tests will be useful in evaluating systems of government or religion as well as economic systems.

Chapter 17
Political Science and Human Relations

Great thinkers have reflected upon the facts of government, and their reflections make profitable reading. But the safest conclusion one can make from their statements is that Society, the State, Rights, Duties, Government, and Law are *words* which may mean admixtures of observable realities with forces either mythical or deeply concealed in the actual flow of life. They tempt students of political science to talk instead of to observe and experiment.

There is a danger of glib plausibilities in general terms. Rousseau wrote that "the strongest man is never strong enough to be always master, unless he transforms his power into right, and obedience into duty"; but if translated into real facts of behavior, are these words true? Moderns write to the effect that government is the means whereby society controls individuals in the interest of the whole; of how many actual governments has that been true? The science of psychology prefers humbler but more objective concepts. Even so slight a change as the use of plurals, such as *societies, states, duties,* helps. Herring ['37] has, for example, used the term "power-units" to direct attention to the pluralism of government. The psychologist is a disciple of what may be called factual and observational knowledge which will describe, predict, and control what kings, presidents, ministers, parliaments, ambassadors, policemen, soldiers, tax collectors, voters, edicts, laws, primaries, warships, post-offices, custom-houses, etc. do, how they do it, and why they do it.

If a principle or law can predict events, the more general the better, and the simpler the elements with which it deals the better. Merriam ['25, '31, p. 129] lists as specially worthy of study the vote, the legislative roll-call, judicial action, administrative process, military forces, and public personnel. These words are many steps nearer to observed reality than solidarity or state with a capital S; but each covers millions of diverse facts.

The psychologist does not require that the data of political science be defined rigorously or distinguished sharply from the data of economics, or law, or ethics. To the reproach that one must define clearly what one is talking about, he replies that we are planning to work with facts before we talk about them; we will know what we are talking about when the time comes.

Realists observing government phenomena less often indulge in over-simplification than absolutists thinking about its essential nature. But they are not immune. Many of them hold the doctrine that government is operated solely for the selfish interests of its personnel, to the limit that the traffic will bear. Many philosophical writers accept this as true.

The opinions of such classical observers as Aristotle, Machiavelli, Montesquieu, Bagehot, Bryce, deserve careful attention, but they lacked knowledge of recent history or anthropological science, and were misled by inadequate biology and psychology, considering man to be a unitary self, possessing a set of faculties which operated in relative independence of the concrete situations concerned.

Anthropological studies have the great merit of being a cure for the acceptance of the customs of Europe from 500 B.C. to A.D. 1900 as laws of nature or of God. As examples they show early chiefs chosen as protectors of the group not so much from bad men, as from bad spirits of nature. It is not a great exaggeration to say that such a "ruler" caused the spring to come, the animals and plants to grow. Naturally his person was sacred and his will potent. Magicians or medicine men appear to constitute the oldest professional class itself subdivided into healers of disease, makers of rain, and so forth, "while the most powerful member of the order wins for himself a position as chief and gradually develops into a sacred king, his old magical functions falling . . . in the background and being exchanged for priestly or even divine duties, in proportion as magic is slowly ousted by religion. Still later, a partition is effected between the civil and the religious aspect of the kingship, the temporal power being committed to one man and the spiritual to another." [Fraser,

J. G., '20, p. 150 f.] Leadership may exist without coercion or subordination, at least in a small tribe. "Even in the absence of any form of
organization which implies subordination, leadership develops. Eskimo
society is fundamentally anarchical because nobody is compelled to
submit to dictation. Nevertheless the movements of the tribe are determined by leaders to whose superior energy, skill, and experience others
submit." [Boas, F., '28, p. 221 f.] Moreover, the particular traditions and
customs of a group may maintain forms of government contrary to what
would be expected. "Regardless of variations in time and space, it is
justifiable to say that the Negroes evince an inveterate proclivity for at
least the forms of monarchical government. Apparently this represents
essentially an old cultural heritage of both the Bantu and the Sudanese,
[and] stocks possessing a different set of traditions depart widely from
the Negro norm even though they may live surrounded by Negro tribes,
that is, in the identical geographical environment." [Lowie, R. H., '25, p.
382]

Many of the elementary facts of government appear in the nursery.
Coercion and cajolery, mastery and submission, war and peace, compromises and revolutions can be studied there. A hierarchical scale of
mastery or dominance can be figured out in any group, as Hanfmann
['35] found among nine five-year olds in a kindergarten.

The observable phenomena of political science are the behavior of
persons. In Walter Lippmann's words, "It is the individuals who act, not
society; it is the individuals who think, not the collective mind; it is the
painters who paint, not the artistic spirit of the age; it is the soldiers who
fight and are killed, not the nation; it is the merchant who exports, not the
country."['27, p. 172]

So biology and psychology should be useful. As Merriam says.
"During the last century politics learned to take cognizance of great
historical, economic and social forces, in the seventeenth and eighteenth
centuries much neglected. It is equally necessary now to examine the new
insights into human nature offered by modern science working in
psychology and biology and other fields." ['31, p. 99 f.]

Human Relations

The behavior of two persons obviously depends not only upon the
nature of each but also upon whether their relation is that of stranger to
stranger, friend to friend, friend to enemy, old to young, mother to child,
leader to led, teacher to pupil, employer to employee. Each of the
sciences of man deals with certain of these relations. Philology is

concerned with the speaker-hearer relation, economics with the seller-buyer and employer-employee relations.

Political Science and Human Relations

Political science is especially concerned with the relations to other men of rulers of all descriptions, but it may study the relations of patrons to beneficiaries, parents to children, or any other. It may even deal with the relations of persons to things, as in the consumption of food in wartime or famine, or the consumption of certain drugs.

The relation between conscience or sense of duty and unpleasant acts of duty is a relation between deep-seated habits and ideals which give orders without giving reasons to the rest of the man. Conscience has urged men to acts which a different training would have taught them to abhor, made one defraud creditors and ruin his family in order to pay gambling debts, made Abraham lay his son on the altar. The psychology is the same in all these cases. Supernatural and abstract entities operate on man by the habits and ideals instilled in him. It is only as God, right, and duty take up their abode in a man that they become political forces in the natural world.

The powerful-powerless relation is a feature studied by political science. The human genes provide apparently a tendency to enjoy dominance. There is also a tendency to enjoy submission to the proper sort of master; the captain may enjoy doing Napoleon's will as truly as he enjoys having soldiers do his own will.

Some environments discourage the exercise of power; a general status of "live and let live," mind your own business," is maintained. Anthropologists have reported tribes living so, and probably some monasteries, research institutes, artists' colonies, and men's clubs could be found where the mastery of others was deprecated. But the rule is the reverse. The powerful commonly use their power.

Without any uncomfortable self-denial, highly intelligent men will use much of their power for the welfare of their followers, compatriots, employees, or slaves, being influenced by the customs of their time, place, and social class. Western civilization at present expects the most powerful one percent to use their power in the interest of the least powerful half to a degree found hitherto in only few and small cultures.

The Brotherhood of Man

The relation of one member of the human species to another slightly favors acts of mutual aid including protection of the weak and care of the suffering. But it is not hard for man to treat other men as he treats non-human animals. There is probably nothing in the genes to prevent it.

Man tends to form a "closed society" in which are men whom he classes roughly with himself; outer classes he treats very differently. These may become an object of hate or exploitation. There is usually some real or fancied reason for his exclusions: a different color, or religion, or nation, or economic status, etc. But the fanatic, the self-confident conqueror or reformer, may at times divide mankind into two classes, himself and all others, and treat his foes as wild animals, his friends and neutrals as domestic animals. So a Napoleon at war spends men who are his fellow citizens and friends as he spends horses or munitions.

Some students of government take so pessimistic a view of power relations that they seriously propose that only such laws and customs should be established by the state as would be established by the arbitrament of war. H. L. Childs writes that it should be made clear that "every law and institution set up by the state reflects clearly what would have been the result had force of arms been resorted to." ['30, p. 180 f.]

A similar view, expressed by Bertrand Russell, was that "a world-State or federation of States, if it is to be successful, will have to decide questions, not by the legal maxims which would be applied by the Hague tribunal , but as far as possible in the same sense in which they would be decided by war. The function of authority should be to render the appeal of force unnecessary, not to give decisions contrary to those which would be reached by force." ['17, p. 66 f.]

So extreme a doctrine underestimates certain humane tendencies in the genes, neglects the strong correlation between intelligence and morality, and risks losing the better by guarding against the worst. But it is useful as an antidote to wishful thinking in liberals and may prevent them from losing their good fight by grossly underestimating the enemy.

The Protector-Protected Relation   The protector-protected or guardian-guarded relation is far older than man. It has roots in the genes. Its early manifestations are such simple matters as holding the child who clings or welcoming the child who runs from a fear. It has developed into an elaborate arrangement of nurses, doctors, teachers, priests, policemen, traffic-regulators, armies, diplomats, spies, sanitary-engineers, and many more. Governments have made less progress than science and engineering in giving protection, especially in protection against outside groups. It may even be argued that such as it gives costs much more than it is worth. The dangers against which feudal lords protected their subjects were largely manufactured by the feudal lords themselves; the same may be said of many rulers of nations. But such protection, until the breed of man is greatly improved, is necessary.

The Ruler-Ruled Relation The ruler-ruled relation is found in the family, industry, and business as well as in government. The ruler as organizer has received least attention from students of government, and his work as appointer, next least. A good ruler is not only one who demands little more power, money, dignity, than he needs to make wise decrees and laws, but is also a skilful organizer of the tribal, municipal, or national affairs for which he is responsible, and a sagacious fitter of men to jobs.

The ruler-ruled relation in a city or state operates in a nexus of things, ideas, and habits. Acceptable customs, especially those of great antiquity, were inviolable even by kings; a truly absolute monarch is a psychological impossibility. If he violates the ideas and habits which his subjects cherish, he will *ipso facto* display himself to them as a bogus king. They may still reverence the divine right of the kingship, but they cannot feel that *he* is a proper king.

This control of rulers, however, is of little practical importance; a ruler can be almost infinitely selfish without overstepping the psychological limits of tolerance of his subjects. The control is so ineffective that the utmost care is desirable in selecting rulers. The able and good are more inclined to spend themselves in offsetting a bad ruler's errors than in getting rid of him. The able and good in general have probably used force and politics less than they should during the past half-century.

For many persons, political power is habit-forming. Small ['32] has shown that even so modest a man as Lincoln worked to increase the presidential power. Voluntary resignation of power of any sort is not common, but abdication by kings, popes, and party leaders seems especially rare.

This effects a neglect of the training of a successor. Few dictators or party leaders attend to this obvious duty. Even the combination of public duty, parental feeling, and the sense that one's rule continues in the hands of one's son have not always sufficed to make an hereditary monarch take pains about his successor.

The Punisher-Punished Relation Recent experiments show that the efficacy of punishment is limited and specialized. It is potent mainly by (1) associating fear or disgust with certain tendencies, and (2) by special situations where freedom from a certain punishment appeals to the subject as a reward, a real satisfier, an adequate outcome of his behavior.

Whether it has any deterrent effect or not, punishment has a shocking effect upon the recipient. These are perhaps as bad for subjects receiving them from rulers as they are for children receiving them from parents, teachers, or playmates. Business has learned that it gets on better by rewarding free men than by punishing slaves. Education is learning that it gets on better by rewarding the good impulses of the young than by punishing their follies and errors. The best excuse for coercion by government is that its coercion replaces more and worse coercion by individuals and small groups.

The Rewarder-Rewarded Relation   There have always been spoils to divide—tribute from the conquered, taxes from the citizens, or both. The government has sometimes had also the income from certain property and the spare time of military and police forces when these were not engaged in war or maintaining order. Any human government will have favorites, and until objective criteria of merits and demerits are established by science no customs or laws can prevent a government from favoring them.

In the present state of the world rewards cannot be acquired by conquest; every war now ends in a deficit for both parties. But a government may hide the fact of the deficit and distribute land, mines, etc. as if they were the spoils of war, which in reality were bought by taxpayers. The wealth of citizens continues as a fund on which governments draw to pay the cost of protecting, ruling, providing services, and also to distribute rewards. Citizens who earn and do not waste are the real benefactors, the government being only a distributing agent. This will remain substantially true if governments own and manage all productive work. The coercion will be applied at an earlier stage, causing citizens to earn and not waste instead of merely to hand over what they or their ancestors have earned and saved.

The Representative-Represented Relation   The idealistic theory is that the representative will set the welfare of the nation far above that of his particular constituents, that he will use his own judgment concerning what will benefit the nation. It would not be unreasonable for a representative to go further and use his judgment concerning what will benefit them; parents, priests, and physicians do so.

The working hypothesis of practical politics is that a man represents primarily the machine which got him the nomination and the election, and the party voters who elected him, and only secondarily the community as a whole. He does what his bosses and those who voted for him ask him to do. They may have at least the sense of dignity which comes from being able to say "I wrote my assemblyman about that. He wants me to drop in to see him sometime." For certain sorts of persons this is literally the cheapest way of increasing one's sense of personal worth.

Election is a reward for party work, and so selects cooperative conformists. The conditions of life and training of representatives doubtless make them increasingly more alike. Politicians, however, may vary from a Coolidge to a Harding, from Cleveland to Al Smith to the two Roosevelts, men alike only in being devoted to politics and successful at it. There is a current doctrine that party machines prevent the public from getting what it wants, with the purpose of getting somewhat more for themselves. The truth seems to be that they are eager to find something that the public wants and provide it, taking what seems a reasonable commission. If the public wants something which the labor leaders, farm bloc, or financial supporters of the machine, etc. do not want, propaganda tries to make the public want what will not embarrass the contributors of money and votes to the political war-chest. The main defect in majority elections would seem to be in the ideas and wishes of the majority, who may think what is not true and want what is not desirable, or in the incapacity of their representatives.

The relation between two sides in a conflict of interests is at the root of government and law. Communities have tolerated a great variety of methods of terminating such conflicts. Many of these methods are grossly unjust, but may be better for the community than a combination of strife and suspense. They may, however, be worse. The older naïve evolutionary view assumed that the survival of the community and its method of settling disputes proved that the method had merit. The culture permits many social mistakes to be made and perpetuated, however. To maintain relations of agreement is doubtless a finer work than to palliate discords, just as preventive medicine is finer than relief from pain. But the latter has been more prevalent in government.

The Lead in Establishing and Using a Relation

In recent years, in some states, the old, the unemployed, and the recipients of charity are making emphatic demands, but the rulers usually lead. The children in a family do not entice the parents to rule them. The populace did not drag Mussolini to power. A small minority leads a political party.

I do not know the history of the origin of new practices in government (the acceptance of a majority vote as final, the party system, the secret ballot, conscript armies, international conferences) well enough to estimate what fraction of them came from the government, from the ruled, from ingenious individuals. My impression is that the masses of ruled are seldom the prime mover, and that the commonest case is an invention by an individual which then receives support from some within the government and some outside it.

On the whole, improvements in the theory and practice of government have been oftenest caused by some relatively impartial persons whose suggestions have been supported enough to obtain a trial. By far the most beneficient cause is the free play of intellect studying reality and adapting it to men and men to it.

Chapter 18
The Psychology of Government

The Scope of Government

What the functions of local, district, and national governments should be is not known. Some argue that when an enterprise becomes very extensive, it should be taken over by government. So Parsons argues for public labor exchanges on the ground that the task of keeping an adequate record of labor needs is too much for any private institution. ['11, p. 131] Walter Lippmann proposes that government should have as one important function to counteract the excess of popular movements. When the people are frantic for war, let the government keep peace; let the government protect the rich when the people assail them; let it be frugal when the people are mad for bread and circuses or for schools and boulevards.

Gerald Heard thinks that representative democracy is a compromise by which men protect themselves against a necessary evil: "Representative democracy, the only form we now know, is in reality not democracy at all. It is simply a device to give individuals or groups not control of but defence against the state, grown strong by vast size and intricate centralization, necessitated by the natural selection of national competition. Representative democracy is a deliberate compromise, not a natural evolution." ['29, p. 136 f.]

283

The probability is that what government can properly do well will be discovered by trial. What psychology has to offer may be put in these statements of probability of fact:

Despite what social psychologists say truthfully about the individual being only part of himself when deprived of the social forces which act upon him, a person is not simply one tenth of an amorphous group of ten. One person can have a purpose, plan for it, work for it, learn how to attain it, profit by his learning, use it, and feel responsible for it, all more simply and effectively than two or ten persons can. In the capitalistic system of free enterprise and under a liberal government, the load of initiative and responsibility is divided among individuals. Groups provide many advantages, but it is far harder to collectivize brains than property.

Second, human nature is adaptable within certain limits about which little is known. To be drafted for industry may be as acceptable as to be drafted for war. The world may learn to get along without the rich as without the nobility. Such a regimentation of genes and men as pictured in Huxley's "Brave New World" may have three or four percent of possibility.

But, third, sudden disturbances of the adjustments already made are more likely to be demoralizing than inspiring. If everybody received a thousand dollars tomorrow it would be a curse to many. If everybody's I.Q. were raised 20 points by a miracle, the sudden increase of intelligence, though a great blessing on the whole, would make some unhappy.

Fourth, individual differences among men are utilized in the present social order and government should increase this utilization rather than decrease it. As Catlin says, "The task of the politician and legislator is to provide a social order in which these gifts may be exercised so far as they are consistent with a balanced fulfilment of the wills of others, and not only so far as they are consistent with traditional conventions and formulae of some erstwhile balance of power." ['30, p. 420 f.]

To these rather trite conclusions from psychology, I may add that the interferences of a labor party with industry will probably be much less harmful than the interferences of a Charles of England or a Louis XIV of France.

Criteria of Good Government

The goodness of a government will vary with its adaptation to the fundamental natures of persons and with the circumstances of their life. The view that good government is scientific government does not relieve us from considering other criteria, for there has never been such a government whose results may be compared with those of traditional sorts to verify the hypothesis.

Scientific students of government have not been permitted to control governments for experimental purposes and the analysis of variation has been applied in only a very small way. Observation is still the main reliance. We start with certain common criteria set up by opinion and observation and test these by more observation.

A consensus of civilized opinion would rate a government good, other things being equal, in proportion as it avoided war, maintained order and justice, cooperated with other governments to maintain international justice, paid its bills, did its work economically and without bribery, promoted science and the fine arts, encouraged freedom of thought, speech, and contract, opportunity in proportion to merit, and good will regardless of race, creed, party, rank, or wealth.

Respectable opinion can be found in favor of certain minor criteria, such as the minimizing of governmental intervention. Governmental intervention is now much more fashionable among thinkers than it was a century ago, but even its proponents would probably agree that, *other things being equal,* the less of it the better.

Manuals of governmental and public administration suggest other criteria on the basis of opinion and observation. Psychology emphasizes the following:

What sort of persons are being born? Are migrating in? Are migrating out?

What sort of persons are rewarded by the government? Are punished by the government?

What sort of persons hold office?

For at least five hundred years, governments have bid for certain immigrants, for the importation of foreign skill. There is much to be said for absolute freedom of movement of persons. The able and good will serve the world better in the countries which are attractive to them, and the weak and vicious will do less general harm in the countries which are attractive to them. But the prudent government will make itself attractive to persons who will be good for the community on the whole, and not import merely to suit the pecuniary interests of employers (or of labor-unions), or the sentimental wishes of the advocates of the suffering, or unwise prejudice, or temporary emergencies.

The sanity, honesty, intelligence, managerial ability, and industry of government officers are important intrinsically and as evidence of the ideals, customs, tone, morale, and other subtle qualities of a governmental system. It is hard to get accurate estimates of the general goodness of governments. It is almost impossible to get governments differing in the feature to be tested but with all other features equal. Common consent provides such facts as that the government of England from 1500 to 1900 was better than that of Spain during the same period, that the governments of Holland and Switzerland have been better than the governments of Greece and Sicily, or that the governments of Stockholm, Edinburgh, and Springfield, Massachusetts, in 1900 were better than those of Constantinople, but there are not enough such. Even if there were hundreds of governments known to stand in a certain order for general goodness, the inter-relations of the features are complex and baffling.

There is a partial remedy in the statistical techniques of partial correlation, multiple correlation, and path coefficients. These are the methods of analysis of variation that promise to be of very great service in political science.

Rulers

If impartial trustees for human welfare possessed of all present knowledge concerning nature and man had to decide who should govern, what principles would they use? They would decide mainly on the basis of past experience concerning the service given by each sort of person who had been tried.

To supplement the findings from experience, what does psychology offer concerning the selection of the leaders in political units from a great nation down to a small village or rural area, who interpret the public's wants and needs, decide on policies, pass laws, make appointments, exercise discretion as judges, members of administrative boards, diplomats, and executives?

Qualities

Character   Psychology adds a warning against excessive demands and over-simplicity; rulers must be chosen from men, not angels. In a sense no man is able and good enough to rule his fellowmen. But somebody must!

The same job may be almost equally well done in many ways by many sorts of characters. Greater honesty in one may be balanced by greater loyalty or cooperativeness in another. Give up expectations of finding characters of distinct types: one character suited to a poet's life, another to a scientist's, another to a ruler's.

Knowledge Competent government depends upon knowledge. Sometimes this is theoretical knowledge of the social sciences. Sometimes it is intimate knowledge of a particular political situation and governmental problem. Sometimes it is knowledge of matters of history, chemistry, psychology, medicine, or economics which, though technical, are so important that somebody in government should know enough about the matter to consult the authorities.

Ignorance caused the nobility to let the burghers take their property so long as they did not imitate their manners. Ignorance caused governments in the early days of the machine age to oppose the general use of spinning machines. [Sombart, '15, p. 166 f.]

Ability All students of government agree that intelligence concerning people and managerial ability are very important. The only disputes will be about their relative importance compared to such qualities as integrity, good will, and popularity, and about whether their possessors should be made rulers in government rather than in industry and trade. In the present state of the world, government should probably have first choice.

Special Abilities Psychology has little to offer here beyond the general facts concerning abilities. "It is rather unfortunate," says Munro, "that nobody has yet undertaken to make a psycho-biographical analysis of American political leaders, big and little. No one has set himself to tabulate their ancestry, their early training, their political and social background, their affiliations, their tactics and methods, their strong and weak points,—in a word, their qualities as a class. . . . That being the case we are altogether likely to be misled by the exceptional because it happens to be conspicuous. General conclusions, when based upon a few untypical examples, are certain to be worthless or worse." ['24, p. 111]

Satisfying trustees for the welfare of the world is not the same as satisfying voters, but a ruler, even if chosen by God in heaven, has to get along with voters and needs the cooperation of men. Indeed mere likeableness may, for the purposes of ruling as for preaching, persuading, or selling, be a valuable ability.

A combination of high intellectual ability and originality is somewhat penalized in government, joint-stock enterprises, and other group activities. The great majority distrust it because it puzzles them; superiors usually look askance at too much of it in their subordinates; colleagues are naturally envious. It has been intimated that a sensible man with an intellect equal to that of the 95 percentile lawyer or engineer will give better service as a congressman or mayor than one of the ablest hundred men in a million because he will have better understanding and support.

Interest   The general rule is that, other things being equal, success will be in positive relation to liking for the work. There is then some loss when persons who take to politics as a business or recreation are turned out to make room for reformers who do it from a sense of duty. Troland suggests that ego leads men into politics. But it seems extreme to say of politicians in general that "He praises his own group, regardless of their personal qualifications, and denounces his opponents systematically, on general egotistical principles, by any means which may come associatively to his mind." [Troland, '28, p. 453 f.]

Goodwill   Genuine kindness and a sense of brotherhood are probably more useful in those who work for or against man directly than in those who do so indirectly by way of growing crops, mining, manufacturing, or distributing commodities. But the difference can be exaggerated. Competent work with things is as truly welfare work as work with people. Moreover, good intentions are no excuse for making silly laws or for slipshod conduct of public business.

Sanity   Abnormalities bordering on paranoia and monomania have not prejudiced the populace against leaders in religion and government. Men in general cannot be expected to distinguish the desirable self-confidence which has its roots in competence and courage from paranoid self-confidence. They should, however, learn to measure men in government by their achievements, not by their promises. This simple rule will reduce the danger of semi-insane leadership and be otherwise advantageous.

Expertise   The aversion to government by experts in the art or science of governing is deplorable, and on a level with human aversions to education, medical treatment, nursing, and sanitation by experts. The expert in the science of government may make certain mistakes in practicing the art; but this will not be due to his expertness in the science. The aversion to genuine expertness is a prejudice explainable psychologically but still deplorable.

One may ask, however, whether there are recognizable experts in the art or the science of government in the sense that there are in electrical engineering and surgery and the physical and biological science upon which these rest. The answer is, I think, that there are, but that the public does not easily distinguish them from mediocrities.

A board made up entirely of lawyers, professional politicians, and men of affairs is, for the world of today, really a rather one-sided aggregation. It is likely to be improved by the addition of some scientists and engineers. As fast as the sciences of man attain settled bodies of knowledge they should be represented.[1]

Men of Affairs   Scholars, men of science, and engineers are somewhat puzzled by the power and esteem given to men of affairs, commonly lawyers, politicians, or business men. Exaggerating somewhat, it may be said that the technical men in a business consider themselves abler than the high executives, that the professors in a university consider themselves abler than its trustees, that the editors of newspapers consider themselves abler than the owners. Indeed many of the high executives, trustees, and owners would agree, and if their salaries were not five or six times as high they might feel a little in awe of them!

Some of them are men of great talents, however, who could have beaten the professors and editors at their own game, who add to high intelligence managerial ability, versatility, and personal charm. The public would think of even the least intellectual of them as having brains enough, but not working them so hard or displaying them so much as do men of science or letters. Men of affairs do not often think for thought's sake; nor do they strain for originality. They are not fascinated by ideas. This policy may keep their minds thus more fit for action than the steady toil of the scholar or engineer or surgeon. They are interested in people, having knowledge of large circles of friends and acquaintances.

They are better practical psychologists than the teachers of psychology, and better politicians than the district party bosses. They tend to be conciliators and compromisers when they cannot be autocrats. They do not whine or sulk; they do not quarrel needlessly, They exemplify the Greek ideal of "Nothing to excess," have notably good manners, properly adapted to superiors, equals, and inferiors, are gentlemen rather than Christians, and have the talent of seeming to do much for others while in reality getting others to do much more for them.

Supposing this hypothetical analysis of men of affairs (for which, I confess, there is little scientific evidence) to be somewhere near the truth, we can see why government should be so commonly entrusted to them.

---

[1] D. C. Miller writes: "We do not recall that the voting public has ever sent a senator or representative to Congress primarily because he was a profound scientist. In contrast, it long has been and is now the custom of the electorate of Great Britain to send representatives to the British Parliament solely because they are eminent men of science." ['36, p. 303]

They are men of ability *with all offensive characteristics minimized*; they can get on with political bosses; they can work in an organization; they refuse to be overworked. Five experts and one man of affairs to keep them at peace and protect them from outside interference, even if he never contributes a single idea, probably make a better team than six experts.

Professional Politicians   It is common to scorn the man who makes his living out of politics as an elected officer, as a paid party worker, as an honest boss taking care of the citizens of his district and being repaid legally. The men who make their living out of politics may deserve more scorn than the men who make their living preaching, or engineering, or teaching political science by reason of being duller or more vicious, but not because they make their living out of politics. It seems probable that they do more good and less harm by working at politics than at preaching, engineering, or teaching political science.

The important questions are whether politics should be a recognized occupation and whether it should be treated as (1) in the class of "gentlemanly" occupations like the diplomatic service and unpaid trusteeships, or (2) in the regular professions like the law, ministry, medicine, and engineering, or (3) in what may be called the "public affairs" group represented by social work, the management of endowed hospitals, museums, etc.

A realistic political science recognizes politics in the narrow sense as a full-time occupation, and puts it for the present in the third class. The only special training for it now is by apprenticeship.

Sex

There are two occupations for which women seem specially adapted, which they have rarely entered—dentistry and municipal government. I think they avoid dentistry because it has been too much associated in their minds with tools and with inflicting pain. They have only for a decade or two had any chance in municipal government. Sanitation, health, education, recreation, and welfare account for about two thirds of the current expenses of a modern municipality. The business of a city or town is thus largely a sort of large-scale home-making and education in which women have the advantages of a stronger interest in people, a stronger impulse to relieve, comfort, and console.

Age   In most social groups the old have more share in government than they could maintain by force or guile. Children form the habit of obeying their elders. Communities form the custom of obeying the old, who were in early days the repositories of knowledge and who now have an advantage in experience.

The doctrine that early manhood is the one period of life when men are easily impressed by new ideas neglects the fact that many habits, including the structure of language which helps decide the ways in which we think, are learned from two to six.

However, the period of early manhood is the time when individuals do usually get ideas in advance of or contrary to the habits and customs of the family and neighborhood, if they ever get such; what a person thinks, does, feels in these years is much more important than his mental life from birth to age eight. This will be denied by Freudians.

Good government in the future should be more a matter of constructive invention and experimentation. This needs an infusion of the young. The best preventive for rash and foolish experimentation is not for the conservative old to defend the *status quo,* but for them to encourage the ablest and best to make scientific and sensible experiments. Another reason for employing younger men is that the facts of biology and psychology tend toward attaching more importance to native ability and less to prolonged training. If we can be sure that we have found the ablest score of men of age thirty for *any* line of work, we may safely promote them as fast as is tolerable to the rest of the organization.

Personal Impressiveness   Size, strength, oratorical power, the appearance of health, determination, frankness, benevolence are potent in winning public approval. This is unfortunate. People should learn to judge rulers by their rule, not by their appearance.

Successful military leaders can rather easily become rulers by popular choice or force. They and their troops may be glad to settle down, and it is prudent to bribe them to do so. Successful military men have energy and managerial ability, and may be fairly impartial after their own wants are satisfied. However, the way to rule an army is not the way to rule a nation.

Sensitiveness to slander, ingratitude, and the like will make life miserable for a ruler and impair his usefulness. Sensitiveness is, however, positively correlated with intelligence and good will toward men; the best solution is to have the ruler learn to free himself from it. This is hard to accomplish, and the combination of great ability with a certain masterful self-satisfaction and insensitiveness is favorable in rulers.

Methods of Selecting Rulers

The great bulk of people do not wish to rule. They tend to give up their political powers. But, if there is a party system with dramatic candidates and issues making the selection of rulers a contest, the people will take part.

Selection by Majorities   The opinion of an unweighted majority, each person counting equally, will be worse than the opinion by any reasonable system of weights.

Weighting is already used, certain intellectual and moral defects depriving persons of their votes. One reasonable form of weighting is more democratic than universal suffrage, namely to weight parents' votes in some relation to the number of their children. Surely a couple with four children have more to gain or lose from government than a childless couple. Sexagenarians should have less weight than men of thirty unless they are found to be wiser.

The unweighted opinion of a population is especially inferior when the question concerns some general policy such as state rights, government ownership, or preparedness for war. Psychology finds little kinship between *vox populi* and *vox dei,* justifying decisions, if at all, on the grounds that they were convenient to obtain, commanded respect and allegiance where they were customary, and were an insurance against pernicious sorts of oligarchy.

Roughly the smaller the political unit the closer the correlation between the majority selection and the best selection. In large elections it would be better if the life histories of candidates rather than their faces and voices were publicized. Purveyors of medical drugs are compelled to relate on the bottle certain facts about what it contains; a candidate's face and voice are roughly like the color and smell of what is in the bottle.

Selection by a Governing Class   In all large political units selection is by a governing class. This may be the party organization of the United States, the inner circle of Russian Communists, the "solid men of the town." It may be a would-be governing class such as a group of zealous reformers. Governing classes select candidates as well as influence votes, naturally selecting them from their own membership, for a governing class rarely can think that it is unfit to govern.

Until very recently governing classes, even in democracies with universal and equal suffrage were more or less coincident with the upper classes. Upper classes have not been studied by psychologists despite their notable contributions to science, literature, and the arts.

Freeman states that an upper-class rule according to the customs of the class reduces the variability of the rulers. Taking the patricians of Rome as an example, he says, "Such a system . . . checked the growth of heroes and of exceptionally great men, but it fostered the growth of a succession of men who were great enough for their own position, but not too great." [73, p. 267]

The emergence of labor leaders as a ruling class is of obvious, but little understood, importance. They seem to be essentially reformers. They are rarely leaders in craftsmanship; such seem rather to become foremen, shop managers, inventors, or the like. They are rarely natural politicians; such are likely to get some political job, and operate along regular party lines. In Europe, however, parties do seek to insert their politicians into labor unions, and the Communist party does so in the United States.

They like to talk much more than the average workingman does. Some of them seem like the volunteer preachers of early non-conformist sects in England and of Methodism in America. Others, though still agitators and reformers, are adventurous "tough guys," like a Methodist "local preacher" only in the possession of a "message" and the craving for an audience.

As the work of attracting workers into the unions gives way to the work of collective bargaining, the reformer becomes more of a business man, a sort of commission-merchant selling labor. As the work of leading strikes gives way to the prevention of strikes until conditions are favorable, the labor leader becomes more of a lawyer.

Their intelligence operates more after the pattern of theology than of science, being doctrinaires oftener than investigators. It is my impression that the drop in quality from the top leaders to those of lower rank is greater than in the professions.

Labor leaders are supposed to be working for the interest of laborers. They can announce this without being accused of sacrificing the country. This lends an engaging air of frankness to their operations and enables them to keep free from the cant and indirection to which employers as a class are tempted to resort.

This description has no warrant in statistical investigations or psychological tests, but I have found nothing authoritative to replace it. If the genes of a Ramsay MacDonald were born to parents in New England today he would probably go through Harvard on scholarships and become a college professor. If the genes of John L. Lewis had been born in Cromwell's time he might well have risen to be a great military leader.

Selection by Blocs   "Blocs" or "pressure groups" operating as parties, or as forces aiding, threatening, and influencing parties, platforms, and candidates, are typical of present-day democracies. Selection by blocs has the psychological demerit of any system which is mainly negative. A candidate who has never said or done anything offensive to any of these blocs is like to be lacking in originality, active interest in welfare, and courage. He is almost certain to have more regard for persons than for facts, which leads him to try to please people rather than benefit them. He is like a surgeon who relies on morphine, not daring to use the knife.

Selection by Trustees for the Public   This heading will excite the derision of practical politicians and experts in political science. Will the public elect them? How can they have any real power over party nominations or official appointments? Will they not be subservient to whoever appoints and supports them? Will they not be so restricted by their training and affiliations as to give nothing better than what voters now receive from various well-meaning organizations?

Consider the least promising case of a national board. Let it consist of a rather large panel from which small groups could be drawn for any particular task, the entire panel to have some such membership, for five or ten year terms, as the following:

All past presidents of the United States;
All past presidents of the American Association for the Advancement of Science;
All Nobel Prize winners;
All past presidents of the American Federation of Labor and the Committee for Industrial Organization;
All past secretaries of the Department of Agriculture;
Four men chosen by lot from past ambassadors to England, France, Germany, Italy, Russia, China, and Japan;
A member to be appointed each by the General Staff of the Army and the Navy;
A member to be appointed by the Federal Reserve Board;
A member appointed each by the Presidents of the Carnegie Corporation and the Rockefeller Foundation;
A member appointed each by the councils of the American Bar Association, the American Medical Association, the National Education Association, the Engineering societies, and the Social Science Research Council;
A member appointed by the Presidents of the six state universities spending the largest sums for teachers' salaries, in rotation;

A member appointed by the Presidents of other state universities, in rotation:

A member appointed by the Presidents of the six private universities spending the largest sums for teachers' salaries, in rotation.

The essentials of the membership should be intelligence and impartiality, not a balanced representation of "interests." Let it be financed by a permanent endowment held by some suitable agent, contributed by the subscriptions from any individuals or groups.

The members should be paid, and a sum allowed for a staff to secure such information as they needed. They should be expected to work full time. They should study and think much, and talk little. Their operations should be a mixture of those of a court and of a group of scientific or business experts.

The recommendations of such a group would be much more impressive than the recommendations of the worthy associations to promote good government. If neither party machines nor voters paid any attention to their recommendations the money would not be wasted; it would be worth a million dollars a year to have that fact demonstrated to the intelligent people of the country.

Citizens

We, the people of the United States, are mostly the descendants of the lower and middle classes of modern Europe, and these were for the most part the descendants of serfs of the middle ages. Very little of the blood of feudal lords and ladies is in our veins; very few of their genes are anywhere in the world today. This is to emphasize the fact that our government and those of European nations arose from governments of, by, and for a noble land-owning class whose genes possibly were unlike ours. It also suggests that modern citizens by traditions of the cradle, and conceivably by features of their genes, are readier to submit to bosses, dictators and the like than the independent and bellicose nobility would be if they had the earth.

Tests of knowledge and judgment about national and international public affairs have been given to students, showing much less knowledge than may be desirable for future citizens. But this is a common and perhaps inevitable complaint, people are ignorant not only of government and public affairs, but also of economics and business, history and geography, science and letters, art and music, philosophy and theology, to a degree that shocks their devotees. The political reformer will deny that any of these others can be so important as the knowledge of public affairs.

To a psychologist it seems absurd that we should specialize productive labor into ten thousand narrow lines, with great gain for welfare, but should adopt an opposite plan for public business. The New England town meeting did badly what is now done much better by specialists and by laws framed and administered by specialists.

The fact that all men have an interest in a certain activity is not necessarily a reason why they should control it. What is necessary is that whoever does control it should consult somebody who knows about it and make proper use of the knowledge. For those to whom reading about public affairs is a pleasure, it is a suitable alternative to other leisure-time occupations. When leisure is used for attending meetings and discussions of public affairs, the use is perhaps more ethical though less healthy than playing games or making music. But why should people who earn an honest living by contributing goods and services which the world needs be taught that it is their duty to learn to mind public business as well as their own, and be scorned because they are ignorant?

It may be admitted that the public needs some defense because the demagogue employs the arts of his classical predecessor, but with the added weapons of propaganda. Organization and social psychology have greatly increased his power. "The demagogue and the propagandist may indeed prove to be a greater menace to the genuine interest of democracy and the possibilities of science than the boss and the grafters." [Merriam, C. E., '31, p. 207 f.] But is not the prudent defense against these enemies of the people a group of the people whose word the public can rely upon?

For each of us to be armed with information enough to detect all lies and inadequacies would require intellects, memories, and freedom from all other duties better than many of us have.

We should note two cases of ignorance which are specially in need of protection. Nineteen of twenty who would make no claim to knowledge of history or chemistry, or law, think that we do know human nature.[1] There is much that people do not know about government. There is also much that they are so familiar with that they take it for granted. In an American city, lighted streets and sewers are expected like leaves on trees. That a child will find schools open and teachers to teach him and

---

[1] Opinions about politics and government have been found rather repugnant to change by ordinary methods of teaching. For example, a college boy seems less ready to alter his opinions about the relative merits of the last ten Presidents as the result of a course in government, than to alter his opinions about the relative merit of ten poets as the result of a course in literature. (L. W. Ferguson, '36)

that the ash-can will be emptied, are expected with little realization of the past efforts and present arrangements which make this possible. So it was a great surprise to many when during the depression schools were closed for lack of funds.

Tax-payers, reminded each year that government takes, uses, and presumably needs their money, are rarely stimulated to find out how it is used. As you can boil a frog to death without disturbing him if you do it slowly enough, so a government can deprive men of liberty, the pursuit of happiness, the fruits of their labor, hope, and life itself without their being aware of it, if the right means are used and used gradually. But present-day governments are usually in a hurry, confident that their acts will win rather than lose votes. So they annex territory, expel Jews, start a war, make a 5-year plan, enact prohibition, make a magnificent gift of money to the farmers and then a magnificent gift of power to the labor unions. Such acts make men aware that rulers rule. Government has been and is to most men and women first an expected order of things and second a spectacle to look at and talk about. These help explain the rarity of rebellions and the tolerance of government by a class.

Ignorance and unthinking expectations help to justify the doctrine that government is usually by the initiative of the ruler with, at the most, the consent of the governed. This statement by Lord Eustace Percy seems to fit the facts both of psychology and history: "... the motive power of government is not popular desires, but administrative initiative, and the source of that initiative will always be found in the conviction of the governor that he has a mission and an authority to govern, a mission far more active and an authority far more imposing than can be drawn merely from a study of the wishes of the governed. Popular desires may be explosive enough, but ... we shall always find that the popular conscience is an intensely conservative thing—conservative, that is to say, in the action which it is prepared positively to authorize at any given moment, and in its reliance on those who govern to show an originality of which mankind in the mass must always be incapable." ['34, p. 12]

Why then do rulers in democracies speak so reverently of the wishes of the people? It is partly flattery, partly a means of keeping themselves in power which even the sincerest may feel compelled to use; it is partly a means of increasing popular interest and zeal, a recognized technique in teaching, selling, and other fields of applied psychology.

The attitude of the public toward public property is psychological rather than logical. The enjoyment a citizen has from sitting in a public park is more like that he has from sitting in another man's garden than like that he has in his own. So a valuable franchise to use the public streets may be given away. Monarchs used to increase crown lands and privileges, but the public in this country gave away much of its land to individuals, partly out of generosity to ambitious settlers, partly to "develop" the country, partly because it did not think the land valuable, but partly because it did not think much about its property.

The attitude of the American public toward public debt is in general that it will borrow any amount it can at any time to buy anything it wants. Local communities have to be restrained by state laws from going head over heels in debt. There was much opposition among the people to the World War but not much opposition to borrowing money to carry it on or to pay the soldiers' bonuses. The restraint of shame prevents many from borrowing from friends and neighbors; when they borrow anonymously as fractions of the public almost all restraint is removed. Little shame or remorse is felt by the people of England, France, Germany, or Russia at their unpaid war debts. The public has no qualms of conscience; it has no fear of punishment. The public may feel sorry that it went to war and grieve for its dead; but it is indifferent to money matters. The "soul" of the public can love and hate, seek glory, and make sacrifices, but it does not pay its bills. We may admire it, but it is not a good business risk.

Eminent reformers and literary men seem often to neglect facts entirely. How, for example, could so able and honest a man as R. H. Tawney write this? "It is idle to expect that men . . . will trust any system in the control of which they do not share." ['20, p. 151] Have not men trusted in deities and religions which they had no idea of controlling? Have they not trusted in feudal lords and the king's justice without the least hope of controlling either? Do they not now trust managed currencies? Do they not trust the solar system which they have no possibility of controlling?

Theorists studying man's political activities are tempted to invent a creature who acts rationally as a conscious cooperator in public business. He started the state by being one of the parties in a "social contract"; he joins his will to other wills to make social forces; he says his say to help frame a policy. It is, of course, true that man as a citizen is not the same as man as a parent, child, employer, merrymaker, or hypochondriac; some abstraction is desirable and necessary. But political man is certainly not habitually cooperative or conscious of what and why he is doing and what the consequences will probably be.

People as Taxpayers

The people support government activities chiefly by forced labor (as conscripts) and by taxes. Their labor may be made pleasant in times of peace and may be more satisfying to some than what they would have done in freedom. However, if military service was made voluntary the number of volunteers would be far below the present number of conscripts, so that for the great majority the service is psychologically equivalent to a tax. It and the poll tax, like government monopolies and import duties on articles of wide and nearly equal consumption, are democratic taxes of which people may or may not be conscious.

Money taxes vary greatly in the sort of persons who pay them, how they are used, and in the effect on the ruler-taxpayer relation. Some assessments are for benefits chiefly to the person who pays, as in assessments on the owners of abutting property to pay for a sidewalk or sewer. Taxes spent for protection against smallpox, yellow fever, or tuberculosis, are a good investment for almost every resident; he may also consider his payment as beneficent charity. Some taxes produce little or no benefit to most of the payers, but yet are tolerated as attractive charities. Such are taxes paid for 4th of July celebrations, municipal golf-courses, or hospitals for incurables. Some taxes are for the self-indulgence of rulers or for the grandeur of the community.

The latter are common everywhere from the too grand City Hall to the great army used more to nourish national pride than to protect persons. Such expenses are akin to those for the palatial offices of company presidents, the caps and gowns of college professors, the too big and too often renewed automobiles of Smith and Jones.

Taxation could be a potent method of reward and punishment. People who do not drink, or smoke, or use gasoline are in this country rewarded at the expense of those who do, but are little aware of the fact. Henry George's proposal would have rewarded those who tried to use land productively at the expense of those who held it speculatively. In most countries, those whose services are valued lowest in the market are rewarded by the income tax at the expense of those whose services are valued highest.

A tax upon items of conspicuous waste is attractive psychologically. Suppose there was a progressive tax upon residential property beginning at 2 or 3 rooms per person (exclusive of servants) and increasing by some scale as, 3000 cu. ft. per person, the normal tax on real property; 4000 to 4999 cu. ft. per person, 1.75 × the normal tax; 8000 to 8999 cu. ft. per person 7.25 × the normal tax.

This would reward families who lived comfortably at the expense of those who used their homes largely as an advertisement of their importance. The latter would not object to the tax so much as people would expect, because the world would know that they were wealthy enough both for grand houses and heavy surtaxes.

Rulers naturally prefer indirect taxation to direct, taxation of the powerless to taxation of the powerful, and taxation which is convenient to taxation which is inconvenient.

The ruler must, as a human being gravitating toward the personally satisfying, favor taxation which saves him from annoyance. As a consequence much of the theory of taxation is how to get the minimum tax with the least trouble to the government. Tax real estate because it cannot be hidden. Tax the thrifty because the thrifty can pay. Tax inheritances because people will pay much to the government rather than resign control of their property while they live. Trustees for the people would make arrangements for taxation very different from these.[1]

The People as Patriots

Most men desire and enjoy the success of some groups or institutions besides their family and friends. The variation in this respect is from the person (not necessarily selfish) who feels very little joy in the successes of his school, team, church, army to the one who exults in them all. This variation is somewhat independent of esteem; a man may criticize his state or church severely, yet crave success for it even in undertakings he disapproves.

A man feels not only that he belongs to the Baptist Church, Democratic Party, and state of Ohio, but also, though more vaguely, that they belong to him. A man tends to enjoy the prosperity of his "belongings," but not in perfect correspondence with the extent of ownership or membership. In fact, any Detroiter may feel the possessive and participative interest in the city's baseball team, and much more strongly than in Detroit's government or population. A hero, an expedition, an army—we thrill at their successes much more readily than at the successes of a law, a constitution, or a science. So nations are personified as John Bull and Uncle Sam, and religions are named for their founders rather than their doctrines.

When men desire "progress" or "social justice" or "socialism" or

---

[1] I conjecture that income and inheritance taxes have slowed down the increase in the general welfare which was so rapid from about 1850 to 1900, but may have increased and improved the schooling of the people.

"feminism" or "true religion," their desires and satisfactions may be none the less potent though these names mean to them little more than a good that all right-thinking persons believe in. Though anything from a nation to a tree, from a prizefighter to the doctrine of foreordination, may be the object of solicitude, the actual objects for most men are restricted to certain customary belongings like his community, church, nation, race, and favorites.

Why does he extend himself to include these? There may be an element of real benefit to his individual life from their success. He may think that a victory for his army may save him from slavery, that converts to the Methodist Church may enhance the status of Methodists including himself. All such calculated bases, however, are probably as often excuses for enthusiasm as causes of it.

More important is the gain to inner self-approval. By extending one's self to share in lodge, church, or party, one makes the personal self a smaller fraction of one's total interest. As a member of A, an inhabitant of B, a citizen of C, a follower of D, I can unconsciously congratulate myself on their victories. In James Harvey Robinson's words, "Paltry, diffident and discontented 'I' becomes proud and confident 'We.'"

A third cause is the tendency of many persons to attain a certain grandeur by possessing themselves of anything appropriable. If they travel on a ship it becomes their ship. Pershing and Foch were their generals; a new King of England becomes their ward.

A fourth cause is a somewhat similar tendency of certain persons to attain the sense of power by behaving as masters of anything masterable. At a concert they feel themselves guiding the conductor's baton; public servants are their servants; they take credit for the promptness of the trains they travel on, or the rise of stocks they read about.

The fifth cause is to take sides in a controversy; it is a very prevalent tendency. Having taken sides one is almost necessarily desirous for and gratified by its success.

There is perhaps also a slight tendency for man to view all things as good or bad, avoiding drab neutrality wherever he can.

The emotions aroused by the fate of one's hero, nation, party may have large admixtures of esthetic emotions. The anxiety or joy we feel for our army in a war may be in part like the anxiety or joy we feel for the heroes in a play. These esthetic emotions are free from certain strains, from certain scruples, from certain demands for practical action, and endowed with certain simplicity and manageability. Most important they are normally entertaining. We go again to see the tragedy which, were it the real life of a real friend, we would wish never to witness.

A man may be uplifted by belonging with the brave and free. But for the practical purposes of personal comfort anything which seems to the person grand and successful will serve the purpose. The useful lessons are that nothing but the truth is entirely safe for man, that he may misuse the holiest social virtues as well as his animal instincts. As events have abundantly shown, rulers will aid and abet such measures to the advantage of themselves or their whims.

Chapter 19

The Methods and Aims of Government: Doing Public Business

A person with abilities to rule and administer should do better with such knowledge of the facts and principles as this chapter will amplify.

1. Reward is usually better than punishment. Experiments with the public would show results comparable to those of Leuba ['30] with children, where a 5-cent bar of chocolate for doing certain amounts of arithmetic resulted in 52% more output than with no reward, and the further addition of rivalry, praise, and social recognition raised this to 65%. No scientific discovery or useful invention to my knowledge has been made from fear of punishment.

2. Prevention is usually better than palliation. The ideal in government, as in education and industry, is never to let mistakes occur. The crucial fact is the existence in the original nature of man of certain cravings for adventure, excitement and success. These cravings cannot be bottled up tight; and if they are, trouble is likely to break out elsewhere.

3. It is prudent for government to prevent a greater evil by a lesser one. Consider the case of gambling and smoking. A state lottery is, it may be hoped, a democratic form of gambling that would satisfy the cravings of the poor and wean them from what is worse. But this cannot be proved in advance, and, as stated earlier, I decide in its favor on grounds of social justice, as giving the poor as good a chance to gamble as the rich.

In the case of tobacco smoking, there is some actual evidence that this petty vice keeps men from worse. There is a substantial positive correlation between the goodness of life in a community and desirable personal qualities in its population and the per capita sales of cigar stores and the percentage of total retail sales belonging to cigar stores.

4. A reasonable government should consider the facts of nature and the consequences of its acts even more than a person or corporation. The state has extraordinary powers, and less unbiased criticism. Moreover, its acts may establish precedents, and usually change things and men irreversibly, even though the governmental act itself may be reversed. If the consequences can only be predicted, they more than ever deserve careful consideration by government. For the people tend to give passion, prejudice, and temporary comfort great weight.

5. All competent students of political science agree that power should be concentrated.[1] Psychology adds that the same knowledge and abilities resident in one head are necessarily much more effective than when scattered in two or more heads.

6. Though concentrated, its organization should be functional rather than hierarchical. The hierarchical system was fairly suitable for the management of a cotton factory, a small railroad, or an old-time army. The persons at each level of the hierarchy could know and do all that those on all lower levels knew and could do. The complexity and specialization of modern private or public business makes this impossible.

7. Governments should make more use of scientific methods in arriving at their decisions. In doubtful cases, a person should as a rule make his decisions after jotting down the facts pro and con, assigning weights to each, and summing the weights. He may include his intuitions and "hunches" with such weight as seems fit. The opinions of other persons should be weighted according to the person's knowledge, expertness in the field, and general good sense.

Science tries to attain the most reasonable decisions, the decisions which a wise future will applaud. Parliaments, assemblies, boards, committees, staffs, try to do this, but also to reach agreement. They will often tolerate a compromise which is worse than any of the alternatives or permit amendments which make the action futile.

8. Other things being equal, publicity is likely to increase the amount

---

[1] A typical statement is Munro's: "It is one of the first principles in the science of politics that governmental authority, to be efficient, must be concentrated. If it is not concentrated in some duly elected official it will be consolidated in someone behind the scenes." ['24, p. 49]

of truth and widen its distribution. A reasonable practice is that of science, which reports its activities freely in such ways that competent scientists all over the world can use them, but that their misuse by greed or folly will be minimized. The mere fact that employers, employees, and nations have not hitherto made their doings public is not an argument against doing so; publicity is not inherent in the nature of scientific men or even a custom of very long standing.

The arts of the advertiser, artist, and literary man are at the service of government. Honest and unselfish men use these arts as they always have done when speech was free. Censorship laws have not worked very well. So long as people care little for truth in comparison with flattery, support for their prejudices, and entertainment, publicity will involve harm. But government censorship is much worse.

9. Almost everywhere predictability is a cause of welfare. The ruled should be able to predict that the laws and customs will be maintained, plus a reasonable progressive shift in a certain predictable direction.

One of the worst features of tariffs, quotas, national-barter rules, and the like was the insecurity they caused concerning what would happen next. It should be kept in mind that predictability is consistent with change, provided enough is known about the direction of the change; for its actions to be predictable does not require the government to be static or conservative.

10. Psychology warns against setting up precedents in emergencies when a proper balance of emphasis is likely to be lost and satisfaction at doing something may take the place of satisfaction at doing what is best. Dicey contrasts unfavorably the legislation of Parliament with that of the courts, largely on the ground that so much of the former is emergency legislation: "Parliament is guided not by considerations of logic, but by the pressure which powerful bodies can bring to bear upon its action. Ordinary parliamentary legislation then can at best be called only tentative. Even ordinary judicial legislation is logical, the best judicial legislation is scientific." ['20, p. 370]

11. Government should be simple. Man's own creations tend to be too much for him to manage. A battleship requires more specialists probably than an entire medieval city. Pasadena, a city of 75,000 and one of the best in the world, has 3400 ordinances. Manufacturing has met the difficulty more or less by the division and specialization of labor and machinery. Government seems encumbered with rules and customs, institutions within institutions.

12. The psychology of advertising lays stress upon suitable slogans in influencing men. Reformers, unhappily, have given little attention to the

science of propaganda, when they have had a meritorious idea to plant.

Terms like proportional representation, segregated budget, and excess condemnation hold back the reforms they embody. Compare them with such self-explanatory terms as short ballot, open shop, city manager. Munro ['24, p. 22 f.] writes:

> In 1898, at a time when no one was accustomed to big figures, we were able to spend what has been estimated at four hundred million dollars in conquering and improving the Philippines. The humanitarian work done in these islands by the United States is amazing. Disease was reduced, social work carried on, living conditions made better, until the population doubled under the improved conditions. Yet it would have been psychologically impossible at that time to have spent an equivalent amount of money on our own poor. The reason was that in the ideology of the time, . . . every American felt richer because the Philippines belonged to the United States. There was an asset to balance the debit. The imperialistic ideal coupled with our natural humanitarian impulses permitted us to treat these primitive people better than our own. We were not afraid of ruining their character because we did not think of them as equals who had characters to ruin. . . . One wishes that it were possible to consider our own country as an asset today. If so, the budget might be balanced by calling expenditures for improvement investments instead of debts. ['35, p. 111 f.]

The general argument is instructive: The names we call things by and the concepts under which we place them influence our attitudes toward them.

13. Rulers should talk less. Lasswell has pointed out that the method of discussion has been much overrated: "The time has come to abandon the assumption that the problem of politics is the problem of promoting discussion among all the interests concerned in a given problem. Discussion frequently . . . arouses a psychology of conflict which produces obstructive, ficticious, and irrelevant values." ['30, p. 196 f.]

14. Rulers should study more. Any conscientious man who holds a government job will study his job and learn from its instructive experiences. There are some associations of civil servants for mutual improvement comparable to those of scientists and teachers. John Dewey could say as late as 1936 that "The resource that has not been tried on any large scale in the broad field of human, social relationships is the utilization of organized intelligence, the manifold benefits and values of which we have substantial evidence of in the narrower fields of science." ['36, p. 464] The statement is extreme; organized scientific observing and thinking is at work with human, social relationships; but the contrast is real.

15. Governments should provide for scientific experiments in advance of wholesale application. We obviously cannot roll communities through business cycles as we roll steel balls down inclined planes, or transpose

two populations as we transpose grafts of tissue. But we may, by sufficient thought and ingenuity, do enormously more than has been done. Many instructive governmental experiments could be carried on in army camps, boarding schools, C.C.C. camps, even in prisons.

16. Government should move toward a more professional and scientific treatment of its problems. At present something which is demonstrably desirable will be cast aside as "politically impossible."

So-called scientific management is apparently "politically impossible." Florence ['24, p. 91] quotes from a law providing that in U.S. Army workshops no appropriations be available for the salary of any person having charge of the work of any employee of the United States Government while making, with a stop-watch or other time-measuring device, a time-study of any job. Why should it be possible to pass legislation which no competent authority approves, waste public funds, and plunge a nation into a disastrous war, and be "politically impossible" to do so many useful things? I think that many reasonable acts of government are politically impossible in the sense that government has to make the best of a rather bad bargain. But I do think that statesmen should ask the questions.

17. Psychology has little to offer concerning the questions of two-party and multi-party government, minority representation, representation of occupations and other interests rather than of geographical units, the totalitarian state, constitutions, and the like. Concerning size, there is commonly supposed to be an inverse correlation between size and effective government. Cities like London and New York are governed as well as cities of a hundredth their size. The largest states are not notably worse off than the smallest. We should not then be appalled by the difficulty of governing a world-state or federation. It will probably be easier to maintain it for a hundred years than to establish it.

Good Government

It is generally admitted that a person should seek the welfare of others, but that a government should seek the welfare of its own citizens with little care for the welfare of others. The general ethics of the conduct of national governments toward one another is competitive within the rules of international law, and in accord with the precept of each for himself.

That the advantage of one is the disadvantage of another in a bargain has been accepted almost universally in national governments. But economists and businessmen understand that the most profitable contracts are those which are equally profitable for both parties.

The enlightenment of national interest *is* a matter of practical politics. A nation should learn not to lie about other nations or work against them for no good reason, just as it should learn not to waste its own substance or ruin its own health. It should learn not to lie about itself. "Each nation, too, has its own defects, and it must come to recognize these defects instead of glossing them over with what the psychologist calls 'defence mechanisms'; Germany, for example, hiding its brutality by its love of culture, France its emotional reactions by its love of logic, England its distrust of systematic thinking and doing by its love of liberty of thought and action." [Myers, C. S., '37, p. 151]

Morality and common sense ask that a government should realize that it lives in a world where political, economic, and social strains and explosions cross oceans. They ask that a government should mind its own business well, know enough about the business and feelings of other nations to keep from needlessly irritating the other, and do its share in world welfare work.

Monarchs, oligarchies, and democracies have all overdone the punishment of bad men in comparison with the reward of good, and democracies have perhaps been worst. In the depression of the '30's, "the United States federal government and many state governments instituted retrenchment policies whose first victims were the publicly supported research centers." [Gray, '37, p. 4] Governments are no kinder to art and scholarship than to science, and seem to treat great managerial ability primarily as a source of taxation or party contributions, acting as if they thought small business men were better than big.

Governments have the opportunity to act with reasonableness, logic, and scientific method. Government maps are good maps; tests in a Bureau of Standards are in many ways model tests; public schools have not been outdone by private schools; government farms have often taught all farmers. If the wage of every postman, policeman, and public-school teacher varied approximately with the purchasing power of money, there would not only be that much gain in justice, but all people would be impressed by certain facts of the utmost economic and political importance.

Governments could be model traders and employers. How can we expect labor unions to keep their promises if governments break theirs? Governments could be models by accepting unchangeable facts and adapting their acts to these instead of claiming to change them.

Peace

Common sense tells us that only a stupid or malevolent government would want war today. But common sense forgets that a government may keep itself in power by assertions which it can justify only by war, and that a government may sincerely argue that an extension of its dominion will be a blessing to the world.

To keep the peace of the world, psychology has a few facts. They are that:

I. The inborn belligerent tendencies in the human animal have very little to do with modern wars between states. These tendencies may be called the instinct of escape from restraint, of overcoming a moving obstacle, of counterattack, or irrational response to pain, of combat in male rivalry. [Thorndike, '13B, pp. 68–73, *passim*] The same irrelevance to modern war holds for the hunting instinct. A person strongly moved by such proclivities would find less gratification in a year as a modern soldier than in an hour or two a week playing football or "rough-housing." Whatever it is in the human genes that keeps a million men hiding in trenches, working machine guns, and wearing gas masks, is mostly *not* what causes ordinary fighting and hunting in boys.

II. Mutual acquaintance between nations is not a preventive of war, as shown by certain facts in anthropology and psychology concerning the closed society and the treatment of strangers. But the facts are against it in the case of wars between nations. Mutual acquaintance in Europe has increased greatly in the last hundred years as a result of literacy, trade, and travel; wars have not decreased proportionately.

III. Some statesmen and historians look for a fairly sudden change, whereby war will go out of fashion. So James Harvey Robinson wrote a few years ago: "To judge from the way in which witchcraft, slavery, and active religious persecution disappeared—all ancient and sanctified and seemingly permanent human institutions—the doom of war may possibly be near at hand." ['37, p. 83] The expectation that another war might bring a lasting peace if it were disastrous enough does not make sense in psychology; it seems more likely that what was was left would be at the mercy of roving armies like those which ravaged China, and of dictators who, in return for order, would do what they pleased.

IV. The orthodox optimistic view is that war can be stopped by an international agreement and court, supported by an international police force. Psychologically it would seem much more advantageous to get nations to join a federation with much wider power than simply to judge disputes and enforce decisions. It should be something to which a person could be proud to belong. If psychologists had been consulted about the League of Nations they would, I think, have recommended that it be given power to hold fairs and musical festivals, to issue money (ostensibly for the convenience of travelers but mainly to make itself known and trusted), and to do other things designed to capture public imagination, make all peoples feel that it belonged to them, and they to it, etc.

V. There is some doubt about the attitude of peoples toward war, the general view of experts being that they are strongly against it. The success of propaganda for war is so much greater than that of propaganda for prohibition, or disarmament, or the abolition of child labor, that there is some doubt. Socialists and intellectuals shift so readily to excuses, then to participation, and soon to enthusiasm, that one suspects that the main aversion is only to other tribes making war. The notions that war is senseless and degrading, that both sides are wrong, that the important thing is not to win a war but to avoid it are so very modern that they exist in few minds, and there only as a thin film covering a feeling established by stories, poetry, history books, and memorial days.

If the aversion to war were very deep it should have produced aversion to those engaged in it. Russian boys and girls ranked a soldier as thirteenth among forty-five sorts of person, above a school superintendent and much above a railroad conductor or postman. [Davis, J., '27] The National Guard in the United States and corresponding services in England and Scotland are eminently respectable. An officer in the army is still looked up to all over the world.

Liberty

Government takes away or prevents certain liberties but makes others possible. On the whole even a rather inferior government adds more than it subtracts, because in our age individuals left to themselves interfere with and frustrate one another to an extraordinary degree.

Some rulers feel it their duty and enjoy arranging the affairs of citizens. Some are happier when they have nothing to do. These attitudes may become traditional, so that German administrators are more restrictive and English more tolerant.

Liberties are multifarious and specialized. Restraint on freedom of speech concerning the orthodox religion and government is indifferent to many who would rebel at compulsion to eat at 6 A.M. and work seven hours daily. Lack of opportunity to make love is a painful restriction to most men in prisons and armies, but not to most women in nunneries. Restrictions of movement which would be torture to a healthy boy of ten are welcome to his grandfather. The freedom we want is freedom to do particular acts, attain particular results, and be particular sorts of persons. In most persons any intoxicating spells of pure freedom give way to the pursuit of some particular happiness.

Demands for liberty are made by persons for themselves or those whose interest they have at heart. Most of the liberties now sought are indistinguishable in reality from special privileges. Liberty for any individual to do what we think he should not do is given very reluctantly. Mill would have accorded liberty to earnest and idealistic workingmen, or to demonstrably humanitarian eccentrics, but probably not to anarchists, free-lovers, or fascists. Men may give it because of a reverence for liberty as a principle, but not if the person takes the liberty to be grossly wrong, or foolish (in their opinion); there is no reason why a person should be given liberty which he misuses, we say.

But there is. This freedom increases the variation of ideas and enterprises. For the sake of one such positive contribution otherwise unobtainable, it is good policy to tolerate a hundred errors. If only the *preservation* of civilization is in question, freedom can be denied to those thinkers who violate the proprieties. But for the *advancement* of civilization it would be desirable to tolerate much liberty. Able people usually advance civilization without shocking it, but ability should be free to shock or disgust us. Because governments may be selfish and deceitful, freedom of speech is one of the best single tests of virtue in a government. A good government is intelligent enough to attach importance to the advancement of truth, and moral enough to be willing to have the truth about itself told.

Equality

Let us examine the consequences of certain sorts of equalization which governments can favor. Since governments tend to aggrandize their powers at the expense of the governed, there is some presumption that a movement of equalization of rulers and ruled is better than its opposite. Since majorities tend to oppress minorities, there is a presumption in favor of raising the power of a minority near its arithmetical share. In proportion as the majority is made up of the same sorts of persons with the same wants as the minority this is less important. But if the majority is largely farmers and the minority factory workers, or if any other important difference exists, some scheme of proportional representation is very important.

Since persons organized into parties, pressure-groups, and the like tend to obtain special privileges at the expense of those not organized and with more or less disregard of the welfare of all, there is a presumption in favor of legislation in the interest of such unorganized groups as widows, old maids, poets, philosophers, and ultimate consumers. The state may well regard these as its wards to a certain extent. Since the young are somewhat at the mercy of adults, the government may reasonably favor their interests. Child-labor laws and compulsory education laws may thus be useful equalizing forces.

Future citizens have very few rights by law. If a government prevents families from improving the world for their offspring by its inheritance and gift taxes, it should reserve at least a part of the wealth for the welfare of future men.

The law and police are probably an equalizing force. In spite of the fact that in a legal contest between a rich person and one with one tenth his wealth and political power, the protection of the former is probably not ten times as great. Moreover protection from assault, theft, or being run over is certainly very much nearer a ratio of 1 to 1.

By any social doctrines held by intelligent men, inequalities are bad in proportion to the lowness of their correlation with abilities possessed and services rendered, hence discrimination against atheists, Jews, Catholics, and other sects is not tolerated now. The same holds true for inequalities based on race, skin color, or titled or famous parents.

There is a fairly widespread feeling that wealth which comes by accident or by the labor and skill of others may reasonably be taken by government and used for the general welfare. But nobody demands that a beautiful woman should be compelled by government to put her beauty to work to buy clothes and jewels to adorn women who are unfortunate in appearance; or that a natural athlete should be compelled to use his strength and skill for other players. Some moralists announce that persons favored by what they call "nature's gifts" should hold them in trust for the common welfare, but they do not state that governments should compel them to do so, except when they have produced material possessions.

Governments do not equalize against the forces of accident, gifts from others, and unfair business practices in favor of the unfortunate, but against the rich and their heirs in favor of the government. What the governments do with the wealth may increase the misery of the un-fortunate and the poverty of the poor, as when it is spent on war or conquest.

Certain facts about inheritance taxes may be noted in this connection. As taxes go, they probably rank fairly high in general merit, although often justified on false pretences. One pretence is that they automatically benefit the unfortunate. Another is that the children of the rich will use the wealth less well, although the correlations between ability, morality, good will, and wisdom in using wealth for welfare and being the child of a person who has accumulated wealth are, I conjecture, in the neighborhood of +.15. What the welfare of the world needs from persons who have the ability to amass wealth is that they and their children who inherit the ability shall continue to do so by honest means. It is better for them to be at work managing industry, even if ruthlessly, than to be devoted to a life of ostentatious entertainment.

The benevolence of a generation ago aimed to provide the fundamentals of bodily comfort—food, clothing, and shelter. Modern theory and practice varies from this in two opposite directions. One is to emphasize prevention rather than relief; preventing certain sorts of persons from being born and certain sorts of habits from being acquired, providing work rather than charity. This is done chiefly by science, education, and industrial progress. The other is to give those near the zero end much political and pecuniary power, trusting that they will use it to help themselves and the general welfare. The former is preferred but we recognize the importance of having the poor help themselves and take responsibility so far as may be.

Reducing "social" inequalities is more important in Europe than in America, more important to women than to men, to the dull than to the intelligent, and to those who depend upon companions than to those who depend upon impersonal interests. The equalization of opportunity for those equally deserving is the kernel of government work in counteracting unfair and undesirable preferences and restraints. Public schools treating equal intellects alike, public libraries and museums treating equal powers of appreciation alike, and public health work equalizing the protection against certain diseases for those who take equal precautions, are cases of equalizing toward a better life. We may hope for public studios where persons of creative ability in the industrial and fine arts may have opportunities corresponding to their abilities.

The general spirit of the United States has been to make great efforts to increase the amount of education, but to pay relatively little attention to its distribution. The plea of reformers has been for more education regardless of who received it, and recommended as a national investment without consideration of the differences which may attach to the investment in certain boys and girls rather than in others. The mere volume of education has been taken as a measure of idealism. The general tendency has been to try to equalize the distribution, by aiding backward communities, increasing the number of days in session, delaying the permissible age for leaving school, enforcing attendance laws.

So long as there were many children who had only a few years of schooling, the benevolent doctrine of changing distribution so as to favor the least educated was rarely questioned. The prevention of illiteracy seemed a wise as well as a humane policy.

In general, a nation's educational resources should be used first to aid young men and women whom nature and nurture have chosen to profit from schooling. Those who can do so much for the world with so little are the very ones who should be given more.

Equality gained at the expense of quality would be a very bad bargain. Care in this is needed because the demands of people often are not to be better off than they would be, but to be better off than somebody else.

Fraternity

Actual fraternity was a potent feature of primitive political life. Figurative fraternity, treating one's fellows more or less as brothers, has never been very strong and probably cannot be. Affection, frankness, and the absence of efforts to exert an influence, cannot easily be maintained with hundreds, certainly not with millions. Something approximating the fraternal attitude often appears when men are possessed by a common interest, in a crowd watching its team or in two citizens of the same nation meeting in a foreign land. Fraternity is allied to loyalty, *esprit de corps,* and confidence; it is an asset in almost any organization, yet so much more has been said and done about liberty and equality in government than about fraternity.

Chapter 20
The Law and Human Nature

In the United States alone there are millions of laws, court decisions, and legal records about which lawyers and judges may need to be informed. The knowledge ranges from details, to broad principles concerning contracts intent and the like, to sweeping theories concerning the rights of man, the powers of the state, and the welfare of society.

The Functions of Law, Courts, and Lawyers

It is clear that the most obvious services performed by the law are protection against badness in men and the settlement of disputes. The law shares the former with religion and education, the latter with business and non-legal government, and both with the activities of men in family and community life.

In protecting against badness the law makes great use of punishment, and thus provides gratification to feelings of vengeance toward the persons in question, and a substantial amount of entertainment to some. Also, the law provides information about what the community will not tolerate, although persons trust the *mores* learned in the home, church, school, and neighborhood, and live in ignorance of legal rights and obligations. They do not separate their obligations as a member of the community subject to its laws from their obligations as gentleman, lady,

Christian, or neighbor. The law also works back to strengthen or weaken customs, to influence the lessons about conduct learned in church and school, the habits formed in the homes, neighborhood, and in business.

Even more important is the power which the law gives us to predict the acts of men and their consequences, and to adjust accordingly. First of all, it predicts what the courts will do. A man having made a promise, and the law being as it is, we can predict with high probability that he will keep that promise. As always prediction favors control. Through the operation of laws generally, much of the uncertainty of the future is banished.

The law does a vast amount of the world's business. Lawyers are busy with agreements as well as with disputes, and much business is done best in the long run by men with legal training. If all human beings were as angelic as, say, Cardinal Gibbons and Jane Addams and as reasonable as, say, President Eliot and Andrew Carnegie, if there were no criminals to try and no civil cases of torts or contracts, the law would still have work.

To these valuable services the law adds some which are questionable. It tends on the whole to preserve past customs. The prudent people in a community by ordinary psychological forces expected little from changed customs, putting almost all their hopes upon maintaining or restoring traditional rights and duties, ethics and religion, manners and codes. After repeated experience of beneficial physical and biological discoveries and inventions the old faith in time-honored customs of public and private conduct is abandoned, along with crossbows, spinning-wheels, amulets, blood-letting, and witches.

The law has not gone so fast or so far. It maintains a respectful, and even reverential, attitude toward past decisions. It does not often search in the other sciences to improve itself. It does authorize changes made discreetly by eminent jurists in whom it has confidence, but in general is conservative and uses its powers of interpreting laws and of declaring them unconstitutional in favor of past customs. A contemporary philosopher, Morris Raphael Cohen, and a contemporary psychologist, Edward S. Robinson, agree in lamenting this characteristic in it.[1] They are probably right, but some defense of the law's tendency to preserve will be suggested in this chapter.

Another questionable service of the law has been its unconscious propaganda in favor of the notion that there exists a majestic being, THE LAW, a spirit of reason, a natural force, or a God. This notion has been

[1] See Cohen, M. R., '33, *Law and the Social Order,* and Robinson, E. S., '35, *Law and the Lawyers.*

thoroughly instilled into conventional thinking about the law. The common man has great respect for the law, much more than he would give to it if he considered simply the judges, lawyers, and laws that he knew; he respects it largely for something which he thinks exists apart from them.

"A law-loving people may criticize, if they have the opportunity, a newly proposed law to any possible extent. But when once it is enacted, they will not only cheerfully obey it, but, by a peculiar action of the imagination will unconsciously attribute to it a quasi-mysterious origin, and banish all memory of the competing views of expediency amidst which it arose." [Sheldon, '85, p. 404]

Attitudes Toward the Law

People are more shocked by corruption among the judiciary than among legislators. They think the law works more unselfishly and uniformly for welfare than does business. It has not, I think, declined in public estimation so much as the church has, although both have lost in dignity and dependability, especially in the opinion of workingmen.

Reformers in 1900 asked mainly for better laws in the interests of children, women, workingmen, and the masses; but those of 1940 are asking for changes in courts, lawyers, and the spirit of the law which will make all more sensitive and responsive, more able and willing to change the world, more devoted to "social justice" rather than to justice pure and simple. Reformers urge that law be in the last analysis an institution for human welfare, that judges be servants of welfare as well as of reason, using their intelligence to develop the law to fit new needs and ideals. They allege that the law is now not nearly so inventive and progressive as it should be.

Law and Science

A science of laws and courts would study them and their relations, especially their causation and consequences, and would test its success by its power of prediction. It would make much use of quantitative methods. Not much like this would be found in the minds of most judges or lawyers. There are few crucial observations, and almost no quantitative relations anywhere in law. There are, however, many facts and principles in the books of historians of law which are much like those of anthropology, psychology, and comparative anatomy, even though the arguments of legal historians often concern very broad questions, depend upon definitions, and resemble metaphysics more than physics.

Teachers of law probably call it a science for the same psychological reasons that theologians call theology science, because it is a very dignified body of facts and principles which can be mastered only by very high intellects; the "science" of law taught in law schools and used in courts is much like theology. Its body of facts and principles is not much like those of chemistry, biology, psychology, or anthropology. They are not inevitable, immutable regularities in nature, but are largely if not wholly made by man, decreed by God, or somewhat vaguely inherent in nature. Since what God has decreed and what the "law of nature" is depends upon the interpreter, it may be asserted roughly that man discovers physics but makes law.

The science of law is in fact more like the science of grammar. The English language being what it is, and the reputable ways of using it being what they are, its grammar has been studied and codified. Similarly the life of civilized man being what it is and the reputable ways of living and doing business being what they are, the facts and principles of law can be stated. As in grammar there is a gradation from very scholarly and deep presentations to mere manuals of rules to obey to have a blameless reputation in speech and writing, so in law there is the range from imposing doctrines of jurisprudence to the everyday advice of one's counsellor at law.

The variety of cases brought before courts is greater than the variety of verbal usages brought before editors and grammarians, their importance to the persons concerned is greater, their average complexity is greater; but the essential mental processes are much alike. In both new customs require new principles. The changes are in the main so gradually made that a man can easily think that he uses language as his parents did and a judge can think that he decides cases as his predecessor did. But in both the accumulated changes are so great that a composition written by Chaucer would hardly receive a passing mark on its grammar in a college-entrance examination, and cases of exemplary filial duty in the past would now be pigeon-holed under murder.

On general grounds a natural science of law, related to the traditional study of the law as linguistics is related to grammar, seems desirable. But its advocates meet opposition. Having spent their adult lives in thinking in terms of verbal statements and in deducing whether a certain behavior comes under a certain category, experts in the law feel ill at ease with quantitative symbols, making experiments, framing hypotheses, and thinking inductively from particular facts to general rules. The main common element in the two sorts of thinking is the use of evidence to determine what happened, and even here the tasks often differ, that of the scientist being chiefly to get it from things and that of the lawyer to purge the testimony of persons.

There is the reasonable fear that the authority and majesty of the law may be weakened by a science which studies it in the same way it might study human food preferences or marriage customs. In the minds of the great majority of men the law has authority from three sorts of reasons: first, because it works well in their experience; second, because able persons whose opinions they trust say that it has authority; and third, because it is supposed to have superhuman origin and support. The great majority of men do think more highly of the ten commandments from thinking that God wrote them rather than Moses; they think more highly of the law from thinking that it is something implanted by a miracle in each baby's soul at birth than from thinking that it is the *jus gentium* of the Romans.

It may, consequently, be good public policy to add one more legal fiction to the present store, continuing to use Divine Law, Natural Law, The Law, and other such honorific titles, but understanding them to mean certain features of human customs and rules found in good men or devised by wise judges, which are advantageous for welfare. It might even be good public policy for science to advertise the laws of Newton, Ohm, Einstein, Mendel, and others as divine laws, letting 'divine' connote truth, importance, and nobility rather than extra-natural causation.

These fictions probably are not necessary. Modern medicine is held in high esteem by the great majority in civilized nations though it is obviously a human product. It may lack law's majesty, but its decisions have even more authority. Law which studies itself scientifically will gain far more authority than it will lose in the opinion of able men, and this gain will probably spread among people in general enough to counterbalance the loss in superstitious reverence for law.

Legal Doctrines About Human Nature

Legal doctrines about man were established and statements of them recorded before the physiology of the brain was understood, before man's evolution from the mammalian stock was surmised, before anthropologists or psychologists appeared. Consequently legal statements about human nature and behavior are old-fashioned, incomplete, lacking in precision, and occasionally absolutely wrong. But for two reasons much less harm results than might be expected.

One reason is that many of the statements are rather vague statements about common facts of mental life which are true enough in a general way. For many purposes of the law, it does not much matter whether the brain is a connection-system of neurones or a gray and white jelly, whether man's abilities are highly specialized or described by a few faculties.

The other reason is that lawyers and judges have been very able men constantly concerned with human thoughts, feelings, and acts, who often took an objective and factual attitude toward these. They developed rules or customs for separating certain sorts of behavior for which a person should be held legally accountable from certain other sorts for which he should not.

Dr. Steuart Britt has examined the concept of intent as used today in the law, and finds many things *said* which sound antiquated and false, but very few things *done* which a psychologist would oppose. Robinson exposes the inadequacies of the law's doctrines about thought and action, but he does not present evidence that they have worked badly, and does not propose substitutes for them.

The law has made up a convenient behavioristic psychology to fit its wants, as follows: It is the business of the law to requite certain persons for certain behavior which can be proved to have occurred. The person must be responsible in the sense (a) that if anybody is to be requited it is he, and (b) that if he is requitable for any behavior he is for this. This simple psychology adjusting man's nature to the felt needs of courts and lawyers is then turned endwise and decorated with verbal distinctions and classifications taken from common usage, theology, and rather ancient psychology, making a certain pretense that the law follows fundamental natural divisions of human behavior. This is still done even by the most eminent; consider, for example, the following argument of Cardozo: "Till now the law has been guided by a robust common sense which assumes the freedom of the will as a working hypothesis in the solution of its problems." [Justice Cardozo in Steward Machine Co. *vs*. Davis, 301 V.S. 548, p. 589, 1937] Just how fully "the law has been guided by a robust common sense" may be doubted; I think that it usually has. The references to determinism and the freedom of the will seem decorative, and also rather dangerous. The Swiss and Scotch and New England Calvinists did not have to give up law or modify it to any great extent.

The law thinks that certain persons should be punished. Whether it gives as its psychology that they have evil spirits or evil intentions is clearly secondary. Until there is a substantial probability that a change in its psychology will make the law a better instrument for welfare, this simple and convenient doctrine may be left undisturbed.

Legal Requitability

All sharp divisions on grounds of age, intelligence, sanity, or any other feature of a person are makeshifts. If a person becomes "responsible" at 21 years 0 days, he was already nearly so at 20 years 364 days. Sanity grades imperceptibly from ordinary persons to eccentrics, to psychopaths, to persons whom not one physician in a hundred thousand would call sane. Law as a natural science would work with sliding scales and degrees of probability, but the law is not adapted to them; and in some cases the game may not be worth the candle.

All, or nearly all, features relevant to requitability are specialized. An idiot's mind is not equally idiotic throughout. Some very insane persons look after their own interests with great shrewdness. Ability in money matters and "knowledge of right and wrong" are notably specialized.

Chronological age is a poor measure of anything save itself; neither physical maturity, nor mental ability, nor moral development is closely correlated with it. John Doe's "mental age" is obviously a much better measure for determining the fitness of a person to be at large, to manage his own affairs, to be a guardian, to give testimony, to serve on a jury, than is chronological age.

A psychologist would be appalled at guaranteeing what a prudent or reasonable man would do and not do in various situations. He might hazard judgments about the median man, in the form of many possibilities of varying probability.

The law does not know how its "reasonable" man compares with the average resident of the United States today (or with any defined real person) in any measurable quality whatever. A judge trusts to his intuition as to what a reasonable man would do, aided by his memories of what judges have said he would do, or else collects *ad hoc* a sufficient number of relevant statements.

The Personal Equation

The ideal judge is absolutely impartial, but that is a psychological impossibility except in treating entirely objective facts. There are prejudices due to sex, age, religion, party, friendships, and many other features of a person's career. Since a judge may be entirely unaware that he has them, they are more mischievous. He can try to know them and allow for them, as astronomers do for their differences in reaction-time. As a man grows older he may well subtract, for each year over fifty, one percent from the strength of his opinions contra the changes in the world. Another useful procedure is to make the *weights* given to facts as objective as possible by writing all down, and making the balance a matter of objective arithmetic rather than subjective opinion.

Common sense, the customs of courts, and psychology until recently assumed that a man was supposed to see what was before his eyes and acted on his retina, to hear what stimulated the auditory cells in his ears. It is now known that the attitude or "set" of a person's mind is very important in perception, that there is a neglect or dampening of some things, an emphasis of others, and even gratuitous additions from imagination. The reports of a hundred witnesses of the same event written down immediately thereafter will vary widely and in unexpected ways. Memory and suggestions from others may easily become incorporated or cause witnesses to omit things really sensed.

The "Legal Mind"

If the ideas, ways of thinking, and emotional attitudes of lawyers are notably different from those of people in general, the differences should be studied. Lawyers form a large percentage of our legislative assemblies and administrative boards, and as judges interpret and modify statutes and constitutions.

In popular usage "the legal mind" is a rather opprobrious term connoting devious ways, unnecessary subtlety, and avoidance of plain facts. Nobody has made a serious study of the qualities of mind which lead young people to become lawyers. I can only suggest probabilities. Young men who become lawyers are highly intelligent and are relatively more interested in words and other symbols than in things. The first is proved by their records in pre-legal studies; the second is indicated by studies comparing early interests of mechanical engineers and eminent lawyers. [Kent, E. B., '03, p. 62]

The intellectual triumphs of lawyers are less in learning more fully the true nature of what they are studying than in contriving to classify it. This encourages what Robinson calls "substantive ways of thinking" to an extent which scientists and engineers consider excessive. Having found reason to classify a hydroplane as a vessel, a lawyer may be content to forget the many respects and circumstances in which it is not a vessel. Lawyers are trained by their ways of thinking to put behind them temptations to be realistic. But if government by rules is better than government by persons, the remedy would seem to be more detailed rules varying with the accessory qualities and circumstances of the things concerned. In medicine we have as an approved doctrine the treatment of each case by itself in all its variety; no competent physician would be content to treat alike all cases which he classified as tuberculosis. We may hope that some of the flexibility of medicine can be put into law and government without damaging other valuable features.

Courts are largely engaged with disputes, and lawyers are often advocates engaged in trying to support one side and win victory. In trials by jury this favors habits of mind akin to debate and salesmanship. A general can lose all the little battles if he wins the big ones. A business man can redeem a hundred ten-dollar mistakes by a sizable success. A literary man can burn all his mistakes before anyone sees them. In law, one slip may lose a case, cloud a title, or spoil a contract. The legal mind is thus a cautious mind.

The law puts a premium upon rules and precedents. The lawyer is taught to search for a formidable number of affirmations that he is correct.[1] This habit combines with his caution to make him distrustful of innovations. Whereas artists, literary men, philosophers, and scientists often pride themselves that their ideas are new when they really are not, lawyers take pride in making their innovations seem the logical outcomes of the old, discovered by superior reasoning rather than by creative imagination.

A lawyer is paid by people to tell them what certain words mean. The rules and decisions he operates with are in words, not equations. I do not think lawyers are mentally prolix, habitually thinking in more words or more technical words than necessary. In ordinary language much is left to be read between the lines or understood in view of a particular situation; the law does not favor such looseness. But their training does make lawyers relatively more careful about words and less careful about realities than men in science or business.

It is in legislators and judges that the legal mind, whatever that may be, most influences government and welfare. One opinion holds that there are too many lawyers in government compared to engineers, craftsmen, labor leaders, scientists, social workers, and other representatives of human interests. There are complaints of too much legislation, legislation incompetent to attain its objects, and unenforceable legislation. But I know of no specific complaints against definite qualities alleged to characterize the legal mind.

[1] A beautiful illustration of this may be seen in a joint publication of a lawyer and a psychologist on the "Psychological foundations for the fiduciary concept in corporation law" [Rohrlich, C., and Rohrlich, E., '38]. Nearly ninety psychological citations are used to support the authors' views, probably three times as many as a psychologist writing alone would have used.

In judges the legal mind is modified by selection for the bench and training for it. On the whole, the selection seems of notably able men, to whom judicial work is intrinsically more attractive than the work of a practicing lawyer. The work of a judge being largely to state authoritative decisions, the forces of occurrence and after-effect described in Chapter 1 make him confident that his official opinions are right. He would be miserable without it, but judicial self-confidence is restrained by the fear of other lawyers. Judges are discomforted when associates disagree, when higher courts reverse them, when teachers or textbooks neglect or deride them.

As a consequence of their selection and training, inventive and creative activity only appears when justice as conventionally conceived at the time absolutely demands it, or in persons of very great intellect and a strong individual proclivity toward it, or when some interest precious in the sight of the judge can be protected only by inventive genius.[1]

On the whole, the legal mind seems improvable by the addition of certain characteristics of scientific or engineering mentality. Psychology warns however against interfering with able minds lest abilities of great value be damaged in the effort to add others. It is safer and probably better to improve the law and trust that the legal mind will adapt itself thereto.

The Improvement of Law[2]

Why do outsiders make suggestions about improving law though they would rarely attempt to improve medicine, engineering, or the sciences? One reason is that law expresses and codifies customs, about which they as well as lawyers should be competent to judge. Another reason is that law interprets and enforces laws which, in democracies, the public makes. A third reason is that the doctrine of lawyers and courts as instruments for welfare is so modern that law can hardly be expected to have unimprovable hypotheses about what welfare is, or how law can serve it best. A fourth reason is that law makes customs as truly as

[1] Such an interest may be that of the nobility or employers, but it may be that of poor children, labor unions, or the ultimate consumer. The inventive genius in Cardozo's famous decision in MacPherson *vs.* Buick Motor Company, by which the ultimate consumer is protected against failure of automobile makers to inspect adequately each part which they put in their cars, acted in the interest of the ultimate consumer, and was probably aroused to action by Cardozo's humane nature. So also in the Wagner case.

[2] The word "law" in this section will usually mean what students study in law schools and what lawyers and courts do, and not the larger total, including all rules made by governments and all activities connected with their enforcement.

customs make law. All workers for welfare are concerned with courts and lawyers as social forces.

We may review briefly the past course of legal improvements: (1) improvements by outright inventions, such as Children's Courts or the "declaratory judgment"; (2) improvements by the adaptation of legislation, lawyers, and courts to new needs and customs; (3) improvements by the struggles of various persons and classes for advantage, from which there emerge benefits to the general welfare.

Legal Inventions   Many of the changes in law are gradual accumulations or omissions, almost unperceived but producing substantial results. By the law of effect, these tend to make law more satisfying to those practicing it, and perhaps to those affected by it. The administration of oaths was originally a very serious matter intended to inspire awe and arouse conscience, pronounced with solemnity. Oaths were so administered as long as officers got more satisfaction thus than they got from a saving of time and effort; oaths are now rattled off. This does no harm if the persons taking the oaths treat them as seriously as they would if the circumstances were more impressive.

In some cases inventors make new law though asserting that they are only applying the old. In others they probably know what they are trying to do as well as Judge Olson knew in his advocacy of Children's Courts. The results are usually good in either case because with men of above average ability and good will, even their unconscious modifications of law will be in the direction of reasonableness and justice.

Students of law regard the judgment in the case in which the rule was set forth that mutual promises give rise to a contract as making new law that was good law. But the treatment of a corporation as a person is regarded with some suspicion, and it may well be that the ignorance of its inventors led them into a sacrifice of the interests of the public.

Besides the danger that legal inventions will favor the wants of courts and lawyers and neglect relatively the needs of women, workers, owners, renters, juries, and others affected by law, there is a danger that abrupt changes will not be made even when needed. This is probably true of all spheres of invention; it is true of law par excellence. In the garden of the law few plants are ever dug up and cast out; few are brought in full grown from other gardens. In general, law abominates revolution and is suspicious of evolution by abrupt mutations.

In their inventions lawyers and judges have been more moved by reason and the desire to make law intellectually admirable than by benevolence and the desire to make it humane. Maine points out that certain beneficial changes in Roman law were not motivated by an interest in the general good. "It was [due] not to anything resembling philanthropy but to their sense of simplicity and harmony—of what they significantly termed 'elegance. . . .' " ['61, Edition of '94, p. 79 f.] Even so benevolent a jurist as Brandeis was convinced that courts should stick to legality, leaving humanity to legislation. This is psychologically sound, maintaining a division of labor by which the expertness of courts and lawyers on the one hand and the expertness of representatives of human needs on the other are used maximally. Benevolence, valuations of wants, and valuations of persons do influence legal inventions, however. If Grotius had had the ideals and temperament of Nietzsche mixed with those of Louis XIV, he would probably not have originated the doctrine that the society of nations is governed by Natural Law, and that commonwealths, like men under Nature, are all equal.

Not all legal inventions made by the profession have been made of its own initiative, and some have been made by outsiders. This seems to have been partly the case with the use of the secretarial bureau of the King of England as a supplementary court, which developed into the Court of Chancery.

Improvements by Adaptations to Needs and Customs   Occasionally the march of civilization simplifies law. Abolishing slavery abolishes slave-law; the decline of feudalism replaces a host of local rights and duties by a widespread law of contract; freedom of religious thought makes many offenses innocent. But on the whole the task becomes more extensive and complex. It probably requires a higher intelligence and more time to master business law alone today than was required for a Roman jurisconsult to master the whole of Roman law.

Both legislative law (enactments) and judicial law (interpretations) have responded to changes in the quality as well as the quantity of human wants. The response is clearest in legislative law, where the improvement of biological knowledge has caused health legislation, and the improvement of sympathy has caused legislation for free education and the emancipation of women. Courts respond also to better knowl-edge and better ideals. They permitted the use of the blood tests of relationship without being instructed to do so by legislatures. They found ways to justify the receipt of money for the use of money by a Christian in medieval Europe when legislation to the same effect would have been difficult to pass.

In law, as in education, lay customs often lead professional improve-ments. In law we have public feeling, pressure groups, agitators, and the like trying to influence what the profession does; experts are not largely left to themselves.

Improvements Resulting from the Struggle of Persons and Classes for Advantage   Legal struggles of persons to obtain what they thought were their rights and to defend them against other claimants have presumably increased the sum total of freedom and satisfaction. The theory and practice of Roman law, of Teutonic law, and of the various European and American hybrids was to settle disputes and prevent interminable strife, and to settle them by the customs of the group interpreted by its legal experts. Retaliation by an eye for an eye was improved on by payments of money damages, because compensation was better for all concerned. Trial by ordeal was replaced by a trial in court, because it was better for the innocent, for the peace of mind of the community, for the encouragement of reason among them, etc. This is not that legal conflicts necessarily evolve toward justice; in England the King's law made rather sharp bargains in the King's favor.

Due process of law probably never worked perfectly for justice, still less for general welfare. But on the whole it favored them increasingly century by century. The orthodox view of jurisprudence assumes that the law bears within itself a motive force for its improvement. Psychologically such a doctrine neglects the important fact that judges were men of notable intellectual superiority. Appeals of reason will correlate very high with intellect, and the correlation of good will with intellect is substantial. If judges and lawyers had been drawn from the population by lot, I warrant that the improvements caused by the conflict of interests in courts would have been less.

Improvement by a Natural Science of Law   From 850 to 1750 European law improved more rapidly than did engineering and medicine. This suggests that the recent advantages of engineering and medicine are related to their utilization of advances in natural science; the law may speed up its improvement by utilizing more fully the facts and methods of those sciences relevant to it. Law should become naturalistic as well as erudite, critical, and historical. In doing so, it will use the sciences of man to change the purposes now assumed by the law.

A naturalistic science of the nature, causes and consequences of law would include descriptions of the instructive laws, written and unwritten, of schools, clubs, factories, churches, armies, games, pilgrimages, hunts, hospitals, stock exchanges, monasteries, oligarchies, parties, along with the laws found in textbooks and histories of law. A naturalist is a glutton for instructive facts, distinguishable from children and pedants mainly by the fruits of his curiosity; the legal naturalist might study the habits which cause customs which in turn cause laws.

The different laws of different times and places will interest him no less than the resemblances. The maximum penalty for incest in Virginia is six months, in Louisiana imprisonment for life, in Delaware a fine of $100. "The guilt of forgery in Kansas is four times that of larceny, but in Connecticut the guilt of larceny is four times that of forgery." [Wines, '94, pp. 325–327, *passim,* quoted by Sutherland, '24, p. 507]

A naturalistic science of laws will be curious about the idea whence the law grew, about what persons and forces caused its enactment or pronouncement. It will wish to know about law caused by thought, by emotion, by reason, by prejudice, by science, and law caused by custom. It will be eager to compare laws made in emergencies with laws made under normal conditions, laws enacted by large majorities with laws barely passed, the decisions of administrative tribunals with those of regular courts, the decisions of sons of the rich and educated with those of the sons of the poor and the illiterate.

It will be most curious about the consequences of laws, studying not only such grand questions as common law *versus* civil law, popular legislation *versus* expert legislation, punitive *versus* reformative intent, but also trivial understandings which seems likely to advance science. Faraday and Joseph Henry did not restrict their curiosity to the consequences of earthquakes and great engines, but played with little magnets and bits of wire, and work like that made the power age. Some little thing may point the way to great improvements in legislation about education, work, or peace.

Valid observations of causal relations in law are hard to make. When we cannot observe directly what causes a certain law or what it causes, we can often make substantial progress by using knowledge of its affiliations or correlations. Variations in customs, laws, courts and the like then become aids. The exceptions which annoy the student of law *qua* classifier and logician become the material for instructive mathematical treatment with statistical techniques.

Improvements by Changing the Purposes and Valuations of the Law   A great lawyer and judge, Cardozo, spent much of his life to promote adaptations of jurisprudence to the purposes and valuations which the social sciences recommend rather than to the alleged edicts of Jehovah, conscience, or reason as neatly recorded in the existing law. "It is the opinion of sociological jurisprudence that if the law continues to follow the method of deriving its axioms and premises from within itself alone and verifying them by criteria which it itself sets up with disregard to the ambient world, it is bound to stagnate.... The sociological jurist wishes to indicate the necessity for jurisprudence of recognizing an extra-legal norm or standard derived from a sociological analysis of the *mores.*" [Aronson, '38, p. 10 f. *passim*] Advocates of sociological jurisprudence are specially interested in a *social ethics* for the law; by studying the social sciences the law will learn to appraise competing values.

The law is to protect the rights of society and welfare as well as the rights of individuals. What sociological jurisprudence accepts as the "social" purposes of the law is stated by Pound, its chief American defender:

... The legal order endeavors to give effect to at least six groups of claims or demands involved in the existence of civilized society. First we may put the general security, the claim or want of civilized society to be secure from those acts or courses of conduct that threaten its existence: ... peace and order, ... the general health, ... the security of acquisitions and ... the security of transactions.... Second, there is the security of social institutions, the claim or want of civilized society to be secure from those acts or courses of conduct which threaten or impede the functioning of its fundamental institutions, domestic, religious and political. Third, we may put the conservation of social resources, the claim or want of civilized society that the natural media of civilized human existence and means of satisfying human wants in such a society shall not be wasted and shall be used and enjoyed in a manner consistent with the widest and most beneficial application of them to human purposes.... Fourth we may put the general morals, the claim or want of civilized society to be secure against those acts and courses of conduct which run counter to the moral sentiment of the general body of those who live therein for the time being.... Fifth there is the interest in general progress, the claim of civilized society to be secure against those acts and courses of conduct that interfere with economic, political and cultural progress and the claim that so far as possible individual conduct be so shaped as to conduce to these forms of progress.... Sixth, we may put the social interest in the individual human life, the claim or want of civilized society that each individual therein be able to live a human life according to the standards of the society, and to be secure against those acts and courses of conduct which interfere with the possibility of each individual's living such a life. ['21, p. 208 f.]

A naturalistic and scientific ethics offers a few reservations, including the principle of weighting wants, according to the kind of person. Law as an agent for welfare will not progress far if it neglects differences in wants and differences in men. Scientific ethics regrets incomplete considerations of the wants of future men. It is also skeptical of assuming the absolute value of all "fundamental institutions," of "the moral sentiment of the general body," and of enabling "each individual ... to live a human life according to the standards of the society," although Pound is probably prudent in advising the law to be a defender of fundamental institutions, the moral ideas of the majority, and the right of each to a certain standard of living.

The criticisms which the legal profession makes of "sociological jurisprudence" are that it introduces subjectivism, relies on social doctrines which are not yet science, extends the purposes of the law too far and too fast, and may detract from welfare by having the law do more but badly.

Social Justice

Somewhat akin to the doctrine of sociological jurisprudence is the doctrine held by many reformers that if ordinary justice were replaced or amplified by "social justice," there would be great gains for welfare.

It is remarkable that so popular a concept should have no accepted definition. In a fairly wide reading during the past five years the nearest approach to a definition which I noted was a statement made by Pope Pius XI.[1] Since he includes the opportunity for all decent workers to have "all reasonable comforts" and to acquire "a modest fortune," it is something which the world has never had. It did not exist in the American colonies for the slaves. Even in the pioneer West of free land it did not exist, because the justice of the pioneer West was the same justice which the East had. The possession of comforts and the acquisitions of fortune came from the beneficence of nature, the gifts of the federal government, the building of railroads, etc., rather than from any special brand of justice. Iceland has something approaching it, but Iceland has a population of superior ability.

The implications of social justice are that it is not ordinary justice, and will cause an enormous increase in material welfare, and comes undescribed and apparently largely by miraculous activities. It is a utopia, a condition of a population in respect of welfare in which the needs of each person and family are regularly and securely met.

R. MacEachen ['31] opines that social justice requires that somebody provide work for those who are willing to work, and pay them enough to live decently. To Alex Mackendrick social justice is something the presence of which will prevent the inexorable laws of the universe from causing the wreck of civilization: "Will the suffering peoples learn that to go on perpetuating social injustice is to defy the inexorable laws of the universe; that it is to pile up a debit-balance that must assuredly one day

[1] Encyclical Letter of March 19, 1937.

be wiped out; that it is to accumulate explosive material that must ultimately, by spontaneous combustion if not by accident, result in disastrous conflagration?" [The Dial, April 27, 1916] In Willoughby's volume, *Social Justice* [1900], he stated the problem of social justice as "the proper distribution of economic goods; and the harmonizing of the principles of liberty and law, of freedom and coercion" [p. 11], and concluded that "A man's rights are measured by his capacity and disposition for good." [p. 201 f.] The most constructive suggestion which I have found is the one made by Brandeis that the provision of a reserve to ensure regularity of employment for workers should be a fixed charge, having precedence over dividends to stockholders.

When there are any statements or implications about social justice as a thing which courts could do, they seem to imply two things. The first is making the treatment of persons and groups correlate more closely with their real merits, and be more independent of accidents of fortune and prejudice. This is merely a fuller and more perfect ordinary justice. The second is the use of legislation and judicial decisions to counterbalance the disadvantages which certain large classes of persons have by misfortune *or any other causes*. There is progress toward better justice by distinguishing merit more correctly, by widening brotherhood, and by getting rules for life which leave less scope for the whims of a possessor of power. Perfect justice of the ordinary sort we approach by getting power used more and more according to rules which requite men according to their merits. Social justice cannot be better than this unless it is something better than justice,—mercy, perhaps, or forgiveness, or a mixture of justice with these, or a system of injustice which is somehow better for welfare than justice.

The treatment of groups to maximize welfare is difficult by any system. Old law was accustomed to dealing with such associations as families and clans, using simple methods of assessing wergild on the kindred and leaving it to them to manage the rest. Indeed the law was slow in learning to provide justice for individuals. But neither the law for family units nor the law for individuals nor the law for the troublesome sorts of associations known as conspiracies is adequate for many modern groups.

If a hundred college students or intelligent adults who read about social problems are asked to give cases of social justice, they are likely to refer to such things as free schools, old-age pensions, votes for women, state care for the blind, jobs for all who are willing to work.

These are either matters of ordinary justice on a large scale; or of what used to be called charity, arrangements to counterbalance misfortunes with disregard of merit; or of things excellent to have but hard to provide. The law should favor justice, including justice to groups and classes; it, or some agency, should provide mercy and charity as needed for welfare. But if a thing is essentially injustice it should not be called "social justice."

Psychologically the words *social justice* seem to function mainly as a demand for more and better justice of the ordinary sort, and secondly as a euphemism for benevolence and charity. The demand is justifiable. No fair-minded lawyer thinks that courts provide as good justice as they might. No fair-minded legislator thinks that existing laws provide as good justice as they might. The euphemism may be justifiable as a means of lessening feelings of inferiority and shame in the recipients of charity, and of preventing smug pride and condescension in the givers. But it has the bad feature of hiding and distorting the real causation of a person's affliction, and of assuming that a world which has only so much to give robs us because it gives no more.

Justice for the Poor

In modern civilized states men of equal merit theoretically are equal before the law, but in practice justice can be bought. Legal counsel and court fees make civil suits a luxury. In spite of Legal Aid Societies, wider use of litigation *in forma pauperis,* the appointment of salaried public defenders, the establishment of small-claims courts with greatly reduced fees, and by various other arrangements, the evil persists.

The bad feeling caused by the misuse of the law against the poor by brutal employers, landlords, and money-lenders is out of proportion to the actual amount of resulting damage to the poor. The suffering of the poor from actual criminals, against whom they do have substantially the same police protection as the rich, is probably much greater than their suffering from unjust employers, landlords, etc.

The robberies by scoundrels who take advantage of the defenseless poor, abominable as they are, did not equal the gifts made to the poor in a single city, New York, from public funds alone, during a year.

On the whole, modern civilization has been beneficent to the poor. Its failure to prevent the misuses of law is, like its failure to prevent various misuses of automobiles, printing-presses, banks, labor-unions, morphine, democracy, and other useful inventions, is important primarily because of its impressiveness to the sufferer and to benevolent citizens in general, who are thereby prejudiced against the law and against a social order which permits such iniquities.

It is well to remind ourselves that this social order, which also permits many gangsters and racketeers to terrorize whole neighborhoods and industries, many robbers and bums to live off the decent and industrious, many feeble-minded to commit arson for pleasure, and many mothers to pawn their children's clothes in order to get drunk, is nearly as good as any that man has yet operated, and that the difficulties may lie more in the persons themselves than in the social order.

Chapter 21
Human Nature and Reform

Our consideration of human nature in relation to welfare promises no miracles, but it has shown that man has the possibility of almost complete control of his fate, and that if he fails it will be by the ignorance or folly of men. Certain sound principles of action I will review here.

Better genes. A man's intelligence and virtue can work for welfare only for a life-span, but his genes can live forever. By selective breeding supported by a suitable environment we can have a world in which all men will equal the top ten percent of present men. One sure service of the able is to beget and rear offspring. One sure service which the inferior can perform is to prevent their genes from survival. The effect of any alleged reform upon the selective birth-rate should be considered.

Better training by rewards. By arranging matters so that the immediate consequences of an action are satisfying to a person, the tendency can be strengthened. So, by unfortunate attachments, horrible perversions may be established; and, by wise training, habits of great value to welfare. Measures to motivate education, business, social life, and government by rewards are helpful.

Better training by sheer repetition. The mere operation of a tendency strengthens it somewhat. If by persuasion or coercion a person is caused to do a good thing, there is so much gained. *Per contra* every error is costly; bad tendencies are rarely overcome by resolutions or by

334

punishments, but only by being displaced by some good tendency. A large degree of freedom may be appropriate for those whose own natures and previous actions direct them into good courses; for the weak wayward, unbalanced, and vicious a benevolent paternalism is indicated.

Adaptation to reality.   A measure for welfare must be adapted to reality. Customs and reforms which are caused by hopes for the impossible and fears of dangers which do not exist play too great a rôle in human affairs. Civilized nations should be beyond the stage of irregular and precarious gains for welfare mixed with useless or harmful accessories made by the zeal of prophets.

Guidance by science.   The social sciences are still weak and insecure, but the scientific method is dependable. Proposed treatments to cure social ailments should be studied so far as possible by the impartial methods of science, and tested in the ways that science tests the effects of a new method of growing crops or a device for reducing friction. Their popularity should not be confused with their actual consequences, assuming adequate governmental and popular support.

Use of the truth.   Since a measure may enhance welfare if it receives adequate support and fail or even do harm if it does not, pressure must be put behind the truth. This is contrary to the hopes of some moralists. But the facts of psychology prove that the naked truth has little power save over those who have learned to honor and serve it, and that governments and people tend most to prefer comfortable ideas.

The able and good should acquire power.   In order to support the truth, defend justice, and restrain folly, superior men should acquire power. Psychology does not assert that they must fight political bosses with bosses of their own choice, or grafters with money, or demagogues with demagoguery, though perhaps they must, but it does assert that they must fight them with something. This is regrettable. But if they do not get pecuniary, political, and persuasive power, not only will they miss a great opportunity to advance welfare by supporting the truth; they, and their like in the future, may be seriously hampered in their ordinary activities.

Power should be in the hands of impartial groups.   The able and good among farmers, factory workers, manufacturers, labor unions, and other special groups will do better for welfare than the dull, selfish, and ill-balanced, but they will rarely be impartial. Impartiality in carrying out laws by courts and police has been a blessing. Impartiality in making laws and customs, and informing and advising the public, would be an even greater blessing.

The following are concerned with improvements in the environment:

The elimination of wars.   War is now almost as bad a bargain for the victors as for the vanquished. Those causes which lie in the inborn tendencies of men can be removed by selective breeding unless they are so firmly linked to desirable qualities that we dare not breed them out. Those which lie in ignorance can be reduced by knowledge. Selecting rulers of benevolent and progressive rather than masterful and aggressive natures will help. Those which lie in the passion of citizens to take pride in national power can be reduced somewhat by diverting this to pride in its health, per-capita wealth and income, athletic records, and scientific and artistic achievements.

The elimination of preparations for war.   Though not so brutalizing as actual wars and not as yet so expensive, these are a deplorable tax. Probably only the abolition of wars will prevent their increase.

Increasing capital goods.   With peace, a birth-rate quantitatively the same as now and qualitatively as good or better, and prudent government, durable capital goods can be made so abundant that the share of the cost of consumers' goods paid for the use of capital goods to make and transport them will be very little more than the cost of keeping the capital goods in repair and establishing a reserve to replace what wears out, becomes obsolete, or is destroyed. Interest rates can be lowered to 3 or 2 or 1 percent. The gain for welfare may be enormous.

Increasing mental capital.   If the hours of labor are reduced to an average of 40 per week the world over, all men should within a short time be able to obtain, at no cost save the use of half of their leisure time, as much knowledge of the essential facts about the world, about man's own nature, and the particular facts of their cooperation as they desire and can make good use of.

The freedom of labor from drudgery.   Machines and power should abolish brutalizing labor and labor where a man does little more than what a fraction of a mule can do. Men should not work at tasks beneath their capacities, except by choice.

Absolute welfare.   Institutions and customs which improve lives over what they would otherwise have been are good. Institutions and customs which improve some lives relatively to others equally meritorious, by restraint or deprivation, are bad. These axioms should be taught along with the law of gravitation and the second law of thermodynamics, perhaps along with $2+2=4$.

Quality is better than equality.   Institutions and customs which seek equality for equality's sake are likely to be pernicious. There is no magic virtue in taking power from the strong and giving it to the weak, or in taking wealth from the rich and giving it to the poor. Power and wealth should be taken from those who misuse them. The test of any proposed reform in the distribution of anything among men is its consequences for welfare, not for homogeneity.

Quality is better than numbers.   A decline in the birth-rate, if selective in the right direction, is good for welfare.

Reasonable expectations.   On the whole the sciences of man and the conduct of human affairs have improved by slow advances. I venture the suggestion that beneficent reforms will come less from governments, churches, and social reformers in search of wholesale salvation than from engineers, biologists, and other scientists observing man and his works with an impartial curiosity and eager for facts no matter how uninspiring.

APPENDICES

Appendix I
The Measurement of Abilities

There are two simple rules: Measure all of the ability. Measure nothing but it.

To measure all of it requires only that the sample be large enough and well-proportioned enough to give the same result that would be had if every item had been measured. If the ability is knowledge of the meanings of English words a test with ten thousand properly chosen should give as useful a result as a test with two hundred and fifty thousand. A test with even only a thousand will measure accurately enough for most purposes the abilities of most persons except specialists.

To measure nothing but it does not require a perfectly pure sample free from any contamination by other abilities. We may manage by determining the amount of contamination and allowing for it. For example, it is difficult to make tests of enjoyment of beauty which are entirely free from contamination by intelligence and knowledge. But with sufficient ingenuity, one can arrange the content of the tests with traps so that intelligence and knowledge lower a person's score as often and as much as they raise it.

Measuring a human ability is usually more like taking an inventory than like using a balance or thermometer.

Science may be able to infer the amount of some traits by a few ingenious questions or even by some biochemical fact. For nearly all

341

traits now, the measurement will be by sampling the behavior and achievements which the trait is or causes. Ingenious investigation will enable us to do much better than merely take a *random* sample inventory. The Stanford Binet test of intelligence is an inventory, but a much better one than a random collection of questions would be. Giving the opposites of words is a better test of intelligence than is multiplying numbers.

Suppose that a valid measure of ability at chess is required. We would waste no time in feeling the bumps on chess-players' heads or applying Rorschach tests. We would proceed at once to create chess problems from the easiest to the hardest, problems representing justly the ability to develop the pieces, to make combinations, to handle the end game, etc.; find how hard each was; arrange them in a series of columns for each sub-ability and levels for amount of difficulty. We would obtain the records of success or failure at each problem of enough persons of all degrees of ability at chess.

Measurement by a Consensus of Judges

To have an ability estimated by persons supposedly competent is about all that can be done with high levels of ability as a sculptor, painter, etcher, singer, philosopher, or poet, or with high levels of tact, courtesy, grace, wit, or wisdom. It is sound practice to correlate the rating by half of the judges with the rating by the other half and to increase the number of judges, if necessary, to obtain a half-with-half correlation of at least .90. Even more important is the prevention of systematic or "constant" errors whereby the judges tend toward certain prejudices. All that can be done is to select judges to represent fairly all the points of view that should be represented, arrange the means of expressing opinions to discourage any general tendency to make like errors, and test the consensus by objective facts in enough cases to expose any illusions.

Rating Scales

Scales to help judges express opinions and to help others to use the opinions may be scales of achievements or scales of persons. Consider judging the quality of handwriting. We may select ten specimens ranging from an excellent to a very poor handwriting and say "Let 100 mean as good as this; let 95 mean as good as this; let 90 mean as good as this"; and so on. Such a scale may prevent certain judges from using eccentric meanings and shifting their meanings during the time they are judging.

It will be much more useful if (1) specimens at each level of "goodness" are provided, if (2) the differences between each level and the next are known with some exactitude, and if (3) the scale extends down to a true zero. The first desideratum requires much labor; the second requires the use of correct theory and much labor; the third often requires much ingenuity.

A part of a scale for quality of handwriting is shown following, with the dimensions of the specimens half as large as in the original scale.

Consider an extremely crude scale of persons for use in judging the ability of a person to rule.

Provisional Scale for Rulers of Nations

9. The average of   Frederic William III, the Great Elector
                                Gustavus Vasa
                                Henry IV of France

8. The average of   Charles XI of Sweden
                                John I of Portugal
                                William III of England

7. The average of   Albert (consort of Queen Victoria)
                                Frederick VI of Denmark
                                Leopold I of Belgium

6. The average of   Frederick William IV of Prussia
                                Louis Philippe
                                Joseph II of Austria

5. The average of   George II of England
                                Henry II of France
                                Humbert of Italy

4. The average of   George III of England
                                Louis XVI of France
                                William IV of England

3. The average of   Ferdinand IV, King of Naples
                                Charles IV of Spain
                                Philip II of Spain

2. The average of   Alphonso VI of Portugal
                                Charles II of Spain
                                Christian VII of Denmark

Such a scale could be improved by determining a value which represents the quality of ruling that would have been had if the ruler had been replaced by an average man of forty, and noting this on the scale. An absolute zero in the shape of a person with just not any ability to rule is

17   Then the carelessly dressed gentleman stepped lightly into Warren's carriage and held out a small card, John vanished be-

15 lightly into Warren's carriage and held out a small card, John vanished behind the bushes and the carriage moved along down the drive

held out a small card, John vanished behind the bushes and the carriage moved along down the driveway. The audience of passers-

John vanished behind the bushes and the carriage moved along down the driveway. The audience

Then the carelessly dressed gentle-man stepped lightly into Warrens carriage and held out a small white

13   Then the carelessly dressed gentleman stepped lightly into Warren's carriage and held out a ished behind the bushes and the carriage moved along down the driveway The audience of passers-by which had Then the carelessly dressed gentleman stepped lightly into Warren's carriage and Then the carelessly dressed gentlemen stepped lightly into Warren's carriage and

11 riage moved along down the driveway. The audience of passers-by which had been gathering about them melted away

along the down the driveway The audience of passers-by which had been gathering about them

John vanished behind the bushes and the carriage moved along down the driveway The audience

9   Then the carelessly dressed gentlemen stepped lightly into Warren's carriage and held out a small card, John vanished behind the

by which had been gathering about them melted away in an instant leaving only a poor old lady on the curb. Albert was sadly

Then the carelessly dressed gentleman stepped lightly into Warren's carriage moved and held out a small card, John vanished

7 card, John vanished behind the bushes and the carriage moved

5   bushes and the carriage

moved along down the

driveway. The audre

not a very important feature of such a scale of beneficial rulers because the scale goes to negative quantities, misrule, interferences with the nation's welfare. We are not measuring the values of various governments versus anarchy, but the abilities of persons assuming the general status of government of their time and place.

Historians and experts in political science will scorn such a scale; and so do I, who made it! Regardless of the demerits of the sample scale, the possibility of such scales is as sure as the possibility of yardsticks.

Scales of persons are generally inferior to scales of mental products or achievements. One reason is the so-called "halo" phenomenon: that in judging a person's status in any particular ability or trait, judges unconsciously tend to prejudice their rating for that ability by their general opinion of him in a totality of abilities.

Appendix II

On the Fallacy of Imputing the Correlations
Found for Groups to the Individuals
or Smaller Groups Composing Them[1]

If the correlation between two traits, A and B (say, poverty and delinquency), in n groups (say, the residents of w districts) has a certain value, K, the correlation between A and B in the individuals or the families composing the groups will not be K, save in very special circumstances. It will usually be very much nearer zero. This is easily demonstrable, yet some able teachers have been guilty of thinking that the two correlations will be closely similar. And it is to be feared that many readers with little knowledge of correlation often misapply correlations between features of states, counties, cities, wards, classes, etc. to their constituent units.

I append an artificial illustration of the general fact, to make the matter clear to students. A is supposed to be intelligence quotient, and B is supposed to be the fraction of a room or number of rooms per person.

Let the scores for sample persons in each of twelve districts into which a city is divided be as shown in Tables 15–26. Within each of the districts the correlation between A and B is zero. If all the persons in the sample are combined, the result is Table 27, and the correlation is 0.45. If the averages for the twelve districts are used, the result is Table 28, and the correlation is 0.90.

[1] This appendix is adapted from a note in the American Journal of Psychology, vol. 52, pp. 122–124.

Tables 15 to 28   The correlation (zero) between intelligence quotient and number of rooms per person for each of twelve districts

The captions at the top of the tables, −4, −3, −2, −1, 0, 1, 2, 3, 4 and 5, represent intelligence quotients of 64 to 71, 72 to 79, 80 to 87, etc. The stubs at the left of the tables, −4, −3, −2, −1, 0, 1, 2, 3, 4 and 5 represent 0.20 to 0.39 rooms per person, 0.40 to 0.59 rooms per person, 0.60 to 0.79 rooms per person, etc.

Table 15

	−4	−3	−2	−1	0	1	2	3	4
−4									
−3				1	1	1			
−2		1	1	4	6	4	1	1	
−1	1	2	4	7	15	7	4	2	1
0	2	2	6	8	20	8	6	2	2
1	1	2	4	7	15	7	4	2	1
2		1	1	4	6	4	1	1	
3				1	1	1			

Table 16

	−4	−3	−2	−1	0	1	2
−4							
−3			1	1	1	1	
−2		1	2	4	4	2	1
−1		1	3	6	6	3	1
0		1	2	4	4	2	1
1			1	1	1	1	
2							
3							

Table 17

	−4	−3	−2	−1	0	1	2	3	4
−4									
−3									
−2				1	1	1	1		
−1		1	1	2	5	5	2	1	
0		1	3	5	10	10	5	3	2
1		1	3	5	10	10	5	3	2
2		1	1	2	5	5	2	1	
3				1	1	1	1		

Table 18

	−4	−3	−2	−1	0	1	2
−4							
−3			1	1	1	1	
−2		1	2	4	4	2	1
−1		1	3	6	6	3	1
0		1	2	4	4	2	1
1			1	1	1	1	

Table 19

	−4	−3	−2	−1	0	1	2	3	4
−4		1	1	1					
−3	1	2	4	2	1				
−2	1	3	6	3	1				
−1	1	2	4	2	1				
0		1	1	1					

Table 20

	−4	−3	−2	−1	0	1	2
−4			1	1	1		
−3		1	2	4	2	1	
−2		1	3	6	3	1	
−1		1	2	4	2	1	
0			1	1	1		

Table 21

	−4	−3	−2	−1	0	1	2
−4							
−3			1	1	1		
−2		1	2	4	2	1	
−1		1	3	6	3	1	
0		1	2	4	2	1	
1			1	1	1		

Table 22

	−3	−2	−1	0	1	2	3
−4			1	1	1		
−3		1	2	4	2	1	
−2		1	3	6	3	1	
−1		1	2	4	2	1	
0			1	1	1		

Table 23

	−4	−3	−2	−1	0	1	2
−4							
−3							
−2			1	1	1		
−1		1	2	4	2	1	
0		1	3	6	3	1	
1		1	2	4	2	1	
2			1	1	1		

Table 24

	−2	−1	0	1	2
−3					
−2					
−1		1	1	1	
0	1	2	4	2	1
1	1	3	6	3	1
2	1	2	4	2	1
3		1	1	1	

Table 25

	−4	−3	−2	−1	0	1	2	3	4
−1									
0					1	1	1		
1				1	2	4	2	1	
2				1	3	6	3	1	
3				1	2	4	2	1	
4					1	1	1		
5									

Table 26

	−3	−2	−1	0	1	2	3	4	5
−1									
0									
1						1	1	1	
2					1	2	4	2	1
3					1	3	6	3	1
4					1	2	4	2	1
5						1	1	1	

Table 27 Combination of all the persons in Tables 15 to 26

	−4	−3	−2	−1	0	1	2	3	4	5
−4		1	2	3	2	1				
−3	1	4	10	12	11	5	1			
−2	2	8	19	30	26	14	4	1		
−1	3	11	25	38	44	23	9	3	1	
0	3	7	21	33	50	29	15	6	4	
1	1	3	12	20	39	26	16	8	5	
2		2	3	9	17	16	12	9	3	1
3			3	4	6	8	8	4	1	
4					2	3	5	2	1	
5						1	1	1		

Table 28 Averages of the twelve districts

	−3	−2½	−2	−1½	−1	−½	0	½	1	1½	2	2½	3
−3													
−2½													
−2			1		1		1						
−1½													
−1				1	1	1							
−½													
0							2						
½								1					
1									1				
1½													
2											1		
2½													
3													1

Bibliography

The quotations in this book are by special permission of the publishers in question; permission to requote should be obtained from the original publishers, in the case of copyrighted books and articles.

Abram, A.	'09	Social England in the fifteenth century.
Adler, M. J.	*See*	Michael and Adler.
Allen, E. P. and Smith, P.	'32	The value of vocational tests as aids to choice of employment. Published by the Treasurer's Department of Birmingham, England.
Allport, F. H.	'24	Social psychology.
Anastasi, A.	'37	Differential psychology.
Andrews, B. R.	'38	Human nature and war. Social Frontier, vol. 4, pp. 158–161.
Arnold, T. W.	'35	Symbols of government.
Aronson, M. J.	'38	Cardozo's doctrine of sociological jurisprudence. Journal of Social Philosophy, vol. IV, pp. 1—44.
Asch, S.	*See*	Klineberg, Asch, and Block.
Ashley, W. J.	'93	An introduction to English economic history and theory. Part II.
Bartlett, E. R., and Harris, D. B.	'36	Personality factors in delinquency. School and Society, vol. 43, pp. 653–656.
Beach, E. V.	*See*	Boder and Beach.
Beck, S. J.	'33	The Rorschach method and the organization of personality. American Journal of Orthopsychiatry, vol. 3, pp. 361–375.

Beckwith, B. P.	*See*	Thorndike and Beckwith.
Benedict, R.	'34	Anthropology and the abnormal. Journal of General Psychology, vol. 10, pp. 59–82.
Bentham, J.	1780	Principles of morals and legislation. References are to the 1907 reprint of the edition of 1823.
Berle, A. A., Jr.	'35	Lasting values in government. Sigma Xi Quarterly, vol. 23, pp. 147–152 and 169.
Billikopf, J.	'31	The social duty to the unemployed. Annals of the American Academy of Political and Social Science, vol. 154, pp. 65–72.
Block, H.	*See*	Klineberg, Asch, and Block.
Boas, Franz	'28	Anthropology and modern life.
Boder, D. P., and Beach, E. V.	'36	Wants of adolescents. I. A preliminary study. Journal of Psychology, vol. 3, pp. 505–511.
Boissonnade, P.	'27	Life and work in medieval Europe.
Bowley, A. L.	'15	Measurement of social phenomena.
Bradway, K. P.	'37	Birth lesions in identical twins. American Journal of Orthopsychiatry, vol. 7, pp. 194–203.
Bragg, W. L.	'34	The physical sciences. Science, vol. 79, pp. 237–240.
Brandeis, L. D.		[Quoted by Billikopf]
Bregman, E. O.	'34	An attempt to modify the emotional attitudes of infants by the conditioned response technique. Journal of Genetic Psychology, vol. 45, 169–198.
Bregman, E. O.	*See*	Thorndike, Bregman, Lorge, etc.
Brolyer, C. R., Thorndike, E. L., and Woodyard, E.	'27	A second study of mental discipline in high school studies. Journal of Educational Psychology, vol. 18, pp. 377–404.
Bronner, A. F.	*See*	Healey and Bronner.
Brown, B. F.	*See*	Taylor and Brown.
Brutzkus, Boris	'35	Economic planning in Soviet Russia.
Bullock, C. J.	'01	Trust literature: a survey and a criticism. Quarterly Journal of Economics, vol. 15, pp. 190–210. Quoted by Hamilton, '19.
Burks, B. S.	'28	The relative influence of nature and nurture upon mental development. 27th Yearbook of the National Society for the Study of Education, pp. 219–316.
Burks, B. S.	'29	Note on Professor Freeman's discussion of the Stanford study of foster children. Journal of Educational Psychology, vol. 20, pp. 98–101.
Burns, C. D.	'21	Government and industry.
Burns, C. D.	'32	Leisure in the modern world.
Burt, Cyril	'21	Mental and scholastic tests.
Burt, Cyril	'25	The young delinquent.

Cabot, P. S. deQ.	'38	The relationship between characteristics of personality and physique in adolescents. Genetic Psychology Monographs, vol. 20, pp. 3–120.
Campbell, C. Macfie	'35	Destiny and disease in mental disorders. With special reference to the schizophrenic psychosis.
Cardozo, B. N.	'21	The nature of the judicial process.
Cardozo, B. N.	'24	The growth of the law, edition of '31.
Cardozo, B. N.	'28	Paradoxes of legal science.
Carver, T. N.	'15	Essays in social justice.
Carver, T. N.	'24	Economy of human energy.
Catlin, G. E. G.	'30	A study of the principles of politics.
Cattell, J. McK.	'12	A program of radical democracy. Popular Science Monthly (now the Scientific Monthly), vol. 80, pp. 606–615.
Cattell, J. McK.	'34	A scientific approach to emotional problems. Scientific Monthly, vol. 39, pp. 536–539.
Cherington, P.T.	'20	Elements of marketing.
Childs, H. L.	'30	Labor and capital in national politics.
Childs, M. W.	'36	Sweden, the middle way.
Cohen, M. R.	'33	Law and the social order.
Compton, K. T.	'34	Science and prosperity. Science, vol. 80, pp. 387–394.
Compton, K. T.	'35	Patterns in our ways of thinking. School and Society, vol. 42, pp. 209–215.
Conklin, E G.	'37	Science and ethics. Science, vol. 86, pp. 595–603.
Cottrell, F. G.	See	Rossman, et al.
Dashiell, J. F.	'37	Fundamentals of general psychology.
Davis, Elmer	'38	We lose the next war. Harpers Magazine, vol. 176, pp. 332–348.
Davis, J.	'27	Testing the social attitudes of children in the government schools in Russia. American Journal of Sociology, vol. 32, pp. 947–952.
Davis, R. A., Jr.	'28	The influence of heredity on the mentality of orphan children. British Journal of Psychology, vol. 19, pp. 44–59.
Dawson, Shepherd	'36	Environmental influence on mentality. British Journal of Psychology, vol. 27, pp. 129–134.
Dewey, John	'36	Authority and resistance to social change. School and Society, vol. 44, pp. 457–466.
Dibblee, G. B.	'24	The psychological theory of value.
Dicey, A. V.	'05	Lectures on the relation between law and public opinion in England in the nineteenth century. References are to the second edition of 1914.
Dickinson, Z. C.	'22	Economic Motives.
Doob, L. W.	'35	Propaganda: Its psychology and technique.
Duguit, L.	'23	Manuel de droit constitutionnel.

Earle, F. M. and others	'31	Methods of choosing a career.
Ellis, H.	'90	The criminal.
Ferguson, L. W.	'36	Attitudes of some Stanford students toward some U.S. Presidents. School and Society, vol. 44, pp. 190–192.
Fetter, F. A.	'13	Sourcebook in economics.
Florence, P. S.	'24	Economics of fatigue and unrest.
Florence, P. S.	'33	The logic of industrial organization.
Ford, G. S.	'36	Some trends and problems of the social sciences. School and Society, vol. 44, pp. 489–497.
Foreman, C. J.	'30	Efficiency and scarcity profits.
Frazer, J. G.	'05	Lectures on the early history of the kingship. Later called The Magical Origin of Kings, edition of 1920.
Freeman, E. A.	'73	Comparative politics.
Freeman, F. N., Holzinger, K., and Mitchell, B.C.	'28	The influence of environment on the intelligence, school achievement and conduct of foster-children. 27th Yearbook of the National Society for the Study of Education, pp. 103–217.
Gambrill, B. L.	'22	College achievement and vocational efficiency.
Gilboy, E. W.	'32	Demand curves by personal estimate. Quarterly Journal of Economics, vol. 46, pp. 376–384.
Glueck, S. and E. T.	'30	500 criminal careers.
Gordon, H.	'23	Mental and scholastic tests among retarded children.
Gordon, K.	'19	Report on psychological tests of orphan children. Journal of Delinquency, vol. 4, pp. 46–55.
Goring, C.	'13	The English convict.
Gortner, R. A.	'33	Others. Scientific Monthly, vol. 36, pp. 435–443.
Gray, G. W.	'37	The advancing front of science.
Hadley, A. T.	'96	Economics, an account of the relations between private property and public welfare.
Hamilton, W. H.	'15	Current economic problems. References are to the revised edition of 1919.
Hanfmann, Eugenia	'35	Social structure of a group of kindergarten children. American Journal of Ortho-psychiatry, vol. 5, pp. 407–410.
Harris, D. B.	See	Bartlett and Harris.
Harrison, J. E.	'13	Ancient art and ritual.
Hartshorne, H. and May, M. A.	'28	Studies in deceit.

Hartshorne, H. and May, M. A.	'29	Studies in service and self-control.
Healey, W.	'15	The individual delinquent.
Healy, W. and Bronner, A. F.	'26	Delinquents and criminals, their making and unmaking.
Heard, G.	'29	Ascent of humanity.
Herring, E. P.	'37	Logomachy and administration. Journal of Social Philosophy, vol. 2, pp. 95–117.
Herrman, L. and Hogben, L.	'33	The intellectual resemblance of twins. Proceedings of the Royal Society of Edinburgh, vol. 53, pp. 105–129.
Hersey, R. B.	'35	Seele und Gefühl des Arbeiters.
Hersey, R. B.	'32	Workers' emotions in shop and home. No. XVIII of Research Studies of the Industrial Research Department of the University of Pennsylvania.
Hildreth, G. H.	'25	The resemblance of siblings in intelligence and achievement. Teachers College Contributions to Education, No. 186.
Hoan, D. W.	'36	City government. The Record of the Milwaukee Experiment.
Hobson, J. A.	'22	Incentives in the new industrial order.
Hobson, J. A.	'33	Work and wealth.
Hoffman, M.	'36	Heads and tails.
Hogben, L.	See	Herrman and Hogben.
Holmes, O. W.	'20	Collected legal papers.
Holzinger, K. J.	'29	The relative effect of nature and nurture influences on twin differences. Journal of Educational Psychology, vol. 20, pp. 241–248.
Holzinger, K. J.	See	Freeman, Holzinger, and Mitchell.
Hooton, E. A.	'35	Homo sapiens—whence and whither. Science, vol. 82, pp. 19–31.
Hoppock, R.	'35	Job satisfaction.
Horst, A. P.	'32	A method for determining the absolute effective value of a series of stimulus situations. Journal of Educational Psychology, vol. 23, pp. 418–440.
Hotelling, H.	'38	The general welfare in relation to problems of taxation and of railway and utility rates. Econometrika, vol. 6, pp. 242–269.
Hoyt, E. E.	'28	The consumption of wealth.
Hull, A. W.	See	Rossman, et al.
James, William	'99	Talks to teachers.
Jarrett, M. C.	See	Southard and Jarrett.
Jenks, E.	'98	Law and politics in the middle ages.
Jones, H. E.	'31	The conditioning of overt emotional responses. Journal of Educational Psychology, vol. 22, pp. 127–130.

Jusserand, J. J.	'12	Wayfaring life in the middle ages.
Kelley, T. L.	'28	Crossroads in the mind of man.
Kent, E. B.	'03	The constructive interests of children.
Kent, F. R.	'35	The great game of politics.
Kidd, B.	'94	Social evolution.
Klineberg, O., Asch, S. E., and Block, H.	'34	An experimental study of constitutional types. Genetic Psychology Monographs, vol. 16, pp. 140–221.
Klineberg, O.	'35	Race differences.
Krabbe, H.	'27	The modern idea of the state.
Laski, H. J.	'32	Studies in law and politics.
Lasswell, H. D.	'27	Propaganda technique in the world war.
Lasswell, H. D.	'30	Psychopathology and politics.
Lawrence, E. M.	'31	An investigation into the relation between intelligence and inheritance. British Journal of Psychology, Monograph Supplement No. 16.
Leroy-Beaulieu, P.	'96	Essai sur la répartition des richesses.
Leuba, C. J.	'30	A preliminary experiment to quantify an incentive and its effects. Journal of Abnormal and Social Psychology, vol. 25, pp. 275–288.
Lindeman, B. C.	'25	Social discovery.
Lippmann, W.	'22	Public opinion. References are to the edition of 1927.
Lippmann, W.	'25	The phantom public. References are to the printing of 1927.
Lippmann, W.	'37	The good society.
Loeb, L.	'37	The biological basis of individuality. Science, vol. 86, pp. 1–5.
Lorge, I.	See	Thorndike, Bregman, Lorge, et al.
Lotka, A. J.	'25	Elements of physical biology.
Lowie, R. H.	'25	Primitive society.
Luce, H. R.	'38	Giving the people what they want. Public opinion in a democracy. Special supplement to the Public Opinion Quarterly, January, 1938, pp. 62–66.
MacEachen, R.	'31	The Church and social justice. Atlantic Monthly, vol. 148, pp. 288–292.
Mackendrick, Alex	'16	Social justice and religious evolution. The Dial, vol. 60, pp. 418–421.
MacIver, R. M.	'36	Society, its structure and changes.
Maine, H. J. S.	'61	Ancient law, edition of 1894.
Maine, H. J. S.	'75	Lectures on the early history of institutions, edition of 1893.
Maller, J. B.	'37	Juvenile delinquency in New York City: a summary of a comprehensive report. Journal of Psychology, vol. 3, pp. 1–25.
Manry, J. C.	'27	World citizenship. University of Iowa Studies: Studies in Character, vol. 1, No. 1.

Marshall, A.	'07	Principles of economics, Fifth Edition.
Marshall, A.	'20	Industry and trade.
Maslow, A. H.	'37	The influence of familiarization on preference. Journal of Experimental Psychology, vol. 21, pp. 162–180.
Mason, M.	'36	Science and the rational animal. Science, vol. 84, pp. 71–76.
May, M. A.	*See*	Hartshorne and May.
Mayer, Joseph	'36A	Comparative value and human behavior. Philosophical Review, September, vol. 45, pp. 473–496.
Mayer, Joseph	'36B	Pseudoscientific economic doctrine. "Abstracts of papers presented at the research conference on economics and statistics held by the Cowles Commission for Research in Economics at Colorado College, July 6 through August 8, 1936. Colorado College Publication, General Series No. 208, Studies Series No. 21, pp. 40–41.
Mead, M.	'30	Growing up in New Guinea.
Mead, M.	'35	Sex and temperament in three primitive societies.
Mendenhall, T. C.	*c.* 1880	Quoted by Miller, D. C., '36, p. 303.
Merriam, C. E.	'25	New aspects of politics, edition of 1931.
Michael, J. and Adler, M. J.	'33	Crime, law, and social science. (Appeared first as a monograph in 1932.)
Miller, D. C.	'36	The spirit and service of science. Science, vol. 84, pp. 297-304.
Mitchell, B. L.	*See*	Freeman, Holzinger, and Mitchell.
Mitchell, W. C.	'35	The social sciences and national planning. Science, vol. 81, pp. 55–62.
Monroe, A. E.	'31	Value and income.
Moore, T. V.	'33	The essential pyschoses and their fundamental syndromes. Studies in Psychology and Psychiatry, Catholic University of America, vol. 3, No. 3.
Moss, F. A.	'24	A study of animal drives. Journal of Experimental Psychology, vol. 7, pp. 165–185.
Mumford, L.	'22	The story of Utopias.
Mumford, L.	'34	Technics and civilization.
Munro, W. B.	'24	Personality in politics.
Myers, C. S.	'37	In the realm of mind.
National Recreation Association		The leisure hours of 5,000 people; a report of the study of leisure time activities and desires. Mimeographed Report, undated.
Nelson, J. F.	'34	Leisure time interests and activities of business girls. Published by the Women's Press, New York.

Nissen, H. W.	*See*	Warden and Nissen.
Nystrom, P.	'29	Economic principles of consumption.
Odin, A.	'95	Génèse des grands hommes.
O'Rourke, L. J.	'38	You and your community.
O'Ryan, J. F.	'38	The family of nations. Addresses delivered on Armistice Day, November 11, 1938. Reprinted by the Carnegie Endowment for International Peace.
Paley, W.	1785	The principles of moral and political philosophy, 6th American edition of 1810.
Pareto, V.	'96, '97	Cours d'économie politique, vol. I in '96; vol. II in '97.
Pareto, V.	'23	The mind and society. English translation of Livingston in 1935.
Parker, G. H.	'32	Humoral agents in nervous activity.
Parker, G. H.	'35	Neurohumors: novel agents in the action of the nervous system. Science, vol. 81, pp. 229 f.
Parker, G. H.	'36	Color changes of animals in relation to nervous activity (especially pages 63–65).
Parsons, F.	'11	Legal doctrine and social progress.
Pearl, R.	'25	The biology of population growth.
Percy, Eustace (Lord)	'34	Government in transition.
Perry, R. B.	'26	General theory of value.
Pigou, A. C.	'29	The economics of welfare. References are to the edition of 1932.
Poincaré, R.	'20	Quoted by Duguit, '23, p. 207, from Le Temps, Sept. 27, 1920.
Pollard, A. F.	'07	Factors in modern history.
Pope Pius XI	'37	Encyclical letter of March 19th.
Pound, R.	'21	The spirit of the common law.
Price, B.	'36	Homogamy and the intercorrelation of capacity traits. Annals of Eugenics, vol. 7, Part I, pp. 22–27.
Ram, J.	'34	The science of legal judgment, American edition of 1871.
Robinson, E. S.	'35	Law and the lawyers.
Robinson, J. H.	'37	The human comedy.
Robinson, Joan	'33	The economics of imperfect competition.
Rockefeller, J. D., Jr.	'18	An industrial creed. Speech delivered before War Emergency and Reconstruction Conference of the U.S. Chamber of Commerce.
Rohrlich, C. and Rohrlich, E.	'38	Psychological foundations for the fiduciary concept in corporation law.
Rorty, J.	'34	Our master's voice.
Rosebery, A. P. P. (Lord)	'21	Miscellanies literary and historical.

Rossman, J., Cottrell, F. G. Hull, A. W., and Woods, A. F.	'34	The protection of patents of scientific discoveries. Occasional publications, American Association for the Advancement of Science, No. 1, January. Supplement to Science, vol. 79, Science Press, New York.
Rowntree, B. S.	'01	Poverty, edition of 1908.
Russell, B.	'17	Why men fight.
Russell, B.	'29	Marriage and morals.
Russell, B.	'38	Power.
Scoville, S., Jr.	'14	The evolution of our criminal procedure. Annals of the American Academy of Political and Social Sciences, vol. 52, pp. 93–101.
Sheldon, A.	'85	The science of law.
Shuttleworth, F. K.	'35	The nature versus nurture problem. Journal of Educational Psychology, vol. 26, pp. 561–578 and 655–681.
Siegfried, André	'31	England's crisis.
Small, N.	'32	Some presidential interpretations of the presidency.
Smith, P.	See	Allen and Smith.
Smith, R. H.	'19	Justice and the poor.
Soddy, F.	'33	Money versus man.
Sombart, W.	'15	The quintessence of capitalism.
Sorokin, P.	'27	Social mobility.
Southard, E. E., and Jarret, M. C.	'22	The kingdom of evils.
Spearman, C.	'27	The abilities of man.
Stamp, J.	'36	The impact of science upon society. Science, vol. 84, pp. 235–238.
Stephen, J. F.	'63	History of the criminal law, second edition, 1890.
Stockard, C. R.	'31	The physical basis of personality.
Stone, C. P.	See	Sturman-Holbe and Stone.
Sturman-Holbe, M., and Stone, C. P.	'29	Maternal behavior in the albino-rat. Journal of Comparative Psychology, vol. 9, No. 3.
Sutherland, E. H.	'24	Criminology.
Tarde, G.	'02	Psychologie économique.
Taussig, F. W.	'11 and '33	Principles of economics, edition of 1933.
Tawney, R. H.	'20	The acquisitive society.
Tawney, R. H.	'31	Equality.
Taylor, C. C., and Brown, B. F.	'26	Human relations: a college textbook in citizenship.
Taylor, F. W.	'03	Shop management.

Taylor, F. W.	'13	Principles of scientific management.
Tead, O.	'18	Instincts in industry.
Thomas, D. S.	'25	Social aspects of the business cycle.
Thomas, W. I. and Znaniecki, F.	'27	The Polish peasant in Europe and America.
Thomson, G. H.	'35	Factorial analysis of human abilities. The Human Factor, vol. IX, pp. 180–195.
Thomson, G. H.	'39	Factorial analysis of human ability.
Thorndike, E. L.	'10	Handwriting. Teachers College Record, vol. II, pp. 1–81.
Thorndike, E. L.	'11	A scale for merit in English writing by young people. Journal of Educational Psychology, vol. 2, pp. 361–368.
Thorndike, E. L.	'13	Introduction to the theory of mental and social measurements. Revised edition of 1913.
Thorndike, E. L.	'13A	Measurement of achievement in drawing, Teachers College Record, vol. 14, pp. 345–382.
Thorndike, E. L.	'13B	Educational Psychology, vol. I: The original nature of man.
Thorndike, E. L.	'14	Educational Psychology, vol. II.
Thorndike, E. L.	'16	The technique of combining incomplete judgments of the relative position of n facts made by N judges. Journal of Philosophy, Psychology, and Scientific Method, vol. 12, pp. 197–204.
Thorndike, E. L.	'22	The psychology of labor. Harper's Monthly, vol. 44, pp. 799–806.
Thorndike, E. L.	'24	Mental discipline in high school studies. Journal of Educational Psychology, vol. 15, pp. 1–22 and 83–98.
Thorndike, E. L.	'32	The distribution of education. School Review, vol. 40, pp. 335–345.
Thorndike, E. L., Bregman, E. O., Lorge, I., et al.	'34	The prediction of vocational success.
Thorndike, E. L.	'35	The paradox of science. Proceedings, The American Philosophical Society, vol. 75, No. 4.
Thorndike, E. L.	'35A	Workers' satisfaction: likes and dislikes of young people for their jobs. Occupations, vol. 13, pp. 704–706.
Thorndike, E. L.	'35B	The psychology of wants, interests and attitudes.
Thorndike, E. L.	'35C	The interests of adults. Journal of Educational Psychology, vol. 26, pp. 401–410.
Thorndike, E. L.	'36	The goal of social effort. The Educational Record, vol. 17, pp. 153–168.

Thorndike, E. L.	'37	Valuations of certain pains, deprivations, and frustrations. Journal of Genetic Psychology, vol. 51, pp. 227–239.
Thorndike, E. L. and Beckwith, B. P.	'37A	Salaries of executives. Personnel Journal, vol. 15, pp. 312–320.
Thorndike, E. L.	'37B	How we spend our time and what we spend it for. Scientific Monthly, vol. 44, pp. 464–469.
Thorndike, E. L.	'37C	What do we spend our money for? Scientific Monthly, vol. 45, pp. 226–232.
Thorndike, E. L.	'38	The influence of disparity of incomes on welfare. American Journal of Sociology, vol. 44, pp. 25–35.
Thorndike, E. L.	'38A	Great abilities: their frequency, causation, discovery, and utilization. Scientific Monthly, vol. 47, pp. 59–72.
Thorndike, E. L.	'38B	Heredity and environment. Journal of Educational Psychology, vol. 29, pp. 161–166.
Thorndike, E. L.	'38C	The psychology of language. Archives of Psychology, No. 271.
Thorndike, E. L.	'39	The relation between the quantity purchased and the price per unit. Harvard Business Review, vol. 17, pp. 209–221.
Thorndike, E. L.	'39A	Education as cause and as symptom.
Thorndike, E. L.	'39B	On the fallacy of imputing the correlations found for groups to the individuals or smaller groups composing them. American Journal of Psychology, vol. 52, pp. 122–124.
Thorndike, E. L.	'39C	Your city.
Thorndike, E. L.	'39D	American cities and states: variation and correlation in institutions, activities and the personal qualities of the residents. Annals of the New York Academy of Sciences, Vol. 39, pp. 213–298.
Thurstone, L. L.	'27	Psychophysical analysis. American Journal of Psychology, vol. 38, pp. 368–389.
Thurstone, L. L.	'35	Vectors of the mind.
Thurstone, L. L.	'36	The factorial isolation of primary abilities. Psychometrika, vol. 1, pp. 175–182.
Tolman, E. C.	'35	Psychology versus immediate experience. Philosophy of Science, vol. 2, pp. 356–380.
Troland, L. T.	'28	The fundamentals of human motivation.
Veblen, T.	'14	The instinct of workmanship and the state of the industrial arts.
Veblen, T.	'17	Inquiry into the nature of peace and the terms of its perpetuation.
Veblen, T.	'19	The place of science in modern civilization.
Wallas, G.	'08	Human nature in politics, edition of 1909.
Wallas, G.	'14	The great society.

Wallas, G. .   '21   Our social heritage.

Warden, C. J.,   '28   An experimental analysis of the obstruction
and Nissen,   method of measuring animal drives. Journal
H.W.   of Comparative Psychology, vol. 8, pp.
                              325–342.

Warner, L. H.   '27   A study of sex behavior in the white rat by
                              means of the obstruction method. Compar-
                              ative Psychology Monographs, No. 22.

Warner, L. H.   '28A   A study of thirst behavior in the white rat by
                              means of the obstruction method. Journal of
                              Genetic Psychology, vol. 35, pp. 178–192.

Warner, L. H.   '28B   A study of hunger behavior in the white rat by
                              means of the obstruction method. A com-
                              parison of sex and hunger behavior. Journal
                              of Comparative Psychology, vol. 8, No. 4,
                              pp. 273–300.

Watson, J. B.   '20   Conditioned emotional reactions. Journal of Ex-
and Raynor, R.   perimental Psychology, vol. 3, pp. 1–14.

Webb, Sidney   '11   The prevention of destitution.
and Beatrice

Webb, Sidney   '36   Soviet communism: a new civilization?
and Beatrice

Wechsler, D.   '35   The range of human capacities.

Whitney, W. R.   '36   Accomplishments and future of the physical
                              sciences. Science, vol. 84, pp. 211–272.

Willoughby,   '00   Social justice.
W. W.

Wines, F. H.   '94   Possible penalties for crime.   National Prison
                              Association, pp. 325–327.

Wolfe, A. B.   '31   On the content of welfare. American Economic
                              Review, vol. 21, pp. 207–221.

Woods, Arthur   '17   Report of the Police Department of New York
                              City, 1914–1917.

Woods, Arthur   '18   Crime prevention.

Woods, H. F.   See   Rossman, et al.

Woodworth,   '34   Psychology, Third Edition.
R. S.

Woodworth,   '38   Experimental Psychology.
R. S.

Woodyard, E.   See   Brolyer, Thorndike, and Woodyard.

Woolley, H. T.   '26   Experimental study of children.

Yerkes, R. M.   '33   Genetic aspects of grooming, a socially import-
                              ant primate behavior pattern. Journal of
                              Social Psychology, vol. 4, pp. 3–25.

Yerkes, R. M.   '37   Primate cooperation and intelligence. American
                              Journal of Psychology, vol. 50, pp. 254–270.

Young, Owen D.   '34   Address at the University of Nebraska. As
                              reported in the New York Times, June 5,
                              1934.

Zimmern, A.   '31   The Greek commonwealth.
Zipf, G. K.   '35   Psychobiology of language.
Znaniecki, F.   *See* Thomas and Znaniecki.

Publication Credits

List of publishers by whose courtesy quotations are included in this book:

F. Alcan, Paris.
George Allen and Unwin, Ltd., London.
The American Academy of Political and Social Science, Philadelphia.
American Council on Education, Washington.
American Economic Association, Evanston, Ill.
The American Journal of Psychology, Ithaca, N. Y.
The American Journal of Sociology, Chicago.
The American Orthopsychiatric Association, Inc., Menasha, Wis.
The American Philosophical Society, Philadelphia.
The American Psychological Association, Columbus, Ohio.
The American Society of Mechanical Engineers, New York.
Apostolic Delegation, Washington.
D. Appleton-Century Company, New York.
Barrows Mussey Inc., New York.
Ernest Benn Ltd., London.
E. de Boccard, Paris.
Cambridge University Press, Cambridge, England.
The Carnegie Foundation for the Advancement of Teaching, New York.
Chamber of Commerce of the United States, Washington.
Clarendon Press, Oxford.
Columbia University Press, New York.
Constable and Company, Ltd., London.
F. S. Crofts and Company, New York.
John Day Company, Inc., New York.
The Dial Press, New York.

Doubleday Doran and Company, New York.
E. P. Dutton and Company, Inc., New York.
Encyclopaedia Britannica, New York.
Farrar and Rinehart, Inc., New York.
Harcourt, Brace and Company, Inc., New York.
Harper and Brothers, New York.
Harvard University Press, Cambridge, Mass.
D. C. Heath and Company, Boston.
Henry Holt and Company, Inc., New York.
Houghton Mifflin Company, Boston.
The Journal Press, Provincetown.
Journal of Social Philosophy, New York.
Kegan Paul, Trench, Trubner and Company, Ltd., London.
P. S. King and Son, Ltd., London.
Alfred A. Knopf, Inc., New York.
J. B. Lippincott Company, Chicago.
Little, Brown and Company, Boston.
Liveright Publishing Corporation, New York.
Longmans Green and Company, Ltd., London.
Longmans Green and Company, New York.
McGraw-Hill Book Company, Inc., New York.
The Macmillan Company, New York.
Marshall Jones Company, Boston.
Methuen and Company, Ltd., London.
National Institute of Industrial Psychology, London.
The New York Times, New York.
W. W. Norton and Company, Inc., New York.
Ohio State University Press, Columbus, Ohio.
Personnel Research Federation, New York.
Princeton University Press, Princeton, N. J.
Progressive Education Association, New York.
G. P. Putnam's Sons, New York.
F. Rouge et Cie., Lausanne.
George Routledge and Sons, Ltd., London.
Science Press, New York.
Charles Scribner's Sons, New York.
Sigma xi Quarterly, Burlington, Vt.
Teachers College Bureau of Publications, New York.
Helen S. Trounstine Foundation, Cincinnati.
University of Chicago Department of Education, Chicago.
University of Chicago Press, Chicago.
University of Iowa Press, Iowa City.
D. Van Nostrand Company, Inc., New York.
The Viking Press, Inc., New York.
The Williams and Wilkins Company, Baltimore.
Yale University Press, New Haven.

Index